# UPRISING

## CRIPS AND BLOODS TELL THE STORY OF AMERICA'S YOUTH IN THE CROSSFIRE

Yusuf Jah
and
Sister
Shah'Keyah

SCRIBNER

NEW YORK LONDON TORONTO
SYDNEY TOKYO SINGAPORE

SCRIBNER
1230 Avenue of the Americas
New York, NY 10020



Set in Adobe Trump Medieval

Manufactured in the United States of America
10 9 8 7 6 5 4 3 2 1

Library of Congress Cataloging-in-Publication Data
Uprising: Crips and Bloods tell the story of America's youth in the crossfire /
Yusuf Jah and sister Shah'Keyah.
p. cm.
Includes index.
1. Crips (Gang) 2. Bloods (Gang) 3. Gang members—California—Los Angeles—
Interviews. I. Jah, Yusuf. II. Jah, Shah'Keyah.
HV6439.U7L734 1995 95-23521
364.1'06'6092279494—dc20 CIP

ISBN 0-684-80460-3

# ACKNOWLEDGMENTS

*We'd like to thank ALLAH for inspiring us to put this book together! This book, "Uprising," was inspired directly by ALLAH, to be used as a tool in rebuilding our nation, our families, our communities, and ourselves.*

To all of the brothers in this book—we thank you for standing up and speaking out to the world. We thank you for helping to get these most vital and essential messages out to the masses. You are today's leaders and you are most important in shaping our future rulers. The solutions and the answers that are in this book came right from within you. You are the ones to bring about this universal change! We believe in you and we stand with you! Together we can do this! May your lights continue to shine brightly throughout the universe! Much love. Much respect.

To all of those who are not in this book and who know *the time and what must be done,* this is a first step to take in the challenge to get with this, to move on this, and to stand up as Black men and women and take our rightful positions within the Black family by implementing these solutions.

To all of the sisters who helped to make this book happen—Veronica, Lynn, Shelia, Kathy, JoAnn, Lisa—you are the backbones, the nurturers, the comforters, the Queens, the mothers of civilization, and so much more. We thank you for being there and may you all continue to remain strong and supportive in helping to bring about these positive changes.

Special shout outs to our loved ones:

Goddess Ah'Keyah—our blessing. Mama Jackson, Grandmama Muhammad, Grandpapa Muhammad, Mema and family, Keyen, Annie, Musa, Rameek, Laney, Kenneth, Elijah, Lolita, Gary, Sandy, Damien, Liz, Ryan, Alicia, Steve, Tim, Novella, Eric and family, Grandmama Penny and family, Shirley and family, all of our uncles and aunties, Khadijah, Neeka, Lonnie, Khallid, Grandpapa Jack and family, Clarence, Shelita, Jordan, Shamel, Michelle and family, Brother Eric "Yarb," Brother Raven, Yogi, Brother Allahjah, Brother Shajee Neptune and family, Betty C., Ran, Li'l Ran, Lori, Brother Link, Mr. Barnes, Mr. Zapata, Paula D., Willie, Sampson, Tasha Shabazz, Lloyd, Floyd, and Troy—the Triplets, Yambu, Rahmaan, Malachi X, Sister Sahara, Reggie B., Roshon, Duane B., Bradford F., Jill L., Robin, Alita, Richard, Juanita, Petie, Debra, Xtina, Brother Quadeer, Brother Meekkaal, Shank, Spice, Darious, Blaine, Joseph, Mama Way, Denise J., Sister Quadeera—much love, stay strong, Queen—Brother Muhammad, Booda, Mark Corey, Johnny Gill,

# Acknowledgments

DeLaSoul, G-Man, MC Hype and family, Rufus Troutman, Charlie Singleton, Eddie Murphy, Wesley Snipes, Christopher T., Carla R., Yvonne, Emanuel and family, Noah C. and family, J. Spady, Mike P., Rich A., Randy S., Ceaser and family, Dewann and Specialized IMS, 125 Black Mecca, L.G. Posse.

Special thanks to all of the people who share the vision:

Harold "Hakeem" Johnson and Wil "Wadee" Wade—we personally thank you for troopin' with us 1,000 percent—and to the staff at Marketing Strategies of America, Walt Hammock, Ice-T, Darlene, and the Rhyme Syndicate, Hamilton "Hamad" Cain at Scribner, Jim Brown, Oprah Winfrey, Marla Gibbs, Stevie Wonder, Danny Bakewell, Brotherhood Crusade, Pam, John Mack, Urban League, Maxine, China, Stenette Kennibrew, Sister Odelle, Touch of Africa, Desperately Seeking Answers, Art Cribs, Akeela, Daude, Rockhead, Manuel, Sister Rasheeda, Traci X, Brother Rasheed, World on Wheels, Compton Billbrew Library, Omar Bradley, 2 Pac Shakur, Afrika Bambaataa and the Zulu Nation, Public Enemy, Chuck D, Flavor Flav, Brother John and Sister Mecca and family, Brother Mike, James Bomb, Crunch, Brother Roger, Brother James, Brother Charles, Brother Shaiykh, Ice Cube, Brother Ron, Queen Latifah, MC Lyte, Sister Jimila, Dr. Khallid Al-Mansour and Sister Sultana and family, Paris and family, Ten Trey, the Last Poets, the Watts Prophets, the Black Panther Party, Winnie Mandela, Minister Farrakhan and Sister Khadijah Farrakhan, Sister Ava Muhammad, Brother Khallid, Minister Ahvay Muhammad, Minister Akbar, Minister Rasul Muhammad, Brother Mustapha, William Muhammad, Minister Conrad Muhammad, Kam, Brother Rubin, Brother Robert5X, Donald Muhammad, Brother Jabril, Brother Abdul Malik Muhammad—keep troopin', Black man—Sister Tynetta Muhammad, the Most Honorable Elijah Muhammad, the Nation of Islam.

To all of the readers, may the words in this book help to inspire you to make a positive change!

Peace! Uprise!

—Brother Yusuf and Sister Shah'Keyah

For lectures and speaking engagements contact:
Black Speakers International c/o ECC
421 N. Rodeo Dr., Suite 15-476
Beverly Hills, CA 90210

# CONTENTS

Ice-T and Big Phil

# FOREWORD

## BY
## ICE-T
### (RAPPER, ACTOR, AUTHOR)

*(This book is the most dramatic and major turning point in American history as far as my life is concerned. The theory of a peace treaty in L.A., the Crips and Bloods trying to get together, this is the most dramatic turning point in American history from my perspective. I can't think of anything else in my life that has happened that meant as much as this, politically. This is going to affect everybody.)*

I had to create a gang peace treaty in my organization prior to the gang peace treaty that hit the streets. I was dealing with hundreds of different people, rappers, etc., from different hoods. I used to have crucial situations in the studio, to where I had to tell people that once you step inside the Syndicate, it's not about that. The Rhyme Syndicate is simply an L.A. version of the Zulu Nation. I had hooked up with Afrika Bambaataa back in the days and had Afrika Islam as my producer. Bambaataa had given me the whole science of the Zulu Nation back then. I wanted to get the rappers together out here in Los Angeles, but the name Zulu was a little too Afrocentric for the brothers out here, and that name at that time wasn't going to work, so I came up with the Syndicate. We're all going in the same direction so we can't compete against each other. Unless you definitely do not want to see somebody else come up, which is evil, there shouldn't be any competition. The Syndicate is a group of businesses with one common goal, moving in the same direction. Which means we could have NWA and the Lynch Mob, and they would all have their own leaders and their own chain of command, but we would all be together. I'm not the leader of the Rhyme Syndicate, I'm just the founder.

Being out on the road rapping, and representing this lifestyle in my music, which has been termed by the press as "gangster rap." When I came out rapping, I was rapping about street life, and it was the white press that categorized us as gangsters. I never said I was a gangster, and if you ask any of the brothers out on the street, they'll tell you that I wasn't really a banger, I was more of a hustler. I wore the khakis and all of that when I went to Crenshaw High, my daughters' mother was a Criplett, she was banging. When I got involved with her, she was down with the Hoover Crips and I started rolling with them, but as far as going out and putting in work, doing drive-bys and all of that, I was never on that level.

# Foreword

By me not having a mother or a father, sisters or brothers, and by leaving my aunt's house when I was seventeen years old, my focus was always on making money, on straight survival. So the gangs to me seemed to be something that at that time, because there wasn't any dope involved, there was no money involved. So I figured I would have to flip this, keep in contact with all the homiez, but get some flavor about myself and get out there and do something. So after hustling, I started rapping.

Back in the days when people from New York would rap, like Spoony G and Melle Mel, they would rap about what they had or rap about going to a party, but they were rapping to other rappers, they were saying that they could out-rap each other. What I did was change the direction of the opponent in rap and direct what I had to say to the people, whether they were rappers or not, which changed the whole concept of the record. It was no longer about taking somebody out on the mic, it was taking someone out period. It got very aggressive at that point, which was totally unheard of in rap, to rap about negative aspects of your life.

What made me start to rap like that was here in L.A., there was no hip-hop scene, but there was a gang scene. While people back East went through hip-hop nightclubs like The Fever, there was no scene out here like that. So what could I draw my experiences from? I could only rap about how I was living. Then later on I did an album called *OG,* which was basically saying that if this is gangster rap, then I'm the original.

I was out on tour, representing this lifestyle, and I got a call that there's a gang peace. I thought it was BS. I thought it was impossible. As long as I had been begging brothers to cool out, because even at the end of the movie *Colors* I was like, "Please stop, 'cause I want y'all to live."

The gang peace was real, and they literally sent me videotape footage from Watts. So I wrote the record "Gotta Lot of Love." When I saw that video of the gang peace with thousands of brothers coming together, kickin' it, I wrote the lyrics:

I woke up the other morning,
I heard a rumor.
They said the gang wars was over,
I told them they was bullshitting.
They said it's real as hell.
I can't explain the way I felt.

I can't even explain it,
Too many years I've seen my brothers die,
And I can't say the shit was really that fly.
But I used to gang-bang when I was younger,
So it's really hard to tell a kid that he's going under.

I never thought I'd get to see us chill,
Crips and Bloods holding hands?

# Foreword

The shit is ill,
But I love it.
I can't help it,
Too much death on the streets,
And we dealt it.

That record was real, coming straight from my heart, and what I did in that record was just try to document my emotions.

There are a lot of shades of gang membership, and the OG has as much pull as he is willing to enforce. You'll see a lot of brothers in their forties who will say that they are this or that, but can they enforce the fact that they are OGs? If they can enforce it on the streets, then they have the power. Some of these older brothers can enforce it, like a lot of the brothers in this book.

I'm thirty-six, I have guys that call themselves my brothers that are twenty-eight, they have guys who listen to them that are twenty-four, they have guys listening to them who are seventeen, so I have to talk to the guys who listen to me and let them know what I want. If they love me, they'll take that, and the enforcement goes down the line. I can never go talk directly to that younger kid. Even though I am from the old school and I have power, my power isn't where I can step to the active gang members, the kids that are out there throwing guns in people's faces, because they're looking at me like, "Ice, you make records. Maybe back in the day you could step, but now you make records. You ain't here right now." So all I thought I could do was make a record. I thought I could just make a record showing these brothers that I have love for them. That's when I hooked up with a brother named Malik Spellman at the Black Expo; he told me what was going on, and he said that the brothers needed somebody to talk for them. He took me to Watts to meet Tony Bogard (RIP) and Ty Stick; these are brothers from Watts, and I didn't know hardly anyone in Watts. So Tony let me know how they needed help, and how they had gotten with different rappers that didn't really come through. Immediately I told them about the song I had made, and because they were so sincere and so real, I told them that I would give them the money from the song. So they invited me to the Imperial Courts to shoot the video for the song, and they put me on the board of directors for Hands Across Watts, to help push the peace treaty.

So then I wanted to help the homiez that I knew from the west side, like Big Phil. I knew what was going on in Watts wasn't really going to affect what was happening on the west side, it's a totally separate area. Big Phil and others were inspired, and we decided to start South Central Love. South Central Love is an organization that Big Phil and I invested in; SCL was built on a lot of good intentions and hope. The problem with South Central Love is that we were unaware that nobody gives a damn. Only in a dream world when you're out there trying to help the community would you think that there's going to be aid from somewhere. That's not going to happen. The bottom line is nobody cares. I went on *Arsenio Hall* and begged for some support; four people called us out of 50 million Americans who saw that show. I had to sit back and figure it out, why wouldn't people call? The first thing I came to realize is that the people who do care are broke. In order for you to care about a gang member, you have to have somebody that's involved in it. Then the other people are victims of gang violence and don't care about them. So the gang bangers' mentality is, "If you don't help us, we'll do this and that."

We then decided that we had to change the scope of these organizations from gang violence to gang prevention. That all of a sudden becomes attractive to somebody who might want to donate. The theory of somebody coming along and dropping a whole lot of money into an organization for our people is not going to happen either, because there are too many "politically correct" organizations. Most people who are entertainers with half a million dollars to donate will give it to AIDS, because it's going to look good on TV.

Eventually, I had to get down and say we have two problems, we have gang violence and we have unemployment. Brothers want to say, "Well, if I had money, then I would stop." That's extortion. You should stop for these babies. The fact that you don't have a job is another problem totally. You can't say that you will stop if you get some money, no, no, no, you should stop because it's wrong. Then on the other hand we can start to figure out how to get you a job.

I realized that any organization has to be based on a business. We have to start businesses, so the businesses will generate money, and then with charity in their hearts they can go out and try to talk to the kids. Brothers have to understand that this is straight, bold charity. This whole problem that we have is going to be dealt with on charity. You can't start an organization that is based on goals to save Black people and expect someone to pay you. You're going to have to figure out a way that you can make money so that you can eat and take care of your families, and then on your free time you can do the saving. That's one of the only ways it's going to happen. Forget the government. The government is not going to help us.

The mind-set of Black folks has to change. I had to do it. I'm Black, and I had to come from zero to sixty. The first thing is that you have to admit that you've been messing up, you have to admit that you BS'd through school, you have to admit your shortcomings. One of the best comments I've ever heard was, "The best weapon against racism is excellence." That says it all. We can sit up and say that we don't have any computer jobs, but if you were excellent in computers, the best, then you'd have a job; if you were excellent in basketball, you'd be starting on the Knicks. Our problem is that we're not striving to be excellent, we're all right, but when you're excellent in something, when you've mastered it, when you are the best at what you do, then you would have a job. You have to be the best.

# Foreword

The last person we blame for our problems is ourselves. Most of us have looked for too many shortcuts. People come to my house and think they can get what I have by next year. They don't understand that what I've obtained is from thirteen years of hard work and sacrifice. I moved from a single apartment, with two pit bulls and puppies, my homie on the floor, and my wife, Darlene, in the bed, back when my first album came out. Then we moved to a one-bedroom apartment with the same two pit bulls, but without the extra person. It was over eight years before we moved into a two-bedroom apartment. Then we moved to another smaller house, and we just moved here to this house up on the hill two years ago. It doesn't happen overnight. Now if you take the same thirteen years and go to school, you'll come out being a Ph.D. and you can do the same thing, or if you take the same thirteen years and focus on what it is that you want, then you will be successful. It's timing. We have to learn to set five-year goals. If you try to get it all tomorrow, you might end up in jail, because it's not going to happen like that. You have to set goals and build, and when you have a good woman, you can do it. The only thing that saved me was when I hooked up with Darlene, she wasn't materialistic, so that kept me from getting in trouble. She was like, "I'm cool, stay down, I'll work, we'll get it." I was with a girl before that who was trying to get me sent to the penitentiary. I was trying to do the right thing, but I had baller friends who were still hustling that I used to hang out with, even though I was working. She had the nerve to ask me one day, "Couldn't you get back with them if you wanted to?" That was when we broke up mentally. She knew what they did, she was caught up in that lifestyle.

Having a woman that's down for the long haul is of major importance. The female has to be as focused as the male. The woman has to respect and help the man so that he can do what he has to do. The nature of a good man is to give his woman anything that she wants, that becomes his dream. If a man loves you, your dreams become his dreams indirectly. Subconsciously you can drive a man crazy. So in order for him to feel that he doesn't have to do anything crazy, you just have to say, "I know we're going to get it, I'm down, it's all right."

As Black people we have a lot of problems with the white situation. I look at it like this: it's going to be twice as hard, but don't we say that we're twice as strong, we're the original people, so it's even. You just have to understand the opponent and the situation.

My role model is Don King because Don King has proven that you can make it with your hair combed straight up in the air. What Don King is saying is that you do not have to be white, you do not have to adapt to their attitudes, you just have to bring to the table whatever has to be brought to the table. I can go into a $20-million meeting with a diaper on if I have what they want, and all they'll say is, "He's a little eccentric." You just have to be excellent.

The white situation almost has to be put into a capsule, it can't be harped on. When you harp on it, that just stagnates everything. We must understand that a lot of the problems we come across are from a lack of knowledge. We always say knowledge of self, but it's general knowledge also. Every time you don't know something, you have to pay somebody. If I was a lawyer, I wouldn't have to pay my attorney; if I was an accountant, I wouldn't have to pay these accountants. Therefore, all knowledge is important, especially when it comes to money and business.

Some brothers are still looking for a shortcut. We can say it's a condition that we've been put in, the jealousy, the envy, but that's just a part of it. What I try to do as a brother coming up is never apologize for my success. I can't do anything for people in the hood by acting like I'm broke. By me showing them that I can get on the hill, that means that they can get on the hill too. I'm still wearing rags around my head, I still talk the same way, I still represent the same thing. It can be done. That goes back to Don King and what he's showing us, it can be done, but you have to have your act together, there's no way around that. The more of yourself that you want to be, that's how much more you have to be together. When you're good like Michael Jordan or Dennis Rodman, you can do anything, because you're that good.

I think another thing we're going to have to do as Black Americans is study the Japanese, because basically what happened with them is they went from America dropping a bomb on them to them now taking over the world and they don't even have an army. They took all their time and aimed all their resources at education. Now what they've done is outthink America and bought the whole damn place. Black people have to develop superior brainpower; we already know that we have the stronger back.

There are a lot of tricks going around. There's a trick going around saying that we have money. That's BS. There's a level of money that you'll see, Michael Jordan, Mike Tyson, Don King, but if you watch, they can take Mike Tyson and throw him in prison, they can take Michael Jackson and break him down. They make you think that Michael Jordan is something, but Michael Jordan does not own the Bulls. Oprah Winfrey is getting paid, but she does not own the network. When you can only count ten or twenty Black people with money, it's still a farce.

I've been on the high end of it, I've hung out with Gerald Levin, Steve Ross, and these ballers from Warner Brothers. Steve Ross, one year, got a $70-million "bonus." When you hit this high level of money, you won't see any Black people, or any Mexican people, the only people coming into that level now are Asians. There's a brain game going on at that level. Sony comes in and buys CBS. They just straight bought it. Until we gain economic power, nothing is ever going to change. Then they have you in another trick bag. The trick bag is "If you get rich, you have sold out." That's a trick bag. It's the same trick bag as "Don't leave the ghetto," if you leave the ghetto, you've done something wrong. That's like telling an Indian if you leave the reservation, you've done something wrong. The ghetto is not a Black community, it's a poor community. There's no such thing as a Black community. Black rich people don't live together. This city has economic barricades around it.

## Foreword

You can go to certain parts of the city and when you cross one block, the same apartment has gone from $500 a month to $1,100. They're economically segregating people. Of course certain people will go toward each other because of language and culture, but it's money that keeps us separated.

Right now we have the situation with the Black gangs and the Chicano gangs. What I think is going on is "the man," and my concept of who "the man" is and what the system is, is that the system can be anybody, even one of your friends, because the system is not a closed room of people. If you have a friend that says, "That's good for Rodney King" or "We don't need these programs," people that have that mindset, they are the system. It could be your mother if she has that attitude. If you have the attitude of, "As long as I got mine, forget about everyone else, we don't want to help people," that's who creates the system.

What's going on right now is that we have a Black-gang truce in Los Angeles, which has gotten really powerful since the Uprisings. I believe that the cops and the people who feel that they can't let this unity jump off, they're pushing the Black gangs toward the Mexicans. The Blacks and the Latinos have never had any beef with each other in L.A. If you go to prison, everybody sides up because that's prison, prison is another whole game. But on the streets of L.A. there has never been Black vs. Latino warfare. What's going on now is the cops are telling the kids that the Mexicans have the dope, so again what they're doing is throwing us poison and telling us to fight over it. They're not coming to Blacks in the streets saying that the Mexicans are getting the jobs, they're not saying that they are getting more benefits, they're saying that the Mexicans have the dope, so kill each other over the dope. If they can get a war going on between the Blacks and Latinos, it will be the most stupid thing, it will not prove anything, it will just wipe out a bunch of poor people. Right now in South Central, if you go to Manual Arts High School, it's 50 percent Latino. Our ghettos are mixing, because it's about being poor. The Mexican kids hang right out with the Black brothers. There's not much difference at all. We low-ride, we say "homeboy," we kick it. There's no big difference, but they're trying to create one, because they're so afraid of the Blacks and the Mexicans bonding. If we bond, this city will be in serious trouble. There are more Latino people in the Los Angeles area than there are Black. It would be over. So a problem between the two groups is something that I don't want to see go down at any cost. I tell the brothers what's really going down, about the fact that there are some people over there with guns and blue suits on, busting your ass, putting you in prison.

The whole thing is based on focus. Why are we mad at Korean people? They haven't done anything. A judge let that lady go who killed Natasha Harlins. The Korean lady shot a sister in the back; how many brothers have shot babies on the street? That's BS. So we're mad because one Korean lady shot a little girl in the back, which was wrong, but our people ride by and kill little babies.

The judge let that lady go, in everybody's face. It's true that there is a lot of disrespect that goes on in the Black community by Koreans, and that's because of the lack of communication. The Korean comes from a different background, their attitude is, "I have a store, I'm in the ghetto." They're not in the ghetto because they're sucking the ghetto dry, the Koreans are like the "niggers" of Asia. They're poor, Korean people work in those stores and they don't leave to go to Beverly Hills, they go upstairs and live in them, about ten deep. Their whole culture says, "I own a liquor store, I hire my son. My son gets married, I hire the brother." They're doing what we should be doing. It's true that they're in the community and should hire a little sister or brother to work there, it's only right, but it's one of those things where we don't have any communication. Spike Lee touched on that in his movie *Do the Right Thing,* when they was sweating the Korean in the community, the Korean said, "I'm Black, we are the same, I'm right here with you." During the Uprisings we struck out at anybody who we thought had power. Nobody moved on any police stations, nobody moved on any cops.

I'm like Superfly, from the movie *Superfly,* when all the brothers were talking about "Black Power," Superfly was like, "Go on with that, when y'all are ready to get out here and kill whitey, when you're ready for the real revolution, I'm right in the front, but until then go on with all that BS." When you're ready to find the real enemy, whoever it may be, and move, I'm with it. The other thing is, you can't say the enemy is just white, because there are a lot of Black enemies too.

We have to be focused. Like Minister Farrakhan and his focus, in his speeches, he refers to "white supremacy," therefore he can't be considered a racist, because it's not like he's calling everybody racist.

Even with hip-hop, I think that the fear of hip-hop at this moment comes from the way that young white kids are embracing it. A lot of white kids are going home and when their mothers say, "Niggers this," white kids are saying, "No, no, kill that s—, I'm not carrying the burden of racism any longer. I like Public Enemy." It's not so much a fear of the words, they are just trying to make it seem like the words are a problem as an excuse, it's not that, it's a fear of the kids looking at the TV and saying, "I like Snoop Dog." Their mamas are saying, "They'll rob you," they push this whole racist thing on their kids, but the kids are saying, "What's the matter with him though? I don't see what you're saying. What's the problem?" This is a major problem for America, because the baton of racism is not being passed as easily now.

Some people believe that there is genetically something different about a Black baby, an Asian baby, and a white baby, but I believe that if you take all three babies and put them together, they'll grow up to be a family. It would take an adult to come and create division and a feeling of superiority in one of the babies. I don't think it would be in their nature. My attitude is that the whole racist thing is something that's taught, that's perpetuated, and passed along.

Back in the fifties rock 'n' roll did the same thing that rap is doing now. Little Richard came out and was doing it, and white kids loved it. That was a real racist time. The scariest thing then was little white girls were screaming for Little Richard, so they had to shut it down. Pat Boone remade all of Little Richard's records, and they separated us. But today you have white kids who are not down with that old shit. In a minute a lot of these white kids that are listening to this rap are going to be sitting on the Supreme Court. You're going to have kids sitting on the Supreme Court with TOO SHORT T-shirts on, not little Black kids, but little white kids. The whole system is going to change.

When I deal with white kids, I let them know that I know what they're trying to do, because they have the money, they are the ones who are going to decide if there's going to be a change or not. A hostile takeover will not happen.

As far as strengthening the peace on the streets, the sisters are really going to have to step in there and support their men. What we're going to have to do in the hood is just make gang-banging uncool, the same way crack became uncool. If the sisters are steadily saying, "It's not happening, that ain't it. I'm not with it. What about our kids?" then the brothers would change. The women have to stay on these brothers. When I used to be rolling and bailing, the girls used to chase behind us, they liked it, and you know we always do pretty much anything that they like. If they chased drug dealers, we wanted to sell dope. So if the woman sits back and says, "I'm not taking any hot money, I don't want to roll with a hustler, I don't want to roll with a banger," brothers would slowly but surely change. The women have to say, "We want you to be men."

A lot of entertainers are into this business for other reasons, so I don't know how much help they will be in helping to bring about peace. I'm blessed to be in this business, and I use it at times as a vehicle to state opinions. A lot of entertainers are just trying to get paid, and they don't care, they're not in tune. I don't really deal with the actual effects that a song has on people, because I think a song is a song. Eazy-E doing a gangster record is nothing more than a director doing a gangster movie, it's just a different way of expressing a story. Away from the records, and the movies, entertainers need to get out here and represent. It doesn't hurt me to go from being the biggest gangster on record, to then turn around and tell the kids that it was an Ice act, but if I try to portray it out like I'm living that kind of lifestyle, then that's when it gets dangerous.

There's a saying, "Each one teach one." Everybody needs to pull in somebody that might need some help and give them some time, look at it like you're sponsoring that individual, helping them to change themselves. A lot of people have so much to say about rappers, but take somebody like me, I'm rapping, just one person on a mic, but I might be carrying thirty or forty individuals, taking them places, letting them see things. Now if these square businesspeople would take one person, they would be doing something. When you see the rappers, at least we role with our crews, we try to show them new things. Most of the people I hire are unskilled, we just help them learn. You have to be willing to take that kid who might not have the dress code and give him the job, bring him or her in, walk them through, and let them see the other side.

One of the programs that they used to have before they cut it off, which used to help me out, was a program called CEDA. How the CEDA program worked was a teenager could get a job, but the state would actually pay the wages. For the employer it was like getting a free worker for your business, and the teenager gets a job that they would have never gotten. I got to work in a law firm like that. They would have never hired me, but I had a CEDA job.

The white community has to understand that either they are going to be good people or they're not. If you're a good person, you're going to care about every situation. The B side to that is *anything that goes on in the ghetto is eventually going to come to your neighborhood.* You cannot continue to sweep dirt under the carpet and think you're going to keep it contained, it's going to come out. The drugs will be in your neighborhood and all of that. Some people say that you better help or it's going to be something bad happening. I don't even go that route; I say if you're a good person, then you should care about situations all over. A lot of money is being sent overseas, and to different places; the same way they sponsor kids overseas, they could be sponsoring the orgainizations in the hood. There are a lot of people in the white community who do care, but when the Uprisings jumped off, that's when they wanted to throw on their Malcolm X outfit and say they're down with us. That's too late. If we have an abortion problem, they'll march, but for a racial situation white people won't march, they'll be down with you in the heart, but you won't see them. What they have to do is be adamant about it, they have to be there, they need to be at our fundraisers, and not be afraid. They'd be surprised at how well they'd be received. Like during the South Central Uprisings, there was a lot of white people down there cleaning up, and they weren't getting knocked in the head. They came down there, said they was down with us, grabbed a broom, and we appreciated that. So in the time of need, show Black people, show your face, don't be afraid. We're human beings and we're all here together and we're trying to get it together. We just have to see who's on our side and down with us. So be down, don't say it, show and prove.

Racism is something that is going to have to be outbred. Unfortunately, what we're doing now as far as gang-banging is not going to help us, because we're going to die and racism will still be here. It's all about the babies. You're going to teach your baby one of two things. Either you're going to teach your children to break up the stereotypes or you're going to teach your baby another thing, which is hate. Hate is a stagnating disease. It's not all about hate, it's about judging a devil by its deeds. Once you size up the person, then you handle them, but you just can't draw a conclusion. If you do that, then you'll think that just because someone is the same color as you that they're your homie, and they may turn around and cross you. So you can't do that, you have to size everybody up. When you're around me talking bad about other people, then when you're not around me, you might be talking bad about me.

I think that right now with the books that are coming out, we're in a renaissance period. To me it's like the rebirth of the fifties.

The first fight right now that we're going to have is with the brothers; before you can get any business going, you're going to have your internal fight. If we removed the drug problem and the violence on ourselves . . . look at us, we're in a pretty good position to do something, all we have to do is do some reevaluating, put more emphasis on school and the family and build family-based organizations. If everybody is just going for self, then nothing is going to happen. I think this time we are in now is going to make history—hip-hop and this whole generation of young people involved with gangs. It's like the second rock 'n' roll era. Rock 'n' roll was the first attempt to join people of the same mind, oppressed people, people who were fed up with BS were joining up, and it was stopped. Now here we go again, this is the tension that you feel, it's not a Black thing, it's the white kids saying, "What's up?" going to see Malcolm X, asking for information. So they're trying to shut down the information between the people of the same mind-set.

Do you understand that there are no more strong Black TV programs. They cut off all the real shows; what they did is create a ghetto on Thursday night. They have *Martin,* but they cut off *Arsenio, Roc, South Central,* and *In Living Color.* What they're doing is cutting off information. They don't want us talking to white kids, they don't want anybody white to understand Black people, they want to dictate to the white kids what we're about.

I didn't become Ice-T until I was around seventeen, I was just a little kid. Then I started picking up my flavor, my attitude, and my ideas. Our babies are us from day one, they're going to be dropping it, the revolution is going to be on. What they are trying to do with rap is what they're doing with TV, trying to shut it all down. They don't like their daughters coming home and taking down their Vanilla Ice poster and putting up a poster of Eazy-E above their princess bedroom set. The people who want to use words like *traditional* and *good ol' days,* they're seeing Body Count come out, and a million white kids listening to Black rage and agreeing with it, yelling "F— the police." "This is impossible. It's okay for the Blacks to yell f— the police, they've been yelling f— the police, but when the white kids yell it about us we have to do something." If you look at the cover for *Home Invasion,* that's what it's all about. They do not care about the impact on Black people, but when we create allies within their own homes, that becomes a big problem to them.

We're going to look back at this time and see how the world was trying to push itself together. The more that certain people push toward each other, at the same time there's going to be people out there that are going to try to tear us apart. The more they see the Black Power coming together, the more you'll see radical whites, because they feel the pressure of people trying to get together.

There's a lot of different ways to approach this, but my particular approach is to unify all the people of a particular mind-set, regardless to everything else. More like on the Panthers tip. The Panthers were like, if you're on the bottom, you're in the Black; if you're on the top, then you're in the white. It has nothing to do with the skin pigmentation.

That's when they really considered me a so-called threat, when I changed my perspective from just anger to actual solutions. As long as you're just angry, you're not a threat. It's when you start coming up with solutions, when you start telling Black folks to move out of the ghetto, to move into Beverly Hills. When I say I want to make this the Black community up here on the hill. They thought that they had branded us with the mind-set of "you stay where you are, you're leaving your hood if you do that." I'm saying f— that, why shouldn't we live on Sunset Plaza, because basically sooner or later people are going to realize that we're not just from South Central, we're not even only just from Africa, we're from Earth, so anyplace you want to live and rest your head you go do it. If you want to live in China, then go to China and lay up, because you're not restricted to any particular place. They have created mental boundaries in us, which say we don't surf, we don't ride skateboards, we don't jet-ski, we don't horseback ride, we don't snow-ski, we don't swim, so what do we do? What have we allowed ourselves to be perceived as doing? We fix up cars and hang out on the corners? I'm like, let's get back into life and expand the Black horizons. You have to expand your brain, because you're from this universe and anything you want to do you should do it. As long as they keep us mentally on that reservation and tell you that Ice-T can't care about you because he got paid, that's like saying if you had AIDS and I had AIDS and I got cured, I wouldn't care about you anymore. I had a sickness, poverty, and I cured myself of it for the time being. I'm not even permanently cured, because they can take this away from me so quick, they showed with Mike Tyson how they can break you. Don't be mad at somebody for coming up, that's one of our main problems, we have to be happy for somebody when they come up. More people from the bottom need to make it to the top. The only place compassion can come from is from people who were once on the bottom and then make it to the top. I run into millionaires every day and they tell me how they used to live in a single house with their mother, they were broke, they can feel you. There's like an underground of people who might be living in this other world now, but who came from the bottom. We have to all push up, up, up, until we're all in there. You're going to bump into your allies. We have to help everybody come up. The kid who was broke the other day is now the guy at the bank approving loans.

What I'm trying to create is what I call on my lecture tour "young urban capitalist guerrillas." This is the opposite of a yuppie. A yuppie went to school, and when you go to school and spend a lot of time at school, you begin to gain animosity against people who didn't. So when they get that job, they're like, "You didn't go to school, you didn't have to spend sleepless nights studying like I did, so forget you. I'm not going to help you." What I'm trying to get kids to do is say, "I'm going to go to school and get that education, but I'm going to retain that love for my brother and sister who might not have been as smart as me or who just didn't take this route." The guerrilla part of it is that we will have to work at IBM, we will have to work within these publishing companies, but just to learn the game. The guy with the big company is not going to teach you, so you work for them for a while and learn the game. But you're a guerrilla because you're undercover, you play along with them, and master the game. Some people say that they don't like the system and that they are never going to become a part of it, and that blocks you out, so you don't learn. I speak at universities like Harvard and I tell them, "You can go to IBM, but you have to remember whose side you're on, and when you get in there, you have to reach your hands out for the rest of us that are out here." The yuppies were taught to forget. I run into Black people that say, "We're going to school and other Black people are telling us that we're trying to be white," and I tell them not to be mad because they don't understand. That's the last thing we need is a bunch of bitter, intelligent Black people to come out of school.

I feel it too sometimes, because this is what I just went through. What has Quincy Jones done lately? Nothing. Right now at Warner Brothers he's getting in the area of $33 million a year for an operating budget. Why is Quincy Jones such a big shot at Time Warner? Because he's Black. A company at that level has to have somebody Black in power. Quincy Jones is loved by everybody, he's not a bad man. But Quincy Jones is getting old. Who did they have over there at Warner Brothers to fill that slot? I do rap, I do rock, I do movies, books, comic books, TV. They had me balling with these guys and they were breeding me to step in, and not just to be Ice-T the rapper, but to one day take the desk at the corporation. Whenever Black people would raise up against Time Warner, they'd be like, "We got Ice-T. He's as credible as you can get. Handle them, Ice." And I'd do it, and I'd make about twenty to thirty million dollars a year. For this, all that I would have to do was in their words, "Tone it down a little bit. We love you, just tone it down a little bit." I made seven gold albums over there, they have no other Black artist over there that has done that many consecutively except Prince. Check the roster over there, nobody else, I was the best over there. I made them a lot of money. Then "Cop Killer" hit, I was riding a Warner jet, they was sending us to Acapulco, fifteen servants, it was jumping off. I was kicking it with these ballers, super-rich, then they tell me to "tone it down." I said, "No." I lost a TV show, *Ice TV,* I lost my DC comic books, my movies, *New Jack II,* I had three pictures, I lost my record deal, my book, all of that, because I wouldn't tone it down. Then niggers say, "Ice sold out." Can you see where the bitterness comes from? The sellout was right there, and I would have been paid, and you wouldn't be able to see me unless you walked through my private police force. But I had to get above that and realize that they just don't know, they don't understand the level of this game. They don't know what a sellout is. They wouldn't know one if it smacked them dead in the face. You get paid to sell out. The sellout is the one that they say, "Do something that you don't want to do and we'll pay you the money," and you say, "I'll do it." I didn't. I'm all right now because I'm doing my own thing my own way, and I can sleep at night. Selling out goes into your heart and you feel it, you know it.

I think Black people as a whole need to get their s— together, we need to learn how to respect achievements and be happy for the achievements of others, instead of being envious and jealous of others. Until we do that, until we give Arsenio his props, and not wait until the last week of his show . . . Arsenio was working at f—ing Paramount, what do you want him to do, come out with an Afro pick in his hair and have a hundred people onstage banging every day? That would have lasted a week, he was on for five years, and he helped a whole lot of people get exposure. Now we have no national outlet to talk. I could say something on *Arsenio* and everybody in the whole country would hear it. That's over and I'll give you five years before that happens again. What's going to happen is they're going to put somebody like Dan Cortez on and give us that. They're going to find a way to try and suck Arsenio's market. When Tracy Chapman sings, represent. Whatever we do we have to support each other, because until then we're just fighting against ourselves.

Once we get the senseless violence down, there will be a lot more networking, it's going to give us a chance to talk instead of fight. I think this gang peace is going to give us the groundwork for us to become a powerful force. As long as we're fighting, and you live on the other side of town, I can't even come over there to talk to you about business. Gang violence and Black-on-Black violence is the number one killer of us, more than AIDS or any other disease, any foreign war, or racism itself. The only thing that killed more of us is actual slavery.

The most unfortunate thing is that there are extremely admirable qualities that are overlooked in gang membership. The theory of being willing to die for one's loved one or friend is something that very few men can even come to grips with, but these individuals don't just say it or pledge love, they carry it out. The theory of someone saying, "I'm your friend and I will die for you," that's admirable, but the misdirection and them aiming it at each other and each other's neighborhood is the big travesty. If we could take that same quality and put it towards positiveness, in other words love each other with that same energy, we could unite and become more powerful than anybody could possibly imagine. That's why I have a lot of love for the brothers, because I know that what they're doing isn't something that's easy to do. Most people probably only look at their baby or their immediate family and say, "If anything ever happens to you, I'll die." But in gang membership you say that to your homiez. Then when something happens to you, they meant that s—, and they move on it. That's a good quality, the question is the ability to redirect that toward protecting ourselves and upholding our families and our communities, that's when we'll really have locks on it. Like Minister Farrakhan says, "These are the soldiers, they're just misguided."

What gang-banging really is, is male love pushed to its limits. It's like surrogate families and brothers bonding together to the death, because it's not all about selling drugs or all about banging, it's about kickin' it with the homiez and backing the homiez. It's love. As insane as it may seem, it's all based on love. I'm trying to bring it full circle, understanding that it's madness, mayhem, and wrong, but there's a lot of honor that goes on in this and there's a lot of qualities that these young brothers that you may look down on have that you ain't got. Somebody will come in your house and kill your wife and your children and you won't do s—, you'll sit on your ass. These brothers ain't having it. A lot of us wish we had it. It's just the wrong direction and the confusion in the world that they live in that causes them to strike out at each other. To the layman it will look like it's a world based on hate, but it's not, it's based on love. It's a love for the hood. Every time you write the name of your hood across your back, or all your dead homiez all over your body, that's some serious s—.

To the reader, if you've gotten to this point in this book, that must mean you care to some extent or your curiosity has brought you this far, but before we go any further, understand that no matter how much you want to believe that this is based on hate, this whole gang thing is based on male love pushed to the pinnacle. Anybody that has picked up this book and read to this point, you gotta care some kind of way, and hopefully you'll gain some insight and understanding.

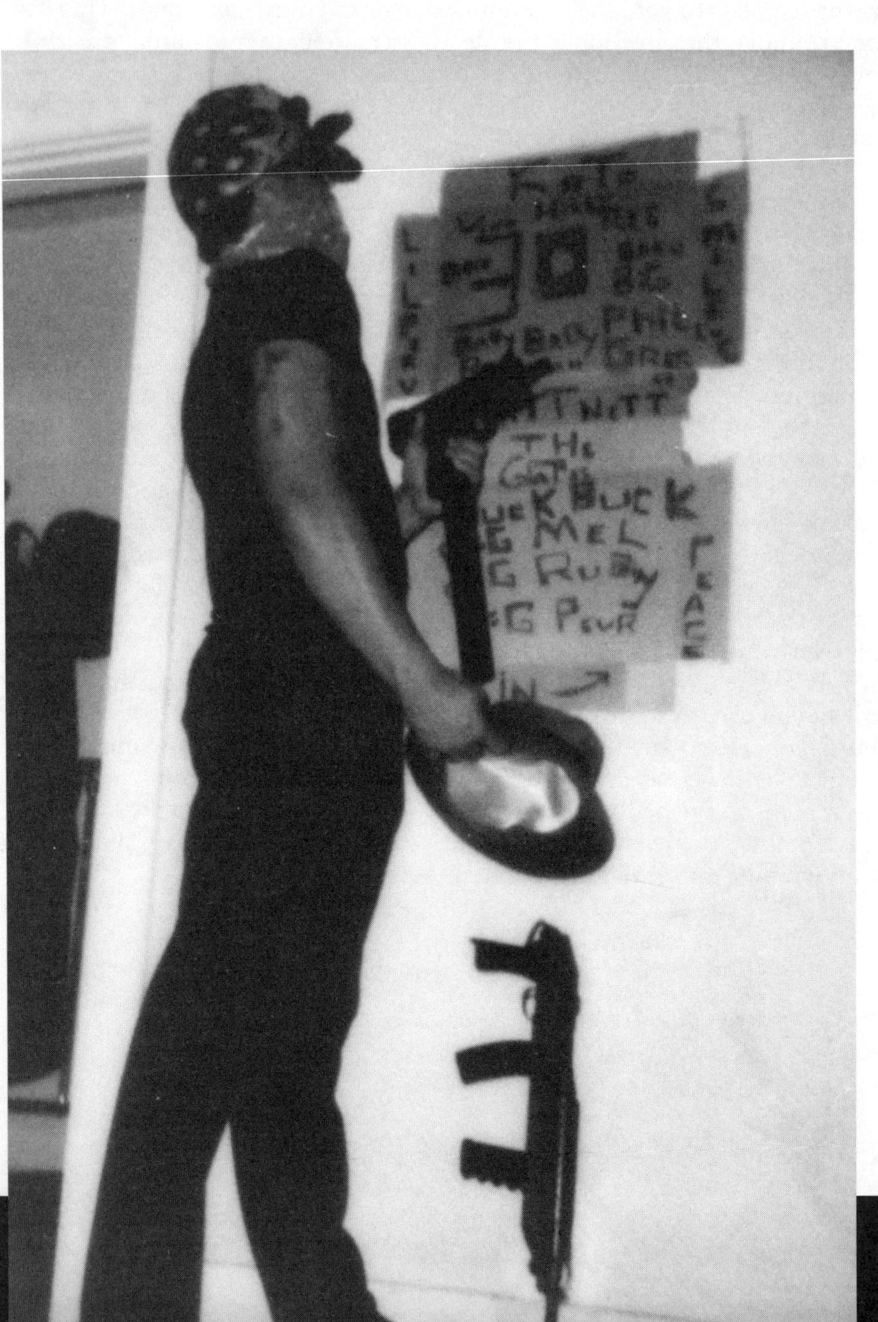

# BIG PHIL

*(This is Big Phil from Westside Harlem 30's. To everybody reading this book, these are the solutions to our problems. We cannot continue with the same madness. I've been through this and I know, if you don't take heed to what we're saying, then you won't make it to the age I am now. The solution is to lay down our guns and all unite together and rebuild our communities, our families, and our lives. We can do this! We have to do this! Peace, Big Phil.)*

**Q:** How did the organization South Central Love come about?

**P:** I had been going back and forth down to KJLH [Stevie Wonder's radio station in Los Angeles] after listening to the program they had on at the station talking about peace in the streets. I had already been at peace, like with my car club, we could ride anywhere through the city. So mainly we were having picnics and stuff, and I was seeing how many brothers was coming through from different gangs without any problems, you know, just kickin' it, having a nice time, no crap or anything. At first I really didn't feel that peace was going to work on the Westside. That was about a year and a half ago, around the time of the Rodney King beating. After that I was out there seeing all the guys getting along with each other, it felt good again, like the early seventies with the homeboys kickin' it and relating to each other.

**Q:** You go back that far?

**P:** Oh, yeah. I started banging when I was ten years old. It was about '71 when I started.

So when I was listening to them on KJLH, I said, "Well, I'm already pushing peace with my car club, the guys are already coming to our functions with the car club." At the time I was having different picnics for the homeboys that are RIP. I was getting a real good response from the gang members. They were coming out to the functions, being real respectful, there were no problems at all. I mean we had a parking lot full, with thousands of gang members, and there were no problems, we were just kickin' it, showing love, no disrespect, just showing love. So I was looking at it, and I felt if I could do it with my car club, I could step to the other side, on the reality side, and just come on with it on the peace level myself, but I still wasn't all the way with it.

**Q:** What made you not want to be with the peace at first?

**P:** I didn't think it was real, I'm talking as far as the true thing. I was down with the car club, but I was still affiliated with my homeboys, which I love, and still love. I wasn't really going down there unless something happened, and even then I would have been going down there to take care of business, you know. I felt that they were my brothers, and if I lose a brother, it was all about the retaliation.

What really made me come to be with the truce was that I had just lost a real dedicated, loved homeboy. I went to his funeral and actually drew down on the police. At that time I didn't care about dying. Then I stepped back the next day, and I said, "Well, what can I do for my homeboys if I'm dead?" You know what I'm saying? I can't do a damn thing for them. So my heart just went straight out for peace. I have to show them a different way. We've lost too many over nothing.

It was a wake-up call. Something woke me up, "You can either die today, or you can bring peace and do something positive for your homeboys so that they may have a better way of life instead of death." Myself, I've lost over one hundred homeboys, and the ones that I haven't lost are in the penitentiary. So there are maybe two of us who are still out here that function, the rest are dead. That's like growing up from the age of ten, and being with one hundred dudes, and there's just two of you guys left, and maybe three in the pen. One has all day [life], and a few are getting ready to get out in a couple of years. So basically I had to change, I had to change for the better.

Also, my nieces and nephews . . . we have our families in these houses, we have our mothers, fathers, and grandmothers in these houses held hostage. They're scared to come out of the house. They're like hostages, so there has to be a change.

**Q:** Did your family ever try to get you to become inactive?

**P:** I was brought up around BGFs [Black Guerilla Families], who are positive brothers on the Black level. I felt that the BGF was for Black people. It's a penitentiary gang that was started, I don't know who started it, but my folks that was around me were powerful, and I just used to look up to them, because they were about Blackness, they were straight powerful. This was before I even knew anything about Crips. I used to see three-piece machine guns when I was ten years old, I didn't even know what they were, I used to just put them together.

That's what got me kind of on the militant tip. I also didn't have a father around, so that right there made me to have to look out for my family. My mother, she's always been a very powerful and militant person, she's just straight militant. She gets along with any homeboy I bring over there, it doesn't matter who. You could be the baddest, you could have killed one hundred and fifty people, you still would have to listen to Moms, because she's going to speak it, she's going to speak the real. So that's what tip I was on.

I just went my own way, which was Crippin'. When I was young, I saw my brother get jumped on by a Brim, and at that time I didn't know what a Brim was, and I just wanted to be the complete opposite. Maybe if it would have been the Crips that jumped on my brother, I might have been a Blood, but the Bloods jumped on my brother and that made me want to be different from them. It's as simple as that, so I became a Crip, living in an all-Blood hood. I was one guy living around thousands of Bloods. So I got beat up and shot at every other day. Then I changed the whole cycle of my neighborhood and turned them all into Crips. The younger ones that was coming up, I just cycled them and turned them into Crips. I came up on Forty-third and Western. The first gang I started was the Four-Tre Gangsters. They had the Four-Tre Avalons and the Four-Tre Hoovers. The Four-Tre Hoovers were in the middle, the Four-Tre Avalons were on the east side, and I started the Four-Tre Gangsters, which there was only about five of us at that time, but we were fighting Bloods every day. I mean we had problems. Then I stepped up and started the Rollin' 40's, which is a big gang now, superbig. Back then there may have only been ten to fifteen of us. I was taking on gun battles with everybody. Then I had some brothers that took me on from the Rollin' 30's, which was one of the biggest, one of the hardest, toughest gangs in South Central.

I had left gangs alone in '78. I was through with gangs. I was through with it. I was into weight lifting. I was around Big Jimel Barnes, which him, Tookie, and Raymond Washington were OG Crips that we all used to look up to back in the day, so they were like my idols as far as on the Crippin' tip, they were my big homiez, and I wanted to be like my big homeboys, you know what I'm saying. So when I started buffin' with Jimel, I blew up to some twenties [20-inch arms], then I got sick with cancer.

That's when the Harlem Crips [Rollin' 30's] took me up under their wing, because the violence was still going on, but they was showing me much love, so I turned over to the 30's. I just started clicking again with the Harlem 30's. So they recognized me as an OG homie, they put me on that status as soon as I came over there. I was Big Phil—"That's the OG"—so we went on from there, and all responsibilities I had towards Harlem I had to live up to.

**Q:** When you came with the Harlems, what gave you that OG status?

**P:** As far as the OG status, once you have eighteen, nineteen, twenty years into it, you're an OG. I mean, I started at the age of ten, and my older homeboys was like sixteen, seventeen. That's why they called us Baby Crips. So we were Original Baby Crips. We were the baby homeboys. There are double OGs that are in their forties now, but we're still known as OGs too, because we were the babies running with them, and we were packing, doing their dirty work. Those were our big homiez, our big brothers. We had to watch their backs. Whatever we did, we did it for them, the love. So my years go way back. I haven't really been active since '89 when I got out of Chino [penitentiary]. I was going to get back active, but it just wasn't in my heart, after coming out of there, and seeing what time it was.

**Q:** What type of things did you see in there that woke you up?

**P:** When I was in there, I was Crippin' hard. I had brothers following me in there. Wherever I go, brothers listen to me, because they respect me, and they know I'm not going to lead them into any bull. I've always been a leader. I've never been a follower. If I have to follow you, I'm going to ride by myself. I'm the type of person that if your ways are not right, I'm going to do things by myself. I didn't need a gang, but the love and respect of my homeboys was way more than a gang.

When I first went to Chino, I was put through all kinds of tests. I had squabbles here, squabbles there. I had a thyroid condition, and I was put in the hole for two weeks for fighting when I went to court, so I really couldn't think. I wasn't in good shape, I was kind of sick. So I went through there being sick, and then I finally got myself to a position where I was almost well, feeling good about myself, and kickin' it with the homiez, going through riots, being involved in different activities, and basically just understanding myself while doing time. You see, I went to the pen for somebody else's doings, and being sick I lost everything I had.

Before I went to jail I had a grip of money, and I had a Rolls-Royce, but I was put in predicaments by the police. They tried to use my being sick, and they tried to take me through different changes, which was wrong. They'd plant a gun on me or get one of my homeboys to plant a gun on me and use me because of my illness. They'd try to get me to tell on a homeboy or something. I wasn't with that, so say one of your homeboys get busted, and maybe they can't do the time . . .

By being in the system and seeing how all the brothers are on one side, and the white boys and the Mexicans are over on the other side, I was like, "Man, what is this? Is this how it is? And we're up in here killing each other? We're out in the streets killing each other like this?" When I got out, I put together a few gang meetings, four hundred to five hundred guys at the gang meetings, you know, getting ready to rally it up again. Soon after that my mother caught a blood clot on her brain, and I rushed her to the hospital, and it saved her life. So that right there really woke me up and told me that I couldn't keep doing this to Moms. I was taking her through too much. So basically it just changed me.

We've been fighting a cause that's a disease. It's a disease that we caught when we were young, and we have to get rid of it. It's worse than cancer, I know because I've had cancer, I've been through chemotherapy, radiation treatment, and everybody that used to take me to the hospital is dead. You know what I'm saying, the homeboys that used to run me back and forth to the hospitals are dead now. It's something else, man. There has to be a change.

**Q:** What are some ways you feel we can change things?

**P:** What we have to do is put ourselves on the line, the OGs, we all have to put ourselves on the line, and re-educate our homeboys and let them know what's really going on. This is a disease, and there's no way out of it but death! If we don't have love, respect, and want peace for each other . . . if we don't honor our mothers, have respect, love, or peace, then next is death.

**Q:** What do you think the root cause is for this disease throughout the Black community?

**P:** I have a buddy named Tim, he has a perfect definition, a poem that hasn't been out yet, he's been trying to get this poem out. He describes it, and when you read it, it talks to you. It's something that got started by a group of homeboys, and it just shouldn't have gone this far. I was thinking maybe it was just a group of homeboys getting together, but my understanding is that it used to be called Community Revolution in Progress [CRIP]. I heard that it was started to stop gang violence, and it turned into gang violence, and that's where the word Crip came from. A lot of guys don't know that we didn't even sag back then. That's the white man's terminology. We didn't wear rag colors. When I first started, we didn't wear rags. It wasn't about that. It wasn't about sagging. We used to press our clothes to the maximum. We had the best clothes in the city. We were like celebrities. Everybody wanted to be a Crip back then, because you were a celebrity. "He's a Crip." "Is that right?" Everybody wanted to be a Crip. But it got out of control.

**Q:** Speak a little more about how the police tried to use you.

**P:** They knew I was ill, and they tried to do something to me because I had so much power. They charged me with crimes and they sent me to jail for crimes that I didn't commit. I may have been at home laying on my couch when a particular crime was committed, but they kicked my door down, three or four times, and charged me for crimes that I didn't even know anything about. Man, they broke the windows out in my house, cut my mother's friend up, took me to court, and charged me with shooting at a young boy. When I went to court, I didn't even know the boy, you know what I'm saying? Because I was going through medication treatment, they were just trying to do things to me to make me flip over.

See, a lot of OG gang members that are not coming out to stand up for peace are scared, because the police probably used them. Did you see the movie *Colors*? There were certain parts in that movie that were real, because the police try to use guys that call the shots, to put the younger guys away. Where they'd do certain things for you, if you'd do certain things for them. Naw, uh-uh. That's what they tried to do with me. I served four years for something I didn't know a damn thing about, because I wouldn't let them try me out. This is reality, no lie, I went to jail for two crimes I didn't know anything about, I wasn't even there, but I had so much power that when something else would happen, they just stuck it on me, bam. They couldn't get me for anything I had done. You see what I'm saying? One of my buddies has been around for years, and all he has is a traffic citation.

**Q:** When you went to court for those crimes, what happened?

**P:** I'm Big Phil, man. "That's Big Phil." I bailed out of jail, a $25,000 case, boom, they kicked my door down again, and charged me with another case. Charged me with kidnapping. I was the first black gang member in L.A. that they called a terrorist, and you can find the newspaper from 1985. It was in the *L.A. Times* on the front page, and they had a picture of Chief Daryl Gates, a gang of guns on the table, and said I was the organizer. Straight BS. I was the first one they called a terrorist in South Central. Things like that happen all the time. They used to get us and take us in a Blood neighborhood and holler out, "Crip," and try to get us smoked.

All police aren't bad, but the majority are f'd up, because they will put you in a predicament and try to use you to get your head knocked off. Then they will lie on you. I feel any brother that's out there, if they charge you with a crime, and they arrest you, don't speak to anybody, go straight to the county jail. Don't say anything to anybody but a lawyer. Nobody. Not even your homeboys. Don't say anything to anybody. If they bust you, go straight to a lawyer, pay for a lawyer, if you don't . . . public defenders, they work for the police. The best thing to do is don't say anything to anybody but a lawyer. Get a state-appointed lawyer. That's it. "I don't want to talk to anybody." If they arrest you, "Charge me with the crime, I'm out of here, send me to the county jail, and we'll go from there." Don't have them take you back in a room and try to interrogate you and try to pick your mind for ideas, because that's all they do is pick your mind for ideas. Don't give them any ideas, just keep your mouth shut, and go straight to the county jail. Wait for seventy-two hours. Don't give them anything, keep your mouth closed.

**Q:** Who were you hearing on the radio station KJLH that captured you?

**P:** I was listening every week, I was hearing Mike Conception, I was listening to him, he's pretty positive as far as if I heard him talking about peace, then I knew there was something in it. I knew it was getting to the real now. Then I had a buddy down there by the name of Russ, who was working at the station, and he was telling me to come on down. So I said, "I'll be down there." I wanted to first hear what they were talking about. I didn't know anybody else. I knew Mike, but when I walked in there, I saw a few people that I knew like Big Al, from Grape Street, I knew him, because he would be out there low-riding with us and stuff. So I said, "Big Al is up in here, I see Mike over there, this looks kind of positive, let me see what's up." So I listened to the brothers talk, and they were talking positive, so I put a little output out there, and a week later one of my homeboys got killed, bam. I didn't go back up to the station for two weeks.

Then one of my boys called me and told me that they were having a gang summit; "Come on up here, Phil." So I went up there, and I caught the tail end of it, and I heard the brothers in there talking about peace. I saw Tony Bogard in there, which I had been hearing him on the radio station, and Brother Ship, from Gardena. I saw Big Jimel up in there, so I said, "I'm starting to see the homeboys in here now." So that's when I put my output down. I just waited till everybody said what they had to say, then I dropped it down to the media. I let the homeboys and everybody out there that knows me know that it's about peace and love, and that I'm submitting myself to this. "So y'all don't have to be scared now, y'all can come on this end." There are a lot of dudes out here who want peace, but they're scared to push up that way, because they are scared of what their gang might do to them. I'm looking at it like this, there's nothing worse the gang can do to you than you being active in the gang, and that's death both ways. I can get killed doing this peace, or I can get killed banging, but I know that if I get killed pushing for peace, that I'm doing the right thing. I'm showing love. I'm trying to get the brothers back together again.

I know there's somebody up there looking out for me, because I'm still here. I've been shot in the head, I've been shot in the back six times, I've been shot in the leg, I've had two stomach surgeries, I've had cancer, and thyroid disease, I've had radiation treatment and chemotherapy. I've been stomped out a hundred times, shot at a hundred times, so I'm like, "Damn, there's somebody up there, and he's calling me." You know what I'm saying? I have to do this. I have dudes right now that's calling me up like, "Phil, I'm with the peace. Can we be about peace?" I said, "Man, if I'm on this end, we can let ours go too." I had a brother that had been hiding from me for seven years, but I want him to come on out and see that I'm real about this, you know what I'm saying. When you turn to peace, I even tell the peacemakers, we've got to let all enemies go.

It's not about killin' and it's not about money. Money is not love. Love is here [points to the heart]. A lot of guys just don't know what love is, they think money is love. I don't know one homeboy that outlasted a dollar bill or outlasted that street corner that we used to hang on. That block is still there, they're all dead. That dollar is still circulating. So when you've got love, you can try to keep the homeboys here. The majority of my homeboys didn't even make it to the age of twenty-one. They're all dead. I've been a pallbearer at over fifty funerals. I've got a gang of obituaries. I've got gang pictures of them alive, smiling, and I've got pictures of them dead. I have about three or four thousand pictures. It's a trip because I've been taking these pictures all of my life. I've got pictures of all my homeboys. The ones that were living, and now they're dead. So they go from living, having fun together, to dying, and I'm still here.

Augustus E. Fields (Pu-Pu), rest in peace

In loving memory of Charles Edward Winston

Lavell Laymond Hughes

rest in peace

## Big Phil

I see the youngsters these days, they're shooting each other over nothing.

**Q:** How is it different now than from back in the days?

**P:** Back in the days when you heard about a killing, it was a big thing. You always heard about somebody getting their butt kicked. I used to get mine kicked, and I used to kick some myself, but now it's like, "What's up, fool?" Buyah [like he's shooting a pistol], you're dead, it's over with. That's not how you do it.

**Q:** Is that why you focus a lot on putting the guns down?

**P:** I'm one of the original pistol packers. So I know this is the solution. The solution is to put the pistols down. Put the pistols down, man, then we can start living again.

**Q:** Inside the peace movement, what can we do to get brothers to put the pistols down?

**P:** The only way it's going to happen, and I'm going to be real with you, man, it's like this: in order to put the pistols down we've got to build trust. It's not going to happen overnight. We have to build trust in the neighborhoods. We have to give the brothers a chance to earn trust. We've got to have it to where if they come to us and say, "Look, check this out, we don't want anybody in our hood." If we can get together with all the other gang members and agree that no hood will go into another hood, tell them that this hood doesn't want anybody in their hood, then they can try to get relaxed. This is something we've got to do. It's got to happen, because if they keep producing those pistols, we're going to keep dying. There's only one way out with a gun. It's either twenty-five years to life, or death, because what you put out, it's going to come right back. Whenever you bust, somebody's going to bust right back at you. Look in the mirror, are you ready to die? Put the gun upside your head and pull the trigger. You might as well kill yourself, because if you go out and kill somebody else, you're going to get it back, it does not matter. I've witnessed it a million times. It always happens. When I'd bust at somebody, bam, it happens to me once again. It's not going to work. You have to put the pistols down. Then we can start talking about what we can do positive in the community.

**Q:** How are brothers responding to that message of putting down the guns?

**P:** Just what I said, we've got to build trust. Nobody is putting anything down until you build some trust. "Keep them out of the neighborhood, this is our neighborhood." That's our main objective, to get our neighborhoods, all neighborhoods in South Central, functioning again, where the gang members in the neighborhood can contribute to the community and make the community feel safe again. Where the community can come back out and work with the gang members and put together some programs in the neighborhoods, and some businesses, where they can run the businesses and get the money functioning where they can get the younger homeboys to work with them.

That's my main objective. My main objective is getting South Central L.A. back communicating and functioning. We have all of these churches. I've never seen this many churches. That's where people think they can hide out at. They go to the churches to hide out. That's not going to do it. The churches are not going to do it. We're going to have to come out of those churches and come into the community and get it back functioning, instead of hiding behind that preacher. God knows when your day is here, you can stay in those churches all day long and pray to God and come home and talk s—, because most of them people that are going up in those churches are hypocrites. They're going to those churches, giving their money to the pastor, and coming home with some BS. So if you guys can go to that church, you can come into your community with the young brothers and see if you can work up something positive together. Let's get this back rolling. Just say if you have five guys on this block, and say the whole block comes on out with them and tries to do something positive with them, maybe you have a lawyer on the block, or a construction worker, you know, something positive, and they say, "Hey, man, let me take you up under the wing. Come on and work with me." Give them something positive to do. Man, it will work. These brothers need something to do.

Basically, the city is broke. These brothers are out here with no money. If there was money circulating in these neighborhoods, there would be less dope selling, less drinking, there would be more positive things for them to do. They have too much idle time, and a lot of these brothers want things to do, but they do not want to work for somebody else, they want to work for themselves. They want their own businesses. They don't want somebody else calling shots on them. These are strong generals, warriors, soldiers, born leaders. "Give me two dollars or three dollars an hour to listen to your funny-looking butt. Work in McDonald's?" Can you see a strong general soldier in McDonald's? "Yeah, I'll come work . . . open the cash register up, I'll work your money." You know what I'm saying? "Give me your money, I'm not working for your crumbs. Don't treat me like an ant."

**Q:** Where do you feel the money that needs to be in the community will come from?

**P:** The money has got to come from ourselves, building, and circulating them dollars back. Instead of going and buying that Louis [Vuitton] and all of that, let's put together a Black product that's going to circulate the money. People will want to get into it then.

**Q:** Where do you think all the pistols are coming from that are being used in the community?

**P:** I don't know where they generate these guns from. I don't know anything about it. They just come up. I used to buy mine out of the store all the time, assault rifles. When I used to buy mine, I would use them the next day. I wasn't buying them to go hunting, I was hunting homeboys. I remember when I bought fifteen guns one day, and I'd be damned if the police didn't come to my house that same night and try to get those fifteen guns.

I had a gang of homeboys sitting on my porch. Somebody called them and said, "He has fifteen guns over there, you'd better come get him." I was so smart I made sure they didn't find them. I used to get mine straight out the shops, but now these guns, I don't know where they're coming from. I feel we do not need any more guns pumped into South Central L.A. We need some money, we need some money to circulate into South Central L.A. The guns aren't doing anything but circulating death. They're not circulating life.

**Q:** How would you explain the way a brother feels about somebody else coming into their hood?

**P:** This is just a different stage of the Indian tribes. Territories. Just like in the cowboys-and-Indians days. That's what it basically boils down to. Apaches, Blackfoot, you know what I'm saying. Really, we don't even own a damn thing, but we think it's our territory. I mean, we feel that this is our neighborhood, this is where we lay our heads down. We feel if you come over here with drama, you're disrespecting us.

That's the main thing we have to understand, we have to bring the respect up, because if you don't have respect, it's not going to work. We have to build respect up first. Basically, just like I said, the hoods are territories, and once you come in our territory with any kind of negative, we're going to get you out of here. As long as you're not coming over into the neighborhood with violence, it should be cool. Just say, for instance, say we're at peace in our neighborhoods; if we're at peace, then you can bring your family over here. Don't come over here by yourself, because we will think that you're over here looking for something to do. Scheming, trying to find out where we're hanging out at or something. If you're for peace, then you can bring your family over here, we can chill. Straight out. I feel like this, the only way we're going to situate these neighborhoods is we have got to do something as far as economics. Every gang meeting I've been to, all I hear is, "Phil, we need some money. We need something to do." We have all these brothers out here that don't have anything to do but get high and smoke Sherm; they need something to do that's positive. If we had a program in every neighborhood in this city, we could get the community back right, man, it would be over with in South Central.

**Q:** As an OG, do you find yourself in a position to bring that unity together in the neighborhoods?

**P:** Yes, with the networking of other Black brotherhoods. It's a human-rights thing that we're about, but we have to start with ourselves first. We're the ones doing this to each other, so if we were able to get on the wrong tip, we can get back on the right tip.

If we go out there telling the media our plans, then we're not going to get anything accomplished, because they're going to blow us right down. That's why I tell a lot of my brothers in here, just speak on what we're about, and when it gets down to the nitty-gritty, we're going to have to do the right thing. We're going to have to start pushing in these neighborhoods, and we're going to have to build the pot up. We're going to have to go from door to door and let them know that this is what we're about. Everybody is going to want to put in that pot if they see something happening.

Like these churches, there shouldn't be five, ten, twelve churches in one neighborhood. If you're going to have a church, have one church in the neighborhood. Have everybody go there and put the Black dollars in that church and funnel it out and build buildings and get with the Brotherhood, and whoever is positive in your neighborhood, and get to work. Don't let anybody know a damn thing but your own folks. You know you're going to have the infiltration, but there's going to be so many heads, who are they going to infiltrate? "Damn, we don't know where to go."

I learned from Malcolm X and Dr. Martin Luther King that you can't lead by yourself, so if we have a hundred leaders, who are they gonna get? Which leader? You f around and tax one, and all the other leaders will get all of y'all, you know what I'm saying? We're not trying to . . . all respects due to Farrakhan . . . we're not trying to be Farrakhan, we're not trying to be Malcolm X, we're not trying to be Martin Luther King, but what we are trying to do is get things happening. There can't be one man calling the shots, because that will not work out here. This is South Central L.A., and it's full of generals. It's *full* of generals. Every man in this city has leadership potential. There are a lot of followers, but there are a whole lot of leaders. When we get all of these leaders together, it's over with, and they're coming every day.

**Q:** Where does the cycle of killing come from?

**P:** Retaliation, money, drugs, a lot of family disputes, women disputes, kids' disputes, jackings, all different kinds of things. Mainly *money.*

**Q:** So how do we build back the trust and the respect?

**P:** It has to start in the hood, it has to start with the OGs putting it down to the youngsters. It's like if the community calls a meeting, say they have a community meeting with the gang members, "We're going to build a pot for you guys," if everybody in the community puts a dollar in that pot, some could put $5, some could put $10, and build that pot up. Then say, "Well, look, we want to pick your strongest members, and have them protect our neighborhood." They're going to make sure that neighborhood stays peaceful. Plus they're getting a paycheck. They're working shifts. They're doing something positive. We're policing our own neighborhoods. I mean, we can make it to where Angelus Funeral Home will have less business, the police force would be able to lay off more then half the officers, because they wouldn't have anything to do.

We have to look at it like this too, what if somebody gets killed over in the neighborhood, what are we going to do? It's a hard call. You have these OGs, they don't want to sell out, nobody wants to sell out, so that's when we're going to have to take it upon ourselves to handle our own business. No twenty-five years to life if you come over here and disrespect this, and disrespect what we're doing, you've already f'd yourself off, because we're about peace, love, and happiness here, and if you're about breaking that bond, you're banished. That way brothers would wake up.

**Q:** What is the response you're getting from the OGs about the peace?

**P:** A lot of them will be with it if you give them something positive to do, because a lot of them are just on the corners smoking crack. A little young homie might come, "Phil, what do you want me to do?" Check this out, I have a job for you. You make this much a week. You want to do it? "Yeah." You know what I'm saying. Don't give 'em no little penny-ante job, let's circulate some money over here where we can pay these brothers some ends. Like $10 or $11 an hour where they'll feel good. There's only about three or four hundred homeboys in each hood. You're going to tell me that all of these thousands of houses in these hoods can't produce five bucks, maybe ten bucks a week to the cause? They can build a hell of a pot, man.

We have to get all the churches to be in it too. We have to get everybody to be in this. I want to see the brothers get into it too. The Muslims, the rap artists, I want to see everybody unite as one. If you're making those Black dollars, circulate them back into the neighborhood. I want to see everybody get involved with it. *Everybody,* because that's the only way it'll work.

**Q:** What motivated you to get more involved?

**P:** Once I pushed myself on that end, it was on, there wasn't no turning back. I remember back in '81, '82, gang-banging kind of played out. Brothers were just into making money. Like these dope-dealing suckers. I don't like dope dealing. They don't have any other way to get ends, but I don't like it myself. I used to get mine by building low-riders. A few OG Bloods used to come by my house, and I was an OG Crip, but we were cool, because there wasn't any feud. They were Big Bloods, and I was a Big Crip. Respect-respect. If I step on your toe, then get me; if you step on mine, I'm getting you. The main thing is respect.

Respect is a lot, because if you disrespect somebody, you're gonna get popped. Say we're all together somewhere, if you don't disrespect me, and I don't disrespect you, how are we going to get into an argument? How are we going to squabble if we don't disrespect each other? We're gonna stay on the same program. A lot of brothers need to learn how to show respect, because they don't have respect, they don't respect anything. The old ethics that we used to have when we were banging a long time ago was when we were going to get somebody, we were going to get *them,* we weren't going to shoot at babies, and mamas. They're way outrageous with it now. These are pistol Crips, pistol Bloods. If you're going to get somebody, go get that man, don't go get his little kid or baby or his mama, that's not straight. They don't even know what they're shooting at, they're just shooting. Sometimes they might be on the boulevard shooting, just to be shooting, just to get something started. They might kill one of their own homeboys and not even know it.

**Q:** What was the structure based on in the organizations?

**P:** My structure was built on me putting work in and calling shots. I wouldn't tell you to go do something, I'd go do it myself. "Well, homie, let's go blast . . . " What you mean *let's?* I'm going to blast. I'd go put the work in, and there was no problem, and I'd be back home drinking some water or something, there wasn't any problem with me.

Basically, when I was coming up, it was a leader thing. It was who was the toughest in that hood. When I put the Crips down over there in my neighborhood, I was that Crip. Basically, when I stopped in the 40's, and went over to the 30's, it was a different chain. It wasn't one man, it was a council of generals, because basically every man over there was a general.

So it has to happen. It has to happen on the positive, because we can't keep doing this.

**Q:** Speak about the process you had to go through to become more positive. What was that process like for you, and how can others also change to become more positive?

**P:** I feel that it takes a lot of discipline and a lot of education. When I first started South Central Love, I didn't know how I would be feeling now about life, and how we have to educate ourselves and do for ourselves. For me as an individual and bettering myself, I've learned that I have to do what it takes to better myself before I can better anyone else. I have to do better for myself as far as getting an education, because education is the key to success. If you're starting something and you're not educated enough to know what you're doing, then you're going to be running around in circles, but if you're educated and you know what you're doing, then you can get things going.

## Big Phil

**Q:** What were some of the steps that you took to educate yourself?

**P:** What really helped me was reading *Message to the Black Man.* That book helped me out a lot, because it got my mind in tune to what's going on in life, and what's going on within myself. If a lot of younger men would read that book and get knowledge of self, then they would actually know what is really going on. We have to educate ourselves. It doesn't cost to read a book; education is one of the easiest things in the world. A Black man can get an education when he can't get some food or water. He can educate himself.

We have to re-educate our children and get our children straight, and that will help our families. We really need strong family backing, because with better family backing we can all help each other.

**Q:** What has the experience been like pushing for peace out here on the streets of South Central Los Angeles?

**P:** You have your ups and your downs. You have the ones who want peace, and you have some who don't want it. [Two youngsters come to where the interview is taking place and ask Big Phil for some change for the ice cream truck. Phil then begins talking about the youth.] All the kids around here call me "Uncle Phil." I try to just take a little time out, like yesterday I took some time out and sat down with them and read to them, to show them something better. Our kids need something better to look at. All the family members need to go out sometimes to a park and sit down amongst each other and chat. We may have feelings or emotions toward each other that are hidden, and once we speak about them and talk about them in a family manner and get them out, then our families can grow closer together.

As far as out here with the peace, I've had a lot of ups and downs, and I've experienced things that I can't even speak about, but as far as peace, you have to have peace within yourself before you can push anything. If you don't have peace within yourself, you won't know what you're doing. You have to also have knowledge about what you're doing, and then you have to have something that you can take to brothers, as far as on the educational level. If you can talk to them about peace, and at the same time bring them some knowledge and let them know the way things are and give them an idea of different routes to take to start doing for themselves, then it would be better. But if we're just going to sit up and talk, talk, talk, then nothing is going to happen. It's going to be the same thing. [At this point another youngster comes to Big Phil to ask him a question.]

The kids look up to me so much that I just want to be positive for the kids and do good things for them. I want to show them by example and show them a different way in life, because if you show them the same old way, it's going to be the same old thing out here.

We need to understand that we have to help better ourselves in any and every positive manner there is. There has to be a better way. We have to get educated, that's the best thing in life, to get educated, because if we don't have any knowledge, then we don't have anything. In L.A. it's like we're all living in a dead zone. We have to really understand that we have to do for ourselves.

The ones out here that want to change their lives can change, the ones that don't, they're going to reach a point to where something is going to make them want to change their lives. But it's hard, it's hard out here. In L.A. life is just up and down.

**Q:** What should someone do when there's all of these negative forces coming against them?

**P:** The only thing you can do is to do all that you can and then give it up to the Supreme Being, because there is nothing else you can do about it, and make sure that He secures your life, because if He doesn't secure your life, you're not secure. God has to secure you.

**Q:** Any further words that you would like to express to the world?

**P:** If I could just have fifty kids over to my house and help them with their education every day, it makes me feel good as a person. That's what I'm really concerned about right now, the kids. You can talk to the older homiez, but they have their own minds. The kids is who we really have to work on now. We have to focus on their education, because they are the future. If we show them love, understanding, and respect, I think they'll grow up to be better people. We can't keep hollering and cursing at them, and calling them names and stuff like that, because if we do that, that's the way they're going to grow up. We have to re-educate our kids and really help them. I don't care what color your kids are, you have to educate them or re-educate them.

To the world, it's all about love. About loving yourself and loving the world.

> ***I know you don't know what life is really worth . . . half the story has never been told—So now you see the light—Stand up for your rights.***
>
> **—Bob Marley**

## SHOUT OUTS

Much Love and Respect to My Loved Ones Resting in Peace:

Big Dexter, Big Melvin, Big Ruben, Shark, Big Peur, Baby Brother, Cadillac Jim, Hucky Buck, Li'l Poochie, Porky, Raymond Washington, Baby

IN LOVING MEMORY
Of
Melvin Banks

In loving memory of Melvin Banks

Rubbin Ray Watson, rest in peace

Dog, Key Stone, Big Fee, Killer Pat, Reggie, Li'l Reggie, Daff, Bert, Andre, Li'l D-Mac, Michael Johnson, Ghost, Dewayne Capers, Mumbles, Pimp, Marlon, Uncle Phillip, Dee Dee, Grand Pow, Bird, Beep, ET, Loco Boy, Moonie, Li'l Man, Box Head, Li'l Bro, Ed Dog, Casper, Nelzee, Big Peru, Tiny Watt, Li'l Rich, Jackie Boy, Herald Mac, Fiddler, Brother, Li'l Dave, Price, Norm, Michelle K., Mom Mom, Li'l Crazy Keith, David Williams, Baby Boo, Eddie Mack, G-Rock, Lee Rat, Mousie, Blue Devil, Time Bomb, Li'l EQ, Shannon, Pistol Pete, Yog, Big Ron, New Birth, Nudy, Michelle F., and Albert Motown.

And a shout out to my mother, JoAnn Gago, the South Central Love homiez, Red, T. Rodgers, Tim, Big Russ, Tow, Greg, Chris, Jimel, Jay, Andy C. To all the hundreds of underground homiez in the South Central Love organization. To the general of all struggles. To all other organizations that I didn't mention. To Minister Louis Farrakhan, to the Black Guerilla Family. To my homie in the pen, Killa Watt, much love, and all the other homiez, especially Big Tookie, the Crip Godfather, for his participation. And those I didn't mention, much love and peace. United we stand, divided we fall.

# RED

*(This is OG Red from Hoover. I'm not saying these things to glamorize myself or gangs. I'm sharing my experiences with hopes that no young man or young woman will go through the trials and tribulations that I have gone through. So I would suggest to everyone that reads this book to educate themselves of their own history, because a people without a knowledge of their history really don't have a future. That's how society keeps you from knowing who you are. So that's why I'm saying these words, in hopes that brothers and sisters will learn about their culture, so that they may hold their heads up high. Peace, OG Red)*

**Q:** How early did you start getting involved with gangs?

**R:** 'Seventy, '71.

**Q:** How did it first get started?

**R:** The gangs back then, the Slausons, the Avenues, and the Businessmen, the youngsters couldn't be a part of those guys, so they started their own little thing, which was the Crips. When they first started, they were going around taking people's leather coats and their money, straight up. They were taking people's things in general. Extortionists, that's what they were.

The gang-banging now is on a whole different level. If you were a Crip, you had to say you were a Crip. The clothes kind of identified you, and having your left ear pierced identified you as being a Crip, and if you were going somewhere, no matter where you were going, you had better be dressed like a Crip. A guy would be like, "What you want to do?" Back then it was mainly a fighting thing, a beat-up thing, where a group of people jumped on one or two other people. So we started making up clichés and stuff like, "Chitty Chitty Bang Bang Crips and Thangs."

**Q:** What attracted you personally to the gangs?

**R:** That's a good question. The excitement, to be noticed. You were somebody, you weren't just the average schoolboy. I was mainly attracted to the excitement. The reason I say that is because if we go back to when I was way younger, I was born in '61, but my criminal record starts in '63. My juvenile record starts there because when my mother would go to work and leave us with a baby-sitter, I would disappear and be off wandering somewhere. Adventurous. There's excitement in that. The average little kid you know isn't going to wander off. I lived in Alieso Village, in East L.A., and they used to find me downtown L.A., wondering how I got past all of those traffic lights without getting hit. So they'd pick me up and put me in McClaren Hall, and then they would have to locate my mother. I was explorative and talkative; my daughter is not even three yet, and she speaks real clear, and concise. I know that's a reflection of me when I was young.

**Q:** Did you have a father figure in the house?

**R:** No. That's why I want to implement a program that they used to have in the 1970s, called the Big Brother Program. I don't know if they still run it, but the type of program I'm talking about would be with ex–gang members that have changed their lives, and from experience they can teach another youngster not to go the route that we went. It won't be like somebody just coming out of the woodworks and saying, "Don't do this, don't do that." A person will be able to show them, "This was my life, and this is how it turned out, and it's only by the grace of God that I'm here to stand with you and even tell you this. You don't want to go through this."

That's what I said on the radio [*Peace Treaty Program* on KJLH]. You think that what you're doing out there is hip, slick, and cool, but when you get behind bars, I don't care who you are, or how tough you say you are, or how tough you really are, I've broken down and cried. Anybody that was a hard-core gang member, when you start getting stripped away from your loved ones, and being put within humiliating circumstances, you might not cry in front of me, but that cover has gone over your head, or you've been in your cell, and you've broken down. At least I have.

I know times when I hurt people real bad, shot people, and everything else, and felt bad. Especially if it was another brother. It's just a bad feeling. Anything I ever did to white people I never felt any remorse for. I've seen my homeboys jump on dudes, and I'll be in there telling them that the guy has had enough, because when you hear somebody's head cracking up against the cement, that sound is horrible. It sounds like a watermelon bursting open, but that's a human being. I know some guys who don't have any remorse over who they do something to, and you can't go to them guys and say, "I really didn't mean to hurt him, or I really didn't mean to kill him, I really didn't mean to do this," because then you invite trouble on yourself. I can say these things now, because these are my feelings, and I can express my feelings today. I used to try to hide those feelings with drugs, PCP, pills, and drinking. Then I started messing with cocaine, not hitting the pipe, but it was still a form of messing with it by putting it in weed. I came to realize that drugs wasn't going to solve my problems. I had to deal with the feelings that I was having about being a gang member, and being in and out of jail, and then to see my grandmother look at me, and you know how grandmothers can look at you and say, "Are you institutionalized?" Penitentiaries are not the only institutions that I've been in. I was in four psychiatric places: Metropolitan, State, USC Medical, and

Gilbert Lindsey. I was young then, I was fourteen, and I was with the banging. I would get violent with the nurses, and they would call the staff on me to rush me and put me in four-point restraints and shoot me with a needle. I used to make vows to kill them. I escaped out of there and came back up there with a gun trying to catch this one dude and ended up having to try to get away from the security guards. I was never the type . . . if I targeted you, you were the person I was coming after, it wasn't going to be anybody else, I was not going to do anything to your mother, your father, or your brother, none of that.

**Q:** What brought you up out of that way of living?

**R:** Believe it or not, listening to KJLH, Stevie Wonder's radio station. He had a program called the *Peace Treaty* that allowed us to all come together and talk about changing things. My friend from Shotgun Crips and I had done time together, we went to Henry Clay together back in '75, and he said, "If I can come out here and do this, and I'm a twenty-year veteran at this," see, that's the type of person I am, if one of my homeboys that I know, and I know that he was real notorious during his days, for him to come out and say that and get up to stand for peace, then I said, "I can come out and stand up for peace too." That was like a dare thing to me.

I'm from Alieso Village, where the Santa Ana Freeway used to come around that bin, we used to call that area Clay Hills, and there's a little island right out there when you come off of the 101 and turn onto the Santa Ana around that curve. When I was young, we used to dare each other. "I dare you to run across there." I was one of the ones who ran across there, and at any minute a car could have been hitting the corner. We used to run from the side of Clay Hill over there, and then run back on a dare. So when I heard him say that, it was like a dare to me.

Hoover is a real big neighborhood. Not knocking anybody's hood or none of that, because I've got respect for anybody's neighborhood, but in the jailhouses, and out here on the streets, I have a lot of homeboys. There are a lot of dudes that go to jail who aren't even from Hoover, but they try to claim they're from Hoover just for the protection.

**Q:** How do your homeboys respond to you now that you're for peace?

**R:** Some of the ones that I used to kick it with, most of them aren't here. A lot of them are doing life, or still in jail, but the OGs I know who are out here are with the peace too, like Big Bam, who came down to the radio station religiously on his own after I brought him the first time. There's only a few more that are on the streets right now that are from back in the day, and now there are others that are younger than me that I've met and grown to love. I'm their Big Homie, so it's like, "You know, Big Homie, that's cool if you're for that," and they'll get to telling me the reason why they're not for it. Then I'll counter with them, I tell them how the hood doesn't move as a collective anymore. It used to be when one homie got killed, all the Hoover hoods moved on every gang in Los Angeles. Every gang that was in the immediate—or whoever they thought did it—that's who the homeboys moved on. They don't do that anymore. So I'd say, if you were to get killed today, a few of the homeboys that really love you are going to want to retaliate for that, but the whole hood is not moving anymore. That's like a dude can come over and kill one of the homeboys now, and y'all really aren't going to respond or do anything about it. So you might as well be for peace, you're not really for banging. It wasn't ever about that in the beginning, but once it got to that level, it was like if one homeboy got hurt, or one homeboy got killed, five or six other dudes was going to die in other neighborhoods. That's how it went, and we stuck to that. They're not sticking by the rules anymore, this is a dog-eat-dog world now, everybody is for theirself, or whoever they might kick it with.

I ask them, what if you wanted to go to a park with your kids? I know you get tired of going to Manchester Park, but that's the only place that I see y'all take your kids, and y'all be out there kicking it, having a good time, because you don't want to go to another park for fear of somebody trying to come out and do something to you. That's no way to live. So I say the reason I'm for this is because I want to be able to take my kids anywhere—even though I do anyway, but it still would be better if the atmosphere in the air was not about killing, because anything can happen. Somebody can see me and if I can't talk my way out of the situation, then I'll be dead. Straight and simple. Even today. Everything that all of us are doing out here is very dangerous. I know Big Phil, that's why I love Big Phil, because I know Big Phil still lives in his neighborhood. I still go in my neighborhood every day. I'm not out there drinking with them, and I'm not out there doing anything harmful to anybody, I just be over there putting something to think about in their ears. I generally try to catch them before they start their drinkin' and druggin', because if they're drinkin' and druggin', they're not listening. They are hearing me, because I've had some of them come back to me and say, "Aw, Red, you're serious about this?" I say we're fixing to try—I have to say *try*, because I can't promise anything, but we're going to try to get some of these businesses developed where it will be Black-owned, and we're going to try to have it where the homiez will own it. Any homie that's willing to go to school, study business management, or whatever they like to do, they will be a part of the business. If you already have the intelligence, or the education, so be it, but if you don't, you have to go back to school. Most of the ones that I've been talking to, they have been coming through, but there's always the ones in the background saying, "F— peace, f— that." That's probably in every neighborhood, but if I can just get to the majority of them and keep doing the one-on-one campaign, which we call gang intervention, and each one teach one, then it will spread. A lot of people are tired of what's going on, and there are also a lot of guys that really feel like they lost somebody that they love through this, and they feel that they have to keep going on with that hatred. A person has to step to those brothers and be real reasonable with them to let them know that they're not the only homeboys that have lost somebody. You aren't the only one who has that hatred, but how are you going to hate me and you don't even know me? Just because I'm from this neighborhood? You don't know anything about me. You don't know that if you needed some money, or if you were in dire need, or if you were to call me up and say you had a problem, that I might be that person to come over there and help you out. We can't hate each other for the clothes we wear, or the guys that we hang out with. Step to that individual and meet him and see what he's about on a communicable level, and not on, "Because I saw him with those dudes, he's automatically my enemy." I've found out from being in jail that a lot of guys that other people hear about and want to do something to, those guys generally are some cool, levelheaded dudes, that are waking up, starting to be about getting a Black consciousness. That's even predicted in the Bible.

I used to read the Bible, and I feel that the Bible is a book about Blacks, written by Blacks, for Blacks, but I feel that everything in there is not the truth because it's been tampered with. As far as the things that were said, and mainly pertaining to Paul's letters. My feeling is, I don't think those were divinely inspired letters coming from God. I think he was a man that didn't want to die because of what he was doing, and he began telling people that he met Jesus. There's just something fishy about that. Then he went three years and kicked it somewhere else before he met the first disciples who walked with Jesus, who knew Jesus' teachings. How are you going to tell the people that it's all right to be in bondage?

**Q:** How did the peace treaty affect you personally?

**R:** I was incarcerated, and I said, "I know my homeboys aren't going to be with any peace treaty, so I'm not with it." I was like, "Man, that ain't going to last." The only reason I felt that way, and it's the same way I feel today—the only way this is going to work is if it is an inside job. It has to be an inside job. Within every hood they have to be peacing with themselves. Then when you're living in peace with yourself, stay in your neighborhood. Stay in your neighborhood for about a year. If you have to go through somebody's neighborhood, have some loved ones with you, a mother, a father, a daughter, and when you pass by those brothers, instead of throwing up a gang sign, throw up a peace sign and keep going, and go to whatever park you're going to, go to whatever shopping facility you have to go to, and then go back to your hood. You don't have any business kicking it in somebody else's neighborhood after all these years of warring. Then maybe after about a year or so of that, of people not coming in other people's neighborhoods to shoot them up, and people not retaliating, then you can build the trust. "Man, I went to the store in this one neighborhood, and some of them was in the store, so I put up the peace sign to them and kept on going about my business, and they kept on talking and going on about their business. They weren't sweating me for wearing this or that."

When we do future picnics, we need to make sure brothers bring somebody with them, a family member, a brother, a sister, a mother, a father, a grandmother, a daughter. A person that's really about peace won't mind that. I gave my mother a ticket for the Truce Jam. That's the reason I gave my mother that ticket, because if I can sit up there and say bring somebody that you love, then I have to be willing to do it too. Phil had his sisters up there. That's how it has to go if you're really about peace. All we need is a few from each neighborhood, and that stops the other neighborhoods; "We can't really do anything to him, because he's with them other dudes from that neighborhood, and we'll be jeopardizing our homeboy's life if we do anything." If your homeboys have love and respect for you, they're not going to jeopardize your life trying to do something to somebody from another neighborhood, when they know that all of us are in here knocking our heads together trying to bring about order.

My homeboys are not shooting at Harlems, and Harlems are not shooting at Hoovers. If they respect me, and they respect Phil, they wouldn't . . . not saying that it couldn't happen, because the youngsters who we are really trying to get at, some of them are just now growing up, and they have heard all these stories about their homeboys who did all this, and they are magnificent feats to them, that doesn't really amount to anything. I go introduce myself to the young homiez and say, "I'm your Big Homie; all of the stuff that I used to do, it's not about that anymore." That's why on the radio I can use my real name or my street name, because back in the days that's what everybody knew you by, as far as the fighting thing was concerned. As it developed into using guns and knives, then you had to change from using your first and last name, for obvious reasons. So people started taking up pseudonyms.

**Q:** How did the fighting and the killing get to the level to where it is now?

**R:** The guns came into the community about '75. I can remember the first person that got shot at a party by a dude from the Figueroa Boys. That was in '74, '75. The way we started building up an arsenal for ourselves was when the burglaries went up. Go look at some of the old newspaper clippings from '70 to '75 in the *Herald-Examiner.* Then you can see how everything started. For some reason, on the news, I remember they used to say, "Burglaries are up twenty-five percent, robberies are up, and homicides are down," they used to give you figures on what was up and down for the week. Then dudes were hitting gun stores and armories. The armory in Compton got hit back in the early seventies, and dudes knew not to mess with Compton.

The only thing that I can figure on how it got to this level is that right there [points to a TV], the idiot box. You have people sitting their

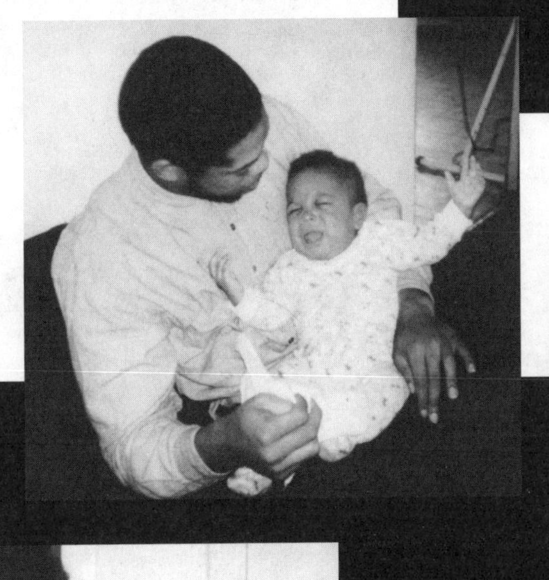

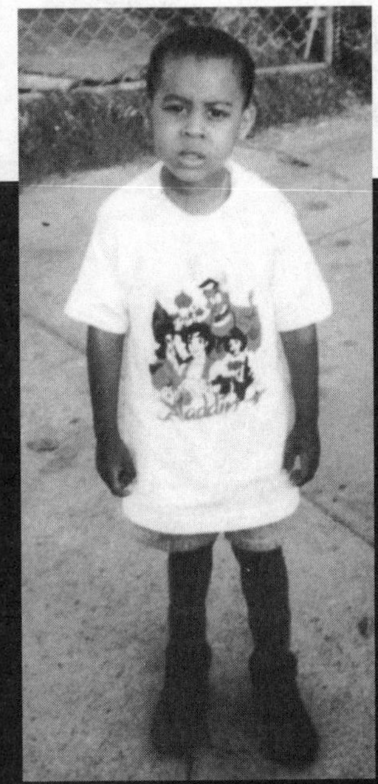

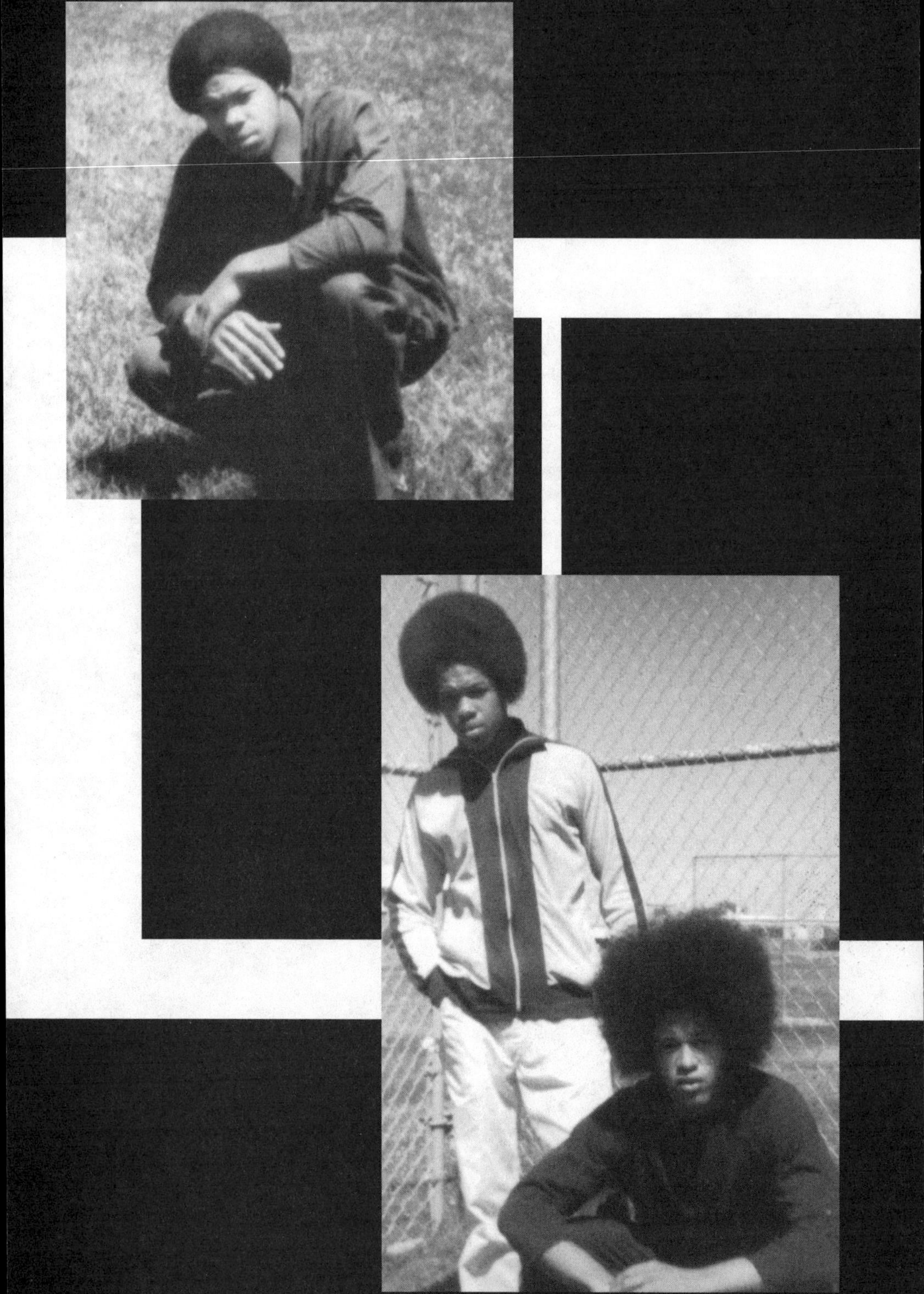

kids in front of an inanimate object that can't show them any type of feeling or love, and here they are watching somebody getting gunned down. That thing can't embrace you and put peace and love in your heart. That thing can't do anything but program a young mind, which it is doing. The parents should know better. When just the radio was around, kids were brought up much better, because there was more communication in the household. There's not much communication in the household anymore. That's why families have to be worked on, to get back to the family unit.

It's a lot, and it's a hard task, but if nobody steps out on it, then everything will keep going on the way that it's going now. You have to have people that are sincere. We have to sit down and write down on some paper what our motivation is. What motivated you to be here? You have to find out what everybody's motivation is, and why they are here for peace. That should be the first thing—like a writing assignment, we have to find out what our intentions are, and why we're here.

**Q:** Why are you here?

**R:** I feel that some of the things that I did when I was young were negative, and as I've always stressed, it's going to be up to us to come back and try to get at these young brothers, to let them know that what they are doing is senseless. I love my people, and I always have.

When Hoovers first started out, we were against white folks. We went down there to Griffith Park near the zoo, where they had a little money. We used to go in the wishing wells and take the money out in front of them, slap some of them upside the head and take their wallets, that's what we were doing. The Hoovers started in 1973. There were Eastside Crips and Westside Crips. Tookie, Big Odie, and Sidewinder were from the west side, and Raymond Washington, Mack, Tommy, and Terry were from the east side. I knew Raymond, but now he's resting in peace.

When Crips started out, we were taking leather coats, because at that particular time the east side of Los Angeles was on a lower poverty level. If you lived on the west side, you were considered living better off than how they were living on the east side. That's going to always be there, the east side not living like the west side. The women looked better on the west side and all of that. Technically, the west side starts at Broadway, but what I would consider the west side was from Vermont, because if you look at it now, all of the houses on the west side still look nice. Then everything from Vermont back east starts looking shabbier. That's just how it is. There are little pockets that are nice, but basically as you go back to the east side, that's where things start to look run-down. The lawns are not kept up, the houses look shabby, haven't been painted in a while, you know, from living on a lower income. So if you were living across Vermont, you were considered as having a little something. The Crips started on the east side, and they were taking people's stuff from the west side. That's the way I saw it; I really can't say for a fact.

With the Hoovers, our basic thing was going in the white neighborhoods doing things. I had a homeboy, he and I personally went to some white people who were still living in our neighborhood, and we kicked in their door, ran up in there, and took their guns, their money, and everything else, and eventually they moved out. We also fought other Blacks, the Figueroa Boys were living right there in our hood, so we had to contend with them. First it was a fist-o-cuffs thing, then the UGs started on the west side, they were a big west-side gang. We liked to do a lot of walking then, so we'd walk into another neighborhood, about fifteen or twenty deep, and we'd end up getting into fights. We'd go to parties, but it was mainly a fighting thing. Nobody was using arms on one another. You would get your respect if you could knock somebody out with one blow, or two. I wasn't ever a person to knock somebody out, but I was swift, because I'm a small person. So I would have hit you about ten or fifteen times without you being able to swing back on me, and I'd have your lip and nose busted. Back then if you felt that you got beat up, the only thing that would happen is the next day if your bruises healed up, and you felt like you wanted to fight again, you'd just fight all over again. Then after a while we would get tired of fighting each other, because this time he might give you a black eye or a bloody lip or something. Then y'all would get to talking about it, "Yeah, man, you thought you would fool me and thought I was going to do this and you . . . " Come to find out y'all like each other, and y'all become friends. At that time we were fighting over who would be hanging out where. The Figueroa Boys lived in our neighborhood, so by us being a self-claimed hood, we were like, "Y'all can't be over here anymore." The average street gang was fighting over a territory, certain streets, and then it generated to the schools. Now they have dudes hanging out in every hood that live in somebody else's neighborhood. Sometimes it escalates into big gunplay, sometimes it doesn't. The thing that I see now is that if you whip somebody up with your fist, you might as well go on and kill him. That's today, because he's not going to take that whipping. That's why *Menace II Society* was so realistic. The dude came over there to fight, but as soon as he got whipped up, he goes and gets guns. That's generally how it is nowadays. I don't know where that mentality came from, but it's a coward mentality. I've been beat up a few times, but it was never to the level where I would go and get a gun and kill the person.

**Q:** What are some ways that you would suggest for us to strengthen our organizations within?

**R:** I've been studying how they got rid of the other organizations, and I would just stress to organizations that we may need to incorporate some of those penitentiary rules that we used to have in jail, in order for the establishments to work out here. I don't mean the penitentiary rules as far as the killing, I'm talking about the silent thing, the not-telling-on-your-fellow-brother thing, because a lot of "loose lips sink ships." Like how the Mafia had the omertà, the code of silence, and they took that to death with them. They would rather die than to give up their friends, and that is what this is all about. Even in the Bible it says, "There is no greater love than a man who lays down his life for his friend."

We must not argue in front of people that are not a part of the organization. The only way that this can be broken up is if they filter somebody in that we really don't screen. That's where the screening process comes in; we have to know that if for the last year or so whoever is trying to come in has been active in the neighborhood as a gang member, if he's still out there doing violent stuff, and then comes and says he wants to be about peace, we have to let that brother in, because we know that he was still out there. Now, if somebody that gets busted for drugs, or something like that, and then all of a sudden they're back out here, and they're trying to come into the organization, that's a person that we really have to look at, because he might be that plant that they're trying to put in the organization to start causing that deceitfulness and treachery from within, causing the division.

**Q:** How did you learn about some of the things that you're passing on to the brothers?

**R:** When I was incarcerated I took advantage of the educational facilities, and I read material about our history. I know that when Shaka Zulu first saw white people, he didn't want anything to do with them, but then after he was hurt, and they came over there with their medicines, which a lot of people don't know was heroin and morphine, once they got him on that, they were able to tell him anything. Just like nowadays when the people get on some type of drug, they're not very coherent. So Shaka gave the rights over. They were scared of Shaka, because he had all of the African nations banding together against them, and they were winning, but the minute he got hurt, they came with their deceit, and they gave him that drug, and that drug had him hallucinating. Then when they wanted the rights to the rich parts of the country, he went on and gave it to them with no problem. Material things didn't play a part to our people over there in Africa, but now they have the young minds, and the young people are coming up today on the material issue, instead of the spiritual issue. They say that knowledge is the key. God said, "My people die for lack of knowledge." Knowledge is king, so to speak. That's why I started reading about our history. I know that over in Africa we weren't a material people, but now since the brothers in the United States are watching television, which I choose to call the idiot box, they are not imagining for themselves. That's why I used to read, because I liked to picture things in my own head. If I'm reading about the desert, and they say it has sand, and a cactus, then I can see that in my own head. I don't need it displayed for me.

**Q:** Did you always read a lot when you were young?

**R:** Basically I have, because I've been incarcerated on and off since the time I was nine years old. A lot of times that was the only thing to keep me going in a cell, was to read, and be in my own world. The world of my own mind, of my own imagination. That's what a lot of these kids need to do now, start picking up more books and start cultivating their own intelligence, and their own imagination, because if you can imagine something, you can make it a reality. That's what they're doing with these movies, they imagine these movies, some of the sick things you see on television now, that's coming out of somebody's mind. I think Stephen King has a very wicked, terrible mind, and Dean Koontz, because I've read some of their stuff, but I can't picture it like they picture it. Some of the bizarre stuff they come up with, my imagination doesn't even want to see stuff like that.

**Q:** What are some of the books that impacted you the most?

**R:** Lance Horner, I think he's a Black writer, and Kyle Onstott, they made the *Mandingo* book. Reading about Mandingo, and why they did what they did to him, I was interested in these writers. I read one, I think the name of it was the *Black Sun,* with Toussaint-Louverture, they wrote about him, and I was like, "Oh, man," because I didn't know that when Napoleon was on his way over here to take over America, he stopped over in those islands messing with those Black people, and five hundred Black men conquered ten thousand of them. A disease came around that was only affecting the white people. I know, because my grandmother was from over there, and I still have people in Jamaica.

When I was growing up, I didn't like the fact that I had green eyes. That was as if you had some white people down in your history. It's true, but there's a whole tribe, the Rastafarians over there in Jamaica, that are light-skinned with green eyes. My hair is real nappy, I have to keep it cut short and brushed; my daughter has the same type of hair that I have, and I tell her right now, "That's all right, because you'll have hair just like me when you get older." I figure I'm going to have a full head of hair when I'm in my fifties and sixties. I have true African hair. When I have braids, it looks good, but I used to be ashamed of myself. That's one of the reasons I became a gang member.

I didn't really like women, my homeboys were more important to me than females. To this day I'm still kind of like that, but only in a different aspect. I go around to the neighborhoods, like last night, I talked to some of my friends, and I know they want to be for peace. They're not going to knock me for what I do, because they know I've been in and out of jail all of my life behind that neighborhood, so they know there's no fakin' and shakin' on mine. They know I'm the type that never had a crime partner. I was always by myself, and the times that I did have some crimeys, we all basically got up out of it by keeping our mouths shut. We have to have a substructure that nobody knows about but us.

The solution that I see is if gang members are out there trying to pass information down one to another. By being positive examples, I can see it working, because one gang member can best know and understand another gang member and what he's going through, and what's feeding the fire in him to do the things that he's doing.

**Q:** What do you say to the other OGs about getting with the younger Gs to make things better?

**R:** I say to the other OGs—not trying to sound sarcastic or anything, but I already know why some of these youngsters are out there wild like that, it's because their OGs may have a drug problem, and the youngsters see them out there loaded, and it makes them feel bad about their neighborhood. They be like, "Look at our OGs, they're all smoked out." How can somebody respect them? They end up beating up some of their own OGs. So they lose respect, and it's like they're bringing up their own brand of comradeship, they're now making up their own rules to live by. So the only thing I can say to any OG is that you thought you were tough when you were in that gang, and you probably commanded respect, so if you're still commanding respect, then talk to your younger homeboys and let them know what it's about. That it's not about shooting one another, because you have brothers killing their own cousins, and their own brothers sometimes. Like me for instance, one of my older brothers is a Black Peace Stone, he's a Blood, but we never let that come between us. That was always an understanding that no matter what I do, or what he does, we love each other, because we're brothers. Just because he's from that gang doesn't mean that we should fight. If these gangs just stop being violent towards one another and start helping their community, clean up their community, fix up an old lady's lawn, have lawn-mower teams or something, or just do something positive that will give them a direction in life, something they can get a few dollars for. It may not be much, but it will be doing something constructive, and instead of having them just run around with an idle mind, they're learning something. They may be able to talk to one of them older people and get some wisdom, and some knowledge. Instead of running around talking negative all the time, about who you want to kill, and getting high, maybe they can go out there and start them a business. That's what I would suggest that you tell your young homiez. That there's more to life than being in a gang.

If you go visit Yosemite National Park, or Sequoia National Park, and see how beautiful it is, see the mountains, and then late at night when the stars come out—because you can't see stars in Los Angeles—when you're in the mountains, you can see millions of them. They are there, you just haven't been to the places where you can see them. Seeing the rivers, fishing in the rivers, swimming in the rivers, like we were meant to do. I know we weren't meant to be confined, because even the Bible tells you that they started trying to build a city to God, and God didn't want them in one place cooped up. He wanted them to inhabit the whole earth. So evidently we were supposed to be nomadic and move with the seasons, the changes of weather. We are a nomadic people. We are not meant to be confined up in regulations and rules. We're supposed to abide by the laws that God gave us. God gave us a lot of laws, and bylaws, and if we just lived by them, we wouldn't have to be trying to rent some land. This land doesn't belong to anybody, this land was put here by God, and it was made for everybody to use, but we just keep taking from the land and not putting anything back into it. When they started building up these little buildings, and setting up these little townships, that's when this place started going down. I don't think it was ever meant to be like this.

**Q:** What are some ways that you feel we can develop our own businesses?

**R:** We can do it. We can start off with the Black banks that we already have established like Founders National, which too many people don't know about, and we can start getting other financial institutions together, it doesn't have to be just that one bank. We can get a contract with them to where we can learn how to run these type of financial institutions. Then once we get them in the neighborhood, when somebody wants to sell some property, instead of them going to the white man, they can come to another brother and see if that brother wants to buy that property from them, and make financial arrangements where everyone is satisfied. There are so many things we can do. Everything that other people have, we can start it ourselves, and instead of spending with them, we can spend with ourselves and let them people spend with themselves. We can control more than half of the money that's in America, but we spend foolishly, and we don't spend with ourselves. That's the bottom line. So, brothers, when you do open up businesses, you don't have to have high, extreme prices, trying to make your profit in one week, because it won't happen. Good business sense is to start off charging a little bit less than the people around you, a few cents less. You can't start off with astronomical prices and expect to get patronage. You can't expect to get patronage if your products are $3.00 and everywhere else they're $2.50. You have to be there and build a rapport, and then a person can come down there and you can let them get things when their money is not right, and they will come back to pay you. That's how you get established, by being there, and not being ridiculous with your prices.

**Q:** What do you see in the future for Black people?

**R:** I believe there is a conspiracy to keep the Black man not only in poverty, but to keep his mind from developing, to keep him from knowing the truth about himself, because as long as they can keep us like that, they can control us. That's why throughout history when a Black man has risen and speaks the truth, and his people start listening to him, then that Black man is immediately dealt with. He's either going to go over to them, or he's going to die. It's as simple as that.

The penitentiaries and the prisons are a big industry every year, built off of warehousing Black men, and other minorities, although we're not a minority. I don't know why they keep telling us that, and feeding that to our kids. We are the majority, Black folks all over the world are the majority. You can believe that. We just don't know how to pool together to make ourselves and our voices heard. It reminds me of the movie *The Spook Who Sat by the Door.* That was way back in the seventies from a man that envisioned—a man who went to the FBI, CIA, and knew how their covert actions were, and then decided to reach out to his people with an underground organization to teach them. Now to show you that we are the power in the United States, if every Black person stopped working for one day, watch what would happen. Straight up. If every Black person in the United States stayed home one day, a week or two weeks, the whole corporate America would come to a halt, and that's real.

**Q:** What do you feel the impact of the gang peace will be here in Los Angeles, in this country, and throughout the world?

**R:** Whatever they start doing in Los Angeles, that's what people look at. If everybody starts peacing in Los Angeles, it's going to have a ripple effect, and then the guys that are claiming neighborhoods they have never been in, living across the country somewhere, they will see that what they're out there doing is foolishness too. Once it can be put out there that it's foolishness, then everybody can live in peace, loving your Black brother and sister. We all know this will take more than one day. It took twenty years for it to get this way. There has always been gangs, but we can start being a gang of peace, a gang of unity, and a gang that respects their mothers, fathers, elders, and neighbors. I can see that today, because if we're not living for peace today, then by the year 2000, they're going to have a permanent plan for all Black people.

It has to start from your own neighborhood. You have to build that rapport with them old people that are scared to come out of their houses during the nighttime, that are scared to go to the store by theirself for fear of getting their purses snatched. The drugs have to leave the community, because as long as the drugs and the alcohol are still around, then the killing is going to stay around.

**Q:** From your experiences, how can people get rid of the demand for drugs and alcohol?

**R:** I was introduced to the fellowship of Narcotics Anonymous.

Through that fellowship is another reason why I'm here for the peace. They have a saying in their format that "the therapeutic value of one addict helping another addict is without parallel." So if you change that over to the therapeutic value of one gang member helping another gang member to realize that he has a problem is without parallel. Gang-banging is like an addiction. Some dudes have to dress up in their garments and go out and pretend to be tough and be thrill-seeking. That's a disease. So we can incorporate a twelve-step fellowship for the gang member. Instead of Alcoholics Anonymous, or Narcotics Anonymous, it can be Gang Members Anonymous, or Gangster Anonymous, you know, GA. We can start on that level, having a place where former gang members can meet and talk about the problems that they are having from day to day. That's why I go to a meeting every day. I didn't go through a recovery, because I didn't feel like I had a problem. Then after talking with an individual, I found out that I did have a problem. I didn't use that much, but it's like they say in their format, "It's not the amount you used, or how little or how much you used, it's just that you're seeking help." So that was never the issue. When a person says "addict," an addict to me was somebody who had a needle in their arm and was nodding, but that's not what having an addiction means. Until I found that out, like I sometimes share in those meetings, if somebody was to call me an addict a couple hundred days ago, I would have killed them. It's not like that now.

I'm an ex–gang member who is in recovery. People will want to know what I mean by that, and I'll say, "I'm involved with a twelve-step fellowship that's showing me how to be at peace with myself every day and get in spiritual contact with a God of my understanding." The reason we say a God of your understanding is as long as that God is loving and caring, then that's the God of your understanding. There are a lot of brothers that have a problem with drugs, that don't really know they have a problem. The reason I didn't think I had a problem was because I was always in and out of jail.

**Q:** How do you suggest youngsters should deal with the police, and the system?

**R:** The only thing I can say is whenever a person gets stopped by the police, and you're Black, they are already going to have a negative attitude towards you. The thing I suggest to do is to just keep a little lightweight smile on your face and answer their questions properly and don't add anything. Whatever the question is, just answer it to the best of your ability, and that's it. Let them do what they have to do. If they're writing you a ticket, don't argue with them, let them write the ticket. Whenever they stop me, they have a gun out, every time, which I don't understand. I've had clashes with them, but what I was doing, they told me, was illegal, and I felt it was legal for me at that particular time.

Back in the days the police used to pick you up in one neighborhood and drop you off in another neighborhood, and dudes had to run for their lives. Just on that "Protect and Serve" thing, they should take that off of the car, because they are not trying to protect or serve. We had only one incident where they protected and served us, and that was at the South Central Love picnic. They came up and asked what they could do, we told them what they could do, and they did it. They didn't make any big problems. So I have to respect that. I can't keep judging all the police by the acts of the police that I've run across, because I used to talk to them crazy. I was one to say, "You ain't nothing but a punk, take the gun off." So I have to look at the part that I played, but when I get stopped now, and I give them the fake smile and the "How you doin' today, Officer? What can I do for you?" that generally puts them in a better mood, where they don't have to try to make you feel less than a man, or try to humiliate you. Just talk to them with dignity and sense, and they can be reasonable. You just can't let them provoke you. When they used to have the choke hold, they would provoke us, and then break somebody's neck. Now they have the Tasers, and they might electrocute you with them things and say that the setting was too high or something. I wish we can get at Willie Williams [police commissioner]; I don't know if he's bought and paid for yet, but I have to admire the man, because he seems like he's equal on his brand of justice, he's not just going to target the Blacks, he'll target the whites, the Mexicans, and everybody else. That's who we need to be meeting with, because he's a Black man out of Philadelphia, so I know that he can understand the oppression and everything. We need to have a closed-room discussion, or out-in-a-park discussion with Commissioner Willie Williams. If he's a real brother, he knows what kind of system he came into out here. He wants to have police walking, protecting, and serving in the community. A lot of police are scared to walk in the community, because of the things that they do. They need to have a lot more respect towards us, then people may have a lot more respect towards them.

**Q:** Any further words you would like to express?

**R:** The thing that I want to say to the younger homiez is that we all try to portray an image that we don't have any feelings, and that we're so hard, when the whole thing that's generating that is fear. Fear to really let somebody know what's in your heart and mind. If you're tired of doing what you're doing, tell somebody. Don't go to the homeboy that you know is a knucklehead, you have to deal with them on a whole different level. Go to a homeboy that has common sense and talk to him about what's in your heart. If you feel that you have peace in your heart, and that's really what you'd rather be doing than carrying a gun every day, then let somebody know it. That's what I tell my younger homeboys. "Check it out, you don't have to say anything to me in front of these guys, here is my number, if you want to talk, I can tell you how to get around all of that, and the same things that homiez try to tell you about why you should be banging, I have reasons why you shouldn't be banging. Whichever one outweighs the most with you, then you make your decision." Common sense, brothers and sisters, common sense.

To the mothers, you can't be scared of your sons. It doesn't matter how notorious you think you are, if your moms slaps you or hits you with something, you're not that crazy to where you're going to do something to your mama, because brothers respect their mothers. Black folk always have that deeper inner love for their moms. Their moms can get away with anything. If Moms chastises you, you're going to let her get away with it. That's what I liked about *Boyz N the Hood.* Even though they were out there doing all of that stupid stuff, when Moms slapped him upside the head, he was like, "What you hit me for, Ma?" I was the same way. My mother broke down the door and ran in the room with one of the canes I used to carry around. I had guns all in the closet and everything, and she came in there and whacked me and my brother all upside our heads with that cane, and we just took that, we accepted that, there wasn't anything we could do about it, that was Moms. So all you moms out there, you have weight with your children, you just don't know. Just give them that basic understanding of God and let them seek out the God of their own understanding, as long as that God is a loving and a caring God.

Also, you brothers have to realize that you have to get some type of skills, it doesn't matter if you've been to jail or not, still get some skills, somebody will hire you. It's geared for the Black man not to have anything, they give the Black woman the job, so when the woman comes home, it makes you feel less than a man, but you have to remember that—don't even bite into that. You don't need to beat on your woman because she's making money, and you're not. You just have to have an understanding and get out there and do something. If your woman is working, get up and take care of the kids and clean up the house. So when she comes home, she feels better. Learn how to cook. That's not too much to learn. Some of the best cooks in the world are men, and they're getting paid top dollar for it, so don't think that these are feminine chores or something. If you like a clean establishment, or a clean place, then you have to put into it too. You can't work your woman to death; she comes home from work, and she has to do more work. Just be productive.

We have to put them Old English cans down. If you've been through anything that I've been through, you know that you don't want to go through it anymore. I'm tired of dodging bullets. I'd rather stick my hand out and do something that us Black men don't do anymore, stick your hand out and shake another Black man's hand and become his friend, a true friend.

This is in the Bible—not saying that I'm a Christian—I believe there is one God, which ALLAH means one God. When Satan went into the garden to con Eve, my impression is that the serpent must have been a beautiful creature if it was crafty, cunning, and subtle—the things the Bible says about the serpent. It had to be standing when God told the serpent, "You will crawl on your belly." We know that something from a seed is going to grow regardless, the seed is going to grow. So when God told Satan that there would be enmity between "your seed, and His seed or her [Eve's] seed," what was He talking about? We all know that a seed is something that's planted, or the seed of a human being. *Enmity* means hatred, straight up. If He told Satan, "Your seed is going to have enmity with my seed," what was He talking about? That was supposed to be the first reference—it said, "And he shall bruise thy head, and your head shall bruise his head." It was talking about Jesus, but it was also talking about Satan's seed, it had to be a spiritual *and* a physical seed. That's what I'm saying. Think about it.

These are people that have caused troubles throughout history, not just to us, but to everybody, and that's a bad seed, regardless. That's a corrupt seed, that's a seed that's highly influenced. When you hear about these maniacal crimes that have been going on throughout history, you might have a few Blacks that are demented from whatever type of environment that they came up in, but the majority of those heinous, vicious crimes are committed by white men. The most bizarre stuff that's coming out on this TV is coming out of the minds of white men. Blacks as a people don't think like that. I know me, and even with what I've been through, I'd rather be out on Waikiki Beach, in a beautiful place with the woman whom I love, and that's it. I don't prefer to be violent, I don't prefer to hurt another human being. That's not in our nature. It's in their nature. Just think about it!

> ***When Black people begin to rebel, and you call it riots, we understand that those are not riots, those are rebellions. People are rebelling because of conditions, and not because of individuals. No individual creates a rebellion.***
>
> **—H. Rap Brown**

## SHOUT OUTS

Tony Stacey, Hoola Ray, Tony Sims, Dennis Shaw, Frank Miller, Marcus Player, Steve Champion, Leon Washington, and all the other homeboys that may never see the streets again behind being involved in gangs.

I would also like to send a shout out to all the brothers and sisters who are down with this peace movement. Love and respect, Red.

Angelo with two brothers on train in New York

# ANGELO

*(To the readers, how are you doing? My name is Angelo. Before you read any further I must say that the "illegal acts" that I and other gang members may have committed arose not from any desire for personal gain, but from a deep philosophical and spiritual commitment, that if a wrong exists, one must take active steps to stop it, regardless of the consequences. What was wrong was in the early seventies when gangs arose, Bloods, Pirus, and Crips, the young Black male was labeled as a potential threat, due to the fact that he was against the same system that has denied us all of our rights that are written in the Constitution. Not only that, he was still being deprived by the political, judicial, and social systems of Amerikkka. With the flourishing of drugs, and weapons, into the city of Los Angeles, the powers that be planned to make fast money and rule the streets of Los Angeles. In quoting Martin Luther King, "The ghetto and plantations were created by those who had power," so in my theory, I believe that the problems Black Amerikkka has were created by this system which is controlled by white Amerikkka.*

*As a victim of all which was created before me, the question is asked, who is truly to blame? The system alone? No. Ignorance alone? No. Bigotry alone? No. I believe that all three take a tremendous toll on the behavior of Blacks in Amerikkka. The system supplies us with all the drugs and weapons, the propaganda is controlled by their media, so that's where all the self-hatred comes from. It is indeed something that has been laying in our faces as Blacks for such a long time, and the only way we can relieve our frustrations is on the people closest to us, which in most cases is another Black. That's where ignorance plays its part. Due to the educational system's way of teaching Blacks, it has failed to allow Blacks to learn our own Black/African history. The fact is 68 percent of Blacks graduating from high school don't have any knowledge of Africa, other than where it is on the globe. This proves that if you don't know your history, you will not have respect for it. There are children out there that don't understand what it is to be Black, and they don't know what their forefathers have done to make this race a fighting force here in Amerikkka. Again, that is a result of the failure of the school system. We can't really blame the parents, because they went to the same schools.*

*I mentioned bigotry earlier—what about it? It's simple: none of us are born bigots. It's the ignorant parents from all races and creeds that embed ignorance and racism into their children's minds and souls.*

*As a parent myself, there have been times when it was hard for me, even when I've had it easy. I was the average Black male athlete in high school, with an after-school job, nice looks, and fair grades. When my girlfriend became pregnant and brought it to my attention, I was shocked, and scared, as if I was the one who was going to carry the child for nine months. The first thing that came out of my mouth was, "It's not mine." I tried everything possible to prove that the child was not mine, and I was wrong. Like a lot of men, for some reason, we as Black men walk out on our sisters once we impregnate them. Why? My belief is that it comes from slavery, when the Black man was constantly taken away from his family, as though his job was only to create children for the enslaver. By that being embedded in us throughout history, we still do it today. We make our children and leave them to the slave master to take care of. Let me put this in street slang, "the county," and brothers tend to joke with the notion that if the county is sending a check every two weeks, they don't need to take on the responsibility. Anybody can be a daddy, but it takes a man to be a father. Fatherhood as a Black man is the biggest responsibility we can take on. It is up to us, as Black men, to challenge the system now, to make it better for our children so that they can have better opportunities. It's time for us to go back to school and learn what we didn't in high school, visit our local libraries, and read books. Sit down with our children and teach them morals and values instead of letting the television do it.*

*I don't believe that rap music plays a role in human behavior. Before rap existed there was gang violence. I know that when I got involved, it was not the result of listening to a record. Now that rap and video are much more popular, I don't believe it is the main reason, it is the television itself that is a major component to child development, and social behavior among teens. I believe each person has a mind of their own, and it's up to them to make up their own minds to do what they want to do. There are cases now that show how behavior resulting from what someone has seen on television has resulted in death. The fact that one responds to what they see is natural instinct and cannot be controlled, due to involuntary muscles in our bodies. I remember as a kid, when I went out to see a Bruce Lee movie, right after the show, me and several other kids would do karate all the way home, and indeed it was the result of what we saw earlier. Although people died via knives, ropes, and sticks, I never had the notion to kill any of my friends. I knew then, like I know now, that it's only television. It was the responsibility of my parents to let me know that what I was watching was not reality.*

*As a gang member, I've learned the streets of Los Angeles like the back of my hand. At this present time, I've learned from the life that I've lived and wish no harm to anyone who I have involved in gang activity. I don't condone gang violence, but I do understand the reason for the behavior. The details about this subject I will illustrate in my upcoming documentary about Crips and Bloods. In this documentary you will get an in-depth look at real live gang members, speaking on their beliefs, on how gang life truly is, and how it is perceived by the public. The documentary will be a sure thing to see in the months to come. I'm also in the works of producing a book of my own. I have been on several speaking engagements across the country, speaking on gang intervention and prevention, and how to avoid gang activity, and what to do if confronted.*

*To the Black families of Amerikkka, stay strong in your role in life on this planet. If you believe that your child is participating with a gang, or conducting abnormal activities, sit him/her down and have a one-on-one talk. Let them know that it is wrong, and that there are other alternatives out there besides gang violence. You must also understand how one gets involved in gangs. It does start at home. A child first loses respect for their parents, due to a father not being present, or a strong enough father. Then they lose respect for other authority, such as the school curriculum, the minister, and the neighbors. That in turn results in them receiving the guidance from their peers out in the streets. That's who he/she will learn from, until someone wakes them up, or they go through the trials and tribulations of true pain and suffering. I wish each parent good luck in their raising of our Black babies. They are indeed everyone's responsibility. Peace to all of you, Angelo.)*

**Q:** What are some positive things that you are now doing in the community?

**A:** I'm working on a documentary that is a lesson in history. It's not to make money, it's to give awareness, to give guidance to individuals who have been misled by this system, saying that gang members are this way or that way, or that youth gang-bang for these reasons or those reasons. I'm here to clear up a lot of myths with this documentary. There's a lot of BS that has been said on how the Bloods started and how the Crips started. There's a lot that needs to be opened up, for the real to be known. The only ones who know the real are the people that started the gangs themselves; no psychologists, no psychotherapist, no lawyer, nobody can tell the story but the gang members themselves. So what I want to do with this documentary is get the gang members themselves—I'm talking about bringing OG homeboys, ex-girlfriends, mothers, fathers, and sisters—to tell the story about how these men were, what were the conditions back in the seventies as opposed to what are the conditions in the nineties, and why we're doing it now, and especially why were we doing it then? That's the only way I believe we can get some type of solutions, from finding out where it comes from, how it started, and why it started.

**Q:** Are you considered an OG?

**A:** No, I'm considered second or third generation.

**Q:** From your understanding, what is the significance of an OG?

**A:** There are many ways that you can consider yourself an OG. I'm an OG to the guys that are up under me, and there are guys over me that I consider OGs. So it's a level of leadership or seniority which you have in the neighborhood. Guys like Pudding and brothers from his generation, they were original gang bangers themselves, so they are the OGs of all OGs. They are double OGs. There are not too many Gs that are out right now, that are living normal lives. Basically half of them are smoked out, or in prison; not many of them out here have themselves back together. The guys out here now considering themselves Gs, they are Gs to a certain degree, because you don't have the bigger Gs, the OGs to come out and check 'em. You have guys that are forty or forty-two years old, that have been doing this from '70, early '68, when it first started, like some of the guys in this book.

As far as names, every gang has come up with different names from their area. A lot of gangs are named after streets. Almost every gang gets its name from its area. The Brims were west from where I was born and raised at. I was born and raised in the Bloodstone Villain Hood, the Eastside Villains, and they got their name from an album. There was a group called Bloodstone, back in the early seventies, and that's how most of the gang names originated. There weren't too many gangs that I knew of back then. The Brims were the known gang when I was a kid, back in '76, '77. I had some knowledge of them, but the most knowledge I had was of the Eastside Crips and the Westside Crips. I didn't actually see Crips back then, because in elementary school, when they said, "The Crips are coming," everybody scattered. That was during the days of the leather jackets getting taken, the baseball caps with the two clubs getting taken. I didn't see a Crip until I went to junior high school. That's when I had my first one-on-one confrontation with Crips.

**Q:** What were some of the early influences on L.A. gangs?

**A:** The research that I've done shows that it came from Chicago, with the movement of the Black Peace Stone Rangers, and the Disciples. When they came into a truce, they were infiltrated by the federal government, who had a lot of guys do things for them under the table, then they would turn around and arrest them and send them back to prison.

Many families got upset, and a lot of guys who went into hiding came west. They came west to California in the late sixties, during the Martin Luther King era, when the riots and all of that stuff jumped off. So they came down here with a movement and got involved with certain brothers in L.A., the Black Panther Party, and organizations like that, and then they branched off. Everybody once was a revolutionary to a certain extent, but in L.A. you just had your regular player, hustler, gangster, or whatever, and they'd see the revolutionaries and say, "Man, we ain't f'ing with those white folks," because they were already down there selling dope for the white man. So they kind of rebelled against each other.

The Muslims weren't moving in L.A. back in the sixties like they are moving now in L.A., they didn't have the recruits that they have now. They were basically back in New York, Harlem, and Philadelphia.

The Disciples associate with the blue, and the Peace Stone Rangers associate with the red, as well as the Black Peace Stone Rangers out of the Jungle, on the west side. From my research, that area of the city was a branch of the Black Peace Stone Rangers from Chicago. Some moved down to those projects and started that gang.

# Angelo

**Q:** What do you think started the colors?

**A:** There are a lot of myths about who wears what. At one time, Bloods wore blue, and some Crip gangs wore red. There are a lot of myths behind the colors, and with all the research I've done there is not one specific configuration to who wears blue and who wears red, and why. It's just like a flag of a state. Certain gangs that once wore blue rags, now wear brown rags, for "hustler," or a green rag for "money man," or a purple rag or a black rag. Red and blue are the two main colors. People actually think that they kill because one wears red, and one wears blue, but we all know there is more to it than that. That's another myth I want to clear up, that Black men are not just killing each other over colors. It doesn't make any difference what you wear as long as you stay in this neighborhood, everybody knows that you stay over here, and everybody knows who you are affiliated with. You can wear pink, purple, green, or whatever, they still know who you are.

**Q:** What are some of the things they are killing over?

**A:** They are killing over the conditions that they are up under. No jobs, the bad education, and growing up in these dysfunctional homes. Basically, the average Black child that grows up in this world doesn't have a father figure, or a father with enough force. You have this kid, and he's in and out of YA [Youth Authority], and he's getting bigger than his daddy every day, so he starts disrespecting his home, he disrespects his teacher, he disrespects his community, he disrespects the authority and the law, then he goes to church and disrespects his minister. He gets lost up in this cycle, and the only person that can teach him or guide him is a person of his caliber, which is his homeboy out in the streets, who's doing madness. So he takes to the streets and learns life that way, because the system has perpetuated him to do so. The average person out there gang-banging, their parents migrated from somewhere else. My parents are from Louisiana. My mother was pregnant with my other brother when they got up and came this way. They were tired of picking cotton, tired of listening to the white folks down there. Everybody was moving to sunny California: "There's love, there's jobs, there's this, there's that." Land-of-opportunity type of thing. That was back in the sixties, during the baby boom. So there are a lot of families with these cats that consider themselves OGs, that went through that same phase, as far as moving to a whole new location. Living up under the conditions with the Watts riots in 1965, '68, and stuff like that, it was just a bunch of madness. We weren't getting the proper education, the proper jobs, the proper after-school training, and that's where we are now. We went into a state where we had nothing to do but rebel, but who were we rebelling against? We started blaming each other, and taking it out on one another. That self-hatred. When you talk to people who are a part of the system, or the status quo, they always say that you can't blame the system. "You can't blame the system, because it is us who is pulling the trigger," but it is you [the system] who is supplying us with the drugs, the system is supplying us with the guns. Since the seventies till now, the weapon availability is like that [snaps his fingers].

To my knowledge, high-tech weapons became available around here in '85, '86. I remember when I ran across a 9-millimeter for the first time, it was around '85. That's when the Uzi first came out. Before that it was just a regular .22 pistol, a .22 rifle, a 12-gauge sawed-off shotgun. I remember back in high school when stuff used to jump off, everybody had the same philosophy, we wouldn't have but two or three bullets, the crowd would come, and we'd shoot up in the air, and everybody would disperse. Now you have youngsters out there spraying people with heavy artillery, due to the fact that the weapon availability has changed. It's easier to get a weapon now than it was back then. It's not that hard to find a pistol or drugs or anything else illegal in our communities.

**Q:** Do you think that's planned?

**A:** Definitely it's planned. America is a business, this is a corporation. They supply the world with everything. They supply us with that which will keep our folks down, so those on top can run everything. Any businessman will tell you, America will find a need and will definitely fill it. So every time there's a need for guns, weapons, or drugs, they're going to fill that need. Until this community, and every community, stops needing that need, then that's when it's going to end. As long as we want it, they're going to keep on sending it down here. As long as there is a demand, they will supply it.

**Q:** How can we as a community cut down and stop that demand?

**A:** Education, that's the basic thing we have to get. We have to get it from the homes first of all, then we have to go out and get it from the schools, whatever little bit we can get up out of the schools. Third of all, we can go to our local library and sit down and talk to people, because they have good people at those libraries that will give you a lot of information. We haven't had that initiative to send a kid to the library, the parents have to do it, so it has to start at home.

We have to learn that we must stand up and fight for each other, because there are no prevention programs out here, no intervention programs. They believe that taking a person to jail is a solution. That's prevention to them, taking them to jail. So we have to set up programs where we can stop our kids from even thinking about selling drugs, and doing wrong. We have to give them an avenue, other than watching that boob tube every day, seeing that stuff on TV, and going out and trying it. We need more educational programs on television, we need to control our own media. We need grassroots role models, because everybody can't become Charles Barkley, everybody can't become Michael Jordan or Magic Johnson. We need guys that have been out there, that have lived their life, to get inside of these schools and start telling these kids what's happening, instead of these movies telling them what's happening. They don't learn a lesson or learn any moral values from watching a movie. There are no positive messages in the movies.

I can do a thirty-minute seminar and tell you twenty times as much as a movie can tell you in two hours and thirty minutes. That's because I'm coming from the heart, and not from a script out of Hollywood. People need to reflect what they see on television and take it in another direction. What I mean by that is, when you're watching a movie, and you say, "That's me right there, that's me," since that's you, why don't you stop doing it then? A bad guy doesn't always die in the end, there's more to it than that. It's more of a psychological thing that goes on when you're out here breaking the law. People think that everybody out here is a coldhearted, don't-give-a-f, don't-give-a-damn killer, just doing stuff. Man, brothers think. They think. I talk to them all the time. They think.

It hurts just being out here. Ninety percent of them can't afford to die. If a brother dies right now, his family and friends are going to be knocking on everybody's door crying, talking about they need money for the funeral. The parents talking about, "I can't bury my baby." The other day your baby was a "punk, mf, stupid, ignorant so-and-so." You've been telling him that all of his life. The education has to start at home. These parents, I hear some of these mothers right now, cussing these kids out every single day. Calling them every name in the book of curse words, and the kids grow up listening to that and internalize it, and that's what they become. If you constantly call a kid a dumb, stupid bastard, then that's what he's going to become. Now here he is eighteen years old, and you tell him to go get a job. "Wait a minute, I'm a dumb, stupid bastard, you've been telling me that since I was two years old. You want me to go get a job, what are you talking about? Give me a break." What's he going to do? He'll go out there and break the law. Go out there and get him a dope sack. Go out there and snatch him a purse. He'll go to the penitentiary, and his mama cries, if he dies, "Oh, my baby, my baby, he never did anything wrong." Your baby was a "dumb, stupid bastard," ma'am, because that's what you made him. The streets don't turn you out, man, your parents turn you out. Your parents, your mother and your father, turn you out. That's what gets you out there, because they can't control you, and so you can't do anything but join a bunch of uncontrollables that all have the same mind-set.

Brothers are not dumb and stupid; there's a lot of brothers out here that are intelligent, that want to go back to school, but they say, "What am I going to go back to school for, I'm not going to get a job anyway." They pick up the newspaper and read it, they know the unemployment statistics of California, and across the nation. When they start seeing other brothers getting jobs, and doing better things, then they may go and try, but basically they're going to stick with the rest of the crowd, because they don't see things happening. Like with this Rebuild L.A. BS. Nobody has seen any change. We ride around, and everything is still burned down. We still don't have any jobs. The police are still tripping, they don't care about a camcorder, they're going to continue to do what they've been doing. Just because of Willie Williams things are not going to change. You still have the same psychos that worked for Daryl Gates there. The mind-set is still there. They've been trained to be racist.

I was at a graduation the other day, and I was talking to some cats just coming out of high school, about ten young Black graduates, and I said, "Why don't y'all go down there and join the police force?" They all started laughing. I said, "You're going to be the same brothers, seven or eight years from now, crying about the police, saying there aren't any brothers on the police force." If there weren't any down there now, we'd be under worse conditions than we are now. So one of my philosophies is to get brothers down on the police force, because we need Black men on the force. There's not enough brothers down there. It's like 14 percent Black, 20 percent Latino, and 3 percent others, all the rest are white boys. White, white, white boys, coming down here knowing nothing about the city. Slaves—slave masters, that's all it is. L.A. would be a f'd-up place, anywhere in the continental United States of America would be a f'd-up place if the whole police force were all white boys, believe me. We need brothers on the police force, *brothers that won't sell out.*

**Q:** Do you think Black police officers would change the system?

**A:** It all depends on which avenue you take, because the only way you can destroy a system is to become a part of it. That's what they have spies for, and infiltrators for. They go in, they seek all the information they can, they bring their people in, and they unweb the web. If we could train brothers, I'm talking from a revolutionary point of view, if we could train brothers and give them the mind-set that you ten are going to join the police force, you ten are going to go join the navy, you ten are going to join the air force, you ten are going to go do this. Like *The Spook Who Sat by the Door.* We must have that type of plan, if you want to take it to that level, because we need Blacks in those positions. My daughter is eight years old. I don't want some white boy from Westwood pulling her over, I want these young cats that I know, that I grew up with, pulling her and her boyfriend over on Saturday night, ten or fifteen years from now. You know, "I know her father, let them go." That's how it works in their neighborhood. We have to start policing our own communities. Every gang neighborhood has its own security, but when the police come, everybody moves to the side or drops their weapons. Whatever goes on here is well protected by the fellas that affiliate with . . . not actual gang members, but just people that live here that are not going to allow anybody to come over here writing on the wall, tearing things up, or breaking in cars and so on. When you speak on that basis, you're talking about cleaning up everything on a mass level. You must have a powerful force to do things of that nature. You have to have people who are willing to agree with what you're talking about.

In our neighborhoods, the number one thing affecting the Black male is the alcohol. Everybody wants to drink. When you come with that philosophy, the first thing a brother is going to tell you is, "I'm not going to stop drinking, I don't care what y'all say," and the only thing the other brother is trying to do is make it better for everybody. The place is safe, but it's unsanitary to a certain degree. When we bring other friends over, or somebody else brings friends over, they see ten or twenty cats out in the alley hanging out, shooting craps, and drinking; every time a sister gets out of the car she gets called a "punk B." So fellas have to come out with a plan and get everybody to agree upon it, because it's hard, it's very hard. The Muslims have been successful in certain areas, but it's very hard for individuals within the community to come out with a plan like that and have everybody agree upon it, but it has been proven that it can definitely be done.

**Q:** How has the gang peace affected you personally?

**A:** It was a turnaround for me, because when it went down, I had just got off of parole. I am against Black-on-Black killing, but I understand why people gang-bang, and I understand how they get caught up in the rapture. I understand the feelings that they go through when their homeboys die, or when they don't have any food on the table. I understand all of that killing, because I have lived that life.

When I got word of the truce, I received a call from this girl, and she said, "They're trucing over there, the Bloods and the Crips are coming together over there in Watts." My neighborhood right here, we're affiliated with Compton. I popped on the tube and saw them at the picnic doing what they were doing, and brothers saying, "Tell Compton to come get a bar of this." So I chuckled, and I said, "That looks pretty good."

All during the looting and stuff I was out there in traffic, and I was running across brothers that I hadn't seen in years. They were like, "It's peace, it's peace, it's peace. It's a Black thang, it's a Black thang, it's a Black thang."

So when I saw this on TV, I got on the phone, called a couple of my partners up, and went to the Crips over there in Compton. We got at them about it, and they said they was with it, and I got at some more brothers, and they was with it, everyone said they was with it, so we decided to have a press conference in Compton. I called some people up, got past all of that red tape, and got permission to use the park, because what was going on before that was every time brothers would come together, they didn't have a permit to use the park. You're talking about one thousand to two thousand brothers in the park. So I just called some people that I had been working with, and they got me a permit to use the park for five thousand folks, and five thousand showed up. Right here at Willowbrook Park, five thousand Bloods and Crips together. That was in April of '92.

**Q:** So the truce was called before the Rodney King situation?

**A:** The brothers in Watts, way back in December of '91, was talking about a truce between the three primary projects: Nickerson Gardens, Jordan Downs, and Imperial Courts. They've been talking peace since December of '91, but the federal government, the FBI, had knowledge of it, and that's when they started sending those FBI agents down here to the city. That was in February of '92 when they first infiltrated Watts. Then they implemented the Weed and Seed program. The Weed and Seed program that they implemented here was to seed in certain individuals, and to weed out other individuals, that's what it is. Plant something to get rid of something else. Just like an antidote for a disease. So what they were doing was hiring individuals, bringing down the FBI to work at getting rid of certain gang bangers who had resources.

They say there was a lot of racial tension going on, as far as blacks and whites, so they didn't want all of these white folks in Los Angeles to get hurt. What happened in the Black community and the Latino community on April 29, 1992, they say was not planned. There have been rumors and speculation that the government itself planned the Uprisings, due to the fact of a new president coming in, a new mayor coming in, and all of these district elections. They needed some type of war within the country so they said, "Wait a minute, we have to spark something. In L.A. we have these four officers up for trial, we're fixing to bring this big hype up, we'll send our FBI agents down there, we'll focus everything on L.A., and we'll bounce Clinton's election from there." That's exactly what they did. Clinton was coming down to L.A. way before the Uprisings, and when all this stuff stirred up, you know what he did, he says, "Hey, I'm down with it, the Bloods and the Crips, and it's a good thing that they're doing this." He went on his election tour with this, all of his other officials, their whole focus was on helping L.A.

The only way they could get the political process going was to have a riot, or something to focus on. They brought the Bloods and the Crips to the inauguration, talking about peace, kicking it with the president. The same thing they did back in '68 when Nixon got elected, they brought the brothers in who were keeping peace at that time from the Disciples, and the Black Peace Stone Rangers up out of Chicago. They're using that same program right now, "tricknowledgy," that they used back then.

They're trying to find out now who are the other Blacks or businesses that are helping these cats right here. They're moving on everybody who has started a business without the help of the federal government; they're getting looked into.

This community where I stay, Ujima Village, we haven't had a drive-by in three or four years. When I was involved back in '85, '86, it was a war zone. Some people would say that when I went to jail, it stopped. I'm not saying I was doing all of them myself, but let the police say, "I was the main man behind a lot of stuff," but I didn't consider myself a gang banger. I was just a regular cat living up in the neighborhood, went to school every day, got proper grades, was in every program there was at the local high school, was in magnet programs, further-education programs, and stuff like that. When I was confronted by this gang thing, I just grasped it and rolled with the punches. I was a motivator, and guys that were running with me took heed to the motivation I was giving them, and we were just out there doing whatever. We were taking care of business. After me and several other cats, we all went to the penitentiary the same year, it just died out. It used to be bad; I mean it was *on*.

**Q:** Did that time in the pen change your thinking any?

**A:** Well, for my first conviction I did twenty-two months, I paroled, and I was on the streets for one month. I was under surveillance, then they raided the house. The first time they just came in on GP, they just kicked down the door, looking for anything. They said that I had robbed somebody on December 29, when I didn't even parole until December 31. So I guess I was supposed to have committed a crime while I was up in jail. After that I went to jail for five or six days and went through all this paperwork, for them to finally release me again with a "We're sorry, you're the wrong guy" type of thing.

About two weeks later my telephone went dead, so I called the phone company to see what was going on. When the man came to fix the telephone, and I asked him what was wrong, he said I had a stereo hi-fi hooked up to it. Right then I knew what it was, so I played dumb to the fact, and I said, "What's a stereo hi-fi?" He said, "Come on, let me show you." We walked out to the phone box, and he said, "Well, they had it hooked up a little, somebody is listening to your telephone." The first thing that came to my mind was that he was working for the police, perpetrating as the telephone man, and he had fixed it for the police. So when he left, I went back out to the phone box to destroy it, to disconnect the wires, and as soon as I got into the phone box, the undercover police hit the corner. "Who are you?" "Y'all know who I am." "What are you doing?" The phone box and light box were adjacent to one another, so I said, "I'm turning on my lights." They said, "No you're not, you're messing with the wires." They arrested me for tampering with AT&T property. I go to court, it gets to trial, and they had changed it around to where they said I was doing the phone tapping. They reversed it. I was six weeks on the streets, was trying to adjust back to society. I hadn't been any further than my doorsteps. They finally kicked it out of court, but I got a parole violation for four months.

I got out again, and I stayed out for two more months, then I get caught with a pistol, go back and do sixteen more months, and I said that was enough. As far as the experience, man, jail, nobody wants to go to jail, and I don't wish jail on anybody, because it's a messed-up place. Jail doesn't rehabilitate you.

When I paroled, I said, "I don't want to come back here." It took for ME to see how I was living when I got back out, and to say I'm tired of stealing, robbing, and running from this cat, running from that cat, because when you're banging, and you're selling dope on the side, doing all of this miscellaneous stuff, it's like you have seven different lives, seven different personalities. When you come in the house, you have to deal with Moms off the top. When you go around your homeboys, you have to be down, with the dope man you have to act a certain way, you can't BS him, and when you're dealing with the clients themselves, you have to treat them a certain way. Then when the police come, you have to act a certain way around them, because they know your name, they know your MO. Then if you have a baby, you have to go around your baby and your baby's mama and act a certain way around them. So a kid that lives that life, he goes through several different things, and he doesn't even understand what he's going through, he's just living.

You just can't be yourself. So you get tired and burnt out. I was burnt out from being all of those different personalities. Every time I went somewhere I had to change; it's a trip. It's a psychological thing, and a lot of kids go through that, but nobody can understand it, unless you did it yourself, that's the only way you can understand.

Jail does not make you understand what you were doing. It gives you time to think about it, but it doesn't change you. Brothers go in and out of jail like it ain't nothing. They designed it for that. That's what they have parole for, to send you right back up in there, because it does not rehabilitate you.

**Q:** You were saying earlier that it was right after the Uprisings when the gang peace first started getting publicity. What type of impact did that have on you?

**A:** Well, I never got into it with the Crips over in Watts, but we used to have a little problem with Nickerson Gardens, they're Bloods too, but there was this thing called "set trip," where gangs get into it with each other. We had a little conflict of interest with them on a few occasions, just power trippin'. We may be a party twenty or thirty deep, and they may be twenty or thirty deep, and we want to clown, so we end up getting at each other. Nothing ever too serious though.

When I first heard about the truce before it was glorified, I was happy, there were a lot of cats over there that had brothers, sisters, cousins, and uncles who stayed up in the other projects that they couldn't go see. So they can now go see their families. The projects are so close together to where they didn't have any choice but to stop doing what they were doing.

There are soldiers that come out of the projects, the "I don't give a f—" type of brothers, so when they said, "Tell Compton to come get a bar of this, come get some," they were calling us out to the truce, and we came out.

There's a lot of flak about who started the truce. The truce started in Watts, then Compton, that's it, but there were other gangs that were coming to Watts, because that's like the Holy Grounds, so you could go over there, Blood, Crip, or whoever. If you're down with Black-on-Black unity, then come on over to the projects. That's how it is. That's how I see it now, like over here where I stay, we're still down with it.

**Q:** How did you help initiate the peace in Compton?

**A:** It was between every gang in Compton. Every Blood gang in Compton is a Piru, and all the Crips are Crips. You have certain types of Pirus, and you have certain types of Crips. You have the Villagetown Pirus and Villagetown Hustlers. When Pirus started back in the days, certain Gs came over here hollering Piru, and we got involved. We all went to Centennial High School, Bloods and Crips, right here off of Vanguard. It wasn't about red and blue, it was about where you stayed. We could snap our fingers tomorrow and say we're going to start wearing purple rags for our new color. If you got four or five cats to do it, the rest of them would follow. It's the domino effect. That's how it works.

**Q:** What can be done to keep the movement for peace happening and free from infiltration?

**A:** Knowledge, and it's out there. Brothers just have to want to get it. They're listening, but sometimes it goes in one ear and out the other. We need tape recorders so that every time somebody starts talking some knowledge, we need to record it and go home and listen to it again. So it can bounce off the wall, bounce back in the tape recorder, press rewind, and listen to it again.

This country is designed . . . the gangs are just like the NAACP or any other organization, there are people watching us all. These brothers are still at peace, it's been two years now. They have people up in there watching, and keeping a tab on everything they do, when they do it, and how they do it, because they don't want us to make a revolutionary movement towards the system. We can have all the parties and picnics, but when someone starts talking about doing something to the LAPD, or doing something to this individual, or that individual, they're going to try and take you out. They have people working within the movement. It's common sense. America has the best security system there is. They're not trying to let anything take them down.

You see how they took that movie *The Spook Who Sat by the Door* off the market. They didn't want brothers getting that visual effect. The only visual effect we get is killing one another on television. We can rap all we want to, because they control all the rap, they listen to most of it, and they buy most of it. White folks own all of the major music companies. They get those demo tapes, "You like this, son?" If their little kid likes it, they put it on the radio.

So we need to start hearing some positive music and seeing some positive programs on television, about education. You have individuals like me and all these brothers who are trying to do this peace stuff, we're going to continue to work, work, work. We can save some lives. I'm quite sure a lot of people have listened to me; I've spoken on a large scale and have been heard by thousands of kids. I'm quite sure I've hit a few of them, and that's all I'm proud of. As far as thinking everything is fine and dandy, and people are going to be happy in the streets, it's not going to happen overnight, we have to put time and work in.

**Q:** What was the process like of getting the peace going on in Compton?

**A:** It was spiritual. It was a force that said, "Hey, y'all need to stop killing one another, y'all need to take a look at one another, y'all need to come into a park or something and just kick it." It wasn't about negotiating, everybody just had that vibe that peace is what's happening. When that Rodney King verdict came down, everybody said, "That's me. They're on videotape whipping that brother's ass, and they walked. That could have been me. We have to do something about this, we have to stop sitting here killing each other every single day for nothing, and stop allowing these police to do us like this. We're allowing the system to just f— us, f— us, f— us." So it was a force right over there in the park. Brothers just kicking it. Chilling. I went and talked to some brothers about getting together, and they said they would bring the music. I went and talked to some more brothers, a brother named Big Ed from Fam-Lee, and he said, "I'm going to help you do this." I was scared to death. We put out five thousand flyers, and we sat and we waited. I thought nobody was going to show up, and he said, "They're going to come," and the next thing I know that park was full. Compton was there in full force.

**Q:** Was it the OGs who initiated the peace in Compton?

**A:** It was basically people who were out here banging. The YGs, the young generation, looking for authority, because they're putting in all the work. You have Gs who are not getting the respect that they used to get four or five years ago. They go to the penitentiary, and when they come home, these YGs have been to YA [Youth Authority] for two years, and they're just as big as them and can knock somebody out and pull a trigger and so on.

So when the truce was initiated, it wasn't really a top-down situation here in this area, it was like a bottom-up. It was the youngsters who were saying, "Wait a minute, we're out here doing all of this killing, y'all used to be out here doing it, but we're going to stop it." In Watts it was basically a top-down and bottom-up situation, where both levels have played a major role. To my knowledge it was coming from both ways. They can speak on it more than I could.

Like I said, here in Compton it was a spiritual thing. It was people who were tired of seeing this stuff happen, and when the peace came it was like a miracle. Like somebody just clapped their hands, like Clap-On, and it was on. Truce, peace, Bloods and Crips together!

**Q:** How many lives do you think have been saved due to the peace?

**A:** I think about three hundred black males die each year in L.A., and they say something like 50 percent were from gang violence in one summer. Every time a Black dies or a Latino dies, they say it's gang-related. You have people that die for all types of reasons. Everything is not gang-related. Here in the streets of L.A. we don't have that status where we're killing each other over stocks and bonds, and politics.

I believe a lot of lives were saved. I can't give you a specific number, but summer was coming up, and usually when summer hits, and school is out, you have a lot of people on the streets. So with the brothers coming together for that whole summer, that saved a tremendous amount of lives. Not just the lives of brothers who were in it, but it gave an avenue for younger kids to see that this is not the right thing to do, and for those who didn't start banging yet, not to bang. For the ones still in the womb.

**Q:** How did that day in the park make you feel?

**A:** I felt so good, man, I was proud to be the one who handled all the red tape. I went and talked to the people down at the Department of Parks and Recreation, the Park Patrol, and the police came knocking on my door asking me what was I trying to do. I was ducking from them, and I got this lady from Drew Economic Development Center to get me a lawyer off the top. She went down there and told them what I was doing and told them to back off. They didn't want it to happen. They did not want to give us the permit to use the park. They would have invaded our privacy if they came inside that park. We would have had a lawsuit, because we had it in writing, by having the permit to use the park. The police had been tripping and coming to the parks, chasing cats up out of there who didn't have permits. I had it all planned out, because I saw how these brothers were getting infiltrated. I remember I was at a park one time, and the police came up to us and said over the loudspeaker, "Y'all are going to be killing each other next week, get up out of here." So this time when we gave this event over here in Compton, it was smooth.

**Q:** How do you feel the peace can be maintained?

**A:** There's a lot of stuff going on now, but it has gotten into the hands of the white mainstream society. All of these unity concerts, unity-in-the-community programs at different parks, they have all of these celebrities coming out. They are not letting the individuals on the grassroots level control the microphone. You need brothers who have been through it to step up and say, "Hey, man, check this out, I've been to the pen, I've lived this, my homeboy got shot, let's stop this madness, let's keep the peace going."

No lawyer that lives over there in the Wilshire district, with a degree from USC, can get up there and tell me to stop gang-banging.

Now a brother who has been shot or has been to jail, has been gang-

Congresswoman Maxine Waters and Deputy Rory Kaufman at Ujima Village Fun Day, hosted by Angelo Adams

Future 'N Action Family at NBC Studios: Glee, Alonzo, Joanne, Jay, Angelo

Angelo with Stedman at 1993 Inaguration in Washington, D.C.

Hangin' in Harlem—a break from the tour

banging, who is an OG, who's known and has bullet wounds, can give me some type of insight, because I can relate to him. So we're the only ones that can talk to a gang member and tell them not to do it, because we are what you see on the six-o'clock news. This is the only thing that they can relate to, because they know we understand.

There's nothing wrong with sharing knowledge, or giving a person insight on something that they don't know anything about. People tell me stuff, and I take heed to it, and I relay it to somebody else. It's about sharing knowledge, and helping somebody else that's Black. Doing something positive, and trying to get everybody to understand what's really going on with a situation that we've been involved with all of our lives, ever since we knew what life was all about. You have kids that are just out here, they don't know what's happening. Then you have those that do know what's happening, who want to do something on the positive tip, but can't because there are so many negatives working against them. They don't know how a brother is going to trip, because of this crap they see on television. "If you quit the gang, you're going to get killed." Those are myths. Man, you can get out of a gang anytime you get ready to. You don't have to go do that s—. You don't have to. Not around here. Not with gangs I've dealt with. If you want to stop, you stop. Other gangs might have a code of ethics that you can't get out, but the average gang, you can get out of anytime you get ready to.

I always tell a little story: here you have a gang of five kids that are doing dirt every day, and they're trying to get you to join the gang. Either they're jumping you or bothering you. As long as you fight that gang back and get somebody else to help you, then you don't have to ever worry about that gang growing, because one of them is going to go to jail, and one of them is going to get killed. That's coming. One of them is going to get injured. That's coming. So when you join a gang, the only thing that you're doing is making that gang more powerful. If you stay out of the gang and don't join, then the gang will never grow.

That's how they start in all of these communities, they get one or two brothers to start pushing on some kids, and the kids never have the education of how to avoid a gang. The only thing they know is how to join them, because of that television. That's what it teaches you, it teaches you how to join a gang. You don't have anything to intervene. He's in school eight hours a day, but the problem doesn't start while he's in school, the problem starts after three o'clock when the bell rings, when he comes home, when he gets presented with all these different things.

**Q:** What are some ways that we can bring about economic empowerment and community development? To provide alternatives for the youth?

**A:** With places like the Playground stores. The Playground is a blessing for L.A., and for the Compton area. The program is a solution. The facility up there, it's a great facility, because what it does is show kids that they can come, and not just purchase shoes, but get an education, learn computers, and also get training in football, weight lifting, basketball, and other activities. It's a start. They need more than just one or two, and I'm quite sure it's going to grow across the city, and to other states. It's the best philosophy that one can come up with, and I'd like to commend everybody that's a part of that program, because they're doing a hell of a job with little capital. They're not working with that much money, but they have a lot of Black people that are coming together, getting together and doing something. To my knowledge there were four or five investors that came together, that were concerned about what's going on in the inner city, put some money together, and boom, started it up. If they can do it, then other people with large sums of money can do the same thing. It's just a program. It's individuals who are taking a chance to get out here and deal with these young gang members.

You have some people out here that want to do something, but can't go to work the next day, "You're giving thousands of dollars to the gang members, I hear." So you have brothers who are holding back, because they'll get flak from the job. We have Black corporations that don't want to touch gang bangers. They won't even help. When the peace treaty first jumped off, and those brothers were coming on TV every single day asking for this and that, nobody, I mean not one big-time Black corporation, came to put a hand down here, at least to my knowledge. There might be some that did something, but they didn't do anything to where it reached out and touched individuals who were actually down with keeping the peace.

Now everybody is trying to be an expert on the gang truce and unity in the community, because it has a price tag on it. When it first started, it didn't have a price tag on it, because the gangs were controlling it, the gangs were keeping the peace, but now you have a few corporations, a few individuals whose names have gained status in the city from working with these gang members, and bringing them into these programs, hyping it up. When I was out there trying to promote concerts, they said I was just trying to get a bunch of gang bangers in the park who were going to start fighting and killing each other, but now they can do it, and they're not even a part of it. They have the money behind them now. There's a price tag on it.

I'm not going to ever put anything in the mix to where it would damage something that somebody else is doing. I don't agree with the approach of all these "truce concerts," "peace concerts," and stuff like that, because the gang members themselves who are out here stopping the violence, and increasing the peace, are not benefiting. Where is all of this money going? Why are these guys not getting to the microphone? It's not all about money, but why aren't these guys given the opportunity, once their name is used, because when you say "peace" in L.A., you're talking about Bloods and Crips, you're not talking about anything else. When you talk about "increase the peace," you're talking about gang bangers. That's the bottom line. So when they have these concerts, why do they have a minister up there, or some other person on the microphone twenty or thirty minutes telling a thousand youth to stop gang-banging? "Stop the violence, increase the peace." As soon as this so-called role model pops up there, the little kids say, "That fool didn't gang-bang a day in his life." When they have one of those fools come up there talking that old Hollywood s—, that's it. The youth don't get any knowledge; they get entertainment, but they don't get any knowledge.

The approach we need to take is, "We have Ice Cube coming . . . ," but before you see Ice Cube, you're fixin' to listen to ten gang bangers telling you not to gang-bang, before Ice Cube says one word.

We really need to be getting together and implementing one big program, vote, select a president, and a vice president, give people different roles, and start delegating some authority. All of these organizations are working for the same goal. We all have resources that we can use coming from different angles.

You need money to make these things run, because you have to have some type of capital to keep everybody happy. When I got involved, I wasn't getting paid. I made a little money here and there. If a brother was to call me up right now and say I want you to come talk to a hundred kids—just have me some water and pay for my gas, and I'll be there.

If you can sell cocaine or any other type of drug, you can start your own business. It's that easy. You don't need all this money to start a business, just like you didn't need a lot of money to start selling drugs. When you're selling drugs, you learn how to do your books, you learn how to save your money, you know how to invest it, and with a business it's the same thing. You can run a corporation. These brothers out here that have seven or eight people working for them, they are managers and businessmen, they're already entrepreneurs. They can turn that right into their own corporation; it's the same thing, the same philosophy, the same movement.

**Q:** What would you like to be doing ten years from now?

**A:** I'm very interested in going into film, but I want to stick with video, because video is much cheaper, much quicker, much faster, and much more enhanced. I believe that by the year 2000 video will take over, because film is playing out, and everything is being done on video now.

I want to have completed at least four documentaries on social life, human development, and social awareness. Videos dealing with stopping the Black-on-Black killing, because when you're speaking of drugs, people say the "war on drugs," the war on drugs is a war on Black America, because we're the only ones losing. We're the only ones going to jail, we're the only ones dying off of this stuff, so the war is really America against Black folks. Black people don't see it that way, because they don't have the knowledge of what's actually going on, and who the drugs are actually designed by, and who they are designed for.

White people use cocaine more than Black people do, they are the number-one consumers of cocaine, but they're not associated with crime, drive-bys, gangs, street-corner selling, or any of that.

So I want to be a mentor for people that are growing up doing that stuff, and I want to provide educational tools such as books, videos, documentaries, and movies, to show kids that there is another way, and that all gang members don't die in the end. Some of them stand up and fight and continue and grow up to be other figures than just a bum on the street, or a name inside of a morgue. I want to be known as a person that has changed and is doing something positive. I want to be on that status just like any other guy . . . I want to never erase where I came from. I want it to be known every time that this is an ex-convict, this is a former gang member, gang leader, dope dealer, whatever you want to call it, that has done something, and if he can change, anybody can change.

**Q:** What are some of the changes that you have made that other brothers may follow your example?

**A:** I went back to school, because when I was in school, I was a part of the magnet programs. I was considered a magnet student in the Compton Unified School District. I had the opportunity to do an internship at Northrop. I had the opportunity to go to summer school two years in a row at Cal State University at Long Beach. I was part of the Math and Engineering Science Achievement program, and several other programs that enhanced kids who were college-bound. I wasn't a dummy, I had high grade scores as far as taking tests, and I was always above average. When I graduated, I wanted to go to Devry Institute, because that's what I was into at the time, engineering. It just didn't work out. I didn't go, I started selling dope and stuff like that, and I went in and out of prison for four years.

I was banging in high school, because when I went to Centennial, I had a one-on-one confrontation with the Crips from other neighborhoods for the second time. At Vanguard we all went to school together and came home together. At Centennial we had kids from ten different junior high schools. So we had Bloods, Crips, and Mexicans, from different neighborhoods and communities. At that point I wasn't a gang banger per se, but I went to school with all the other homiez, we went to school together. So you have this crowd that's banging and going to school, and you have this crowd that's not banging, but we all got up at seven o'clock in the morning and walked to school together. So if we were confronted by some Crips, we all had to fight, because you never know when these bookworms were going to get confronted by themselves, so we had to help them, because we were going to need their help. You just get inside that channel, and that's how it happens sometimes. It's like, "Where you live at?" "I stay over in Ujima Village, but I don't gang-bang." "I saw you walking to school with those fools this morning, and they had their red rags." "I had my books in my hand, what are you talking about?" Bow, you get fired on. What are you going to do? The average kid is going to fire back, some will, some won't, and some will go home crying.

You also have the situation where the police will pull you over and just label you. This is exactly how people get labeled as gang bangers.

Everybody doesn't like to be called a gang banger. You have brothers who will say, "I haven't gang-banged a day in my life." There are different definitions of what they consider themselves as individuals, but society just says, "You're a gang banger," that's it. Here you might have ten or fifteen kids going to school, half of them gang-bang, half of them don't. You have another set of kids across the street that are from another neighborhood, and they get into this big gang fight. Half of them fight, half of them don't, then the police pull up, and everybody is getting labeled as a gang banger. They have a rap sheet on you. That's how they come up with all of these gang-banger statistics, because the police themselves make it look that way, because the more gang bangers they have the more officers they need on the streets. It's a game that they play with society, and they're always winning the game.

**Q:** Have you seen agitation and instigation by police?

**A:** Basically the federal government in their funding of these nonprofit organizations is one of the biggest moves of infiltration there is. You have certain brothers who are in the gang for the money, and they will do anything to get the money. When you have zero dollars, and two weeks later you have $250,000 in your account, people start to think. It's highly impossible for a Black to get treated that way in the nineties from white folks, or from private entities, without their own agenda. So every time I get knowledge of an organization that has taken that route, or is affiliated in that fashion, I don't deal with them. I don't want to get involved with something that is not working for the best interests of the community. When you deal with these organizations that come into the community and they do this or that, the bottom line is they just want to use you, so they can get money from the federal government. You have a lot of grants where they say you don't have to pay them back, but they're going to have somebody to come down there and say, "We need to know this, and we need to know that, and the only way we can get this information is by your organization coming out with a survey." Just like they were doing during the riots, with those surveys that said, "What are you going to do?" "What do you feel about the Uprisings?" They're getting paid off by the cops because the cops need to know everybody's attitude. What's the best way to find out their attitude? Have other Blacks go door-to-door and ask how they feel about what's going on. When they get that survey, they turn that over to the system. They know our attitudes, they know how we feel, they know how many of us are unemployed, and everything else. Again, when I look into an organization, and they work in that fashion, I don't have anything to say about it, and I don't have anything to do with it, because it's all about infiltration.

The only way they can infiltrate you is to find out where you're at. To get involved with you, to get inside you like a disease, and just tear you down from the inside. They'll work with you, they'll give you all the money and all the press you need, put you on TV every day, do this and that for you, but in the end they're going to take you out. They're going to use you until they can't use you anymore. Then they're going to let everybody know you were working for them on top of everything else.

I think that every man needs to take control of his own destiny. I feel that every individual out here has the opportunity to reap all of the benefits that are here. I think people need to take time and look back at the history so they can understand what's going on right now, because if it wasn't for history, we wouldn't be in the position we're in now. People need to re-educate themselves and re-educate their parents and get their parents involved in their schooling, and upbringing. I think every man and every child should respect their parents, their elders, and sit down and listen to what other people are telling you. If you can sit down and watch *Martin* every night, you can sit up and listen to that brother on the corner, because there are a lot of people out there that do have knowledge that you might not think have knowledge. A television is not the key. I don't watch TV, a lot of stuff on television is all BS, if you look at the news, it's all BS. You can't get anything from television. Television is not real. If you're watching a basketball game, it's not real, you're seeing a tape delay of something that went on.

So kids need to get away from in front of the tube, get inside of some books, pick up a newspaper and read it. Go to your local library and get all of the knowledge you can. Regardless of where you live, or how you're living, you need to get out there and get you some knowledge, that's the bottom line. If you don't have knowledge, you will never have any power. A lot of things that are going on out here, you may not know about, but it's right there in your local library, right there in your newspaper or your magazine. If you don't read, or if you can't read, you have to get out there and learn that you *can* read. There are a lot of illiterate people out there who are afraid to even say that they can't read. They street-talk every day, they can get up and hold conversations with you, but they can't read. So people need to say what they cannot do, quit saying what you can do. What you can't do is what we need to know, then we can help you with that, and you can make yourself a better person.

For all of the little brothers out there that are still gang-banging, y'all need to stop it. Y'all need to Hotep and have peace, because there's nothing in it, there's no future in it. I've been involved for ten years, and I didn't get anything out of it. I was never paid for shooting at somebody, or helping to take another brother's life. I've never been actually paid for selling cocaine to somebody. I was just killing my own self, destroying my culture, and bringing the Black race down. It's not all about that. We need to wake up. Everybody just needs to wake up, because when you're out there selling dope, doing wrong, you're not doing anything but working for the white man, because you're taking lives and denying another brother his innocence. It's genocide. You're making individuals get further and further in the hole, because you're not helping anybody when you're out there shooting up folks, and robbing folks. You're not helping yourself, you're just making it worse, all for only a

Honorable Mention at Howard University

Thanks to all the brothers and sisters who gave peace a chance

March on New York for jobs, peace, racial harmony

couple of bucks in your pocket. You have these brothers out here car-jacking—y'all need to kill that. There's not any money in car-jacking, there's not any money in robbing an old lady at the bank teller, they can't get but $200 to $300 out of there at the most. You're going out there blowing people's heads off for no reason at all, but it's not all your fault, and I understand that. Knowledge is the key.

**Q:** Who are some of the people you respect?

**A:** I respect a lot of my homiez who were once gang-banging who are not gang-banging right now. I respect a lot of our leaders who are here in our community. I respect everybody who was involved in the gang truce. All the Bloods, and all the Crips. I respect the brothers out of Watts, Tony Bogard (RIP), High T, Ray Ray. I respect the homiez over there in Nickerson Gardens. The homiez from the west side, the homiez from the east side. I respect those around me every day who represent what I represent, which is peace and unity among Black men, women, and children. It's a trip that we're here together, trying to stick together. It was very much unheard of, and it's like a dream come true to a lot of people. So everybody that has been down with it, I respect those that are down with the program. You can't do anything but respect those who are down with this, because there's no other solution to gang violence but to stop it. The only thing that you can do is lay your guns down, lay your hands down, and hang your rag up. Other than that it would just keep going on and on. So we've got to take that stand to stop it!

**The man in the mirror**
**got power**
**it's now or never**
**more than ever**
**Black people have to stick together**
**But yo, let's hear it for the Bloods and the Crips**
**I gots to admit it**
**ya'll brothers did it**

**—Kam, "Peace Treaty"**

## SHOUT OUTS

I would like to thank Brother Yusuf and his Queen, Sister Shah'Keyah, and their daughter, Sister Ah'Keyah, for giving me this opportunity to share a lighter shade of brown with you.

A special thanks to the Creator of the earth, to my mother. To all the wonderful people in Ujima Village, the homiez, and all my friends at Continental Cable of Compton and Los Angeles.

Thanks to Alonzo Williams of Zolo Inc. A special thanks to Brother Cli N Tel, for his guidance and support. The great city of New York, the

Martin Luther King Commission in New York, Aaron Dare and Eric Eve, the New York State Assembly and Commission for giving me the opportunity to share my vision and wisdom. To all my friends in Washington, D.C., thank all of you for putting the Truce Is On tour together, and all the beautiful sisters of the National Council of Negro Women, Dr. Dorothy Height, Kim Julian, Samantha of Washington, D.C., all my friends in Atlanta, the King family, all of my friends from Future 'N Action, and a special thanks to the late John "Jay" Hunter for showing me new avenues to positive leadership, Joanne Beck for giving me the opportunity to share my dreams and visions with her, and Brother John.

Thanks to everyone who has been part of my life, all of my old schools from East 56th Street, the Bottoms, and to my Compton comrades. Thank all of you, peace for '95. I'm outta here.

Don "Playmate" Gordon and James Brown (of Wellness Center) sending out message

# PLAYMATE

*(My name is Don Gordon, and I'm a former gang member from Grape Street Watts. My reason for wanting to participate in this book is because I want to give people the insight and the knowledge of what goes on down here in Watts, in the Jordan Downs. So people that are reading from all across the world can understand what we're saying, and what we feel, and how we're living. That we do think about other places than just here. We are concerned about the development of the rest of the world. Playmate.)*

**Q:** How did the peace first come about in Watts and what was your involvement?

**P:** The truce that has been going on right here, we started to build the truce back in 1990. That's when we first started having our meetings. The reason for the truce was to stop the killings and the drive-bys and all of the negative things that affect our community daily. We took the first initiative, our side. Grape Street Watts [Crips] took the first initiative to sew up that bridge, that dispute that's been going on for decades. We went over to the Crips in Imperial Courts, which is where the brothers who shot me three times with an AK-47 live. We went over there and talked to them, and once we established that neutral ground between us and them, then we went over to Nickerson Gardens, which are Bloods. We united with them, and then we went over to Hacienda Village, where they have Pirus [Bloods]. These are four major project developments that control everything on their outskirts.

So by us taking the initiative to come at them with peace, we found out that everybody in these gangs have been wanting to stop the killing for a long time. I found that out from a lot of brothers that I speak to, that I had never had a chance to hold a two-word conversation with, that everybody has been wanting to stop the killing and stop gangbanging.

**Q:** What happened here inside Jordan Downs when you all came together for peace?

**P:** A series of killings had taken place . . . for a minute the neighborhood was calm, even with the gangs, and without the peace treaty. Then the crime rate had gone up so high, to where people weren't safe. I mean I couldn't even trust people that I knew. It was that serious. Everybody basically stayed to themselves.

We formed the peace treaty because we said, "We can't just sit back and live like this, we have to start doing something." We started realizing that this is a cage. I've been here all of my life, since 1966, and basically nothing has changed. *Nothing.* We still have to bathe in bathtubs, because we don't have showers in these projects. So we started addressing these issues, like how the police used to ride through and basically do whatever they wanted. They tell us not to break the law, but they break the law every day. Who knew that the police—I didn't ever know that the police weren't supposed to stick their hands in my pocket. I didn't know that. So it was just a series of things going on, and the older we started getting—I'm twenty-seven now—we started to find out that the problems with gangs wasn't even in our age category anymore. It was down in the younger generation, and it's getting younger. So when we started focusing on how we're living, and how we're teaching our kids, that's when we got together, as individuals, it wasn't everybody at once. We got together as individuals and started communicating. Myself, and this brother by the name of Charles Harris, we went and started doing interviews around the neighborhood, just being concerned. After all the interviews we did, we went back and watched over all of them, and we found that people were constantly talking about the gangs, talking about the educational system, the government, and all of these different issues, but nobody was talking about the kids. It sounds harsh, but it's the truth. Out of all the interviews, out of all these people, nobody said anything about the kids. Which is why we came up with our game plan, which is to deal with the youth. That's how we organized our youth club.

Back to the peace treaty, and how we formed it. We had a lot of problems, because some brothers weren't with it. We had people that had killed other people's cousins, homeboys, and brothers. There was a lot of animosity in bringing about this peace, because everybody wasn't down with it. It was like, "It has been like this, let it stay like this." We weren't going for that. So slowly, but surely, we started having our meetings, and we started having our ciphers. We learned about a cipher, and how you say the prayer, and we'd sit back and talk and start communicating with each other. We had to bond first, because we were so broken apart. So a few brothers bonded back together, and we started bringing about a change.

We found out that if we change ourselves, and it's so true, it's not philosophy, it's a fact, that if I change my life, I change the people around me. So as this change was being made, more and more brothers started coming. Then we started learning something new. We started learning about ourselves. We started learning about being focused on ourselves and our own beliefs, what we live for, and what we stand for, not just what the set stands for. It's what *you* stand for.

We started taking these classes up at Jim Brown's house, which is the Amer-I-CAN Program, which teaches you responsibility, and self-determination. That alone gave us the knowledge that we didn't get in school. All through school they would tell me about goals, but nobody ever sat down and told me that my goals had to be realistic, they had to be worthwhile, attainable, timely, and manageable. They didn't tell me that my goals had to be accomplished with perseverance, and understanding. They just told me that you need a goal. It's a trip, because the schools never even told me how to respect myself, first. How to use my own mind.

I had a bad condition—I call it a condition, because it was something that I learned at a young age—and that was being abusive towards women. Not just towards women, but people in general. I found out that the reason I was really abusive towards women was not because I hated women or disliked women, but all through my life I was my mama's baby, her youngest son. I had three brothers older than me, and lots of cousins and homeboys, and I witnessed each and every last one of them beat up on their women. It was a control thing. Then I found myself in that predicament. Until I understood this, I was still in that same predicament where I'd be abusive towards women, as a form of my conditioning, something that I had learned at childhood.

People who study human behavior say that in our earliest childhood, beginning as young as perhaps two years old, our fundamental basic attitudes and behaviors are determined by our total environment. This includes home, school, church, family, and the immediate community. They didn't teach me that my attitude was a condition from my total environment. I can't say Mama taught me how to gang-bang, or Daddy. It was when I left that secure place and went outside and dealt with all of the negative in the world that we deal with every day, this is how kids learn things. Me, as a product of this system, that's how I grew up, and that's why I did the things that I did, and that's why a lot of people are still doing it, because they don't understand. They've never had a chance to get knowledge of self. When I went to school, I went because if I didn't go, I was going to get my behind whipped. I didn't go because I wanted to go. I went to school for somebody else. I never had the opportunity to develop my own self.

I graduated from Jordan High School in 1984, and I was totally illiterate. I could not read a lick, but I graduated from high school. How? How did I graduate from high school and couldn't read? As I started developing myself, started getting knowledge of self, started understanding the words *focus, determination, responsibility, respect, understanding,* and *communication,* I mean really started understanding the actual meaning of these words, then I was able to make that change.

I'll never stop stressing that change is healthy. I don't care if you're eight, eighteen, or eighty. It's never too late to change. Change is healthy, and it's something that we constantly have to do in everyday life. Every day we have to sacrifice something for something else. We can't just sit back and expect and wait. I trip off of AFDC [Aid to Families with Dependent Children], social security, general relief, and food stamps, because I believe that those are forms of manipulation.

I live for my people, and I see what this system is doing to them. It's allowing them to sit back on their ass and not care or think about anything. I can't even get them to help me do something for their own kids.

This is how bad it is, because they've been sitting back all this time getting those free checks. Work? They've never had to work. This is what's going on. They'll sit back and write me an AFDC check or a social security check because I have legal custody of my oldest son. I've had him since he was six months old, he's ten now, and every month I received a check on the first, and the fifteenth, to take care of my son. If I was to go out there and get a job—you know something else, I've never been convicted of a felony—but if I go out there and try to find a job, they're going to find some reason not to hire me. That's the way it is, man. Why? Is it because of where I live? We can't even get cable TV around here. I thought everybody had cable. You can go right across any one of these streets outside of the projects and receive cable television. Why is that? Because they know that there are Black stations that talk about what we're talking about. Changing things. Changing all of this negative. It's not that hard. The thing is you have to be willing to make the sacrifice. Sacrifice is something we're not conditioned to do. If we do something now, we want to get paid. That's why I tell people all the time, in my job that I took for myself and for my people, money is not important to me, because I live for people. Money doesn't make me. What is money? I make money, money doesn't make me. The love of money is the root to all evil, but we know we can't live without it. I live for my people, and I stand strong for my people, and anything I can do, anything I can say, anyway I can help create positive for my people, that's my stand. I'm capable of enhancing any individual or organization that wishes to effect a positive change.

**Q:** What was it like going over to Imperial Courts after getting unity here first? What are some of the things that made y'all successful?

**P:** Let me tell you, it was a scary situation. I thank Almighty ALLAH for having me here right now. I said it once, back in the days when them guys finished shooting me up, they left thirty-two bullet holes in my car, and three in me. This is what happened—it was early one morning after the rebellion, one of the young Crips from Imperial Courts came over here to Jordan Downs. . . . During the rebellion, nobody cared if you were a Crip or a Blood, everybody was straight up together. So after the National Guards left out of the projects, and out of the area, one of the young guys from over there came over here, and some of the young guys from over here was going to trip on him. Then me, and one of my homiez, Poncho, and a few more of us, we stopped it, and we told them we're not with that anymore, we're going to sew this up. All this time, the peace treaty was already being formed and developed, before the rebellion, before Rodney King and all that. So when he came over here, he saw that nothing happened to him. We told him, "It's all right man, y'all are cool to come over here," but still nobody trusted it. That weekend we all got together, and we sent a message that we were going to roll over there to Imperial Courts, and they gave us the okay to come on, they said that everything was cool, but it was scary, because everybody didn't go at one time. It was a few individuals, then a few more, and then a few more. Now when I got there, there was a lot of people outside. Then they started having homeboys come out that didn't know about it, so there was a little argument that got started. "Well, there can't be a peace treaty without me saying so." So what they did was, they got brothers older than me and put them together. They went in the gym and started talking, while everybody was outside waiting. We didn't know what was fixin' to happen, they had their whole crew, I mean these are some big gangs, they were kickin' it on one side of the street, and we were on the other side of the street. It wasn't an official peace treaty yet. We were over there though, and I was just hoping they wouldn't trip. Then a whole lot of their females came out, a whole lot of women, and mothers.

When they opened the gym up, it was the most beautiful thing that you could ever see in your life. It was what we had been working for. When they opened the gym up, and our big homiez and their big homiez came out hugging each other, and kissing each other, all the people started hollering, and everybody just collided, because everybody knew each other already. We know everybody from their hood, and they know everybody from this hood. It's just like with the Bloods from Nickerson Gardens, we all went to school with each other, but because of the gangs and because of the sets, we had to stay apart from each other. When they came out, everybody just collided, it was on. It was just beautiful. Talk about power. Talk about strength. Man, they made a long chain of all hugs and handshaking.

**Q:** Were those older brothers that went in the gym considered the heroes of the neighborhood after that?

**P:** Well, I'll tell you, I wouldn't have ever learned anything about banging if those other brothers would have never taught me. So now with them uniting, they have all the respect in the world. I'm glad that I had a chance to be a part of this, because at least now we have a chance. There are a lot of brothers that are dead and gone to prison for life behind this s—. Some have a chance now to see what they created, what they made of us, and what we are making of our next generation, and of our kids. There are a lot of people that haven't had a chance to see that. The peace treaty is so strong now that it is even spreading throughout the jail cells, and do you know what's coming out of it? Change!

You have people coming down here now to find out for themselves, and not just what they've heard. Man, wouldn't anybody come down here and talk to one person in Jordan Downs on any level, about anything. If they were going to do a news report, they would do it on the outskirts.

I've been here long enough to see Jordan Downs go through many changes. Once upon a time this place was a big ol' family. There wasn't any gangs, no sets, it was one big family. If you messed with the next-

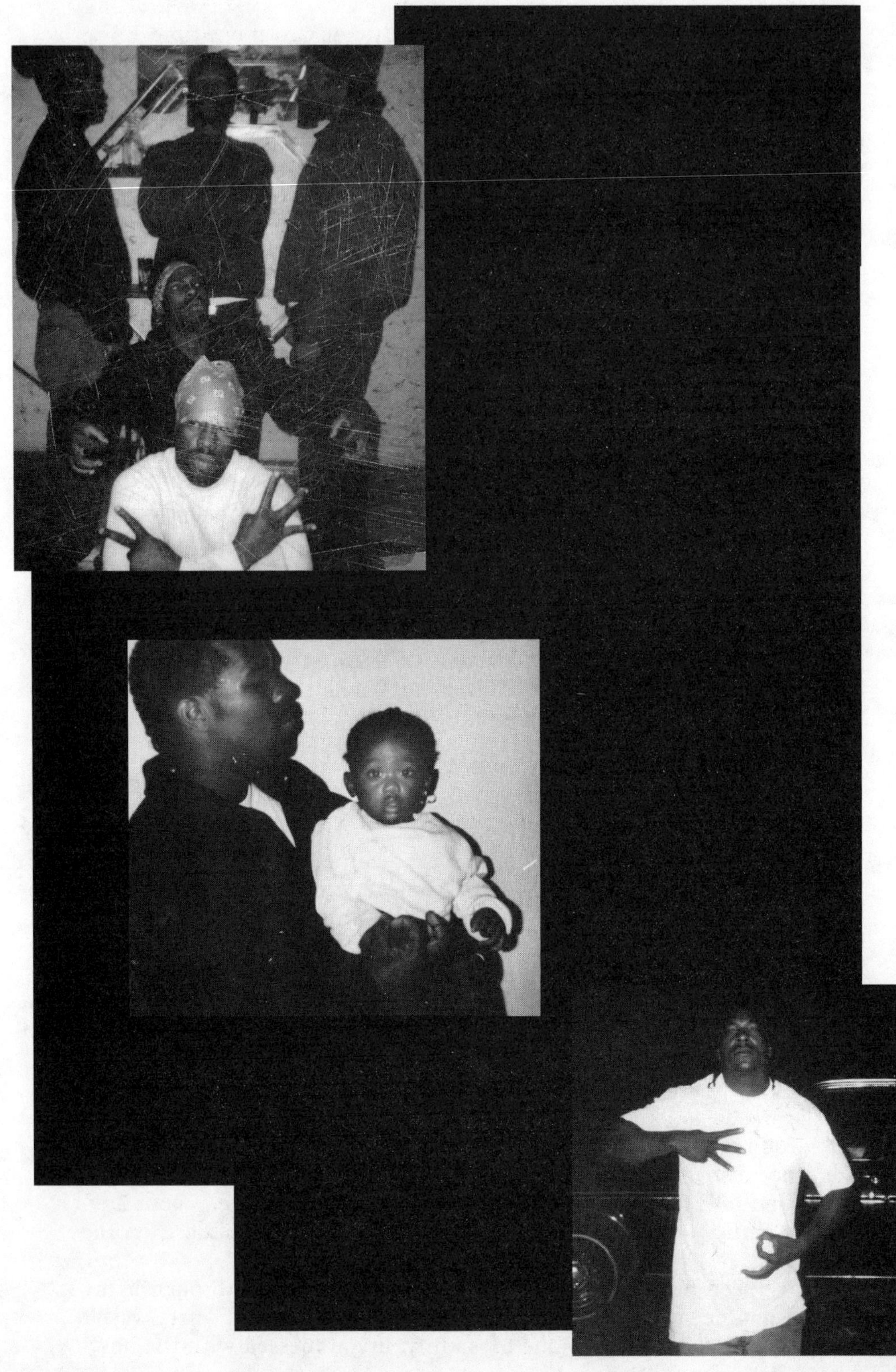

door neighbors, here came everybody from that side of the projects, and guess where they're coming? To get you, because you couldn't hurt anybody in here. I've seen it go from where next-door neighbors were brothers and sisters, uncles and aunties. Right now, the majority of these people are kin to each other, because there are generations and generations of families here. It was a trip when the peace treaty came about, because there were people over there from our families [Imperial Courts] and over there too [Nickerson Gardens]. Then when we finally hooked up and got together, we decided that if we can peace up with each other, after the killing that went back and forth between us two, then we might as well go on and unite with the Bloods.

Everything almost went haywire. They weren't going for it. Even right now to this day, you have certain Bloods that just stay to their self. They won't mess with the peace treaty, they'll speak to you, "What's up, Blood," or "What's up, Cuz," but that's it. They won't do any more conversating with you or anything, but they have respect. There's respect. It has always been about respect. If I can come to your neighborhood, your city, your community, or to your home, and show you all the utmost respect in the world, how are we going to feud? How are we going to misunderstand each other? It's about respect. When we went to the Nickerson Gardens, they gave us so much respect, because they had been with the peace. They was with it when we first approached a couple of their homiez. What you have to do is get to the people that everybody else looks up to. Once we got with them, they gave so much love I couldn't believe it. I got on the telephone, and I was telling one of my homeboys to come over, he was like, "Where you at, man?" "I'm in the Nickersons." "Man, I ain't coming to the Nickersons." "Man, come on over to the Nickersons, the peace treaty is on." "What?" "I'm telling you I'm in the Nickersons right now, brother, come on over here right now." Here came cars and cars, they started coming from all over. It was on. Then we hit the Haciendas. Another neighborhood we used to war with.

You know what tripped me out, all those different projects that we went to, when they came here, the Imperial Courts and the Nickerson Gardens came . . . I thought it was strong when we went there but, man, when they got here, you should have seen all these people coming outside. "What's up? What's going on?" Like they didn't know what was going on.Then we had a big ol' party, and what happened was we started partying too much. Not us, not the major projects, because notice our peace treaty still stands strong today. We had people coming from the west side, people coming from the north side, the east side, and from all over South Central Los Angeles. People who weren't even down with the peace treaty, didn't know how it was formed, how it was created or anything, came through.

They was just like, "If those brothers down there in Watts can peace treaty, we can too." Yet all the time they didn't know that it took some bonding. It was a process. It took a process of three years to create this. This just didn't happen. It started in 1990.

In 1988 little things started happening. That's when the communication started evolving. Right now to this day, you will find that the outskirts of Watts are feuding again. Not at it like they used to be, because during the peace treaty when it first jumped off, a lot of people had time to come together. I went to Compton last week and got jumped on. For what? There wasn't any argument or fussin' over nothing.

**Q:** Why do you think that happened?

**P:** Right now with the peace treaty going on, brothers need something to do, other than kickin' back, chillin'. Right now you can go where you want. If I go somewhere that's not with the peace treaty, and I tell them I'm from Grape Street, nine times out of ten, I'll be asked to leave, instead of a fool just taking off on me. I don't know why they did that. I don't represent myself on that level anymore, and I know how to carry myself respectfully now, so when I go places, nobody usually bothers me. The thing is, these brothers don't have anything to do. Only a fool walks backwards, and I'd be a fool to get a gun and go somewhere to retaliate and kill a brother I'm trying to save. That doesn't make sense.

**Q:** What would you say now to those brothers who jumped on you?

**P:** What happened, happened, but I truly believe that what you do to people shall be done to you. In my heart I truly believe that. Brothers have to be aware and be responsible for the predicaments that they put their own lives in. When they did that, anything could have happened. I'm not the one to do it, but the same thing you did to me, eventually it will come back to you, somewhere, somehow, some kind of way. What I would say to them is to think before you act.

**Q:** You spoke about a process of learning about yourself. Talk about that process. What was that process like and what do you feel others should do to learn more about themselves?

**P:** I spoke on it once. We have something called the Amer-I-CAN Program. It teaches the responsibility of self-determination. It allows you to learn about yourself. I came to learn about it just after I moved away from kickin' it with the hood, when I stopped hanging out. I mean I'm always a part of the neighborhood, because I've been here all my life, but I had basically moved to an area where I was to myself. I kept a pistol on me every day. The brother I talked about earlier, Charles Harris, is actually responsible for my learning process, because if it hadn't been for that brother approaching me every day . . . *every day.* He would call me by my real name: "Why don't you come and see what we're doing at Jim Brown's house. You're not doing anything right here." Which he knew it. All I did was sit on that porch every day, waiting for something to happen, or waiting to get into something. So every day he approached me. One particular day he approached me, I was mad, and I pulled that gun on him, and only by the grace of God he didn't get shot. He looked at me and said, "What are you going to do now? Are you going to shoot me? Go on and shoot me then, I'm standing here living for you anyway, it's the same thing. So if you want to shoot me, go on." When he said that, it was something else. I just thought about it. Here I am with a gun on this brother, and I've been knowing this brother all of my life. A brother that would do virtually anything for me, and I have a gun on him, fixin' to shoot him. I dropped the gun, and I don't own a gun right now to this day. I went with them up to Jim Brown's house, and when I got up there, I found out that I didn't have to act any particular way, all I had to do was be myself, and I was respected. Then I started learning about the classes that they were having, learning about the responsibility of self-determination. So I started taking those classes.

Once we started taking the classes, we got a brother named Aqeela from our hood, he is now the director of education for the Amer-I-CAN Program, that's our homeboy. We brought the class down here to the projects, and we started teaching amongst each other. It doesn't matter if you can read, write, or spell, we get by all of that. If you can't read, we have tapes.

We had a feelings session every day, that's how we got that bond. We had so many fights, you wouldn't believe it. The brothers that were in that one room, twelve brothers having a feelings session, talking about respecting somebody's opinion. The bonding process—man, we got kicked out of buildings [starts laughing]. I'm serious, man, it's funny now, but it was a serious process to get to know each other, to get to trust each other, to learn what we're really about, learning to speak the same language. My vocabulary has gone way up, now I speak what I feel and understand what I talk about. At first I could open my mouth and talk, but then I didn't know what I was talking about. I could elaborate on certain things, but to just open up and talk and conversate, I was limited. It wasn't the limitations I had put on myself, it was something that wasn't even given to me during school. I had to re-educate myself all over again—that's what we all have to do.

There was a brother named Chopper, who could read something one time and never forget it. So Chopper started reciting our books, and the chapters in our manual. I used to trip, because I was listening to the tapes as much as he was. Then he taught me that I could be the same way if I wanted to be. He said, "All you have to do is take all limitations that disable you, up off of you."

When I started with my youth club, I went through so many merry-go-rounds. During the process of re-educating myself about myself, I learned that I love kids. Yet I never knew that until this change took place. Then once this change took place, and I started dealing with my kids—automatically I knew what I wanted to do with them. That's why my youth club is unlike any other, because I allow the kids to make the decisions on whatever we do, as long as it's positive. Whether it's a cleanup, a field trip, or whatever. I let them make the decisions. We teach them Hooked on Phonics and all of that.

This is what's happening now, but when I first started, people took advantage of me, and they used me, because I didn't have full knowledge about what I was doing. So I went back into our manual. I started back to studying, because I got depressed and frustrated. They had yanked me out of a $150,000 contract, they utilized my kids' names, their addresses, phone numbers, our time and everything. Then they kicked us out. So I got frustrated and started to quit. Then I realized that a quitter never wins, and a winner never quits. I started studying massively, by myself, and I found out that nothing worthwhile is easy. If you're creating a business, organization, or whatever, nobody is to know more about your business than you. If I knew more about the business that I was in, then they couldn't have yanked me for the $150,000. Only because I didn't have full knowledge about what I was doing, it was easily done, and it's being done to people every day.

There are no youth centers around here. There are no Boy Scouts or Girl Scouts around here. There has never been anything like that around here for kids. I've been around here since 1966, and I can speak on that fact. YMCA, where at? There are no YMCAs around here.

**Q:** Speak on the importance of the youth, and why you focus on them.

**P:** One thing that I have found out by listening to the kids is that they speak, and they talk real heavy, they're smart, and very intelligent. Kids these days, growing up, you learn everything you possibly need to know by the time you're twelve years old. If it's about drugs, sex, gangs, guns, anything. Before you're twelve years old you know about it, and you understand it.

What I wanted to do is give the kids an opportunity that we never had, and that is to do something good, something positive. They never had anything positive to do, because I didn't show them how to do anything positive. I used to run around here and show these brothers how to gang-bang and show them how to be hard, and how to be an OG.

I found out in my change that an OG is not really an OG until he dies for the cause. So I'll never reach the status of being an OG alive, not now, because we have a chance to change. See, the brothers that are dead and gone, they can't change their lives, they lived their life, and they died for their cause. They are the OGs. You can do anything you want to do, go on and get life or whatever, but you're not fixin' to be an OG until you're out of here.

I wanted to do things for the kids that weren't done for me. Nobody ever cleaned our sandboxes for us. Nobody ever took us on field trips. Nobody ever told us that we were not supposed to curse at grown-ups. Nobody ever told us that we had to respect ourselves. That is what's going on right now, kids are being born, and they're just growing up. I look around here and it's sad, but I'm glad to say that I have the opportunity to be effective in the change of our youth. They just don't know . . . you've walked around my neighborhood, you see the sandboxes, they've been like that since I was a kid. We can't play in those; if you get in those boxes you will get ringworms. Every sandbox we cleaned out had little bugs that bite in them. So the new sand we got, we sprayed it with lime, to kill the bugs. Basically there has not been anything around here for the kids, not for me, not for those who came before me, and not for those coming after me. This is exactly why we are now doing these things for ourselves and for our future generations.

**Q:** Was it your own children that made you really get serious about this?

**P:** What really triggered it was when we were watching the videos of the interviews that we did with the people, and nobody was really concerned about the kids. So I walked around and started asking the kids, "Y'all want a youth club?" "Yeah. Yeah." Quite naturally, because they never had one. So when we came together with the kids, we had a feelings session with them, and we let everybody have a turn to speak. It could have been about anything, negative, positive, messed up, happy, however they felt, just talk about it. They talked about their feelings, and I asked others to respond to their feelings. What tripped me out was this one girl, when she was talking, I felt sorry, because she didn't have anything. Then I looked, and I tripped, not off of my kids, but my nieces and nephews. I have a gang of nieces and nephews. One of my brothers has eleven kids alone. I looked at my nieces and nephews, and I found out that my brother was having some personal problems, and their mama was also having problems, and it was affecting the kids. It made me mad, but then it really drove me to being sincere with what I'm doing now, because when we were coming up, our mamas and our dads weren't like that. Not mine. We took care of our babies, our sisters, and our brothers. Today, they're not taking care of their kids right.

Then I went around, and I started looking at what was going on. Mamas be dressing up real tough and neat, and their kids are tore up. Daddies running around here driving these nice cars, and their kids are tore up. Nobody is disciplining them, nobody is talking to them, or spending any time with them. That's why when we walk around, you hear all the kids say hi to me. Do you know why? Because I talk to them, I listen, and I care. I never tell them, "Don't do this, don't do that, you little stupid . . ." You should never verbally abuse a child. Do you know what that does to their self-esteem? I know what it did to some of my people. I've seen people move here from somewhere else, with expectations to go to school or go to college, do things with their lives. Then when they get around this, they forget about school and college and being a lawyer or a football player. They forget about it, because the manipulation here is so strong. It's not even really the manipulation, as much as it is the conditions that we've been having to live in for all of our lives.

What conditions you to be comfortable? I have lived here all my life, I was always comfortable here. I've never said that I wanted to move somewhere else. I'm only here because I choose to be. I don't have to live here. We don't have to live like this.

It's just like back in the sixties, before the civil rights movement, when colored folks had to sit upstairs to watch the movies, and white folks had to sit downstairs. Years after the segregation laws had passed, Black people still wanted to sit upstairs. Even though we could come downstairs. Why? Because it was a condition that was comfortable, and the surroundings were familiar.

**Q:** What happened to make it go from that love and family vibe, to fighting each other, and allowing the banging to get started?

**P:** My own experience, and my own view of when it all started, is when the unity broke.

**Q:** How did the unity break?

**P:** It was disastrous. The police came through here, and they called us terrorists. They called the Grape Street Watts gang a terrorist gang. You could have been from any other gang, but if you were from Grape Street Watts, they would take you to jail. They said, "We're going to come through here and tear Grape Street down." They got these young dudes that didn't know any better to fill out these white cards, saying that they were from this gang, from this set, and for how long, the whole thing. What they did was set them up. That little white card that they signed said that if you got caught doing any kind of crime, you'd get the time for that crime, plus three years for being in this gang. They had a lot of people sign those cards. After that came the sweeps, and the pickups. There are more people sitting in jail from around here for something they didn't do than there are people in jail for something they did do. They just came through sweeping, picking up people. Another thing, don't you ever think that gangs are the only ones who do drive-bys. Police do drive-bys too. Well-known people started getting killed, they started getting robbed and held hostage and kidnapped by the police. They were taking people to jail, and just snatching away the unity. While they were snatching the people that were born and raised here, and bled here, they were taking the original people out, and moving other people in. So now you have a lot of phonies and fakes in Grape Street. We know for a fact that the Hispanics living here are snitches, but so what. You can be a snitch all you want: if you don't have anything to snitch on, then what?

That "Weed and Seed" woke a lot of our people up. When the Weed and Seed program became active, we went to the town hall meeting to shut it down, but we know it didn't really get shut down, because all they did was give it a different name and stick it right back out here. It's here right now in full effect. They were moving people in, two to three years ahead of time. These people were moved in by the police, to stay here and monitor us. Keep an eye on this, and keep an eye on that. It was organized. They get in and try to be your friend and kick it with you, sit back, smoke weed, and drink with you, and they even did a couple of drive-bys, but all the time he's a police officer. All the time. That's how they knew who to get, when, where, and how. Once that happened, these new brothers got in and started perpetrating the game, and they started jacking each other. We never jacked each other around here. People never broke into your house around here, people would go somewhere else and break into somebody else's house. The only way you would get your house broken into in these projects was if you were moving in, and like a dummy you moved your stuff in and then went back and got the rest of your stuff, and left everything here without somebody watching out.

I'm telling you, since they broke that unity, I can't even truly say that I have a brother that would stand by my side and die with me. Back in the days, there was a time when I could say, "I'd die with you, brother," because I knew he was going to die with me. But when you have situations where this fool passes by you and other homeboys and shoots the youngest brother, somebody that he could have bent over his lap and spanked, shoot this brother, step on him, and you tell me that's your homie, that's your people, and you allow that to happen? You tell me that you love that man, who shot that fourteen-year-old boy, who wasn't any bigger than that [snaps his fingers], and you didn't even try to stop him? Then you watch the other man stomp on him, after he shot him. That tore me up, man. I was on my back with bullet holes in me, and it tore me up. I'm the type of brother, I was real when I was banging. Everything I did, I was real about it. I stand for peace now, for my people, to save lives. I'm real to the fullest. I'd die for what I believe in right now.

When the unity broke, everything broke. When I started my change, I was becoming a loner. I was by myself, and I took care of myself, because I found out that I didn't need someone else to stand for me, a man stands alone. A man always stands on his own two feet. That's what he has his woman for too, his wife, because when he can't stand on his own two feet, that's where she's going to support him at, and she's going to be right there for him.

That's why we have to learn to respect the Black woman and help her to learn to respect herself. I trip off of these "Daisy Dukes"; they be wearing these shorts, biker shorts, and these little crazy outfits. They have our women buying garbage. They're manipulating and exploiting our women.

You wonder why somebody wants to call you this or call you that. All our women around here wear pants. What happened to the dresses and the long skirts and the shoes? My woman running around here wearing stretch pants? For how long? Let me take you shopping. Let me show you how I want to see you. Let me show you how I want to respect you, and how I want to treat you. When the next man sees how I treat my lady, he's going to want to treat his lady like that too, he's not going to want his lady out there in those Daisy Dukes. That's garbage. They wear that for attention. You don't need attention like that. You want them to respect you for this [points to the mind], and for who you are.

That manipulation is exploiting our women to the fullest. Look at the videos that the rappers make. It makes money, that's cool, but watch what they rap about, and watch how they exploit women. There are a lot of rappers out there that contradict themselves with the words, and then with the video. It's a trip. Our conditions are something that *WE* have to change. I love my people, and I stand strong for my people. I stand for what's right. I'm not a racist, I don't alienate any race, but I stand strongly *first* for mine, for my people.

Somebody can easily sit back and say, "What are the problems?" The first thing you will hear is, "Gang killings, political corruption, the destruction of our educational systems, joblessness, homelessness"—the list is almost endless. However, there is hope. There are positive programs that will reverse the downward spiral that society faces today.

Let me tell you something about what's really unique with what we do. We have ex–gang members, Bloods and Crips, in various states teaching state police officers the responsibility of self-determination. Something that has never been done. We are in more than seven state penitentiaries, where we have Muslims teaching the Aryan Brotherhood, and they don't even know that they are being taught by Muslims. We're going to make the change, but it has to be done on an individual level. Once a person can change, and I'll keep saying that, because it's the truth, if you can truly look inside yourself and change yourself, you will change the people around you, because you project an image. That's what draws the kids to me: it's the image that I project. The kids love to be around me. We have fun. Last week we took 179 people to the movies. Imagine 179 youngsters walking in the door, getting a big bucket of popcorn. That's too much popcorn, man—the popcorn fight was on. It wasn't supposed to happen, but it did. You talkin' about a serious popcorn fight [begins laughing]. Them people were glad when we left. We went to go see *Meteor Man* by Robert Townsend. It got three thumbs-up from everybody on all four of our buses.

**Q:** What keeps you motivated, inspired, and strong?

**P:** First of all, I always have to remember that nothing comes out of a negative but another negative. I get approached every day, at one time or another, with the negative. It only takes a minute for something negative to happen, and it takes a half a second for you to react to that negative. So I eliminate the negative off the top. That's the first step: establish all the facts, then you pick your best option. It's having full evaluation of the problem, and full evaluation of the consequences of the problem. Tough, honest, and mature judgment of the problem. Knowing when and how to act on the problem. For every problem there is a solution, and when you stop looking for a solution, anything is subject to happen.

I'm a man, I speak my opinion, and verbally I defend myself, as long as it doesn't have to get irrational. When it starts getting to that level, I'll walk away from the whole situation. I'm not the one you're going to hit on the cheek and then turn for you to hit the next one. So before any of that happens, I'll leave. The one thing that really keeps me motivated is the fact that I had a chance to change my life before my mother passed away. My mother passed away on the eighth of May 1993, and I had a chance to change my life and start doing positive things for her to see. I was learning new things that I had never learned in my life and indulging into areas that elevated me. From that change I was making, I know that I truly made my mother proud of me. So I'll never turn back. I get frustrated sometimes, where I just want to kick it, but what I do is eliminate the negative, establish the facts, and pick my best option. If the problem is still there, then I go into prayer, or I just stay to myself. If you think, and if you've had the experience of having to spend a little time in jail, because that's all you have to do in there is think, you just sit back and think—that's what I do, when I get frustrated, I sit back and think to myself, and I think about everything that's frustrating me. As I'm thinking about the things that are bothering me, I think of solutions. The first thing I do is say a prayer. A prayer is always answered if it's done honestly. Don't just start praying because you feel something is about to happen, or because you want something. I pray all the time.

You can't walk around in fear—fear is a negative, and it's something that we don't support. So to walk around scared is just like walking around dead. If you were born, then surely you will die. I try not to worry about things I can't control, like earthquakes, or what the weather is going to be like today or tomorrow. I can't control the weather. It's interesting because I was just talking to somebody last night who was reminiscing on their grandmother, and I told him if you need to cry, then cry. That's what tears are for. Don't ever feel like you can't cry. If you really want to reminisce on her, just look in the mirror, because she hasn't really gone anywhere. Just look in the mirror and reminisce on everything that she taught you. Then start living like she wanted you to live. Start really paying attention.

I told my brothers and sisters, I have five brothers and sisters older than me, I lost one brother in 1980, and I tell them, if y'all truly miss Mama, then it's time for you to start living the way she was talking to you about, because she's in you, all you have to do is search for her. You have this little spot in your brain that's called the subconscious, and it's a little piece of your brain that remembers everything you feel, see, touch, say, think, everything. If you go back deep enough into that memory bank, you can acquire all the knowledge you need to go and do anything you want to in this world. A lot of people don't know how to search that far, they have a limitation, they'll hurry up and say, "I can't." Once you say you can't do something, then you automatically put a force up that will disable you from doing what you really want to do. So I try to never use the words *I can't.* There's nothing in the world I can't do. Education is what? A kin relation to knowledge and facts. I can do anything I want to do. There's no limitation. If I have a will to build something, I'm going to build it. If I have a will to help somebody, then I can help them. I'll tell a man in a minute, if you feel like crying, cry. Do you want me to cry with you, because I feel your pain, I know what you're talking about, I know how you feel. I've lost a lot of people, man.

**Q:** What was the process of your forgiving, and how does one come out of the pain from loved ones they may have lost.

**P:** I have this one brother—when I started my youth club, I started out with seven young women and nine young men. Out of those nine young men, I had one particular brother that stuck and stayed with me, that knew he wanted to change. This brother was one of the most diverse young brothers I have ever met in my life. He didn't grow up under me, he grew up under his uncles. All I basically did was deal with him every day. How? The same way I'm dealing with you right now, that's all I did. I took him closer to me, because I saw the way he had adapted to me was something like the way I adapted to the Amer-I-CAN Program. The program manifests through me, so I was talking to him and dealing with him on a level that he liked. Reg is back in school, he's in the eleventh grade right now, going into the twelfth grade. He has all Bs on his report card. What tripped me out was that at first he didn't want to go to school. I allowed him the time that he needed to make up his own mind to go back to school. Out of the other brothers that dropped out and didn't go through with our program, we have three dead, we have one in San Bernardino that has recently been shot and beat up again by the police, and two in jail. When I talk about these brothers right here, these are brothers that really inspire me to go ahead, because they adapted to me. Reg was the only one that didn't grow up under me, out of all the brothers. They were brothers that I had taught personally how to gang-bang. For the ones I actually taught, it tripped them out to see my change, and they felt, "Maybe he's getting older or something." A few of them got put into predicaments that they didn't have knowledge about, they were exploring off into areas that I didn't take them into. Whoever was responsible for that didn't teach them right, didn't show them right, and because of that, those brothers lost their lives. I knew these young brothers, what they used to talk about and how they used to live.

Recently, I lost a brother real close to me, and the day that it happened, a lady came to me, and she said, "When we do what's good, and we start affecting people in a positive way, Satan doesn't like that." It's like a good-versus-evil struggle all the way down the line. I understand that, because there are people that say they care, and they don't. There are people out there who do certain things, when all the time it's only for theirself. What's wrong with doing something for somebody else? Why should I have to get paid for doing something for my babies, and for your babies? Why do you have to get paid to get up and do something for your babies? That's our responsibility. Our children are our responsibility. We shouldn't have to get paid to take care of our own responsibilities. You want me to pay you to deal with your kids? No way. Then how are our kids going to think when they grow up?

**Q:** How do you think it got to the point where fathers—?

**P:** Not all of them. I already know what you were fixin' to ask me. The system is designed like that. They won't allow me to take care of my family, they want my woman to take care of my family. So they put brothers in predicaments where they have to sell drugs to survive. I told you already, we don't have anything around here, we never did, so you get into s—. You might steal something, do something to somebody, or get a felony, which automatically allows the system to discredit you for a job that you can do and get paid the right money for. I went to YTS recently, and we did a little thing on our program at YTS. We had a lot of young homeboys in there that have been in there for five, six, or seven years. When we went there, it tripped me out, because I saw something else. Nine out of ten times every young man around here has been to jail—you go to jail, you get out, and then you're on parole, probation, or something. Any contact with the police—and before this peace treaty you didn't have any other choice—I couldn't walk up and down the street without getting jacked by the police. They'll take you to jail for a crime, talking about how they're going to rehabilitate you. They will pay some man, I don't know how much money, to find out what makes your brain tick and let you out into a predicament worse than when you went in. Now, look what they do to us, they have so many of our young men, and they take older men away, so they will not be here to discipline the young men. You know mamas get frustrated too. I know this lady didn't just suddenly start smoking drugs, when she never used to smoke dope. She wasn't out here like that when her husband was here, or when her sons were out of jail. You have brothers that come out of the penitentiaries with trades, that can do the job way better than the next man, but because he has that state number, or that felony, they are held back. That's what our organization is all about, allowing those who are resented by power to attack power. Our whole executive board is set up of ex–gang members, Bloods and Crips, and this is who we chose. We prefer not to deal with people who have college degrees and all that, because they are going to come at us with their philosophy. We stand for humanistic existence. What's missing is people having knowledge of self, people being responsible for self, people understanding and respecting self.

I can understand and respect your comments, whatever you say, because you're a man or a woman, and by law you're entitled to your own opinion about anything. Who am I to stand up and pass judgment on you about how you feel about something.

See, they didn't tell us about the primary and secondary social needs. I always lived on my social needs. I always worried about what people thought about me, what they felt about me. I didn't know that I was supposed to take care of my food, clothing, shelter, and all that first. Then I have to get my self-esteem, my peace of mind, my rest. I have to eat right.

**Q:** What are some things that can be done by brothers who have skills and have no limitations except those that are self-imposed, to create opportunities for themselves?

**P:** First thing you have to do is find out from inside yourself what it is that you can do, that will affect other people, and you can make money from it. It's coming up with a game plan. You come up with a game plan, and you take action to achieve it. Once you set your mind on something, you can do it. We've had a tendency to set goals, and when we pursue those goals, and when it starts getting difficult, and rough, we'd quit. We can't ever quit. You have to find out what you like to do, not what somebody else would like for you to do. Create your own. Create your own, no matter what it is. We need to create for-profit organizations. You don't want to be a nonprofit, because when you're a nonprofit, you are controlled. This is what I had to learn about nonprofit and for-profit organizations. When I told you I had to go back and be re-educated, because I got yanked for a $150,000 contract, I found out that if I was a nonprofit organization, and I dealt with x number of kids, and I wanted to have an event with the kids, I would have to write a proposal, let my board sign it, and send the proposal in to whoever I want to get some cash from. I would have to wait for a contract to come back with however much money I want, and then I would have to do exactly what I said I was going to do with that proposal, and with every dollar. That means that by me being the director of my youth organization, I can't get paid unless I take a step down and be an employee in something I created. Not only that, you would always be like this [sticks his hand out], with your hand out, looking for somebody to give you something. Why do you want to work for somebody else? They have this thing going on now in the projects saying that everything that comes and goes through Jordan Downs has to go through the board. The board is doing their work, but in the board's documents, it states that they can't get paid. Why do you want to work for free? If you want to work for free, come and work for me. Why are you submitting to working for somebody else when you can create your own job? It's very easy. Find out what you like to do, what you do best, and market it. It's easy. These are things that are not taught down here. There are certain brothers that I talk to with certain skills, and I try to hook them up to do things. It's going to have to happen on an individual level. You can talk to them, and we can come up with all kinds of problems, and all kinds of solutions, but if we don't take action—if we don't take action—if we don't take action with these solutions . . . like the saying goes, it's 10 percent inspiration and 90 percent perspiration. It's sweat and work, that's the bottom line. Nothing worthwhile is easy. For something that you really want, you have to work for it. Changing a well-conditioned attitude will be one of the most difficult things that any individual will do in their life. Changing yourself will be the hardest thing you're ever going to do in your life, especially if you've been well conditioned to function in a certain way.

That's why I talked about the condition of my people that are on AFDC, on general relief and on social security, because they've been conditioned for so long to just sit back and not work. There are people that stand out there on corners, and they'll stand out on that corner all day and sell oranges and apples. Do you know why? Because when they get finished, there are around nineteen hundred of them, and they're all going to come together and put their money together. Economically, if we come together with an economic plan—I have an economic plan for my family. I took my brothers, my sisters, my nieces, and my nephews, all of them. All of us have an income coming from somewhere. Imagine this, say if we were all getting social security, AFDC, general relief, I don't care where the money comes from, if we take all the money and put it together, then you take the food stamps and put them all together, and you make sure that every household has food. You make sure that you know what you really need to spend money on, your rent, light bill, telephone bill . . . Everybody gets their rent, lights, and telephone bill paid. How much money do you think would still be left? Take that, and put it in a credit account. That's besides the money you're going to spend on your accessories. The rest of the money is put up in the family's name. All the heads of household, all the grown-ups, have their name on the account. Nobody can withdraw money from the account without the other one's signature. That's so the money won't get misused. That was done on a three-family level. Imagine the whole projects, just these complexes right here, all following up in that game plan, with all the trust and respect in the world. Do you know we could do whatever we want to do around here? We could remodel; we wouldn't have to have anybody else come in. We would not have to wait for them, twenty-seven or twenty-eight years to remodel the projects, we could do it our own selves. We don't have to be sitting back complaining and crying about cable television.

The economic plan, it's going to have to be a serious plan. People get money, and they don't know how to use it. Money is being misused every day. A good three or four years ago, if you would have given me a million dollars, a year later I would have been broke, because I would not have known how to invest it right. It would have been dealt with foolishly. You *have* to have an economic plan, I don't care what kind of situation you're in, how much money you get, or where it comes from. If it's not utilized for the right purposes, we'll always have problems.

We only live as good as we choose to live. You can only make as much money as you want to make. You can sit back and say you want this or that, but what are you doing every day to get it? You have to do something every day to work towards what you want out of life. That's where you have to make those sacrifices.

I had to give up a lot. My life has done a 360. I am my exact opposite, that you see sitting in front of you. I was my exact opposite. Everything about me, from my conversation to the way I looked, was negative. Everything. I mean, when I got out there in that sand today, and whenever I start digging in that sand, people look at me, they see us out there in that sand with the kids, redoing the playground, but what do they really think when they see us hit that sand?

I think about them brothers in the old days, that used to get whipped to do this. They would get beat across their backs to do it. They were made to do it. Made to dig in the trenches and fight fires.

I think about the hard work, and what's going to come out of it. Those playgrounds are going to be beautiful when we finish with them. I don't want to just do the playgrounds in Jordan Downs. I want to go over there and get the brothers from Imperial Courts to get involved in doing theirs. Then get the brothers in Nickerson Gardens, and the brothers in the Haciendas to get involved in doing theirs. They tripped off me when I came through here with my cleanup team. I do videotapes of my cleanups. We rolled around and picked up the trash by the trash bins. Sometimes when people's yards are tore up, we'll go out and clean their yards. They look at me, and they trip off of me. "How much y'all gettin' paid?" "We ain't gettin' paid, we're just doing it. We're being responsible for our own community." There's not anything wrong with wanting to be around something clean, something nice. The projects aren't bad, it's the people here. If you can change the people in the projects, then you can change the projects. It's the people that make 'em.

Like these colors that they have around here, these crazy colors, do you know what lead does to you when it gets in your blood? Lead alters your thinking, slows down your thinking capacity, it stops you from competing with other people. We've been trying to get everybody around here to take their kids to get checked for lead. What we found out is that there's lead in the paint, lead on the window seals, on the doorframes, and this lead has been affecting us for years. It's in the water, and in the pipes. They're just now changing the pipes, from since the projects were built. We tried to get a truck to come down here and get all of our people tested, and some kind of way they stopped it legally, but we told everybody to start taking themselves, and their kids, to be tested for lead. We're not supposed to be paying rent, because they have poisoned us with this s—. Straight out. There's fixin' to be a lawsuit. This sister came to me today, and she showed me this white paper, her baby is four years old, and he has so much lead in his body that he has to take treatments. Now how much lead do you think is in me? I've been here all my life. It's not a joke.

When you go to school, do you know what they do? They put you in this little class, way in the back of the room, and say, "He's a slow learner." There's no such thing as a slow learner. Where did they get that from? Calling kids slow learners. I may not learn as fast as he or she learns, but I'm not a slow learner. Let me work at my own pace, my own time. That was before we found out about this lead too. Lead affects your learning ability, and it gets in your blood. These projects used to be an army base way back in the days. They were built for servicemen. Then after the wars were over with, they moved people in. The trip is, it has never changed. It has been just like this. It's not just here; go to Chicago or New York. I know, because HUD is everywhere. HUD owns these projects, and HUD owns those projects, so I know they're the same way. Do you think they're not scared that somebody is checking these projects for lead? They're just now remodeling these projects. We had to go on national TV and talk about how the roaches climb on us at night. You're laying down asleep, and all of a sudden a roach is climbing on you. You can exterminate and exterminate, but because they have so many big holes in the walls, you can't ever completely get rid of them. I don't know anyone who has gotten rid of all the roaches in their house.

I'm about to change apartments from a three-bedroom to a five-bedroom, because I just got legal custody of two kids. So they have to give me a bigger apartment. I've been exterminating for three days. I don't want to move the roaches with me, but it's impossible to really get rid of 'em all. What they need is for everybody to move out of these places, one building at a time, and put tents over them to *really* exterminate them. They come in here and use something that smells like water, feed your roaches, and then leave.

Now if we had a brother around here that wanted to start an exterminating business, which makes money, and he comes and signs a contract with the Housing Authority to exterminate all seven hundred units—it's very easy to organize and get the contract—when that brother comes in, he knows where to spray, because he lives here. He'll know what to use to get them. You have somebody coming from the boondocks, he stays in your house three or four minutes, and he leaves. They tell you to stay out of your house for four hours, and he was only in your house three minutes. Where did he spray? What did he do, just spray in the corners? Roaches are smarter than that. Our roaches are so smart now, they know not to come out when you have company. They wait until you're at home by yourself to come out and kick it and bother you. It's a trip, but I'm glad that I had the opportunity to change my life and now be effective and positive towards my people regardless to their living conditions.

Now, with me being in tune and focused with self, nothing negative will stay around me. How can I miss it? How could you whisper, and me not hear you? Now I know how to read body language and read facial expressions. I come from the heart with what I do. I used to think that it wasn't important to read people's body language, and their facial expressions, or to really hear a side conversation. I'm sitting here talking now, and I hear conversations outside. I'm focused, and I'm in tune with self, and with nature.

**Q:** How do we stop some of the madness that's still going on, and what do we do to keep this peace tight and spread it to the places where they're not peacing?

**P:** I invite people to come down and see me. I had a lady come down here from Australia, and she was talking about the same things that are going on here, are going on over there. First, to keep the peace, we have to talk it, live it, and spread it. How do you do that? By bridging the gap—communication, understanding, and respect. We have to communicate with each other. Don't let this interview be where we start and finish. We have to talk and keep on talking. What we're talking now, we need to relay to other people. That's how we spread it. Communication.

The media will take everything and switch it around. They did that to us before. We did an interview for the media, and they got to talking about something that had happened with other people somewhere else, but they used our picture, as big as day, like we had something to do with it. It really tripped me out, because I was dealing with this guy from USC, and they wanted to do a little something on our youth club, because we have an arts center. He came down here and did the report, but he switched it up.

Talking about solutions, if I communicate with you and other people about the solutions, nine times out of ten we're talking about the same problems. We have plenty of solutions, but the main thing is, we have to teach our people and re-educate them.

First of all, re-educate them with knowledge of self. I don't care if you want to be a religious person or not. I think it's very important, and this goes for Christians, Buddhists, and Muslims, to sit down and really acknowledge what you're learning. As far as the spiritual level, I think that Buddha is ALLAH, and ALLAH is God, and Jehovah is ALLAH. All these people are talking about the same person. So somewhere there is a Being higher than our own selves, but a lot of people put limitations on themselves, due to the fact of their religion. From what I read out of the Holy Qur'an, it says some of the same things that it says in the Bible. Somebody told me, "If you really want to be smart, take the Holy Qur'an and the Holy Bible and put them together, and you'll never see those two books bump heads." It's the philosophy that man adds on after he reads the books that causes the division.

The peace treaty is alive, and it's important. It's history. A lot of people keep saying, "Keep the truce alive, don't let the truce die," but what they don't understand is that this truce will never die. It will never die. Of course you're going to have differences, but now they've gone back to just fighting if they have a dispute, and even then it's going to be just those two individuals fighting. It's not like, just because you had a fight with my homeboy, you can't come over here anymore. Y'all had your fight, and now it's squashed. He knows he can't go get a gun, and the other one knows that he can't go get a gun. If you're from my neighborhood, and you go get a gun for a brother over there, then our own neighborhood will discipline you.

**Q:** What do you say to the older homeboys about helping to keep the peace strong?

**P:** Now I have to talk about Dreamer. Dreamer is a guy that just got out from doing five years in the pen. All I said to Dreamer is the same thing I said to Black, and V, when each one of them got out of jail. I said, "Here is a manual." They had heard about us in jail already, so when they got out, I gave them a manual. I know everybody that gets out of jail comes out a little smarter, and all of them can read. I explain to them what we're doing, and what we're about. When Dreamer got out, he said, "Yeah, I was hearing about y'all in the pen, I heard y'all had it going on, I want to get with that." What I did was I found out that we could develop relationships with their parole officers—like with this one brother, he gave his parole officer my hook-up, for him to call and investigate me. So I let him know that when he gets out, this is what he's going to be doing. All they have to do when they get out is deal with me, and if they deal with me, I can guarantee anybody that there is no way they would go back to jail, because they're going to truly find out what it's all about. The system gets paid anywhere from seventy-five to eighty thousand dollars a year to house each brother for one year in a state penitentiary. The psychologists and the doctors that they have, because they automatically think you have a problem, they get paid half that much annually. Why don't you pay me to go and talk to gang members in jail? Who is better to talk to a gang member than an ex–gang member? You have brothers sitting up there, talking to a fool that has never gang-banged, who doesn't even know where to start with gang-banging, picking at your brain.

You want to pay this fool a bunch of money to talk to me about gang prevention, and he doesn't know the first thing about gangs, how they function, what started them, how they came about, and what they really do. He can't tell me anything. The police didn't stop this killing. The police ride around here so comfortable now, they give us the utmost respect in the world, because we made their jobs so easy. All they do is ride around in their cars now and wave at people.

How are they going to counsel the kids that they have in juvenile detention centers right now? Do you know who they have counseling them? People that have never indulged in gangs, drugs, or none of that. Never smoked a joint a day in their life, and they want to tell you what marijuana will do to you. How does he know? He never smoked any, but why won't they pay a brother like me—don't even pay me—why won't you allow me to go in and counsel? I'll do it for free. I'll do it for nothing. Just let me in there once a month to talk to whoever I need to talk to. I want your most notorious ones. The ones that you say are in high power, the ones that you want to send to the penitentiary as soon as they turn a certain age. Those are the ones I want to talk to, because they will deal with the younger ones that come in.

All that I've been taught on the negative level—notice I said that I've never been convicted of a felony a day in my life. When I had people showing me how to bang, I had people telling me not to come to the pen. I have cousins sitting in Folsom. They'd tell me, "Don't come here, this ain't no place for you." I didn't need them to tell me that. I went to jail, I stayed for a minute, and I knew that wasn't where I wanted to be. So if I did something, I made sure that I'd get away with it. Even the best get caught, but anybody in their right mind knows that a jail cell is not where you want to be. There's a lot of people sitting in jail right now under circumstances where they were just at the wrong place at the wrong time, who just didn't think, they just acted. A lot of people act without thinking. That's just like a mechanism, as if they don't have control over what they do. Like when you get mad and swell up and blow your temper, you act like you can't control your temper and calm down.

Just don't take things personal. What I mean by that is, if I take my relationship with my wife personal, it would be affected in a negative way, because I would become insecure, overprotective. So I can't take it personal. I love her and give her all the respect in the world, just like she loves me, but if I take a human relationship personal, I'd start catering to your feelings, and what you think. I'd start thinking more about you than me, and I always have to think about me first, because how can I take care of you if I can't take care of me? How can I take care of my kids, how can I provide for my kids, if I can't provide for myself? How can I give to my kids if I don't have anything? That's why I don't like to split things up with kids; if you buy for one, you should buy for the next one. If I buy one something, I'm going to buy the next one something. It's only being fair, because it plays with their minds. Just like these colors. Certain colors affect the way you think. People don't know that, but it's the truth. Somebody told me once before that life is a game, and you have to learn how to play it to be successful.

Notice that a lot of people use time: "I don't have time for that, I'll do it later." That's drama, BS; the last thing you should be worrying about is time. That's one thing you'll never run out of, because when you're dead and gone, time will still be ticking. Only a fool thinks he can destroy something that he didn't create. Man thinks he's going to destroy the world. He can't nearly destroy this world with anything he has built. All you can do is destroy yourself, and you can play out your own existence. You can't touch this world. You can get rid of everybody on the planet, and everything; this world is still going to be right here spinning [laughs].

**Q:** Talking about the world, speak on the importance of the gang peace, and its potential impact worldwide?

## Playmate

**P:** Let me explain something. First of all there's nothing but strength here. Strength and power. It's always been here, and it has never been able to be tampered with, by anybody. Anything that happens down here in Watts is going to have an effect everywhere else. Not just in Watts, but anything that happens in any ghetto, because that's where the strong people are. The strong people, the intelligent ones, the ones who will bring this world out of the hole that it's in, are in the ghettos, and in the jail cells. The brothers, the people that are going to come first, are down in the ghettos, and I don't care if you're Black, brown, Mexican, Chinese, or whatever, if you're in the ghettos, it is truly written that those who are last shall be first. Look at it. Look at what's happening right now across the world. Look at the problems that are occurring. Right now we are living in the days of Revelations. For any spiritual person, you understand what that is, it's the truth, and it didn't just start. It's a cycle. The world is going through a cycle, and only the strong will survive.

Let's talk about racism. A lot of people that don't understand racism say that it's stupid, or dumb, but you really have to delve into it, because just think about it. If I had a baby by a Caucasian woman, and my baby came out looking half-Caucasian, but has my blood, and my genes in her, when my daughter grows up and she has a baby by another Black brother, that baby is going to come out Black. We'd automatically play out a race of people, because of our genetic makeup. Our genes dominate. Let me ask you this, when was the last time you physically saw a pregnant woman that was white? They're taking sperm out of somebody else and putting it in her, so they can have babies. We can just go and have ours the right way. There're at a zero birthrate right now. It takes research.

Why do you think they're talking about, "We're going to kill this, and kill that." They're marching and everything. We didn't f you up, you f'd yourself up, by f'ing over other people. America has destroyed and f'd up everything it has touched. Who said this was America? When Caucasians got here, they gave it a name. They were looking for India when they got here, and they said, "We're going to call this place America." They didn't ask the people who were here, "What do you call this place?" They came and gave it a name. What did my brother Farrakhan say, "That's what white people do. They just come and start naming things."

This is a punishment that they're getting for destroying everything that they have touched. America was built on other races' blood. Not just the Black man's blood, but the yellow man, and the Mexicans. This is America's punishment. Not only that, the ozone layer alone is killing them. We didn't put the hole in the ozone layer. We don't own any factories. Show me one Black-owned factory that's manufacturing something, that tears up the ozone layer. I can't find a Black man that's producing toilet paper. That is chemically making it, producing it, and putting it on the market. We don't own oil wells. That's also killing the environment. You don't see any Black people over there tearing down the rain forests.

**Q:** Speak on how the alcohol and the drugs have been used to destroy our communities.

**P:** We have a map in our office, and we can show you from 1980 to 1993 how many businesses have come up in Los Angeles. You have over five thousand liquor stores that have come up since 1980 to 1993. They are on every corner. It's a map that shows the few liquor stores that we had to how many we have now. Alcohol, I'll tell this to anybody, drinking will alter your thinking, you can't function on liquor. You cannot be focused and function on alcohol. I know, because I drank the other night, and I found out. I can sit up and smoke weed from here to next month and still stay in tune and focus with self, but once I take a drink, and I take another drink and another drink . . . and people around here don't drink in moderation, they drink to get drunk. Once you get that liquor in your system, brother, look here, you won't know anything until tomorrow. I'm trying to stop drinking. I took a drink the other day out of frustration. I realized that was not going to help me, so I went out there and worked in the sand, until I worked it off. When I was out there sweating, all I could see was that liquor just dripping out of me. Alcohol is one of the main reasons why our people cannot develop today. If you have someone drinking in your home, and if you drink, I don't care if it's just a small drink, you are jeopardizing the positive process. Even me, when I took that drink the other night, I jeopardized what I was doing, what I live for. I did that, and I know it, and that wasn't being responsible. If you're going to be responsible, you have to eliminate that. How do you eliminate drinking when you've been doing it so long? Well, I can tell you this, Alcoholics Anonymous can't help you. How do you get off drugs when you've been doing them so long? I'll tell you, this place they're trying to send you can't help you, *it's all in yourself.* Everything negative that is affecting your life, if you want to change it, you can. Say you want to stop drinking and get rid of that negative, you have to replace it with something positive. If I don't replace liquor with drinking juices and water and stuff like that, I'll drink liquor. If I want to stop smoking cigarettes, I have to put something else in its place. That's how you do it. That's the process. If you want to get off drugs, no matter how much that dope is sitting up there talking to you, it can't talk to you if it's not in front of you. How is it going to ask you for a hit, if you're not around anybody that smokes it? Drug dealers hang around drug dealers, gang bangers hang around gang bangers, people who go to church hang around people who go to church; it's a trip, but it's the truth. If I'm trying to get off drugs, what in the world would I be doing sitting up in a crack house watching everybody smoke and know that the dope is going to tell me to come here. "Hit me."

Richard Pryor's story on his life wasn't a lie. Drugs, that's one of their weapons too. When you talk about drugs, you're talking about liquor, and cigarettes too. All of them are drugs, all the way down to the miseducation.

Positive change—brothers supporting the Amer-I-CAN Program and Youth Club. These young men believe that change is healthy.

Opening Day at Art Center with LAFD and youth of all ages

Opening ceremony at Art Center—Congresswoman Maxine Waters and Don "Playmate" Gordon presenting awards

FEELINGS FROM THE AMER-I-CAN YOUTH CLUB

IN OUR MEETINGS WITH OUR KIDS WE HAVE SOMETHING THAT WE CALL A GROUP DISCUSSION. IT'S A LOT LIKE THE FEELING SESSION IN THE AMER-I-CAN PROGRAM. THE ONLY DIFFERENCE IS WE LET THE YOUTH DO ALL OF THE TALKING. KIND OF STRANGE THE THINGS YOU FIND OUT WHEN YOU SIT AND LISTEN TO KIDS.

KIDS SPEAK OUT BUT THEY ARE NOT HEARD. IN THE GROUP DISCUSSIONS, WE HAVE FOUND OUT THAT THE KIDS WANT A CLEANER COMMUNITY, AND THEY WANT TO SEE PROGRAMS LIKE THE AMER-I-CAN YOUTH CLUB IN THEIR INNER-CITY SCHOOLS.

THE AMER-I-CAN YOUTH CLUB TEACHES YOUTH TO BETTER THEMSELVES, AND TO HELP ANOTHER PERSON TO BETTER THEMSELVES. AMER-I-CAN ALSO TEACHES RESPECT FOR SELF AND FOR OTHERS. THE YOUTH IN THE CLUB ARE INNER-CITY YOUTH THAT DON'T HAVE ANY ALTERNATIVES OR POSITIVE THINGS TO DO. THROUGH OUR CLUB THE YOUTHS BEGIN TO FEEL BETTER ABOUT LIFE AND ABOUT THEMSELVES BECAUSE WE SPEND QUALITY TIME WITH EACH OF THEM. WE HELP THEM TO DEAL WITH THEIR PERSONAL PROBLEMS.

THE STAFF OF THE AMER-I-CAN YOUTH CLUB HELP THE YOUTH THROUGH MEANS OF INSPIRATION, TIME, ATTENTION, AND BY HELPING THEM TO FIND THEMSELVES. WE WALK THROUGH THE COMMUNITY WITH THEM AND SEE THEIR LIVING CONDITIONS, WHICH IS EXACTLY WHY WE CAME UP WITH A SOLUTION TO ATTACK THE PROBLEMS THAT OUR INNER-CITY YOUTH HAVE TO FACE IN THEIR DAILY LIVES. THE YOUTH AND THE PARENTS ALL BENEFIT AND REALLY APPRECIATE OUR YOUTH CLUB.

FOR THE BABIES IN OUR YOUTH CLUB, WE FEEL THAT IF WE CAN GET TO THEM IN THEIR EARLY LEARNING STAGES, WHICH BEGIN AT THE AGE OF TWO YEARS, WE CAN DEVELOP RESPONSIBLE A.D.U.L.T.S. WE HAVE TO REACH OUT TO ALL AGES OF OUR YOUNGER GENERATIONS, FOR THEY ARE OUR FUTURE.

IF YOU ARE WILLING TO EFFECT POSITIVE CHANGE IN OUR COMMUNITY, IT HAS TO START WITH THE YOUTH!!

BY PLAYMATE

**Q:** Have you seen a relationship between the heavy drugs and alcohol in the community, and the escalation of violence?

**P:** Since the peace treaty jumped off, we've been slowly but surely chucking that poison out of our neighborhood. Let me tell you this, back in the days, you name it, it was here. Cars used to line up to buy Sherm. That was Sherman Alley right there [points to a back alley]. People used to come through in hearses and drop the Sherm off. It wasn't Black people either, I can tell you that. That's the *only* time white people ever came in here. If they were police, or if they were dropping some drugs off. Drugs, you talk about drugs, I'm talking about from pills to paint. Our people don't even sniff paint, but they had it all: pills, Sherman, cocaine. The escalation of violence? How many people got killed in 1988 alone? How many people got killed just in 1978? The majority of the killings are behind what? Not just gang violence. What does the violence come from? *Drugs.* Nine times out of ten, when somebody shoots somebody else, they're either drunk or high. They always go out and get high before they do something like that.

**Q:** Any further words of wisdom that you would like to express?

**P:** I say this to all it may concern, young, old, rich, poor, known, or unknown. Change is healthy. It's never too late to change any predicament or any circumstances that you face in your life. The successful completion of a goal represents the heart and the guts of the Amer-I-CAN Program, and we accept nothing less. What I mean by that is, whatever you want, you can have it. No matter who says you can't, always remember that you are your own individual, you have your own self-respect, and your own life to live for, *first.* Nothing—nothing worthwhile is easy. Remember this, I say this to all people, nothing will be more difficult in your life than changing a well-conditioned attitude, but you can do it. You can always change!

> ***You better listen, WORLD! You better listen/listen/listen to what I'm saying. WAKE UP, WORLD! Because tomorrow, world, tomorrow might be TOO LATE! Change you/change them, change it, change ME, changes, changes . . ."***
>
> **—Watts Prophets**

# GENERAL ROBERT LEE

## (REST IN PEACE)

*(My name is General Robert Lee. I am one of the founders of the L.A. Brim Blood Army. I've been through two generations of gang-banging, and my purpose now is to be one of the founders of bringing the peace, and stopping the gang-banging. My goal is to start programs for the youngsters, and the gang members, so that they will have a better way to live.)*

**Q:** When did gang-banging first get started in Los Angeles?

**G:** Like Farrakhan said, ever since I can remember, there has been gangs in L.A. When I was a kid there was the Rabble Rousers, Gladiators, Businessmen, and the Blood Alleys. I was a baby Rabble Rouser. It was the same as it is now, but just not as much killing. We used bottles and bricks, but now two carloads will pull up with gats, Uzis, AKs, and 9s, when back then, two carloads of people would pull up with bricks, bottles, sticks, baseball bats, bumper jacks, and maybe a knife or two. This was back in '62, '63, '64, '65. When the Watts riots jumped off, that helped to stop the gang-banging from '65 to the end of '68. Nineteen sixty-nine is when the Brims started.

**Q:** How did the brothers get classified as gangs?

**G:** Like I was telling my brother, I never considered myself a gang member, I called myself a soldier in the Brim Army. The other Brims would say "Brim gang," I would say "Brim Army," because I felt I was a soldier for the hood. The police department is the biggest gang to me.

[General Robert Lee's wife of twenty-one years, Shelia, was present at the interview and was invited to comment.]

**Shelia:** If you look back a long time ago, they used to call white groups "the mob." It goes way back to when they used to lynch and kill Black folks. They had gangs of white folks get together, dress up, and lynch Black folks, but it was all right then, because it was white against Black. Now they're so afraid because it's coming back on them.

**Q:** How did the Brims begin in '69?

**G:** The Brims were started by a brother named Eddie. He was the originator, he started it, and then he just disappeared. I don't know if he got killed or if he's in the pen or if he just doesn't want anybody to know that he created this monster. We haven't heard from him in about fifteen years.

**Q:** How did you become active?

**G:** I've always been a soldier, even before the Brims. I was into everything, my mama could tell you. I was holding my hood way before that. So when the Brim era came out, I had already been through one gang. It was about protecting the hood and gettin' a girl, drinking the "Rainy El," and smoking some weed. I was slanging weed and Red Devils when I was seven years old. I had been out on the streets, so I fit right in. I had met the Brims when they were called the Hatboys. I was in juvenile hall on a violation, and about seven or eight guys came in there all at once, making all kinds of noise, kicking up dust, having fun; it was just like a little family. I was like, "Who are these guys?" I ended up getting real close with them: Pumpkin, James, and Felix. When something happened to one, they were all there for each other at once, they didn't care if he was wrong or right, they were with him. Whatever it was about or whatever he did, they didn't care, that was their family member. So when we got back on the streets, we just hooked up, and the rest is history.

**Q:** What was it all about when y'all hit the streets?

**G:** Big fun. That's when we would hide behind the cars and the bushes at Freemont High School or Manual Arts High School, and when it got dark and the record hop let out, we would come from behind the bushes and the cars and start jumping on the people, taking their coats, their money, and their watches, and then we would just disappear. We would go buy some weed and some beer, kick back, and laugh about it.

**Q:** What effect did the riots that took place in Watts have in stopping gang activity back then?

**G:** The same thing with the South Central Uprisings, the Watts riot was in August 1965; I'll never forget it. It was hot, I was on Slauson and Denker, there was about ten of us walking down the street, and we saw these fires popping up from everywhere, ambulances and police flying up the street; we didn't know what was happening. So when I got to the pad, my mama said, "Come in here, boy, there's a riot going on." I looked at the TV and saw all of these brothers cutting up. Moms said, "Go to bed." I went to the bedroom, went straight out the back window, and got straight into it. I had to be nine or ten then. I went out there and started breaking into jewelry stores and liquor stores, looting, drinking, and throwing Molotov cocktails at everything I could see.

By the end of this time, the police started killing ten- and eleven-year-old young brothers; they were blowing their heads off. Then brothers started to see where white people were coming from, mainly the police. That's when they realized that there was no longer a need for us to fight each other. That's when the Gladiators, the Businessmen, the

Ditalians, and Blood Alleys came to peace. They weren't going to fight each other anymore. That was from August '65 to the end of '68. There weren't any gangs fighting each other at that time. Everybody came together. It was a Black thing. So when I heard that the rebellion was jumping off in '92, I said, "That should help bring about peace, but I hope this time they don't get tricked by the white man," because the white man will go and dress up like a Blood or a Cuz, and do a drive-by and holler out to your set to kick it back off again. I was just hoping they wouldn't be tricked again.

After the Watts riot we had teen posts. Every neighborhood had a teen post. We had a counselor there, we had a basketball coach there, we had a boxing team, a karate team, and pool tournaments. We had activities, we had somewhere to go. Nobody had to hang on the corners anymore. The teen post was the thing. We had talent shows and everything. So the teen posts really kept the youngsters from gang-banging. The teen posts were everywhere. They did a lot for the Black youths back then, a whole lot. Everything was about fun back then. When they killed the teen posts, that made us sprout out again. That's when another era of gang-banging sprouted. There was nothing to do. They killed the teen posts. That's what made it kick back off again, but it wasn't meant to be like it is now.

**Q:** How do you think it escalated to where it is today as far as the shooting and killing?

**G:** When Li'l Country got killed—Fred. We had a confrontation with the Crips, and Li'l Country from the Brims was killed, and that's when the gunplay really came in. I think that was about '71 or '72. When he got shot, that's when the retaliation of the gunplay came in. His coffin was in a Crip neighborhood at the funeral place, and the Crips went in there and turned his casket over and wrote crazy things in the sign-in book, and then wrote up his casket. That's when the war started. After that we made a bond that every year on his birthday, and on the day he got killed, we had to go out and kill some of them. It was just something that went on for years, because he was a hard-core little youngster that we loved. So that was when the killing really began between the Brims and the Crips. We tried peace treaties after that, but they just wouldn't hold, because of that killing, we just couldn't let it go. There really wasn't any problems between us and them until then. When that killing happened, it was on. You can say that was the first gang killing with the Brims and the Crips. After then it was straight trouble, and it just got bigger and bigger and bigger, and it got way out of control. When we were shooting at each other, it wasn't over a rag. We were shooting at the Crips because they had killed Li'l Country—Fred. That's why we were shooting at the Crips.

When I first started, they hadn't become the Brims yet, Harvard Park was our headquarters, and our first rags were blue rags. When I got shot, I had two blue rags in my back pocket. A lot of Bloods don't know that we used to have blue rags. The blue was for the Brims. The "B." Back then the rag really didn't mean anything, it was just a style. When the Crips were first trying to get an identity, they wore blue rags, so we said, "We have to change our rags, the Crips are starting to wear blue rags now." So that's how we switched over to the red rags.

Our identification was one cuff up, one cuff down, and a rabbit's foot. If you were stopped by some Brims, and they said, "What set are you from?" And you said, "I'm a Brim." "Well, where's your rabbit's foot?" If you didn't have that rabbit's foot, you were beat down immediately. Red rags and blue rags didn't mean anything. The Brim hats meant something. The one cuff up, one cuff down meant something. For the Crips, they had canes, and acey-deucey hats; that was their identification.

It was mostly based on fun, and going head-up. I'll never forget—it was on Thirty-ninth and Western, the Gladiators and the Rabble Rousers got into it with each other, two guys from each set had a beef with each other, and about sixty gang members came from the Gladiators, and about sixty to seventy came from the Rabble Rousers, they met up and let the two who had a beef go head-up. After they went head-up, they shook hands, and one went one way, and the other went the other way. There wasn't any shooting or stabbing. Back then if someone pulled out a gun, it would be a shotgun, but that only happened every blue moon.

Everybody was down with the Brims. The Brims were well loved, and still are well loved. The Pirus could have gone with the Crips; the Bounty Hunters, the Avalon Park Boys, the BSVs, all of them could have gone with the Crips, but they got down with us. We set the path for gang members. We don't get the credit now, everything is Crips now, but if you talk to any OG, they know. A long time ago when you said "Brim," they knew, "You don't want to mess with them Brims, they're deep, and they don't care, they're killers."

Then the gunplay came into it, and that just messed everything up. It went from fun, where you couldn't wait until the next day came, to the point where you didn't know if you were going to be here the next day. My wife, when she would open the door, I used to have two pistols pointing at the door. I went to church with my pistols. I went to the police station with my pistols. I took my pistols everywhere.

I've been in this wheelchair nineteen years. When I got shot, I got worse. Usually when somebody gets shot, they just lay back or kick back and call the shots. I was involved, I was out there, getting in the cars doing everything in a wheelchair. I'd be in my wheelchair with my two pistols, the sawed-off shotgun, the Godfather hat, and a natural this big [holds his hands way above his head]. I had people from my set calling me the Godfather, then the player homiez called me Black Rob, some called me Robert Lee; it was according to who I was hanging with.

All the girls were attracted to gangs, so guys who were never able to get a girl before turned into a gang banger, dropped his pants down to his butt, turned his hat to the side, got an earring, changed his walk, then he had all the girls coming to him. Most girls do not want good guys; I don't care what they say, the badder you are, the more they like you, most of them. They'll say, "I don't want him, that's a good guy, I want that guy down there with the pistol hanging out of his back pocket, who has fifteen women." So gang members would get all the women; everybody in the neighborhood looks up to them, and that becomes hooking.

**Q:** What would you say to the younger homiez that are fighting over territory?

**G:** These hoods are not ours, they are the government's hoods. I'm buying this house, but this house ain't mine, it's the government's. They can come and get this house anytime they want to. "I'm fightin' for my hood." All of this, we're fightin' for the government's hood, that's it. I could pay fully for this house, yet I still have to pay taxes every year. You never really own it. If you stop paying taxes, they're going to take it away from you. It's never yours, it's always the government's. You're fighting over the white man's property, period.

**Q:** What did you first think when you heard about the peace treaty?

**G:** I was elated. It was a high that I had been waiting to get for years. When I saw the Bloods and Cuz hugging each other on that stage and waving those rags, I didn't want it to ever end.

I figured that Black people would be sharper than they were in '65, that they wouldn't be crossed and go back into it. I wanted to see peace so bad that I overlooked a lot of that. I overlooked the fact that they weren't taking the time to learn each other, and taking the time to communicate. They were just getting high and partying, celebrating the Uprisings. They really didn't sit down and say, "Here's a time for us to communicate, so we won't do this again." That's the time when the Gs should have really come in. The Gs should have really hit it. The real Gs, the old Gladiators, the Rabble Rousers, they should have been right there to say, "Hey, look, it's a party now, but what are y'all going to do when the party is over?" You can't party like that every day. You can't get drunk like that every day, picnic every day. That doesn't last. We can't get high at the meetings, because if we don't get to learn each other and know each other, then we're going to be right back to the same crap again. So I had just overlooked that part, because I was so happy about what was going on, that they was together, and I didn't want it to end. I overlooked a whole lot of stuff that should have been spoken out on. I know you can't party and get high every day; I don't care who you are, your body won't stand it, and the money won't stand it. We can party on Saturday, but from Monday through Thursday we're going to get to learn each other and keep this peace going.

**Q:** How do you feel about what just happened here in L.A. with the white supremacist groups coming into the Black community?

**G:** They want some war. They're ready for war now. They're in the mountains shooting every day, building up their arsenal, but they don't have hearts, they can't handle anything. When that heat comes back on them, when the Bloods and Cuz turn on them, they're going to be crying a whole different song, because we know how to do it. They don't know how to do it, they've never done it and never will do it. They've never been through a war zone. We've lived through many war zones, and when we focus our energies that way, they're going to change their song, I'm telling you now. They don't know what war is. They have someone calling himself Metzger or something, he calls his organization WAR. White people will never win another war; their army cannot even handle a ground war. The white man will never win another ground war. Never. Their whole attack has to be from the air, or that big bomb. They should have realized that from Nam. They got whipped. They couldn't do anything with them Vietnamese on that ground. We do guerrilla warfare a lot; we specialize in it.

Now a lot of Bloods and Cuz are saying, "Hmmm. They're coming into the hood now. They were going up in the mountains and burning crosses and stuff, but now they're coming to the hood." If the Bloods and Cuz focus their energies on the Nazis, and the Klan, by next year this time the skinheads wouldn't even be claiming. Their hair would be so long, they'd look like hippies. They'd be telling each other, "You don't want to look like a Nazi or skinhead. No boots." Their sign is those boots. That's why I don't like those boots. You see a lot of brothers into those type of boots now; I can't get into that, because I remember when the Nazis used to have them a long time ago.

**Q:** Why do most young brothers join gangs?

**G:** There are a lot of reasons. Some people join for the protection, because they're scared; we call them cowards. There are some that join for the family, for the unity. They don't have any family, they don't have anybody, and they see the unity of family when they see gangs. They see the laughing and the hugging. They see that when something goes down, how they all run to each other's defense. It's those strong family ties. Then you have some like me, who come in for leadership. I know people who have mothers and fathers, but they need shoes, they need clothes, because their mother or father would rather go out and get beer, wine, weed, or dope. When a gang member sees another gang member who has run-down sneakers, they'll ask him, "Hey, man, you need some sneakers?" and they'll kick him down some. They get support that they don't get from their families, even as far as clothes. If he's hungry, they'll give him food. They keep each other going. I knew brothers who didn't have anyplace to stay, and the homiez would say,

"Here's a hundred dollars, go and get you a room, and some food, and kick it for a couple of nights." When they couldn't even go to their own relatives and get a penny.

**Q:** How can that unity be transferred into positive?

**G:** As far as the Bloods and the Cuz . . . I can't speak for the Eses [Chicano] and the white gangs, but I know for a fact that there's more good in the gangs than the bad that the media is showing us. There are way more positive things than there are negative. Like when one gang member is in need of food or clothing, he's taken care of. Even down to when a gang member has a problem, when they're feeling low, the other gang members build them up. There's a whole lot of good. There's more to it than them just going out and being violent. When one brother or a couple of brothers have a problem, or when they have a beef with each other, they are counseled to work it out.

**Q:** With that being the case, what are some ways to generate it to become more positive and what are some solutions to stop the killing?

**G:** We have to get things like the teen posts going again. So when a brother has a problem, he doesn't have to rely on a gang. He can go to a teen post, where they have counselors, or he can go and get in a ring and box his frustrations out. I would recommend for everybody to have a punching bag in their house. So every time you get frustrated, you can go hit that bag for ten to fifteen minutes, and just with that bag alone your frustrations will almost be gone. With a bag to punch on, a speed bag, a jump rope, running, and some sparring, you will release any kind of pressure. That's what we had back when the gangs had stopped from '65 to '68. That's what we had to keep our frustrations down, because of the circle. We're locked in that circle, and we take it out on each other.

That circle is just like jail. If you keep somebody locked down in jail, their frustration and their stress is going to build, build, build, and they're going to begin hating theirself, and when they start hating theirself, they're going to take it out on others. When you can't get out of that circle, it becomes a problem. It's like, if somebody locks you up in a room, and you're trying to get out. If you can't get out, you're going to get madder and madder and madder. If there are drugs there, you're going to take them. If somebody else is there, you might hurt them, or you might kill them.

When I was in jail, I wanted to kill everybody, because I couldn't get out. The police looked at me one day and said, "Damn, I can just see the hate in your face." I could feel it too, it was just beaming in me. I would whip a white boy every day. I got off by hitting a white boy, and then looking at his hair fly up like a porcupine. Every time I hit 'im, his hair would stand up like he had gotten electrocuted, and that was my thing, that made my day. I did it every day. I had white boys saying, "I sure don't want to see you when I get out on the street." It really wasn't that I hated them that much, it was just that frustration. I was in a double circle. It's that hate; when you get out, it's a whole different thing. You're frustrated on the street too, but I'm telling you, you can look at people in the pen and say, "Damn." You can look at their eyes and tell they're about to bust. They're time bombs walking around in there. I hated everything when I was in jail. I had gotten to the point where I didn't even believe in God. So you couldn't come at me with God. I was like, "God wouldn't allow anybody to go through all of this here." Plus I had never seen him, so I was like, "I ain't going to believe in something I haven't seen." Before I went to jail I did believe in God, but when I got in there, I didn't even believe in myself. You have people in the pens that kill people daily. We don't hear about it, but there are people who get killed in the pen every day. Every day somebody comes home in a box from the pen.

**Q:** What do you think is the cause for that frustration, and for the hatred?

**G:** That goes all the way back to our ancestors. That goes all the way back to slavery. That's where it originated, when we were kidnapped from Africa and brought here to be stripped of our culture, our family, and everything. That's when it began. Before that, the circle didn't even exist. That's what started the circle. It goes way back, and brothers don't know that. They don't understand that their problems came through generations. We came here with zero, that's when our problem began, and that's when the circle began. There's not even a hole in the circle either, because if you think back, even the guys like Magic Johnson, Michael Jordan, Kareem Abdul-Jabbar, Michael Jackson, and Bill Cosby, they're still in that circle too, they're just doing good in the circle. They're still considered a "nigger." We have a lot of work to do. One of the only ways I can see us getting out of that circle is for brothers that are doing good to work as a team in helping the other brothers that are not doing so good. We need our own radio stations, and our own TV stations, so we can present ourselves and not be portrayed as white people represent us. Everything you see on TV is the way the white man represents us, not as we really are. They stereotype us. We have to get our own food companies, our own producing companies, so we won't have to depend on them or go to them for anything. That's the only way we're going to get a hole in that circle, that's when the circle will bust. As long as we have to go to them for everything, that circle will still be there.

**Q:** What would you say to a young brother who's in that circle?

**G:** That's where the zero comes in. If you would just examine where we've come from being stripped of everything, we're the only people in the whole wide world who have been stripped of everything. You can look at us now, and we still smile, we still have that pride. We have a lot of faults, but we've come from zero, when everybody else had thirty, forty, or fifty, some had eighty or ninety, to start from. They know their background, they know their history, they've never lost their family, they can trace their family from the beginning. We are doing damn good to have come from zero. We have to push that and let the brothers know that we are somebody, and if we use our knowledge, we can't be touched. The white man knows that. They're like, "The way we've stripped these Black people to nothing and took them from their country, raped their wives and their mamas, killed them, tarred them, and they still have that pride, they're still strong, still fighting. The average race would have given up." We've come a long way. Everybody else had a head start, and we're giving them a run for their money.

Right now they are scared. We're coming together, and they can see that the circle is about to bust. That's why they're so scared of our unity. They'll go out of their way to kill that unity. They don't want Black people to get together, because they know how well we've done being divided, and when we come together, it's all over. It's all over, and they know it. That's why they want to keep us in that circle. They'll let a few brothers have big money, but they want to keep the masses of us in that circle. I don't think there's anyplace in the United States where Blacks own their own TV stations; we have plenty of money. We're always complaining that they don't show on TV what we want them to show, like the rappers were complaining about not being free to say what they want to say in the rap business, so they started getting their own record labels. We have to do the same thing with the TV, so we can school the brothers about the circle, and how we've come from being stripped of everything. Look at Michael Jackson, Bill Cosby, Sugar Ray Leonard: they are some of the richest people in the world. White people didn't have any idea that brothers would come that far being divided. So once we come together, there will be no stopping us. Once we can get that unity and start trusting each other and put our money together, then we will be in a position to purchase TV stations. White people will sell to us when we come up with enough money. They might overcharge us, but we can get it. We need our own, because the way they do us when we do have a good Black program, and we don't have that many, but when we do get a good Black program that comes on every week, they'll mix it up with another good Black program. At first one will come on a Thursday, and the other one will come on a Wednesday. They both will skyrocket, with white people, Mexicans, Blacks, and everybody looking at it, then you know what they'll do, they'll put them both on at the same time, to split their ratings, and to knock their ratings down in half. They know you're going to have to choose one. Black people cannot see that old tricky stuff. They do it every time, to make us end up losing one of our shows. Like *Martin* [Lawrence], another station will try to find something . . . *Martin* is skyrocketing now, so what they'll do is find another Black picture to put on at the same time *Martin* comes on, to knock his ratings way down. His ratings are going through the roof right now. You can't help but love his show, because it's so real and down.

**Q:** Speak on how we can stop the cycle of retaliation of killing each other.

**G:** The police beat us up and kill us all the time, but we can still tolerate to see them every day without shooting at them, yet once we see that blue rag, or that red rag, we think that we have to kill somebody? You're looking at a people whose families have raped our ancestors, killed them, and hung them up by the testicles, tarred and feathered them—that stuff was true. I was looking at a show last night where they were taking pictures of this dude with a gun, and he had a Black man laying on the ground butt naked where he had killed him. They had this Black dude that they had beat, cut, and killed, and they were standing over him like he was a winning prize. Now if we can forgive and walk around people like that every day, then we ought to be able to forgive each other easily. I don't know one brother that has skinned another brother alive, put salt on him, boiled him in oil, and killed him. I don't know any brother that has done another brother like that. White people have done us like that a lot, and we forgive them. So if we can forgive things like that, then we sure can forgive a brother for shooting another brother, who really didn't even mean it. He may think he meant it, but he didn't. Our killing of each other has been strictly stupid, killing over nothing. We've got to forgive each other, we've got to let everything go. By any means necessary, we have to forgive each other, because we're getting short, we're killing each other off with drugs, guns, and alcohol. It's critical that we forgive each other soon, or there won't be any more Black people, or we're going to be so short that everybody is going to run over us.

**Q:** What are the steps to get brothers to forgive?

**G:** We have to push communication. The communication brings understanding, the understanding brings respect, respect brings love, and love brings peace. A true peace treaty that will hold. We can't just say, "Okay, let's truce, let's stop killing each other." We have to get to know each other and get the communication, the understanding, the respect, and the love amongst each other, then it will hold. We have to get that communication going.

**Q:** What alternatives can we offer for young brothers who want to come to peace?

**G:** Brothers like that 99 percent of the time are very talented. All you have to do is sit down with him and bring out the other talents that he has, things he can do just as good as when he was jacking or killing. Ninety-nine percent of the time he's a sharp brother, with all kinds of talent. Find out what talent he is best at and help him to use it. Tell him to go use that talent the same way, and with the same seriousness, as when he puts that ski mask on.

**Q:** What would you say to brothers who have lost their homiez and haven't been able to let it rest?

**G:** Me personally, I would name thirty or forty homiez that I've lost, and how I dealt with it.

**Q:** How did you deal with it?

**G:** That goes back to the circle again. That was before I got to the understanding of why. So now I know if I can deal with these people every day that have done what they did to us, then I can deal with a killing easily. I mean, you're going to feel it, but instead of having to go retaliate, once you find out where it's coming from, you will understand why a brother does certain things. It's all because he doesn't even understand. So I'd just run the circle down to a brother.

The only way it's going to work is by speaking to them individually. If I got fifty Bloods and Cuz in here, and I try to tell them why they're banging, they'd say, "Oh, no, that ain't why, we did that because homeboy did this here to us. If he wouldn't have shot my homeboy, I wouldn't have done anything." But how did it get to that point? That's why you run that circle down to them individually. You have to do it individually, because there are egos involved, that "gangster thing" they call it. So you get them individually to explain the circle to them, how the circle started from the day we were kidnapped from Africa, and how we were brought here and stripped of everything. Tell anybody with common sense, and it's going to register, 99 percent of them are going to understand it, and they will come in with perfect harmony.

Out of any gang there's only one guy who is an actual killer. I've been out on missions where there was five to ten of us, and if you really peep it out, you will see half of them shooting up in the air, one shooting with his eyes closed, and another one shooting at the ground, but then you have that one guy who has one eye closed and one eye open, aiming straight at someone's head trying to blow him away. He has that much hatred, he hates himself that much that he really wants to blow another brother away. If you take one hundred gang members, you won't find but two actual killers, if that many. Two killers that will kill at will. Two killers that want to kill, that want you to die. Most gang members if they shoot you, they will shoot at your legs or your arms, they will not try to kill you. Two out of a hundred really want—when they pull that trigger, they really want you to cease living.

I know I've shot at a lot of brothers, but I hope to God that I never killed anybody, taking a brother's life for some stupid stuff like that. You have some who will say, "I sure hope they came up missing."

That's really a sick person. That's not a gangster. Killing for nothing, that's not a gangster. A true gangster wouldn't want to kill a brother over nothing. You have good leaders that are fair who are really down, and they don't really want to kill anyone unless there is a harm to their set. Then they will get busy. You have some whose homeboys have never been shot, killed, or beat up by another gang, but they want to get that reputation. They're not gangsters either, they just want to "get a rep," like Gangstarr said.

**Q:** What were some of your early positive influences?

**G:** I was with the Black Student Union, and the Black Students Alliance. I stayed on Forty-ninth and Western then, and the Black Students Union was on Forty-fifth and Western, and the Black Students Alliance was on Forty-seventh and Western, by the Jerry Lee Amy Center. That center was named after the brother that was killed by the police on Fifty-ninth and Denker. The police shot him about fifty to sixty times when he was playing with his niece on the front lawn with a water gun. The police came and shot him all up and said, "Well, we smoked us a nigger tonight." There was a little riot behind it, so they named that center after him.

See, the militant thing was kicking out here for a minute. Black Panthers were everywhere, US [United Slaves], the Nation of Islam. To me, the Black Panthers did more for Black people than anybody in L.A. and the West Coast. I don't know about the East Coast. Malcolm talked good, but he didn't put in action. To me, a person that didn't put in action, I really don't give them any credit. Huey P. Newton, he talked that talk and walked that walk. He put a shotgun in his car and patrolled. He had his little black book, the law book, and when the police stopped a brother, Huey was right there behind them, making sure everything was cool. Then when they did that stuff on the steps of the courthouse, I knew those brothers were down. They went gun to gun with the police, and the police backed up off of them. It showed us that we didn't have to be run over. They had the Black Panther newspaper; we have to get that newspaper going again, because a lot of Black people don't know what's going on.

I remember when fifty of us would be on the corner, one police car would pull up, and everybody would leave. When the devil pulled up, brothers that didn't even do a thing were breaking their legs, tearing their pants, and jumping over cars to run away. They would have their IDs on them and everything. It's just that white people have put that fear in them. Huey P. Newton stopped that. He said, "You have a right to stand here and talk to each other. When the police pull you over, just put your window down a little bit and stick your license through the window like white people do; you don't have to get out of your car—you haven't done anything." The Black Panthers did more for Black people, they just didn't talk it, they got out and got into it.

I joined the Panthers, and I was ready to put in some work, I was ready to go to war. They had the morning breakfast programs where they would feed Black children who were hungry, and that's how I got kicked out of the Panthers. They said I had to wash dishes. Wash dishes? I wasn't washing anything. They said, "Well, it's a positive cause; if you're not going to be with this positive cause, the whole thing, then you can't be with it." I was out of there. I wanted to straight get militant, get out there and get busy. Now that I am older I understand, but I had just gotten out of jail from washing dishes, and I wasn't going to wash any more dishes.

I was down with George Jackson. When I was in jail, I lived by his rules. If you down one brother, three of y'all are going to pay. When George Jackson was living, nobody messed with Blacks in the pen, nobody, not even the police. That's why they killed that brother. If that brother had gotten home to the Panthers . . . man. They said, "We can't let this nigger get out, and we can't let this nigger stay in here, we have to kill this nigger with the pistol." They say he had a gun in jail; they just killed George Jackson. George Jackson was deep; he had those brothers so down—he talked that talk and walked that walk. When the police talked bad to him, you might not see that police the next day. They was taking Nazis out, they was taking them out so much, and teaching the other brothers how to take them out, that after a while they didn't have to take anybody out, because nobody messed with them. If you were Black, nobody messed with you. "Man, if we mess with them, three of us will be automatically gone, and we don't even want that." The white supremacist groups, they didn't want that. The Mexican mob, they didn't want that. It held for a while too, but it faded when he was killed.

I followed brothers like George Jackson, Huey P. Newton, Bobby Seale, H. Rap Brown. Everywhere H. Rap Brown talked, there was a riot, he juiced brothers up so much. Everywhere he talked back in the day, when he left, the brothers were rollin'.

The Black Panthers and the US had it going on. US was the type of group that was intelligent. They were sharp, karated down; when you talked to them, they were proper. US was so down, and the Panthers were making such a big difference, that the CoinTelPro conspired against them. They were out there, and they were tired of just talk, because white people don't understand talking. You just can't talk to white people. It's just something about them. I remember when I was in jail, every day when we had to march, this white boy would get on my heel, and I would tell him to get off my heel. So one day I didn't tell him to get off my heel, I turned around and knocked him out, and I didn't ever have to worry about him getting on my heel anymore. A lot of them you really just can't talk to.

I know who made a difference, I saw for myself. It wasn't something I read in a book or heard somebody say, I saw what Huey did for the hood. Huey and Bobby, Eldridge Cleaver, and all of them back in the day, they were out there. They didn't sit behind a desk or just give a good speech, they backed their talk with action. To me Huey P. Newton was the greatest Black man that ever lived. The way he went out, I just can't believe that the Black people in the pen are letting the boy that killed him live in there.

Do you know why the feds didn't kill Huey P. Newton when he was in his prime? I'm going to tell you why they killed Malcolm X and Martin Luther King, and why they didn't kill Bobby Seale and Huey P. Newton back then. If they had killed Huey P. Newton at that time, they would have made him a symbol. They wouldn't kill Malcolm X when he was talking separation and doing for self, they wouldn't have touched him then, because if they would have touched him then, they would have made him a symbol. They make him a symbol now, as if he's a symbol of peace. If they would have killed him at his prime, he would have been a symbol of strength. The reason why Martin Luther King was killed is because he was a peaceful guy. They said, "If we kill this guy, while he has all this juice, we'll make him a peaceful symbol."

"Turn the other cheek." How can you bring a thousand kids and take them out to march and let dogs chew on them and let beasts throw water all on your kids, and your wife, and you don't fight back? I didn't like Martin Luther King for that. I couldn't believe how he did Black people, taking them out there; that's like committing suicide. Turn the other cheek, when bricks and stuff were being thrown at them. The feds said, "He has all these Black people, whites, Mexicans, Indians, and everybody behind him, if we kill him like he is now, that will make him a symbol," and that's just what they did. He's a symbol, and Malcolm X is a symbol.

Huey P. Newton did more for Black people than anybody. If they would have taken him out at his peak like that, brothers would have been living like, "We ain't taking no s— off white people, we're going to be like Huey P. Newton." That's how we'd be living. Every time the police stop us if it's not fair, we're holding court. If a brother gets hurt, we're going to the courthouse with gats. We're just going to hold court right there. They didn't want that, so they let him live until he faded, and now you don't hear anything about him. Not only Black people, but white people loved Huey P. Newton. You see, he had Jane Fonda taking care of him for five or six years, in a penthouse up in San Francisco. She paid for everything. White people were mad about that. Jane Fonda was just like that.

Geronimo Pratt, he's in the pen for nothing. He was a hell of a Panther. When he was in Nam, they used to drop him off behind enemy lines, come back and get him a week later, and when they'd come back to get him, they didn't think he would be there. When they would see him, he would be bloody, to where he had went through there and just handled business. When he got home, they said, "This man right here, we can't have him down with the Black Panthers, he'd be killing white people, and we won't even know it." I was around those type of militant brothers.

The FBI sent in a brother to infiltrate the Panthers. He said that J. Edgar Hoover had told him to go in there and start some s— between the Panthers and US with the UCLA event. The Panthers had won the election over the US to be the head of the Black Student Union, and somebody from US pulled out a gun and killed the two Panthers right at the event. So it was on from there. The whole thing was started by the infiltrator, because he said, "You're going to let these niggas come down here from Oakland, into your area here, and win the election?" They started to spread rumors saying, "Maulana Karenga said this about Huey P. Newton and Bobby Seale, and Bobby Seale said they're coming to L.A. to take over US's thing. Pretty soon there won't be any more US, it's just going to be all Panthers." The US was hearing this and believing it, and it caused the US to kill a couple of Panthers. The FBI got a victory on that, so then they said, "Eldridge Cleaver is calling you a punk, Huey." They believed 'em on that too. What makes it so hard is they get sell-out Blacks to do it. They figure, "This ain't no white dude telling me this, it's a black guy," so we believe it. We have to become more wise and stop falling for the same old tricks.

I used to follow Elijah Muhammad. My wife will tell you, I had stacks of *Muhammad Speaks.* I used to have Muslims come to my house. I was fixing to join the Muslims. You know the only thing that stopped me from joining the Muslims? When Elijah Muhammad was gone, and Wallace D. Muhammad took over and started letting white people in, it broke my heart. Ever since I was a little kid, I remember the Muslims who were on Exposition and Western, and a young brother came up to me and asked, "Do you know who the devil is?" I said no, and right then we saw a police car passing with a white boy in it, and he said, "That's the devil right there, the blue-eyed devil." And I believed him, I knew he was a devil because when I was younger I was attacked by the police.

We were going eastbound on Forty-ninth towards Harvard, the police just came out of nowhere and stopped us and started questioning us about some stuff that we didn't even know about. At that time I always had a smile on my face, I was always laughing. I was laughing when the police came, so he was like, "You have to stop laughing." I was steady laughing, and he put his pump shotgun in my mouth and said, "Smile now, nigger." It didn't dawn on me that it was racism then, because I was so young, around thirteen or fourteen years old, but as I thought back on it, a grown man doing that to a kid was racism. He was trying to put that fear in me right there, and it didn't work. My laughing was intimidating him, because I wasn't scared or shaking like most brothers. Everything he said, I was laughing about it.

**Q:** Do you feel that there is a conspiracy to keep the brothers from uniting?

**G:** I know there is. Like the police would go get a low-rider from another town, or an area not close to where you're at, put on the red rags, and go shooting. When there's too much peace for them, they start some trouble. They're professionals at doing that. Then they'll tell another gang member, "You know who killed your homeboy? That was so and so. I got a transcript right here where his homeboys snitched on him." It's a big conspiracy, with the government and the police starting much of the trouble between us.

**Q:** Do you think a lot of the young brothers know that they are being infiltrated?

**G:** No, they can't see it, only a few of them know it. When I had the shoot-out with the police, they had people in there with us who were working for the police when they tried to kill me.

**Q:** When was that?

**G:** February of 1974.

**Q:** What was that all about?

**G:** The police came and shot 256 times, and they threw four tear-gas bombs which were made to ignite the house as soon as they enter.

**S:** They came and positioned themselves in the alley between the garages. The dog woke up, and he was moaning to get out. As we started scuffling in the room, we heard somebody running around making noise outside. So Robert said, "Who is it? Who is it?" They wouldn't respond. Then we heard them kicking in the back door, so Robert pulled his gun out and started shooting at the wall. After they came in the first door, they were on their way in, they were no more than about four or five feet from the bedroom door. We originally thought it was gangs, but it was the police.

**G:** They set it up to be like that. A week or two before that happened, our house was shot up by some Crips. So I was thinking it was them coming back, but coming back harder. I had a lot of juice in the neighborhood, I was uniting 'em real tough. I was making them work out, hit the iron, and box every day. Preparing them for war. The Crips were hearing about this so a lot of them said, "If you get rid of Robert Lee, the Godfather, then the set is gone, because he's the one pumping 'em up and keeping 'em going."

So when the police came to the back door, they hollered out, "We want Robert Lee, Angel, and Sugarbear." Angel and Sugarbear were in jail, so it didn't dawn on me that this was the police. That's when they started coming through the back door.

**S:** Even the judge, when we were in court, he said, "If you came to my back door at four o'clock in the morning without announcing yourself, I would have shot at you too." They lied and said that they had approached us at the front door with a search warrant. We didn't see a search warrant until we went to court. The only thing that saved Robert from doing time was when I went and took the pictures of the positions and the angles from where the bullets had been shot. I stood where the police were, and it showed that the back of the house was the only place where they could have shot from, through the rear window into the bedroom. They couldn't have done it from the front serving a search warrant.

**G:** They said they knocked on the front door and presented a search warrant, and I started busting. They had told my homeboy that night, "We're going to kill your homeboy Robert Lee and his dog." They wanted to get me because we were getting into some deep stuff in the hood. There was a drugstore, a market, and a corner cleaner's that we were making pay for protection. That's why the police really started investigating us. They had been investigating us for about three months. They said they would have never bothered us as long as we were killing Black people. Brims on Crips didn't fade them, but when we started making Jews and Koreans pay, they came at us. Two hundred fifty-six shots, and four tear-gas bombs.

**S:** They never could understand why that house didn't catch on fire, and this was all in one room, a small bedroom.

**G:** The tear gas was so strong that when the police was driving us to the station, they were leaning out of the car. When we went to the police station, they showered me, and it still didn't kill the smell. All of the police had to get out of the police station. Then they ended up having to put me outside in the parking lot. That's how strong the tear gas was, and how much tear gas they shot into our house. Two weeks later my cousin went to the house to get some stuff out, and when he came out of the house, his eyes were swollen, he couldn't even breathe. That lets you know that they pumped a whole lot of tear gas in there.

**S:** They shot the whole rim off the window. What was so strange about that was we had just lost our baby right before that. If our baby would have lived, they would have killed our baby, because the baby's bed was right there at the window that they shot through.

**G:** I would have been dead now, because I would have gone on a serious mission if they would have killed our baby.

**S:** That showed me how God can foresee things that we can never imagine. I remember when the baby died, I was like, "Why? Why not me? Why not Robert?" If anybody, the baby hadn't done anything. After that happened, it made me realize that God foresees things that we can never foresee. The baby's bed was right by the window. I was so glad after that, it was like a relief to me. I was really bitter at first, but after that happened, it was a relief, because if I had to live with that, knowing that my baby could have gotten killed by the police—that showed me that they could care less. From the way they were acting, I don't think it would have even mattered to them.

**G:** They knew my wife wasn't involved. I know the informant had to be telling them that she wasn't in it. She was steady talking against it.

**Q:** So if y'all didn't fight it, they probably would have tried to lock you up for a long time?

**G:** Yeah, because when I bailed out, I had one attempted murder on a police officer. When I came back, it was four attempted murders on police officers, nine receiving stolen goods; the list was real long. Outside the court there was a list of names with the accused charges, so I asked the bailiff, "Can you come here, I'm looking for my name and I don't see it. There's another Robert on here, but it's not me." He asked me for my booking number, I told him, and he said, "Well, that's you." They had tried to sock it to me, but the way we got the pictures of the angles on the house, and when we presented the pictures to the judge, it killed all of that.

**Q:** What made you do that research? [question directed to Sheila]

**S:** The lies. When it got to court, they lied, saying they had served a search warrant. I went to the law library, and I found out that a search warrant has to be presented before they can enter your property. Then since we hadn't been served the search warrant, I found out that there were certain penal codes where if they don't abide by the law, the case can be dismissed. So I got records of different cases that had been dismissed because they didn't present the search warrant. Then I took the pictures of the bullets, because they were lying, saying that they knocked on the front door, served the search warrant, and that we started shooting at them, and all of this they said took place at the front of the house. Well, if all of this took place at the front of the house, how come the bullets were in the back of the house? There was no way all of these bullets could have just ran all the way through the walls. There were no holes in the walls, except through the back door. I took pictures of bullet holes down along the floor. They were shooting down in case we were crawling. I crawled through that hallway, and how those bullets missed me, I'd like to know. I know God had to be there with us, because we wouldn't have crawled out of there. There was only two or three bullets that went all the way through to the front, and went all the way into an upstairs apartment across the street—I mean, a big wide street like a main street.

On the receiving-stolen-goods charges, the judge asked if any money was passed, and they said, "No, we didn't see any money passed." So the judge said, "How can you have a receiving stolen goods unless you can prove that he paid for it? Case dismissed."

Then for the attempted murder charges on the police, we had a public defender. The public defender fought the case, and we got a hung jury. When we got a hung jury, the public defender told Robert, "Well, you can cop a plea to a lesser charge, and you'll only do about a year or something, but if they decide to run another jury and you get convicted, you're going to do some time." So Robert was ready to cop a plea, and I told Robert not to cop a plea.

**G:** When she told me don't go for the okeydoke, I said, "Are you going to be with me if I go to jail?" She said, "Yes." So I said, "Let's do this." We went back into court and told the judge that we weren't going for it, and he said, "Case dismissed."

**Q:** What impact did your wife have on cooling you out some?

**G:** I've been married to her for twenty-one years. If it wasn't for her staying on me and riding me and not having fear about riding me, I'd be dead or in the penitentiary, or a whole lot of other people would be dead. I know a whole lot of other people would be dead, and that would have probably led me to getting killed, or being put in the penitentiary with double life. I used to think about massacres, and she would help me avoid it. Not because of a rag or anything like that, but behind me getting shot. She kept preaching that forgiveness.

**S:** When he got shot, it didn't only hurt him, it hurt me. I'll suffer for the rest of my life from what happened to him, because of what somebody else did. They think they were just hurting him, but they hurt the whole family. Not only do they hurt the whole family, but they hurt our whole race, because we're all one family; whether we want to accept it or not, we're all one family. We're all brothers and sisters in one way or another.

**G:** At that time when I got shot and I was put in a wheelchair, anybody that knew me didn't feel too bad about it, because it was really a blessing. They knew I was on my way to getting killed, because I didn't fear anything. Just fearless—didn't fear anything, so a person like that usually ends up getting killed or ends up going to the penitentiary for life. When I was in the wheelchair, I still cut up, so they just imagined, "If this boy hadn't been put in this wheelchair, people would have been in trouble." Anybody that knows me would say, "That's the best thing that could have happened to him." The gang was mad, but most people felt that was the best thing that could have happened to me.

**Q:** What role do some sisters play in getting gang wars started?

**G:** They play key roles. Most drive-bys and most trouble is usually behind a woman. "I ran into these Bloods at the swap meet, and they disrespected me. They called me all kinds of names because I told them I

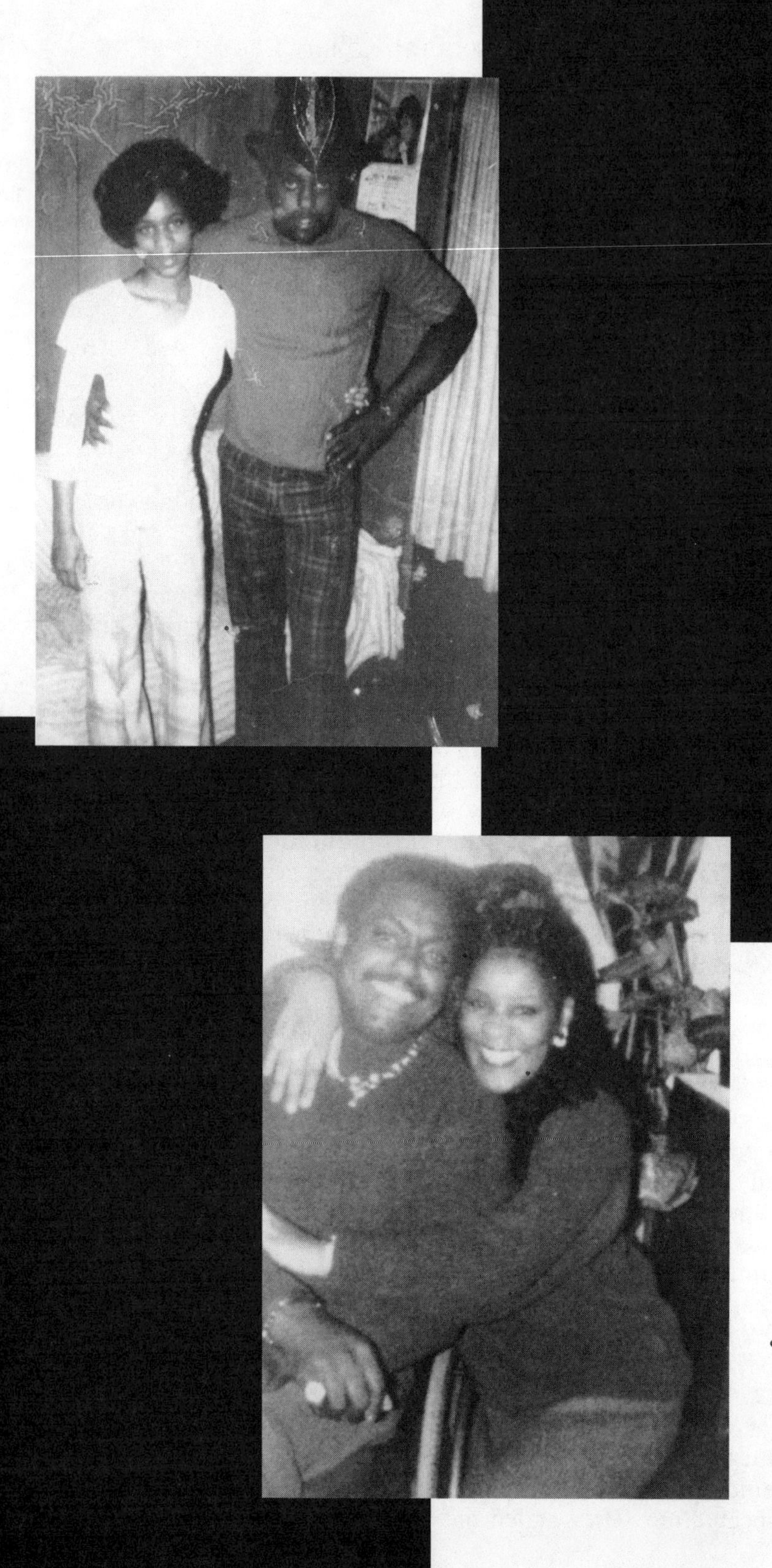

wouldn't mess with Bloods, I'm a Crip lover," or whatever. "What, they dissed you like that? We're going to get them, we can't have them disrespecting the homegirls from the hood." There goes some more shooting. Then it goes back and forth through retaliation. Sisters play a key role.

**Q:** What would you say to sisters who have played a key role in instigating a lot of the fighting and the killing between brothers; what could we say to them now to get them to help keep the peace going?

**S:** I look at it like this, you have to stand up and stop being afraid. A lot of sisters are afraid of standing up to their man, because the first thing he'll do is threaten them. "I'm going to kick your behind." There are a lot of men who do that, but to me, if you really love a person, you're going to stand for what's right. Any weak person can back down and say, "Go ahead." But you have to look at the loss. Somewhere along the line we're going to lose. We might figure, "Let them go their own way and do whatever they want to do," but we're going to lose. We're going to lose a brother, we're going to lose a husband, we're going to lose a father, we're going to lose a son. Somewhere along the line if he gets killed, then through retaliation somebody else's brother or father is going to get killed. That's why we have so many fatherless children right now, and when a lot of mothers get older, they don't have their sons there to take care of them, because the fathers and the sons have died in these gangs, or from drugs or something.

First they were killing us in the wars, then when they couldn't get us to volunteer for that anymore, they started the draft. Now they have the gangs and the jails.

Women just have to learn to stand up and not be afraid. For years we've been beaten for speaking. So we just have to learn to stand up for what is right. What makes you stand up is that love. Just like a mother with a child, if you love that child, and that child does something wrong, you're going to discipline that child. You have a lot of mothers that are afraid to discipline their children, because they think the child won't love them. If you genuinely love your child, you're going to discipline that child, because if you don't, somebody else will. The closest one to you is the one that you love. It's the same thing with our husbands or our men: if you don't stand up to them, then somebody else is going to discipline them out there in the streets, and nine times out of ten they're going to kill 'em. A lot of times the mother won't say anything to the sons, or the sister won't say anything to her brother, or the wife doesn't want to say anything to her husband, or the girlfriend won't say anything to her man, and in the long run they lose. So they have to start standing up to make that change.

**Q:** What is the significance of brothers tying their rags together and calling for peace?

**G:** If you can get L.A. to come to peace, the impact will be nationwide.

If L.A. can do it, anybody can do it. L.A. is the gang capital of the world, harder than Beirut. That's why the government is going to fight hard to stop the peace from happening, because they know how strong the impact will be—not just in L.A., but everywhere else that follows the trends that are set in L.A. New York or Chicago never even got to the degree that it has gotten to out here. L.A. set the level, and now everybody else is trying to get to that same level, and they're doing a damn good job. So if L.A. can put their rags up and get with the peace and get into that unity, then it will be a big impact.

**Q:** What things should the peacemakers of today look out for?

**G:** They should know how the government tries to keep the peace from happening. They should look at the Black Panthers and the US, and how the police and the FBI infiltrated them. There was much love between the Panthers and the US; they were two organizations, but they were like one, fighting for the same cause. They were going the same way, they just had two different styles, that was the only difference. The police saw that each organization had tight unity, so they got with the FBI, and they went in to spread rumors and to cause killing amongst the two groups. The instigation and the agitation by the FBI and the police brought the brothers to war. So study our history, and study your brother and sister, because everybody Black ain't Black.

**S:** When I run across gang bangers, I try to help them to understand that Satan wants us to believe that our fight is against one another. He's behind the bitterness, the hatred, the division, and all of that. We can't see that he's pushing us to hate one another. We can't see that he's pushing us to fight one another and destroy one another in whatever way he can. We can only see each other; that's why we kill each other, because we can't see who we're really fighting. When I share that with gang bangers, it really helps them to relate. The fight is really not against each other.

**G:** I know that my study of religion, and what I have learned, has helped me to overcome drugs and alcohol and to live a cleaner life. It has helped with me a whole lot.

**Q:** How long have you been at peace?

**G:** Since '82, '83.

**Q:** How were you able to kick it with Crips with no problems?

**G:** There just wasn't any fear. I wasn't scared of the brothers. They were brothers just like me, humans just like me. What did Public Enemy say, "I never ever ran from the Ku Klux Klan, so I shouldn't have to run from a Black man." So it was that kind of thing. We just didn't have any fear of each other.

**Q:** At that point you didn't have fear, but you also didn't have any beef with them, right?

**G:** That's right, because we knew they were Crips. Maybe that's why there wasn't any fear, because we really didn't have any beef with them. They really weren't our enemies. If we had felt they were our enemies, we would have probably been trying to do something, or we just wouldn't have been around them.

**Q:** So some of your homeboys had been killed and everything else, but at that point you had no beef?

**G:** It was that forgiveness, which is a good role for our Black sisters, to push that forgiveness to their men. Sooner or later with most brothers, it will register. Not with all, but with most of them it will register. That's a big role that the Black sisters can really play on the positive. If they would push that forgiveness, it would have a big, big impact.

**Q:** What would you say to other OGs?

**G:** Get involved quickly. Don't just kick back and say, "It's their thing." It's not their thing, it's your thing, because you started this thing. You made the pathroad, they're just keeping it going. You carried the ball for years, and you passed the ball to them; now you have to help kill that ball. You can't try to run over them because you're an OG, you still have to treat them with respect, treat the young Gs with respect, and you will get your respect.They know where you come from, you don't have to prove to them or carry yourself a certain way because you're an OG. Give them their respect, and your respect will be due. You have to give respect to get respect.

**S:** If you even look back in the days with the older people, when they respected young people, then young people gave them respect. Nowadays older people will curse you out. I tell parents all the time, "You don't know how wrong you are to curse your children the way you do, and then expect them to respect you." Once you start cursing them, you lose control, and you lose respect. You've lost it, to the point where you have to curse them in order to get their attention. Back in the old days people didn't have to curse their children to get respect from them. Respect only comes from where you give it. If you give respect, you get respect. If the older guys want the younger ones to respect them, then they have to carry themselves in a respectful way.

**Q:** What would you say to the brothers locked up in the pens, who are saying they are not with the peace? How would you get them to be with the peace?

**G:** They're frustrated. They've done time, and they are mad. They have a chip on their shoulder, because the brothers are trying to come to peace, and when they were out here, they was warring with each other. Now they're in jail for defending their set or from putting work in for their set, but once they get out, that will end with most of them. The ones that put in work for their Gs might be mad, because they may have gotten ten years, and now everyone is talking about peace. You have brothers that have murders, that are on death row, or have double life in the pen, and now there's talk about peace, so you know they're not with it. Then you might find some of them who have a true heart that are with it. A lot of them think about what they did once they get in that pen and they hate what they did. They say, "I wouldn't have done this." Most of them that say they're not with the peace while they are in the pen, when they get home, 99 percent of them will be with it. You have some of 'em that are with the peace in there. The other ones that are not with it is because of the frustration they have from being in there. They are mad at theirself, they're mad at everybody. They're doing time for a Blood or a Cuz.

**S:** You know how that *Scared Straight* program worked. They say that helped a lot of kids. I think that if they applied the same situation to the gang bangers out here and let them go in the pen to talk to some of those guys that are going to spend the rest of their lives in jail, it might help. Let those that are really sincere about wanting change tell the younger ones about the situation. They were a part of creating the problem, so they can be a part of solving that problem. The same thing with Robert: when guys talk to him and see that he has been through it, and he's talking from actual experience, they listen. A whole lot of OGs might be able to help a lot of those youngsters.

**G:** *Scared Straight* was deep, but they had something that was even deeper than that. They had this thing where they would take the gang members to the morgue and show them where somebody's head was blown off by the Bloods, or somebody that was shot nine times by the Crips. They were taking them to the morgue and showing them the damage, and it was blowing their minds, because a lot of them don't know what damage they really do. They would show them bodies with their heads blown off or their backs blown off or their whole chest or stomach blown out. They were showing them just like it is. They said some guys were fainting and throwing up.

Let's just say I'm riding down the street and I start shooting at some brothers on the corner. I take off and I don't see the damage that I did. When you go back and tell your homiez, they don't know either, all they know is you shot somebody. But if they go and see it, if they go to that morgue and see the body, I know that would be a big impact. That would help a whole lot of people. Those gang bangers that went through that program, they ended up saying, "I do not want to shoot anybody, and I most definitely do not want somebody shooting me." That program had a big impact, but they killed it real quick. They really need that down in South Central now. All the schoolkids, all the gang members, anytime they go to jail, or if they're put on probation or parole, take them there and let them see the damage that their homeboys are doing. That would have a big impact. That would make a big difference.

**Q:** What can be done to get the drugs out of the community and to cut down the demand?

**G:** That's where the rappers, the Kareems, the Magics, the Michaels, the Cosbys, come in. We have to write to these people, because we're the ones who made them famous. They wouldn't have a dime if it wasn't for us—all the public should write to them. Tell them that we need some money in the neighborhoods, we need positive programs so we can bring out the positive in individuals, instead of the negative. We need alternatives.

**S:** One way to get them involved is to withdraw our support from them. If people stopped supporting them, then they would listen.

**G:** Stevie Wonder blessed us with that radio station where we could get our words across. We really need to get that *Peace Treaty* program back on KJLH, or another program like it on one of the other radio stations that cater to Black youth, because that program saved a whole lot of lives. We should definitely get support for another program. Anybody who's not down with helping, then we're not down with buying their records or going to their movies. That will put them straight in check. Then they'll have to support us.

**Q:** What are some ways to develop our own businesses to do for self?

**G:** That's where the celebrities come back in. They have to put that money into the community. What we need to work on right now is getting our own TV stations to get that communication going on the positive.

**S:** Again, you have to withdraw support from certain products, because even the TV stations are sponsored by certain companies. The controller is really the one who supports it. If people are not buying the product, no matter who is distributing it, if Black people are not buying the product, it won't matter who's distributing it. The purpose is to bring in the money. So that means if the Black community doesn't buy the product, it's going to become obsolete. The same thing with the TV shows: if we don't watch them, then they're going to have to take 'em off the air.

**G:** We need to "shut 'em down," like Public Enemy says.

A lot of people say, "What's the use in boycotting; if we don't give them another dime, they're still rich." True, they're rich now, but they have mansions and Rolls-Royces, and stuff that they have to pay for, so when you cut them off, they can't continue to live like that. We have had a lot of millionaires that have gone broke.

**Q:** Talk about how alcohol affects the Black community, and how it affected you?

**G:** Personally, I can honestly say that if I had never drank, I would have never went to jail. Drinking has gotten me in so much trouble, man, I mean terrible trouble. I did terrible things when I was on alcohol, things that I wouldn't have done if I was just on a natural high like I am now. I know there are millions of other brothers that can relate to the same thing. That liquor has hurt us more than drugs have. Believe me, that liquor is the "king" drug. Alcohol is the king drug in the neighborhood. Everything comes after that.

**S:** That's why they have so many liquor stores in the Black community, because we're already oppressed and stressed out, so in order to relieve ourselves we're going to reach for something. They have the drugs here, they have the guns here, and they have the alcohol here. Alcohol is much easier to get than anything else, as far as expenses, and alcohol will eventually lead you to the rest of the drugs.

**G:** I remember once when me and my wife went into Beverly Hills, we were trying to get some liquor, and we went from store to store, and they didn't even sell liquor. They had mellow wine, and some beer, but you couldn't find liquor. The alcohol is in that circle. You can't get St. Ides or Old English 800 up in Beverly Hills, or neighborhoods like that. They don't even know what you're talking about.

**S:** In Kentucky they have "dry counties" and "wet counties," where you can't even buy liquor in the county, you have to totally leave the county in order to get liquor. Even down in Arizona, there are certain counties where you can't buy liquor, but here in the Black community you can get it on almost every corner. Children can actually go in the store and buy liquor. I remember when I was a small child, I went and bought six-packs of beer for my grandmother like it wasn't nothing. I wasn't asked for ID or anything, and I wasn't more than twelve years old.

**Q:** Any further words on how we can bring about this positive change?

**G:** Really, the Black woman needs to push the forgiveness to her Black brother, because coming from a Black sister, he will listen. It hits the right spot coming from their women or their sister, more than if I tell them. So keep pushing that forgiveness, Black sister, and it will make a more peaceful Black community.

To the OGs, you have to come out. You have to come out of your comfort zone. I know you've been through all kinds of trials and tribulations, but we have to help these young brothers to come out the same way we did and prevent the other ones from having to even start going that way.

To the youngsters, just stay away from the gangs, don't even get in a gang, you don't have to even go that way. You don't need gangs for protection for the family thing. There are other organizations that are more positive that you can reach out to and get that same family thing from, without going out and killing each other. I'm talking about the ones that have never been in it. The ones that are already in it can keep it, keep the Blood and Cuz, keep that family thing, keep that unity, but just make it positive.

**S:** Instead of keeping the Blood and Cuz, I think they need to make it something more unified. If you have it where they are all unified under one group with a totally different name, that would eliminate the division.

**G:** I believe they can get to that point to where they probably could give the names up and take on another name as one. I think that will be coming. Anytime you get notorious gangs like the Grape Streets, the Bounty Hunters, the PJs, and all of them to come to peace, it's coming close to where they can come to one name. Watts is not as big as South Central, but they're just as notorious, or more. So if you can get those brothers to not fight for over a year, then we can do anything.

***Police in our community couldn't possibly be there to protect our property, because we own no property. They couldn't possibly be there to see that we received due process of law, for the simple reason that the police themselves deny us the due process of law. So it's very apparent that the police are only in our community not for our security, but for the security of the business owners in the community, and also to see that the status quo is kept intact.***

**—Huey P. Newton, Black Panther Party**

## SHOUT OUTS

Big shout outs to:

Al Dog , Alexis Goudeau, Ant Dog, Bartender, Big Bubba, Big Country, Big Dennis, Big Shot Butch, Big Smokey, Black Joe, Bobby Seale, Brandi Alvarez, Bubba Davis, Buckwheat, Busy Lizzie Martin, Cadillac Bob, Camille Alvarez, CoCo Demers, CoCo, Connie Young, Damieon Long, Daryl Alvarez, Dawayne Preston, DeAngel Alvarez, Del Alvarez, Denette Martin Johnson, Eddie Watson, Essie Johnson Haywood, Fat Daddy—Lloyd, Francis Williams, Fright, Frog, George Jackson, George

Williams, Geronimo Pratt (Freedom Fighter), Hilda, H. Rap Brown, Huey P. Newton, James Sanders, Jehovah's Witnesses (for preaching, Good News of Peace), Jerry, Jewel Williams, Jimmy Celestine, Jimmy Williams, Johnnie Martin (Pops), Jon Lockett, Keisha Jordan, Keshone—K.B., Little Country, Little Johnnie, Little Rob, Louis Lovely, Lynn Lockett, Makeitha Christon Sr., Makeitha Christon Jr., Margaret, Mark Gallen, Marquis Gains, Mary E. Williams, Mary McClain (Mama), M.C. McClain, Michael Grundy, Michael Williams, Michael Young, Michelle Alvarez, Mike Mike, Mitchell Williams, Monique Alvarez, Nat Turner, Ne Ne Goudeau, Paul Lockett, Peabody, Rainbow, Redd, Richard Williams, Ricky Jacob, Sampson Cunningham, Shawn Williams, Sheila Alvarez, Sheila Foster, Shirley Alvarez, Stokely Carmichael, Sugarbear, Swig, Terry Goudeau, Tom, Tremell Parker Alvarez, Vassa Jones, Vernon Hickingbottom, Virgil Davis, the Wallace Family, Walter Chamberlain, Wanda, Wibburn, Willie Blu, Yvette Cunningham.

All Other Families
All Other Friends

Authors' note: To our brother—General Robert Lee, in these words you live forever and we pray that through your words here in this book that your dream will become a reality in helping to SAVE some of these lives out here, and to change some of these lives for the positive. We really, really wanted you to see this finished book get released. This book and this work will hold your memory for always.

Live on, Black man! ALLAH-U-AKBAR!

Photo by Orpheus

# GODFATHER JIMEL BARNES

*(Along with my homeboy Raymond Washington (RIP), I am one of the Godfathers of the organization known as the Crips. My purpose for speaking the words that you are about to read, and telling the history of the Crips and the Bloods as I know it to be, is because I want to see the day when the Bloods and the Crips come back together. I'm a very spiritual and personal individual, and I don't like the idea of babies, children, and senior citizens getting hurt. So read these words and think about what I'm saying, because our unity will bring about a universal change.)*

**Q:** When you describe yourself as a Godfather, what does that mean to you?

**J:** When I say the "Godfather," that means the person that started the gangs. When Raymond Washington came to me and made that walk up Avalon Boulevard to Avalon Gardens from his house and said, "Jimel, I'm going to create a gang called the Crips," that was the two Godfathers. That was the beginning of the Crips. There were a lot of gangs before the Crips. There was the Slausons, the Businessmen, the Spook Hunters, the Avenues, and then later you had the Brims. What made the Crips so unique and stand out is that day when Raymond Washington wrote *Crips* on the wall, and he told me, "Check this out, Cuz, Crips will never die, they'll multiply. One day you will see, from generation to generation the Crips will be worldwide." I looked at Raymond and thought he was lying. I thought that the Crips would just die out like the Businessmen, the Slausons, the Gladiators, and other gangs. It seemed like he had a vision, so from that day he was the negative, and I was the positive.

**Q:** Explain what you mean by he was the negative and you were the positive?

**J:** Raymond had so much power over the youth, and Black people, it was incredible. He loved the power, but he used all the power to become negative. He liked me and respected me, because he knew that I was a positive person with power. So he used to come to me with the negative and see if I agreed with it. What he was speaking on when we created the Crips would eventually start killing up Black people. That's what I saw when he spoke this and wrote *Crips* on the wall. That had to be in '68.

**Q:** What did the name Crips mean?

**J:** When he came over to me, he pulled out a picture of a baby's crib; he said, "This is what I'm going to call our gang, Crips—like Cribs. It's from the cradle to the grave, C-RIP, may you rest in peace. Chitty chitty bang bang, nothing but a Crip thang, Eastside Cuz. This is going to be the most notorious gang in the world. It's going to go from generation to generation." I looked at him; I was stunned, because he seemed so happy and so delighted, like he had found the mothership. Raymond always wanted his place in gang history.

**Q:** What was your vision when he said that to you?

**J:** I looked at both sides. I thought we would just go out and take some leather coats, get in some fights for six to nine months, and that would be it. There was something inside of me saying, "Let this gang go, because it will die out in nine months just like the other gangs." So for six to nine months we got into some fights and took some leather coats. We had a macho thing going on.

**Q:** What positive did you see as possibly coming out of the gang?

**J:** On the positive side I felt we would be able to unite the youngsters and get all the brothers to come together and get more into a positive Black situation. I wanted to get the youngsters involved in sports: football, boxing, things like that. I saw a positive and a negative aspect. I had both thoughts going at the same time. At that time I was a guy who wanted to play professional football and be a heavyweight champion. When I was confronted with this, I was stunned.

**Q:** When did the gang violence start to escalate into gunplay?

**J:** In the beginning it was more of a macho thing: fighting, taking leather coats. Raymond went out recruiting from different areas in L.A. and Compton; Mack Thomas, Ecky, No. 1, Batman, Mad Bull, Mad Dog. Then he went back through Compton and recruited Pudding and Tam. Then it seemed like the police infiltrated us with guns. That's when all of the killing started, when the guns started.

**Q:** Back then, what was it that attracted young people to gangs, and even today, what is it that attracts young people to gangs?

**J:** I believe what attracted people to gangs when Raymond first started the Crips was that everybody wanted to identify. A lot of youngsters don't get love at home from their parents, so they go out in the streets or go to the gang and look for love, and get that bonding.

Later on after Raymond passed away, I wanted a twin brother, I wanted somebody to replace Raymond, so I went out and found this guy named Tookie and built him up from a little small guy to be a gladiator like me. From the day that I met Tookie we started going to every concert. The Parliament concert where there was one hundred thousand people, Tookie and Jimel was there, we were there together. "Those are Crips, that's the way a Crip looks." We would bully police, move people out the way. So kids saw us and they could identify with that. We went on from concert to concert, stars to stars, east side to west side, Carson, Compton. All you heard was, "Tookie and Jimel, two buff Crips. They look like gladiators." Women would just go crazy over seeing our bodies. I believe that's what really glamorized it and glorified it, because when Raymond went out, we went everywhere parading around, flexing muscles, all through Compton, everywhere. So rappers saw that, kids saw that when they was with their mothers, they saw how we wore our clothes, how we talked.

**Q:** What was your dress code like?

**J:** Raymond had the beige khakis, with the blue croakasacks, and a beanie. I'm the one who brought the overalls in. Long hair, long earrings, plaid shirts, we were clean. We had a whole wardrobe of that.

**Q:** So with the Crips having started as one unified body, how did all the different sets start to form and how did the division come in?

**J:** I believe that the root to all of that is the system, and the genocide on Black people. I believe that the Crips and the Bloods, and the young generation, are the smartest and most talented beings of the century, but they don't realize that. It comes from how the rappers—Ice-T, Ice Cube, Dr. Dre, and all of them—are so talented. I believe that they are the cream of the crop, and before the cream of the crop can unify together, they divide you and conquer you.

**Q:** What are some of the tactics that you've seen used to divide and conquer, and how do we counterattack that?

**J:** First of all, since it first started, everybody has gained their titles of Godfather, OGs, Gs, which means a lot to the young people, so therefore I think everybody that has power in their different communities should get together and start showing each other love. Show each other love by sharing, hooking each other up, sharing money, and showing these youngsters that we can get along. There has got to be a group of older OGs that get together and show these youngsters that they can work together. For instance, I heard recently about Jesse Jackson, Minister Farrakhan, Maxine Waters, and the other people that are older than us are coming together in unity, when they used to didn't get along. So therefore in order to be a role model you have to practice what you preach. Love is the key. Everybody should get together and show love. Then start showing each other that we can share money and help each other. That's originally what a person got into the gangs for. To share and to show that love and that unity.

I was the guy that if you got pass Raymond, you couldn't whip me. I was the guy backing up Tookie. Raymond and I had a lot of love for each other. Remember what he said, "One day you will see, Jimel, this gang is going to be the biggest gang in the world. It's going to be famous all around the world. You will see."

A lot of people are mad at me now, all I've been hearing lately is, "Jimel has never gone to the pen." Well, Jimel never went to the pen because God made it to where I kept beating the system. It's not about going to jail. The parents, the mothers, along with the gang members and the churches, have to get involved and work to re-educate themselves, the youngsters, and each other. It's not about who killed the most people. Killing somebody doesn't mean that you have a reputation. It's about respect.

I just went to jail over some traffic tickets. I didn't have any problem with the Bloods that were in there; they respect their elders. That's what we have to get back to. Raymond, as notorious as he was, he respected people's wives, mothers, and families. So if he was after you, and if you were around your mother or your people the rest of your life, he never would have said anything to you. So it's about respect and love. That's basically what I think has to happen. We have to get back to that respect.

**Q:** How does that process take place?

**J:** I think we have to go to them, to the youngsters, because that's how the gangs were started in the beginning, we went to the youngsters to recruit the gangs, so we have to go to them again. When I go to youngsters, and they're gang bangers, and I start talking about doing something positive, they listen. I believe you have to go to them, take the initiative, and take charge over the situation.

**Q:** What do you say to the youngsters now who are active in gang-banging?

**J:** I can only say something that's positive. When I go to youngsters, I say to them, "I have a lot of love for you, and I respect what you're doing, but it's not about that anymore. It's about trying to do something positive, and coming back to Black. You have somebody right here who will help you to the end. When I get some, you will get some. With you and me working together we can get some. So you go out and get your other li'l homiez and come in with me, and we'll all do this together. Either we'll make it together, or we'll starve together." You don't ever have to worry about Jimel Barnes, the Godfather OG, because I've never crossed a Crip or a Blood. I've been straight up with everybody. I feel when you are straight up and real with everybody, no matter how long it takes, everything good will come back, because it's like a circle.

**Q:** Who are some of the positive influences in your life that helped you to stay positive?

**J:** The most positive person in my life . . . he worked with Mayor Tom Bradley for twenty years, his name is Lonnie Wilson. I used to take Raymond Washington to see Lonnie over on Eighty-fifth and Broadway, and he used to talk to Raymond and I. That man was like a father to me when I didn't have a father. He was one of the main ones that when I was on my way to the penitentiary, or on my way to the grave, he kept running down to City Hall, to get Chief Gates and the CRASH unit off of my case. They were going to straight kill me. So he was one of the most positive influences in my life, and right now he's still in my life. All of the pain and suffering that I'm going through right now, of being a Godfather, he's in my corner. So he's making ways and opening doors for me for the positive.

**Q:** Economics—when you talk to the younger brothers on the street, what do you say to them about economics?

**J:** South Central L.A. has a lot of money in the community. That's the reason why the Koreans and the Japanese are all over here running businesses and taking the money out of the community. So Black people that are in the community, along with the church people, and all of the celebrities that have come out of the community, they all have a responsibility to put something back into the community. They should stop blaming the White House, stop blaming the system for the conditions, because this is our town, our residence. We need to be accountable to ourselves for what's going on.

If every Black person that has something shows the love and gets with another Black person, and helps a young person, you will see a big difference. That goes all the way back to the beginning. Most young people say they are gang-banging because they don't have anything, and nobody is ever going to help them or give them anything. So therefore, "Why don't I just deal dope? Why don't I just do this or that?" It's a system, and it's steady turning.

Just recently I saw my son who's seventeen; I didn't even know I had this son, because he was hidden from me by one of my ex-girlfriends. My thoughts are in his head. So from the way I've been preaching about boxing for years, he's now talking about boxing. He wants to pursue the gold medal in the Olympics, and he's surrounded by gangs. His cousin is in a gang, and his best friend is in a gang. He doesn't want to join a gang, but he wants them to start making money too. This is the cycle repeating itself. So I've gotten with him, and I'm showing him how to get out of this system and make it, so he won't have to go through what I went through. Everybody is not able to make it out of the system, because it's too vicious, and too violent. He's thinking about boxing, and everybody else around him is thinking about killing.

The youngsters must realize something: if you kill somebody, that does not mean that you're tough. When you can deal hand to hand with a man, you whip him or you lose, and you respect the man and leave, that's making a man. That's what makes you hard. That's where the reputations came from. Raymond Washington could whip everybody there was. That was the message. *A man* can accept a whipping from another man. *A man* can ignore somebody trying to do something to him. A lot of youngsters don't realize the difference between a man and a teenager. A teenager will react to anything without thinking. *A man* will think before leaping and then decide. Life in this circle, in this world is about overlooking the dumb s— and striving for the positive. Nobody ever told me that. I figured it out by being on the street, and going through it. Being able to learn how to forgive.

**Q:** How do you deal with someone who says they lost one of their loved ones and it's hard for them to forgive?

**J:** I hear that all the time. I say to them, where does it end? He killed your brother, or he killed your uncle; where does it end? It has to end somewhere, or there won't be any Black families left. The Black male is disappearing at a rapid rate. Either they're incarcerated, smoked out, or dead. It has to end now, you have to grow up and recognize that.

I forgave the person that shot me before the peace treaty, way before Amer-I-CAN, way before any program. God told me to forgive them, because God told me that if I didn't forgive this man and let him leave with his life, I would be cursed, and not blessed. Life is based on pain, forgiveness, and striving for your goal, those three things. So you have to make up your mind on what you want to be the best at. It's easy to kill somebody, but it's harder to overlook what they've done to you, shake his hand, and show love. I think the new generation, the new banger, can do that, because I've seen it done. I've seen it happen with the peace treaty, I've seen it happen in Watts, I've seen it happen with a lot of people.

**Q:** What role did you play in the peace going on in Watts and in parts of South Central L.A.?

**J:** I used to help through Jim Brown's program, the Amer-I-CAN Program. I would come and speak to the brothers about the history and tell them that they can all get along. I'm here for South Central Love, Hands Across Watts, wherever I can be used.

**Q:** What can be done to increase the peace in more neighborhoods, and in other states?

**J:** Getting those who are at war, getting both sides together, and starting communication between them.

**Q:** What happens when you get two sides together that have been warring for a long time; what is that experience like?

**J:** There's a lot of tension at first, but when they find out that each other left their guns at home, then they mellow out and be themselves. You must remember something, we are all from the same gang. We used to all get along with Pirus. Crips, Bloods, all of us got along, and got along for a long time. It seems to me now that more of the Bloods are trying to get with the peace than the Crips.

**Q:** Why do you think that is?

**J:** From talking to the Bloods, their Gs put it down to the young, that you respect your elders, you respect this person. They did a hell of a job teaching that from generation to generation. It's locked in. They show me love. Just like with Raymond, he has a daughter, I've been talking to her lately, she's fifteen, and they live in the projects, her and Raymond's ex-girlfriend. The whole projects are Bloods. They know she's Raymond's daughter, and every Blood in those projects respects her. They say, "Your daddy started the Crips, but we love you." That's deep, brother.

**Q:** What's the potential power when those two forces, the Bloods and the Crips, come together?

**J:** When those two come together, it's unlimited. They could deal with the system on any level, as far as being educated. *You have gang members that are brilliant. That's the cream of the crop. All they have to do is recognize that, get with each other, and get with the peace.* Once you forgive a person . . . I've been shot up and almost died. People are saying I didn't pay my dues—because they wasn't there. They were not there when I got shot at fifty times. When my windows were blown out, and I thought my head was off of my body. They wasn't there when I got shot up twenty times. They wasn't there when twenty redneck police beat me down—having shoot-outs with the police. They wasn't there, because they weren't born yet, because they're not OGs. All the things I did, I did early, thank God. They look at me—I'm forty years old, I don't drink or smoke, never got high in my life, I look like I'm twenty-five years old. They think I'm perpetrating. I'm not perpetrating, all that s— you see from Raymond, Tookie, the riots; the first riot, and the second riot, all of that is instilled in me. It's just that now I'm in control of it, I'm trying to do positive things with it, I'm trying to box. I'm doing everything positive, using what I have within myself to come up.

See, the youngsters don't realize that when the system gives you thirty-five years, or forty years to life with no possibility of parole, you become just a number. They move on to the next person. If you're twenty now, you look up and you're fifty years old, locked up almost all your life—you're history. All you're going to do is end up downtown Los

Angeles, homeless. People will be laughing at you, talking about, "That used to be the homie that held down the set."

What hurts the system is when you're making money, being successful, taking care of your families, bringing up your kids. That's the key. That's what life is all about.

**Q:** What do you say to young brothers that say they want to change? What is their first step?

**J:** The right type of program can really help a youngster. They need somebody older—it gets back to the Gs, you have to get with somebody older that's positive, somebody that has been where you are at now. You have to respect your elders, then get back with them and listen to them. What a lot of youngsters don't understand is that even though I'm a Godfather, a notorious ex–gang banger, I listen to older people. I listen to people that are fifty, sixty, seventy years old. I just recently listened to Milton Berle about some things, and he's eighty something. So as I listen, I get longer life and slowly come up. The key is listening. I listen well, and I respect people.

**Q:** Talk about the importance of developing the spiritual side.

**J:** That's one of the things that I work at perfecting, seeing what people are going to do before they do it. I can feel people, the way they're thinking. A lot of people have homiez, but you have to learn how to feel your homiez, feel what's real, and what's not real, especially in South Central L.A. This town is the most dangerous town in the world. I say that because you can know a person fifteen to twenty years, have eaten with him, stayed with him, know his whole family, and all of a sudden somebody will give him some money, and he will sell you out. So you have to feel, when you're talking to somebody, you have to feel the vibes of where they're coming from. Some people give positive vibes, others give negative vibes. You have to go with the positive and don't go with the negative, or you'll get "crossed out," like Kris Kross says.

In California you have very few people who are real, you have people that are not real, and then you have people that are totally scandalous. People out here don't come directly at you. If they don't like you, they come around the bin in another way to let you know. They can come at you, and say for instance they give you $10,000, and any person would think that's a friend, but not me, the Double OG knows that you're just giving me that because you want me to go the wrong route, you don't want me to find the pot of gold. That's a cold method that's being used. He's trying to take you out, but he's trying to do it in an L.A. kindness method.

My grandmother used to take me to church all the time. I was in church all my life. They don't understand that I believe in God right now. Back when I was with Raymond, and then with Tookie, a little angel used to come into my head and say, "You're going to be here, and nobody is going to be there, because you believe in God." Don't go out and do stupid things for no apparent reason. It's a spiritual thing, which I even believe that the whole thing with the Crips and the Bloods is a spiritual thing.

**Q:** What do you think makes it spiritual?

**J:** Crips and Bloods, Black parents, and Black people in general have gone through so much, it's like a testimony of strength. Only the strong will survive, so therefore I feel that it's all connected. There was a reason why Raymond said this gang was going to be so big, and so notorious. He saw something and felt something. I felt something. Every day of my life I felt something. So nobody can tell me that I haven't paid my dues. They don't know what dues were paid, because they're not an OG, they're not a Godfather, and they're not original. All of the originals are dead or smoked out or buried or locked down for life.

Sometimes when I'm riding home late at night, I say, "God, why did you just leave me here? Why haven't I ever been to the pen? Why didn't you make me just start killing people?" Then it comes to me, it gets back to, "We want you to be the example. We want you to be the positive person, because from you the kids will be able to see that you can suffer, take pain, and eventually come up. You owe them." It's not a self thing, it's a universal thing now. I'm representing a university now. When I was in jail last week for some traffic tickets, youngsters from the Bloods and the Crips were all coming to me, because they can feel the love, and the realness. I believe that the key for gang-banging to cease is to go back to the beginning. People have to start showing that love, because the young people can see straight through you if you're phony, they can read you and feel you. Even with my children that are ten and nine, I'm teaching them how to read and feel people. That was the main topic with my son this weekend, about his homiez. He's trying to become a gold medalist, and people are going to start tripping on him. So get ready and be willing to sacrifice, and let certain people go, in order to better your life. You have to surround yourself not only with Crips, but with Bloods too. It's very important, because when you can learn how to deal with both sides, it makes you a greater person.

The bottom line is that greed and money will kill you. I can share with my brothers. Most people don't do that. They're just about self. Self—that's it. When you're Black, it's not about just you, it's about us in this system.

**Q:** How would you say you've been treated by the system?

**J:** I was treated by Daryl Gates, CRASH, all of them, just like I wasn't human. They would pull me over and say, "We're going to play this game." They'd pull a throwaway gun out of their boot, put a bullet in the chamber, and say, "Watch this." Put it to my head and burn the trigger. I was young, I wasn't scared of anything, but they were trying to kill me, intimidate me. Then they used to grab some of my homiez and take them from a Crip hood and put them in a Blood hood and leave them there with all blue on. They would take a Blood over to a Crip hood and leave him. They were like instigators of making the madness grow. Recently it has gotten out of hand, that's why everybody is scared now. As long as it was in South Central, it was cool. Now it's everywhere, like Raymond said: "Crips don't die, they multiply, Cuz, you'll see, Cuz, all over the world, Cuz, one day you will see, Cuz. Eastside Cuz. From the cradle to the grave may you rest in peace."

**Q:** What are some of the solutions to get the gang members to come to peace and to realize they're not the real enemy to each other?

**J:** I think that books and movies will help, but they have to be done right. There are a lot of other books coming out right now, and all they're talking about is who killed who, and just negative, nothing positive. You have movies coming out and all they're talking about is negative. We need to see movies with positive thoughts. Parents, movies, and books like this can play an important role, then the schools and the churches, in that order. Also rappers, the rappers owe gangs a lot, because they're making a fortune off of the images, and now it's time to come back. So when you rap, you can rap about something positive. From what I hear, the record company makes them go negative. [To the rappers] Once you get in and make you some money, you should be bigger than that. Start studying how to form your own record companies, to do our own thing, to distribute our own music. It gets back to the love, and the sharing.

**Q:** What's your vision for the future?

**J:** I see the brothers showing love and affection for one another. I see Tookie and all of us getting back together and showing the love and affection like it's supposed to be. Getting back with these young people and guiding them in a positive direction, into a powerful, positive Black entity that can go worldwide.

**Q:** Any further words that you may want to say?

**J:** To the parents; I want to focus on the parents. The females and the males—the females are going to have to stop taking their children and trying to use the children to get back at their men. Just like the men are going to have to stop doing that with the women. They are going to have to start playing a strong—like in the old school—positive role in their families' lives. It gets back to family. The family is going to have to get back strong like it used to be. If that happens, you'll see a dramatic change, because back in the old days, your grandma or granddaddy wouldn't have let you be around here gang-banging. The next-door neighbor wouldn't have let you be out here gang-banging. The parents and the older people are going to have to stop being scared of the younger people. They brought them in here, they're going to have to recognize that, and they're going to have to deal with them. If that happens, we will see a great, great change in the young people. What the young people are looking for is some direction, and some love. Every day of my life I try to give a youngster love and guidance on a positive tip. No matter how people come at me, I still come positive with them. I feel that makes you stronger and greater. That's what I see for the future, with all this talent coming together, getting Black, and coming together on a worldwide scale.

> ***. . . there will be a Universal Change. . . . Showing a blue star beside a red star means removal of a world that doesn't correspond with the Original World.***
>
> **—Honorable Elijah Muhammad**

## SHOUT OUTS

I want to send a special shout out to Lonnie Wilson for being there for me and Raymond, and for keeping me from going to the pen. Also to Raymond Washington (RIP) and his family.

To all the Crips and Bloods, wherever you are in the world, it's time to stop the fighting, connect, get with one another, and get back to Black. That's coming from an Original Godfather. Peace!

Photo by Orpheus

# BRUNO

*(For those of you who are unfamiliar with my existence, my name is Curtis. A lot of people know me by Bruno or Big Man. At one point in my life I was heavily engaged in gang activities. When I first involved myself in these activities, I was under the pretense that it was cool and the thing to do. However, after damn near losing my life to gunshots from head to toe, and to the prison system, I've realized that the gang trade is a waste of life. I say this because from experience I've learned that there are only two things that will come out of the gang scene: (1) death, and (2) a life sentence for taking someone else's life. Either way, you're assed out. So definitely take heed to the contents of this book. Stand tall and remain solid!)*

**Q:** How did you first become involved with gangs?

**B:** Basically, I became a product of the environment. I grew up out there in the streets, that's all I knew. That's what I grew up with. It just happened to be the Brims that I joined. The set I'm from is the Brims, which are Bloods. By the time it got to me it was broken up into various sets. It wasn't the L.A. Brims anymore. It was the Six-Deuce Brims, Six-Four Brims, Five-Nine Brims. I fell into the Six-Four Brims first, then with the park being right there on Sixty-second Street, which is where all the Brims hung out, we decided to go ahead and make it one set, the Six-Deuce Brims. The Six-Deuce Brims were already a set, but we also had Six-Four and Five-Nine, so we all came together as one.

**Q:** What attracted you to go that way? You could have gone other ways, right?

**B:** That's right. That's true. That is something I've tripped on in the past. While doing time, I used to kick back and reminisce and ask myself that same question. What I always come up with, is instead of me kicking it with the fellas that were playing basketball, and running track, I chose to run up and down the alleys with BB guns, shooting at pigeons. Then the BB guns turned into pistols, which made things escalate. We had clubhouses, and that led to hanging out at the park, and shooting dice.

I was watching the older brothers too, like Robert Lee and them. Those are my OGs. They're considered Triple OGs. I was young, and I just fell right into it. Plus a lot of them used to hang out at my pad, because I have some sisters that are older than me, and they were little cuties, and the fellas were right up in their age, so a lot of the G homiez used to come over to my house and kick it with my sisters. That's how I got started so early.

**Q:** How early did you start?

**B:** I was about ten years old when I started hanging with the fellas. That is when they started to let me roll with them. They'd throw me in their little Chevys, and we'd hit the corners.

I looked at them dudes as being tough. I think that was what attracted me. I saw coolness. Nobody would mess with them, they were like the leaders of the neighborhood. They were looked up to, so I went that way.

The other dudes that weren't hanging around us were playing ball, and we looked at them as punks, as hooks. Back then we used to call them hooks. So the way I went was the way I thought was more down, more in, which really it wasn't, but I didn't realize that until way later on in the game, until years later.

**Q:** Were there any positive things that you were being taught by the Gs at that young age?

**B:** No. Honestly speaking, no. They gave me weed. They took me with them to steal. I can't remember any of them even telling me to go to school. As a matter of fact, those dudes would be ditching school and throw me on the handlebars of the bike, to take me up to Manual Arts H.S. with them. I was only in the fourth or fifth grade at that time. So I can't say that those were positive things.

**Q:** At that young age what part did you play in the set?

**B:** There is one positive thing I can say about my older homeboys from the Brims: they didn't ever try to take advantage of me. Today you have a lot of older dudes that are still in that life, and they get those younger dudes and try to make them sell dope for them, make them break into houses, make them do different things. My older homeboys never did that to me. They never tried to take advantage of me. My role with them was that I was just a young homie, and I was there. They just had me with them. They never tried to push me into somebody's house, even though they probably could have, because I was looking up to them, and I was hanging around them. I wanted to be around them, and they were embracing me. I compare what goes on today with back then and what went on with me and my big homiez. Everything I did was because I wanted to do it. They basically took care of me.

**Q:** What made you realize that wasn't the way to go?

**B:** Time. Doing time. I didn't realize until afterwards. I was stuck in the penitentiary with eighteen years. That's when my eyes started opening. Then my moms passed, and my eyes really started opening. I started righteously, truly realizing that I had basically messed up. I went the wrong route. Plus, when I got to Folsom, a straight level-4 pen, I was in new Folsom, B facility, which was supposed to be the hardest line in the system, until they opened Pelican Bay.

When you're climbing their ladder, they have level-1, level-2, level-3, and level-4 prisons. Level 4 is the highest. I started out at level 3, and then I worked my way up to Folsom, which was supposed to be the hardest line.

All before I got to Folsom I was gang-banging, fighting Crips. Then as soon as I got to the Folsom line, all the OG homiez, the Muslims, and everybody was saying, "We don't gang-bang here." So at Folsom I had to role and kick it with the Crips. I had to walk the track and kick it with the Crips, because my people had told me, "We don't gang-bang here. Up here it's all about fighting white boys, and the Mexicans. So we need each other."

I go to my cell, and I kick back, and I say, "Damn, this really doesn't make any sense." We have all these young brothers messing their lives up, catching life sentences behind killing each other, and then when we get to the pen, and get to the top level—you can't go any further than a level 4—you get to the top level of the pen, and your people tell you, "You can't gang-bang here. If you gang-bang here, you're going to be causing problems for all of us here." When a Blood goes and disrespects a Crip, the Crip is going to come back to the rest of the Bloods and say, "Your homeboy is tripping." "What is it about?" "We don't know what he's tripping about. He's gang-banging." We'll pull him and say, "Look, homeboy, we're not doing that here." Nothing is personal really, everything is a collective. That's if you're cliqued up. If you're a loner, then you handle your business. If you're a Blood, then what you do reflects on all of us, so we won't let you trip, because some of us have dates to get out, and a war at level-4 pen is a war. That's straight war.

**Q:** How did that make you feel being in the street all that time and feeling the Crips were your enemies, and then when you get there to the level-4 pen, you realize that's your brother?

**B:** I had a reputation for doing whatever needed to be done, as far as in the banging field, so it was first brought to me as soon as I hit that line. My homeboys immediately pulled me, we walked the track, and they said, "Bruno, it's like this here, we're not tripping up here. It's off-and-on war with these Mexicans and white boys; we don't have time to be fighting each other." I understood it, but it also kind of f'd me up. I understood it though, and from then on it stuck with me.

I felt real good that I didn't get a life sentence, because I was up against life. They were trying to convict me on a first-degree murder, but I got it down. At that point I started feeling real good, and thanking God that I didn't get a life sentence, because immediately I started saying, "Damn, it really doesn't make any sense now." I was locked up for a gang-related murder, and my own homiez tell me no gang-banging anymore. All that time I was out on the streets, getting shot, shooting people, going through all these changes—let's just say I would have gotten a life sentence, then I'd get to Folsom, and my homeboys would tell me that I can't fight the Crips. "What do you mean I can't fight the Crips? I just got a life sentence behind a Crip. My whole life is messed up."

**Q:** What would you say to the homiez that are out here now who feel the same way you felt when you first went to Folsom? How do we get the young homiez to understand what you learned in there, without them having to get locked up themselves?

**B:** That's a good question. Let me tell you something that I learned from when I was in the pen. Do you remember when the Uprising broke out? I was in the pen when that happened. They started talking about the peace, so I kicked the issue in the pen I was in. As far as a peace treaty, they said, "Okay, peace." I was happy, but I learned that a lot of those youngsters are straight up into banging, they're too deep into it. This is what I started feeling from dealing with them. This is my experience with them, because I was pushing the line, and I had a certain percentage over here saying, "Yeah, we're down with the peace," then there was a certain percentage over there who wasn't down with it.

I came to the conclusion, after trying to talk and talk to them, that they just really didn't understand what the Uprisings were all about. They didn't understand, because if they would have understood, they would have been game for the peace treaty. They just wanted to impress each other, and I found that there was a few who there just wasn't any getting through to. I thought about how we could put the law down, as far as to stop the gang-banging.

What I came up with is that it will have to come from the penitentiary, with cooperation from all the Gs in the pens that are pushing the lines. We would have to get some kind of media coverage, to put the word out to the young homiez that are banging, and tell them, "If you come up in here behind a gang-related murder, *we* are going to deal with you in here." Everybody has to be solid, and stick to that. We know when you're coming, we already know what's going on in the streets. So me being a Brim, I get with all the Brims in the pen, and we push the line with all the Brims. We deal with our own though, to keep the conflict down. All the Crip sets deal with their own. We already have Gs from every set on the streets in the pen. So we have to get with all the penitentiaries just about. We have to get cooperation from the Gs in the pen, to put the law down here on the streets, and it will travel.

So if the Brims on the street know that if you go kill a Crip, which is a Black brother, if you go kill another Black brother, behind gang-banging, regardless to where he's from, and you come to the pen, the Brims are going to deal with you. Who are you going to run to now? You're going to think about that. If you're a Brim, and you're not going to be accepted by the Brims when you go to the pen, that's deep. They'll think about that. That's where I think it has to come from. The Uprisings did some good though, that simmered a lot of things down, but you still have some tripping. The Uprisings put a dent, it did some good. That's where I'm comin' from.

I used to kick back and watch all of these talk shows, with all these youngsters out here talking about a truce, and I already knew right then that it was not going to happen like that because we all basically know of each other. We know something about each other, or about each other's hood. Some of these dudes that were going on the talk shows, with all red on, talking about, "Yeah, we're going to have a peace treaty," we never heard of them. When I went out on the yard, all the homeboys that I know have put in work, with life sentences, twenty years, ten years, in and out of the pen. In the heart of their hoods they have put work in, and none of us even knew those dudes on the talk shows. So everybody was wondering who they were. Who do they think they are? Just on that alone, others were rebelling against what they were saying, because it's like, "How is he going to call a truce? Nobody knows him. F that." Then they'd go the other way. That's what I watched. With that, I knew it wasn't going to happen like that. I used to just observe and check it out. I was for the peace treaty, because I started realizing that banging is not about anything, it's not right, it's genocide. That's all it is. That's why it's so messed up out here today.

I've been home about three months from an eight-year bid, and it's all messed up out here. All the brothers, the solid, true brothers, are gone. I run into a handful at each spot. Before I left, we had them out here. Brothers were out here doing it. They were out here standing tall. Over the years they have fallen. That's what I'm seeing.

**Q:** What do you think it is that makes them fall like that?

**B:** I know those drugs are powerful. That's what has most of them, those drugs. They are tore up. Everywhere I go they're panhandling. Some of them are in the gas stations pumping gas.

**Q:** What do you say to them when you see them?

**B:** I talk to them. I say positive things to them. I try to get them to leave the dope alone and get right. I tell them that they're better than that. I shoot positive words at them all the time. I let them pump my gas, and I give them money. I let them wash my car, and I give them a couple of dollars and shoot some positive words at them and go on about my business. I know the drugs are powerful. That's about all I can do, is get at them and keep rolling. Now, if I had the money, and the space to pull them, to try to rehabilitate them in my own way, I would do it, but I don't have that. So all I can do is deal with it, because it hurts.

**Q:** What type of economic alternatives do you see for brothers that are out there selling dope?

**B:** I haven't really been pushing this issue on the homiez too hard, but I've been pushing it on the sisters pretty hard. Some people say it's hard, but it's really not that hard. Self-discipline; go and learn something. I'm not going to ever tell a brother not to get his money, it's just a shame that we have to sell it to each other. Sell it to white folks, sell it to somebody else, whatever you do, just get your ends, take your money, and use your head. Take your money and go enroll in a school or apply for a grant. There's a whole lot of things you can do. Take the little rock money and go to school and learn something.

Learn something first, because you're going to need to know something before you open up a business. You can't just open up a business and not know anything about it. So whatever you choose to get off into, just go to school and learn about it. Get whatever paperwork is necessary to keep the system off of your back, then go ahead and handle your business.

**Q:** What have you learned about this system that we're living in?

**B:** I think they're some cold mf's. They don't give a damn about us, and they're only going to let us get so far in life. Regardless to how much money or education you have. You can get far enough only to be comfortable. They'll let you get far enough to be comfortable, but that's it. They don't let you go any farther than what they want you to go. I think they're full of s—. They've been taking from us all the time, and they're still taking from us. I'm talking about countries. You see what's going on over there in Africa, in Haiti, and in Somalia. They even put an American flag up over there. That is not America's country, that's their country; leave them alone, and let them live like they choose to live. That's the same thing they did way back in the day. You know the story, they took this land from the Indians. They're still doing it. That's what they're doing over there now, taking s—. It's just more modernized. They're a little more cool about it, and they're good at making it look like it's right. *Deceit.* How are you going to kill somebody to help them? Not fight them, they're killing them.

**Q:** What are some ways we can counterattack what we're up against?

**B:** Come together. That's the only way. We have to come together, we need some self-discipline.

**Q:** What made you become more disciplined? What was your process like?

**B:** In the jailhouse I started reading and talking to some of the older brothers. I read a lot of Black literature. I read some of Elijah Muhammad's literature, *Message to the Black Man;* I got a lot out of that. I kicked it with a lot of brothers that had been locked down for a while. I'm talking about eighteen, nineteen years. I did a lot of time in the hole too, at Pelican Bay. I had a celly, a brother named Grant. I think he had been down about fifteen years, and I used to straight kick it with him. I used to pay attention to the brother. The brother had knowledge. So that, with my own little common knowledge and common sense, made me start becoming aware. I started waking up.

**Q:** What are some of the things we need to develop that discipline?

**B:** One thing I can think of off the top is strength. Will power too, you have to have that. You need strength just to deal with life, period. Everyday life. To know what's good for you, and what's not. Especially when you become an adult. You don't have Mama watching over you, smacking your hand, telling you to put that down. I think will power and strength are important.

I think the family unit helps to keep you strong, when you have a family. Again, I'm going to go back to the pen on you. A lot of brothers in the pen that fall off, as far as their strength and doing the right thing, I think a lot of that comes from lack of family support. A lot of them will stress out and be quick to go after somebody that they've had a problem with. For a lot of them it's their own fault, because when they were out here they burned bridges. You know how that goes, they get on dope and start stealing from Mama, stealing from their brother. Then when they go to jail, their mama and brother are like, "You don't have anything coming."

Everybody needs some support when doing time, because you're doing time in a cell that's no bigger than five by seven feet. You have two beds, a toilet, and a sink in there. Then it's you and another brother in there, and y'all are just there. You get two hours a day on the yard, and you're right back in there. Every day mail is passed out, so those brothers that just watch the mailman go by—or if you and I are cellies, and I didn't burn bridges, so I get mail constantly, from my girl, my moms, whoever, after a while that will start to get to you. There will be some envy there. A little jealousy, and it can kind of stress you out. It depends on the type of person you are. You have some brothers that it doesn't faze. I've experienced brothers where it has fazed them, and you can see it in them. That will affect their attitude. They'll come out for breakfast mad. I may have just got some mail, pictures, or a money order. These dudes don't have any money. That plays a big role in a lot of the problems in the jailhouses. That causes a lot of stress, and a lot of distress in the jailhouses. Sometimes people will just wake up with an attitude, or at chow time, they will get dressed with an attitude. You won't know why they have an attitude, and they'll come out with that attitude, and anything is liable to happen. If they would get mail, they'd be happy. You get three or four letters from your baby, a few pictures, you'd be going to chow smiling at the fellas, "What's up, homie." That support and unity in the family is very important.

**Q:** What is the potential impact when the Bloods and the Crips realize that it's not about them being enemies, but the unity between them?

**B:** I see them all together socializing. I just think it will take a while before they honestly trust each other, before they honestly go in each other's neighborhoods and just be totally content, before we can start saving money and making plans. When the Uprisings jumped off, and they ran all the Koreans out, the only thing I fault us on is not rebuilding the community ourselves. I think the Uprisings were cool personally, it has done some good in a few ways. I'm just glad Rodney King had enough strength to endure and still be cool. I know he suffered pretty bad, but he's still living. I think it was good that the Uprising happened, and again, like I say, the only thing I fault us for is not rebuilding the community ourselves.

Some people say we shouldn't have burned down our own community. I think it was cool to get them out of here, because they come in here and get our money and take it back to the hills. So get them out of here. We have to rebuild it though and keep our money in our own community. If that was to happen, where all the brothers could get established, we could get together and start making plans. Then we'd probably get somewhere. That would be a good start right there. Basically what we need is to come together, where there would be worldwide peace.

It's not something we just want, it's something we need. It would be beautiful. It would have a great impact. I think people would be a lot stronger, because they would feel safer just being out. We're only scared of each other. I don't go in certain neighborhoods, only because of my own people. I'm not scared to go into a white neighborhood, that's straight up.

It's evident though, because the average Black family has sisters that are older, around my mom's age, in their fifties and sixties, and they're tired of what goes on in the ghettos, which is brothers stealing from brothers. Somebody snatches their purse, and then they want to leave. Where do they go? They all move out to Caucasian neighborhoods; Cucamonga, Diamond Bar, that's where everybody is cutting out to. Nobody is really scared of the white man physically. They mainly do you harm mentally.

**Q:** Break that down, the kind of damage that they do mentally?

**B:** They keep us down. They keep their feet on our necks. They keep us in a rut. They keep us poor. They keep us stressed out. They mislead us a lot. They teach us lies; you can see where they aren't putting the truth in the books in the schools. That's one of their tactics. They put lies in the books. They miseducate us.

They can't really teach us about ourselves, because they don't really know about us. They have their own perception of us. That's just like the saying, "A woman can't teach a man to be a man." She can teach what a woman expects of a man, but she can't teach a man how to be a man.

So therefore they just hook up their little books and only teach us what they want us to know. Through their TV and their movies they continue to portray us in a negative image, and a lot of us just suck it all up and stay down. We stay down from their teachings. They have some cold tactics, lots of them.

**Q:** What role do relationships play in strengthening the brothers and keeping them positive?

**B:** It plays a big role. I think it goes back to what we were saying a minute ago. Having that support when you're down. Your woman or your fiancée or your wife would play a big role in keeping you strong during that time. So I guess it's the same on the streets too; it should be.

I'm going to tell you what I think has a lot to do with our problems today. The dope. A lot of brothers have strong women behind them. A lot of brothers already have that, or had it, but they get ahold to these drugs, and alcohol, and they abuse the support their woman gives them. I think a lot of our sisters are strong; when they have a man who is taking care of business, they'll get behind you and support you. I think the majority of the sisters do that. I think the majority of the females are reflections of their men. If you're positive, and talking positive and taking care of business, then your woman will be positive and take care of business. If you're tripping, swaying, and grabbing dope, she's going to follow you, unless she's an extra-strong woman. That's the extra-strong women. That's just how I'm categorizing them, extra-strong women, that are able to cut you off if you're tripping. It takes strength to do that when they love you. I think a lot of brothers have strong women, because a lot of our Black sisters are strong already. They just need a strong Black man with them to keep them strong.

**Q:** What do you say to your younger homiez about some of the negative things they may be involved in?

**B:** I tell them about my experience in going to jail, and then being told by your own people that "you can't bang in here, which is what you were doing on the street." Which is something that causes you to lose your freedom for the duration of your life.

**Q:** How do they respond when you tell them that?

**B:** They think about it. I've gone to them, and they tell me that they think about it. When I first got out, I went over to my relatives' house. I have some relatives that are Crips, they were out there with their blue rags, they was kickin' it, but they have big love and respect. I've heard of fellas who have opposing gangs in their family, and they let the gangs come between them. One may be a Crip, and the other is a Blood, and they trip on each other. That's one thing me and my family never did. I have a couple of relatives that are Crips, but we have straight love for

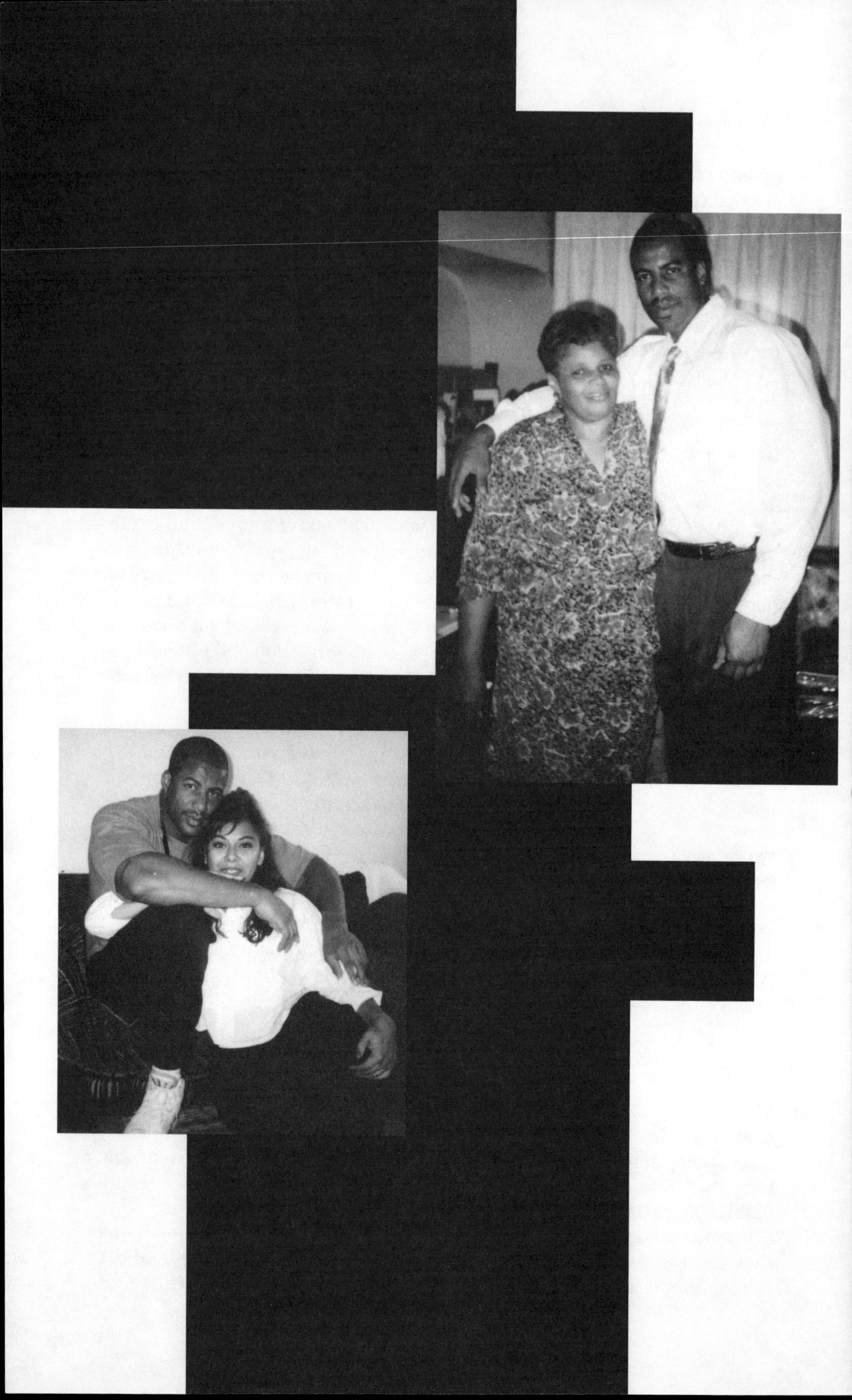

each other. We have that family love, and we never let that come between us. I went over there and kicked it to them, and I shot that right at 'em, and one of them pulled me to the back and said, "You know what, Bruno, that makes a lot of sense." From the way he told me that, I knew what I said had penetrated. That made me feel good, because that's what I came out kicking to them. I told them straight up, because they were talking about AK-47s, and all this madness, so I shot that right at them. I said, "If you go use an AK and go kill some brothers, you'll go to the pen, and when you reach level 4, they're going to tell you, 'We don't bang up here.' "

In a level-4 pen, Bloods and Crips get stuck in situations where they share with each other. If you're a Crip, and I'm a Blood, it's possible that there can be a war, and we can be in lockdown for three or four months. They don't care anything about guns, it's all about handling your business, kill or be killed. If you're in there, it's time-out for that Crip/Blood madness. If I can help you with something, I will, just on the strength that you're Black, plus we need each other. You need me, and I need you. That's the atmosphere. The bottom line is, it doesn't make any sense to be out here gang-banging and killing each other behind the color of a rag. It doesn't make any sense, because when you mess your life off, and you get up there, you can't do it there. Anybody that can't understand that has got to be far gone.

The problem now comes in with the youngsters that don't understand what's going on. You have a lot of youngsters that don't want to listen. We have a lot of youngsters that are just straight illiterate. I've kicked it with a lot of dudes that couldn't read and write. I used to get mad too. I was talking on the phone to my girl one time, and a little brother came over and was asking me about some coffee, because the jar he had he couldn't even read it. He had his pants sagging, and his Jheri curl hanging, and with his little earring, he was the coolest and hardest dude, to himself, in the penitentiary. Running around with his pants sagging, fresh crease, and he couldn't even read. I peeped that automatically, I picked up on that, and I immediately told my girl, "This dude needs to be in school somewhere, at least trying to learn how to read." A lot of the youngsters don't understand, and they don't try to understand.

When I was trying to push a peace line in the penitentiary, during the Uprisings, all the brothers out here were pushing the issue too, and we started kicking it in there. But some of the youngsters just don't listen. That's when I learned that a lot of those dudes just don't understand what's going on. They're not that far advanced. They haven't gotten to that point yet. I understand that too, because I was there before. There was a time in my life when I wouldn't give a brother the time of day. I had Muslim brothers try to talk to me on the streets, when I was a youngster. They used to try to pull me and just try to wake me up. "Look, young brother, you're tripping. This is what's happening." They would start kicking it to me, and at that time, I didn't understand what they were talking about, but I think part of the reason was because I didn't try to understand. I didn't want to hear it. To me it was like when my moms used to scold me. Trying to tell me to do what's right. I didn't want to hear that. "I'm into this, I'm gone. Don't lecture me." A lot of homiez take it like it's a lecture. You know they're speaking the truth to you, and what they're telling you is only going to help you, but you don't want to hear it, because it's like a lecture. You want to hurry up and go. That's what a lot of those young brothers are doing. I honestly feel that if they understood, if they was aware and understood what's going on, and what's happening to our race, then they would be with it.

**Q:** What do you think are some ways we can try to get them to understand, without having that lecture approach?

**B:** Honestly speaking, and I'm not trying to butter y'all up or anything, but people like y'all. Doing what you are doing right now.

**Q:** Like us. You're down with this too?

**B:** Right on. Things like this. This book. Things of this nature right here. This is good. I don't know about those talk shows, because there are not too many youngsters that watch those talk shows. Dudes don't have time to watch talk shows. I'm going to tell you something else— a lot of them like those little gangster flicks. When I got out, I went and saw *Menace II Society,* and I really didn't see too much positive in that. Right when it went off, I told my girl, "They shouldn't even put that out for these youngsters." When they watch all that violence, the killing and shooting, if that's what they see, then that's what they want. That pumps them up. When they leave the movie, that's what they think about. Just like when they watch karate movies, they leave out of a karate movie doing karate. So the average youngster leaves out from the movie fantasizing. Just like the old men who watch those old movies and then ride down the street fantasizing. We all do it. So they need to start putting more positive books out, and more positive movies out. Have little youngsters from the hood in the movie, but all throughout the movie, just make it more positive. Real positive. You don't have to have all of that gunplay to make a nice, decent movie. If you put some real, true OGs and Gs from out of these neighborhoods up on the big screen, their young homiez are going to go watch that movie, regardless to what they're doing. The young homiez are going to watch, just because Robert Lee is in a flick. "Man, that's the homie." They will go just so they can sit there and say, "That's my big homie." So I know we can make it just straight positive.

**Q:** When you was out there banging, what did the neighborhood mean to you?

**B:** The hood meant life or death. It was that deep. If you said, "F Six-Deuce," I'd try to kill you. It was that deep. "Don't come in the hood with a blue rag, or we'll try to kill you." Even though we already knew that in the course of trying to kill you, we were taking a chance on being killed too. We know when they made one gun, they didn't stop making them. It's also obvious that someone won't come in a Blood neighborhood, knowing it's a Blood neighborhood, and be a Crip and not have some type of protection. So to sum it up, it had to be straight life or death.

**Q:** From the way the neighborhoods are taken so serious by the homiez, what are some ways to get them to build up their own hoods?

**B:** The problem is that dope. I think the dope has a lot of us confused. Dope is holding a lot of us down. If we could get the dope out of our lives, then we would be able to accumulate the money necessary, because we need money to build the community. That's where we have to start at, with ourselves. The dope has a lot of brothers confused, and spending all of their money. Every dollar they get, where is it going? They're not thinking about anything but that dope. That dope is what's tearing us down. Which comes from you know where.

If we could get the dope out of the hoods, then the brothers would think better. All of the brothers from the hoods that go to the penitentiary, they're sharp. The ones that educate themselves. They think good, and they talk good, they think along the lines of businesses. The average brother that you go out on the yard and kick it with, that has been down seven or eight years, their heads be fresh and clear from the drugs. They use their minds, they think. That's because they are clean. When you're out here on the turf, you don't know your capabilities, because you get to messing with that dope and alcohol, you stay full. Everything else becomes unimportant to you.

**Q:** What makes brothers begin to use dope and alcohol?

**B:** Everybody has a certain amount of weakness in them, but I think the problem is because it's so available. It's there. It's everywhere in our community. The Caucasians make sure it's there. They put it right there under your nose. The temptation gets you. It's just too available. That's why they keep it down in the ghettos. It's not available to their kids where they live. That's why a lot of them try to keep us away. They try to keep us out of their communities, because they don't want us bringing to their kids what they put down here for us. They make it nonavailable to their kids, but they give it right to us. Like I said, everybody has a certain amount of weakness, them as well as us. It's just too available here.

**Q:** What are some solutions and some ways we can strengthen the peace?

**B:** I think discipline is necessary. Not just self-discipline, but discipline from our own people. That's why I came up with the idea of putting the law down from the penitentiaries. I think it's necessary. Basically what we're talking about is organizing our people, right? In any organization there has to be discipline. For example, take the Mafia, or the Mexican Mafia in the pen; I watched them function, and they have straight discipline. If you don't take care of business the way you're supposed to take care of business, they get you out of there. Brothers argue with each other. If a Mexican in the pen tells another Mexican, "You have to go and handle him," they go handle him. If a brother tells another brother in the pen, not always, but in a lot of cases if a brother tells another brother, "You have to go handle that, it's your turn," "Fool, what you talking about, it's not my turn." They go at it. A brother just won't let another brother tell him what to do. That comes from lack of unity. Not being organized. Nobody wants to have a chief in command, when it is really necessary sometimes, because otherwise you have everybody trying to make decisions. You have to have that chain of command, and that's being organized right there. That's how other dudes function. They fall right in line, right in place. If they don't fall in place, they're gone. I must say this, they are tight. Any brother that will speak the real, that has been in the pen, will tell you, "The Mexicans are tight." They are even kind of tight out here. They're coming up.

**Q:** Any further words we didn't ask you about, that you would like to say?

**B:** I'm going to get back on that dope issue. I think a lot of the OG homiez are responsible. The OG homiez that are not smoking dope, but that are getting the dope and selling it in the hood. I think they're halfway responsible, because they're getting it from the Caucasians and bringing it into the hood and feeding it to the young homiez. They're distributing it in the neighborhoods, and who's getting it? *Our people.* That's steadily confusing the young homiez. My message is to a lot of the G homiez, to start pressing the issue on people, and themselves, to not bring the dope in the hood. That's where we need to start. If we can get that out of the way, if we can not bring dope in the hood and get as many of the young homiez' minds clear, get them to thinking right, that would be a start right there. We would have less problems out of them, and we would have them cooperating with us. As long as we're bringing dope into the hood, and giving it to them, then they're going to want to rebel, because of the dope. It keeps them confused. We need to clean our hoods up and get the dope out of our hoods, then we can take it from there.

> ***The white man has broken every law known to man to establish America, but he'll put you in the state penitentiary, he'll put you in the federal penitentiary, for breaking these same laws.***
>
> **—Ice Cube**

## SHOUT OUTS

Shout outs to *all* my brothers and sisters of the world.
Special shout out to all my homiez from Six-Deuce Brim and a double shout out to my little brother Li'l Man!

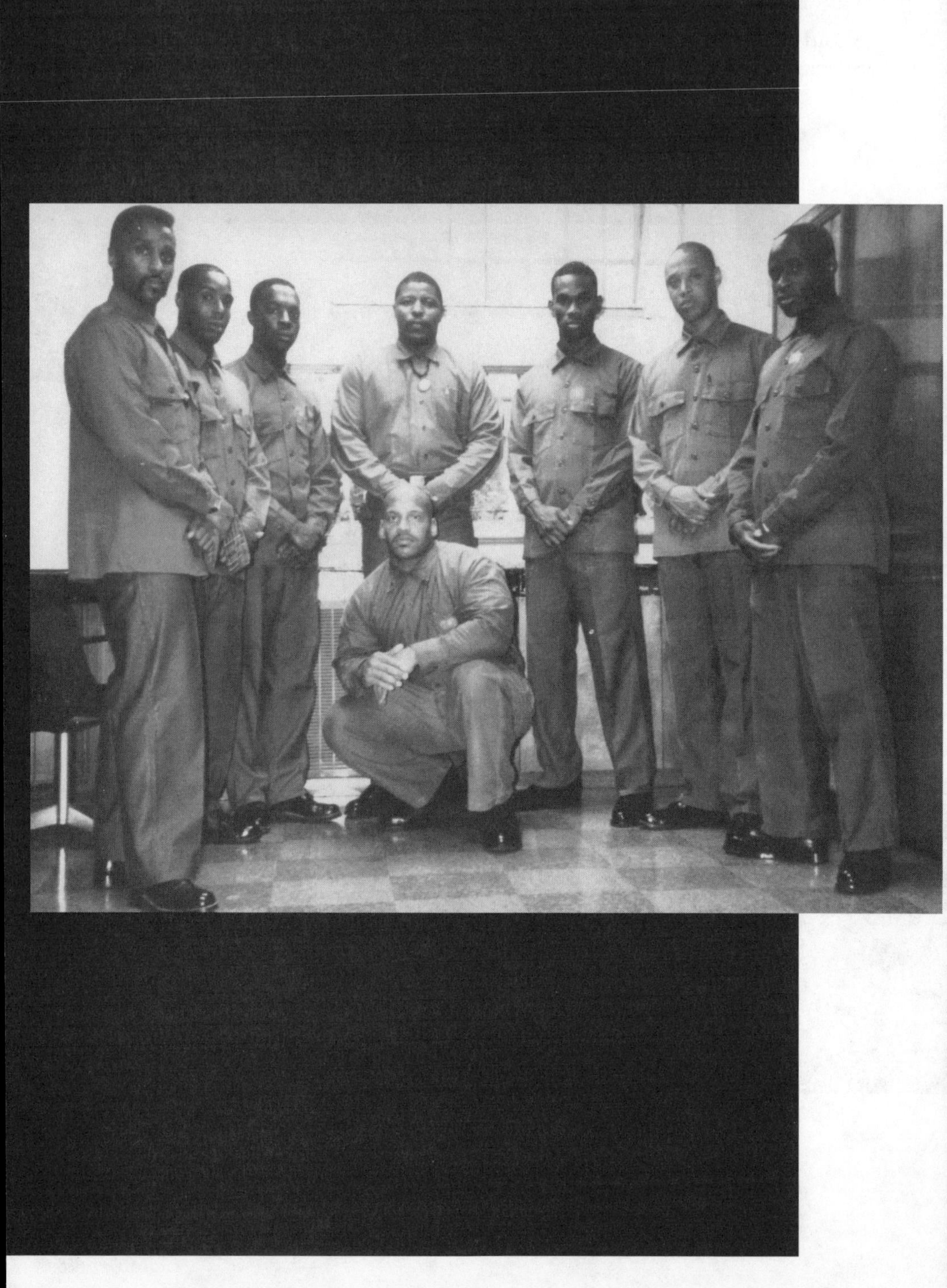

*(I'm your brother, and like an older brother talking to younger siblings in his family, I'm like the Prodigal Son. I have went down that road, I've traveled that street, and I know that block, and you don't have to go down that street. I know another way that you can get to your goal without going down that road. I'm just an ordinary brother out of Front Street Watts, trying to keep the peace with the brotherhood. We have to unite or we're going to perish. We've been through major penitentiaries, YTS, federal time—we've been exposed to that criminal element. We've busted caps, we've done it all. Everything any other brother out there surviving will do to protect theirself. We're your brothers, and we know we're your brothers now. You would have been an enemy four or five years ago, or somebody was going to die, but we're coming in peace now.)*

**L:** Before I say anything, I'd like to say, in the name of ALLAH, the beneficent, the most merciful, all praise is due to ALLAH, the Lord of the worlds. I bear witness that there is no God but ALLAH, and that Muhammad is His Messenger.

**Q:** How did you first come to Islam?

**L:** I met a brother out of Compton, his name is Marvin, he's an original Piru, and I was telling him how I used to buy some bud from these Jamaicans on the west side all the time, and how I bought this pouch with a star on it, I think it was the Star of David. I tripped off of the star and how it looked, and the symbols on it. I felt it was some kind of linkage to my past. So when I was telling the brother about it in jail, he said, "No, brother, you need to get hip to the star and crescent." I said, "I don't know anything about a star and a crescent, but this star I have is deep." I was only doing a year violation at that particular time. When I got out, I ran across one of my childhood friends that I grew up with from the neighborhood. Back in the days this brother was straight in the church every Sunday, he never missed one day. So when I saw him, he said, "I'm down here at Mosque #54, I'm into Islam." I was shocked. He told me I should check it out. Then I ran across this other brother named Joe who took me down to the mosque, and I started going. Then I started seeing brothers at the mosque that I was in the penitentiary with. It was on after that. I stood up at the mosque one day and told them that me and some other brothers wanted to open up some hospitals, some banks, some grocery stores, and some schools. I think Minister Khallid was there that day, and it was really on after that.

**Q:** What kind of change has that made in your life?

**L:** I never got taken out of my reality, it just made me see my reality in a different light. The way I grew up in gangs, drugs, the street life, prostitutes, base heads, the drug users, the drug sellers, I saw them all differently, not as those titles. I saw them where they could be teaching the people, helping the people, raising the people. All the institutions in our community, we could open them up ourselves, our own schools, we don't have to deal with L.A. Unified, or the police department, we can have our own security. It changed my whole perception. I don't see another brother as an enemy, but as a comrade in a nation of people. Instead of us killing one another we should be concentrating on the enemy who is keeping us down, our oppressor.

Me and my people grew up low-riding and stuff. Islam took me out of thinking about just individual low-riding, of trying to glorify myself, into bringing it to where I'm doing it in the name of God. So I can attract the people, and I can discuss things with the people on another level now. When I wasn't into the light like that, I was bangin' and slangin'. Now I can meet a girl and not even think lustful of her. I'm into what's in the sister's head. I want to hear what the sister is talking about now. "What's happening with you? What are you doing for yourself?"

**Q:** What was it about the teachings of the Most Honorable Elijah Muhammad that brought about that change?

**L:** It was the tapes, and it was the reading. Brother Sharieff, he made me think, because when I hooked up into Islam, I hooked up with him. He took me to meet Minister Farrakhan in Chicago. He used to stress to me, "Get a firm root." I never knew what he was talking about, but the way I took it was by going to get a tape of Minister Farrakhan explaining about Master Fard Muhammad, and ever since then I've never been the same.

**Q:** What was that like coming from the streets of Watts, bangin' and slangin', and then going to meet Minister Farrakhan?

**L:** I didn't believe it. We were going to help pay Brother Sharieff's way to Chicago so he could go, because we were fired up, we just didn't have the basic understanding. Then they was like, "You brothers can go too." I didn't believe it. I never grew up thinking I would meet Farrakhan. I didn't know anything about Minister Farrakhan until '89, '90, maybe '91. I heard people speak about him, but I don't think I had ever saw a picture of him. It just wasn't me. Then when I met him, the things that I was expressing to him at the table, I don't even know where those words were coming from. There was a lot of brothers that were there from Watts, that was from different hoods. I took to certain people at the table, like the Minister's son Mustapha, I was mostly talking to him, then I would say something to the Minister, but I didn't really understand what was going on. Right up to this day I flash back to the things that he said, the points he made, and I try to grasp the different things, because it affected my life. It slowed me down. The way I was raised, we were just out there. We were providing for self and getting our money the best way we could.

**Q:** At what age did you really start hitting the streets?

**L:** About nine. I had some cousins that were from Four-Tre Hoover, and we used to go to Hollywood and bash windows out, just going for self in the streets. My mother and my stepfather . . . my stepfather was a conscious brother—you can say he kept me from killing a lot of people when I was growing up. He gave me a certain conscious level. I still had my temper, but he guided me.

The gang thing came up in my neighborhood with people like Big Jimel, Tookie, Big Jackie, Raymond Washington, Ricky, Mack, Dee Dee, Bare Foot Pookie from the west side, and all of those brothers, they used to be in the hood every day. Between Central and 76th, all back there, up on 104th and McKinley. The majority of them are dead now. I'm telling you it was all of the OGs. There wasn't anything but Crips. There were no Hoovers, no East Coasts, or any of that, it was just Crips; west side, east side, and Compton. Mack and them moved to Compton and started C.C. Riders.

I was put on the set in '74. Going through elementary school we were claiming, but we were officially put on as Crips in '74 when I was like twelve years old.

**Q:** What was it about the OGs that attracted you to banging?

**L:** When you ask me that question, it pops into my head, it was the unity. It was the strength in the unity of the brothers. I used to sit in my window and watch them walk down the street to the park. They used to be four hundred to five hundred deep. I'm talking about Big Moon, the Allen Family, Crazy Crip, Mad Dog, all of them. I was a little boy, and I used to watch them go to their meetings deep. Most of these hoods now are new hoods. The Rollin' 60s have been around, East Coast Crips have been around for a long time. Really all East Coasts are East Sides; they turned from East Side Crip to East Coast Crip. That was back in '76. It was more of a unity thing then; I don't know where it broke off at. I used to be able to go on the west side, and there wouldn't be any problems with the brothers over there. The same thing with Compton, there wouldn't be one problem. It's like a phase, or going through classes. I don't know where it swung to. When I got out of the pen in '87, it was wild. When it first started, it was more about the unity, but then they started taking leather jackets up in Hollywood and stuff. Like I said, I was a young buck, and in those days they wouldn't let everybody just roll out. You had to go home, unless you sneaked off or something. I knew all of them. Like my little brother, they used to come pick him up and take him off with them. My little brother didn't turn out to be a

Crip either, he's a Blood from Cedar Block in Compton. He's doing twenty-five years to life right now. He just started that bid in '90. So I have to go get at him sooner or later.

**Q:** What do you think started the sets to tripping on each other?

**L:** We know that it was the government; agents and provocateurs, but at that time the people were ignorant on how to avoid that, so it mushroomed.

**Q:** What tactics did you see being used?

**L:** My neighborhood is a close-knit hood, they call it Front Street Watts now; when I was banging, it was East Side Crips. It would have to be how they deluded the people's minds in the community, because there was a lot of strong antiwhite feelings in my community. Like if some of my OG homiez caught white people in the hood, it was over for them. I actually saw them drag white people out of their vehicles, and out of their places of business. If we had white people living in the hood, they would run them out of the hood. That whole neighborhood used to be white, prior to me growing up over there.

When we had problems in our hood, it was from the shoulders, we would just fight. I don't know where the gun and pistol play came from. I know it occurred, because I have experienced those things myself. I can't say exactly where the agents and provocateurs came from in my neighborhood, because you would have to know an agent when you see one. It's hard to find one, because they are like hypocrites, they say they are with ALLAH, but they are not, or they will say that they are a Crip and they're not. They'll be with you in the hood, and then when they get where they're going, they have their secret agenda. There was warfare amongst the brotherhood, because that's actually what the Crips and Bloods were, the brotherhood.

I know that some of my OG homeboys tripped on other people in different neighborhoods, and communities, causing a riff. I know one of my homeboys, who was probably one of the first brothers to shoot and kill a brother from Compton. Pirus used to be Crips, the Compton Piru Crips, and from what I understand, the feud that they had with the brother from my hood caused them to switch up. Back then it was like everybody used to be unified. You also had envy and jealousy, which was a factor on top of everything. The idea of taking what's natural, and turning it into mischief. I got that understanding from Minister Louis Farrakhan. I can see it now. We're taking what's natural and turning it into mischief, and it can cause problems within the brotherhood, and between the brotherhood and the sisterhood. There were many different causes that made things escalate to the level we're at now.

**Q:** Did you see any relationship between the increase in pistol play and the infiltration of the drugs?

**L:** I remember this brother in the neighborhood was telling me that they had found a vanload of weapons, .22s, .25s, .32s, and .38s, by one of the projects, just sitting there. The police had confiscated the vehicle. It's a good thing that nobody ever went and bothered the vehicle, or they would have come up on a lot of cheap artillery. He was saying that under the Freedom of Information Act that they traced the vehicle to some white supremacist groups. I guess they left the guns in the community for us to find, so we could shoot and kill one another.

As far as drugs, there was always drugs in the hood from my recollection, it's just that the older brothers that were dealing with it didn't let the younger brothers get involved. It wasn't like it is now. You can catch one of the li'l homiez now, and he doesn't even want to go to school, he wants to sell some dope, come up on him a car, and some Daytons, some sounds, and he's straight. Back then it wasn't like that. I would say that things got worse when cocaine hit the streets in '83, because prior to that all the brothers that were slangin' were selling "water," "Sherman," angel dust, PCP, or whatever you want to call it. About '82 or '83 is when rocks hit the streets hard. With rocks hitting the streets hard, and the money that was generated, two years after that, about '84 or '85, guns hit the streets hard. Around '86, '87, it was on. You name it, you could get it. You didn't hear that much about 9-millimeters, M16s, M14s, and AKs unless you were hooked up and was high on the echelon, but after 1986 they were available to anybody. When I got out of the pen in '87, it was on. Brothers had Uzis, AKs, and like the Minister said at Savior's Day, it gave brothers a false sense of invincibility.

**Q:** Did you go to the pen behind gang-banging?

**L:** I wouldn't put in work in the name of the hood, because what hood would I be representing? There was no more East Side Crips, because they all turned to East Coasts. I was one of the li'l homiez that was die-hard like, "It's always East Side Crip on mine." Then there wasn't that many brothers that were down with East Side Crip anymore. So I mostly did what I had to do for individual survival. People knew where I was from, and if they didn't, it really didn't matter to me, they knew who I was.

I've been in situations where I would be somewhere with brothers from the hood, and they would take off and leave us there. So I was never hung up on the hood, as much as in having a good true friend that I could trust, and that was loyal to me, and vice versa. If I scrapped and got with somebody head-up, they would know what hood I was from, so they could come through and see me, I was right there. I would never say that I didn't put in work on individuals that have done something to somebody close to me from the neighborhood, but I wasn't just going out and doing things senselessly for the hood. I always tried to keep myself thinking, because some things you have to do for self-survival. I wasn't an instigator who went out to start mischief. It was more like, if you come to get me, we're going to do something, and it was for a right cause, or what we thought was justified at that particular time. I've never been just a hothead, "We're fixin' to go do this for the hood." I like to just deal with certain people in the neighborhood anyway.

The brothers under me were the ones who were to be the future leaders, so they didn't have to honor me. All I asked is that they respect me. If you don't know me, give me my respect. If you disrespect me, I'm going to disrespect you back. I wasn't tripping off of ego, so if a brother said something to me, I could let it go. Words never bothered me, but don't put your hands on me or seem as though you're trying to harm me, that's something different. That's just me. I've been around a lot of so-called gangsters or killers, who for something that wasn't really about anything, they would go off the deep end. So I always tried to look at other brothers and see the types of mistakes they would make and learn from them. A lot of times they are protecting something, or hiding something about theirself, so they don't want you too close to them. I'm just as human as anybody else.

**Q:** What are some of the things that you feel brothers are protecting or hiding?

**L:** It's a false sense of security sometimes. A brother feels like, "I see somebody weaker than me, and I'm going to oppress them." That's the same thing that the white man did to our whole nation. You have some brothers that are just tripping off of ego or the image, and he's thinking more of himself than he should, and he feels like we all should submit to him. Some people are tripping off of leadership. They may have the ability to lead, but they're not letting ALLAH use that ability, and they'll try to take it their own way. Most of the little brothers don't have real respect for a lot of the OGs, because of what they've done. If the OGs truly had concern for the brothers in their hood, then they would never have done certain things. You don't ever hear anyone talking about those brothers, because those are the brothers that the youngsters leaned on for guidance.

A brother that was putting in work for the hood was a protector of that hood, protecting the hood from an outside enemy, but never oppressing the brothers. A lot of the brothers that were following them were scared and were following them because of an intimidation factor. So each individual brother that reads this book will understand within himself what it is that made him do whatever it was that he did, and he can't hide that fact.

Like that brother right there, Moon [Moon joins the conversation later on in the chapter], he's the only youngster I know that was in L.A. County Jail at the age of fifteen, in the Crip module, with brothers like Mad Dog from Front Street Watts, San Fernando Valley, stretched out; Chino, from ETG; Stan and them from East Coast 76; he was in the module with brothers that didn't care. That brother right there is no different now than when he was fifteen, as far as being a natural individual.

Instead of having false ego and pride like, "Yeah, Cuz, I did this or that," he's still himself, looking for guidance and understanding from God. He's a humble brother, when most brothers would take that in their mind and oppress a person like, "Don't you know who I am?" It's to the point of, who are you? We know you, and we hear you, and you represent a certain hood or community, but what? What are you really about?

**Q:** So do the younger brothers look for guidance from their OGs?

**L:** That's right, and if you're not providing that, they'll jack you. If you're in a certain neighborhood, the li'l homiez will be like, "Man, we have to do something to him." They're young, and they really don't care. They look at it like, "I'm sixteen years old, and I don't have anything to live for." So when a lot of them get shot, they do what they have to do to stay alive, like a baby has survival instincts, and that's from birth, embedded in the fiber of our character. A lot of them are tired. They're tired. "I'm tired, I don't have anything to look forward to. I don't have anything to live for. My mama is smoking crack, my daddy's not around, my uncles are tripping." If there is a family net, it's barely hanging by the strings of economics, so he has to go out there and get his. So he's doing things, trying to come up on some paper. The first thing that comes to his mind is, "If I do this, I can take care of my people." If the proper respect is not there, or if the younger brothers see any type of weakness in that character that you're portraying, then they will eat you up. There's an intimidation factor that older Gs have over them anyway, and once they see beyond the intimidation factor, they're let down. The younger homiez look for truth all the time. They don't know what they're looking for, but that's what it is. They look for that realness. It's just natural that brothers are aggressive; that's all it is, just aggressive behavior.

**Q:** Speak on the importance of economics in the hood.

**L:** We need that. We need an economic platform to help elevate the younger brothers and sisters. For example, say a brother is representing Hoover Crips, you are a name behind a street called Hoover, and then if you take that name to a deeper root, you'll find out where the root of Hoover comes from. If you're a Hoover Crip, and you love your community, you should buy it. The same neighborhood you're kickin' it in, you should buy that neighborhood. All it is, is taking the money that you scrap up in the streets and channeling that money in the right hands, because you know the government is not going to let the brothers take that money and make anything with it, because they want that money.

**Q:** What connection will make that happen?

**L:** What we need to do is get back to the family. The breakdown and destruction of the Black family is what has caused us to be disunited and divided. These Crips and Bloods, and these so-called dope dealers, they all come from a family. Their family unit has been destroyed, so they went outside of that biological family and formed another family, which the white man labeled as gangs. If we can get with some of those people from within our families that are professional businesspeople, and get them to come to the community without the intent of robbing and stealing from the people, then we could lift ourselves up. It's no different than the Italian American or the Irish American or the Jewish American, who by the backing of Meyer Lansky, Lucky Luciano, Frank Costello, and all of these big-time mobsters, they didn't do anything but take that drug, alcohol, prostitution, and vice profit and start the state of Israel, or support the Italian government. It's no different than what they did, it's just that our people are so disunited, and fearful of the system, that they turn their backs, for the slaughter of their own children. They're calling for the death of the youngsters, who therefore are turning their frustrations and anger back within, destroying one another. So we have no respect for anybody. "I don't have respect for your woman, your mama, nobody but the brothers from the hood." And since they see each other every day, it's easy for them to destroy one another, because they're so tired of each other, they just don't know how to vent that frustration out on the real enemy. I talk to a gang of brothers in the hood, and I let them know, "You see me, and I come through your hood, and I can have on blue or red, if I'm in the wrong neighborhood, y'all are ready to bust a cap on me, but let onetime hit the corner, you're throwin' straps, breakin' and runnin'." It's the fear. They're intimidated by the white man. If we went ahead and broke down all these barriers of this hood, and that hood, and formulated a brotherhood, we could look out for all of them brothers and give them something else to do.

The reason a lot of brothers are banging, it's like on a football team, and the team is good, and y'all are winning, but you're just on the team with a uniform. Well, a lot of brothers are like that about banging. They want to be down with a team; some may have never banged a day in their life. There are some brothers I see in '94, from when I was coming up, there was nothin' happenin', but when I see them now, they're so hard they don't even speak. When I was out there, it wasn't important for everybody to know what I was doing, as long as I knew what I was doing, and where I was coming from. You have to deal with each brother on an individual basis, because there are some brothers in the hood that won't run from the police and will blast, but they don't kick it in the hood, because they know they will get some of their own people killed. "I'm not going to kick it in the hood. I know how I'm thinking, and how I feel, and when I see onetime creeping through, and I have the opportunity to get 'em, and then I move on 'em, I'm thinking about if I get these two, and I will get away, what about the homeboys? If I love my hood, how are the police going to respond to the community where the incident happened?" There are some brothers that will do it, but the majority of the brothers out there are banging because of *Colors*,

*Boyz N the Hood, Menace II Society.* It's a fad thing. Just like when dope came out, only certain people knew how to manage drug money, how to make it, but then other brothers, not knowing how, but wanting the image and popularity, they would submit to being a worker under this individual. Which would stagnate them on their own growth and development. Bangin' and slangin' is a phase. Especially when you're bangin', that's a step that you go through in your development for identity out in the streets.

**Q:** In your experience, was the gang more positive or negative for you?

**L:** I've had positive and negative happen. I've lost a lot of people. Then there's the camaraderie, and the brotherhood, the extension of that love that you get from the formulation of the gang. It's like friendships in all walks of life. You meet brothers, and besides Crippin', or Bloodin', they can do something else: fix cars, some are scientists. Once you get to know the brother and get beyond that image and tap into that raw talent, then you get to see who that individual truly is. It's like a mask: a brother is acting one way, to throw people off another way. Once you get to know that brother, there are some beautiful things going on in these hoods with these sisters and brothers. They're reaching out for the attention and love that they're not getting from anywhere else.

**Q:** What can be done to bring some of their greatness out?

**L:** To me, you have to let everybody be, and let them grow. Don't oppress them, but correct your brother and sister when you see a mistake. Talk to them, and don't talk about BS; be real, and deal with the truth, so they can recognize what you're saying, and never leave God out of it. If you leave God out of it, there is nothing that you can do with them. These are God's people that have extended beyond the level of family, these are human beings, they're individuals, they focus on self, and they will self-destruct at any moment from the pressure, and the stress of white supremacy.

You can't deny that white supremacy has put us in the condition that we're in. We have to elevate and gravitate back to the level of a family. "Sister, will you excuse yourself from my presence and put some clothes on. You'll look better if you did." You have to make the Black woman feel more important about herself. A sister would get with me because I'm Leibo. They're impressed by an image that they see, without ever knowing what I'm thinking in my mind, how I see them, or anything. They just see an image.

It comes from the media, it's Hollywood. I used to sit up in the morning and watch gangster movies as a child, because that's what they were pumping into our minds. If you talk to any brother that grew up in L.A. from the sixties on up, they watched gangster movies. The flip jumped off when *Scarface* came out. Man, it was about being a major drug dealer. So the media portrayed the image. The media portrayed the image in *Colors* and brought out a whole different level of gang-banging. They made it more popular to gang-bang.

Then the police used to ride around: "What hood are you from? Let me take your picture?" All the time they're setting you up. They'd write their hood down, with their name, and they'd tack it on the board. Then they created OSS, which is Operation Safe Streets, with the Los Angeles Sheriff's Department, and then the LAPD started CRASH. Knowing the intent and the direction of that idea was to lock up masses of Blacks, then they created the Crip module and the Blood module in the jails. Back then it was row forty-eight and forty-three, then they broke it down to where row twenty-seven, twenty-six, twenty-one to twenty-three was the Crip module, forty-three and forty-six was the Blood module, that was in the county jail. The sheriffs instilled certain concepts and thoughts into their minds by walking these brothers to visitation all gaffled up. Making them feel like they were true criminals, gangsters, and murderers. It was just the image of being incarcerated, shackled down like an animal. It was the media, and they controlled that idea. The sheriff department is something else. They really created a monster.

I think about Turtle, from Compton. I remember I was locked up when one of the twins came through from Santana Block and said, "Cuz, Turtle got killed." I was like, "What, he just got out." "Such and such faction of this and that did whatever." When I think about it, CRASH, OSS, they're like the gestapo. They've done some serious damage, they know how to destroy that unity. They kick up a lot of drama. They have intelligence, CIA information, and they can cause a rival gang war if they kill the right people and leave the right evidence around. They flipped the script on us. The police was so familiar with a lot of the brothers from different neighborhoods that they would actually get out and talk to the brothers on the streets to set them up. So what kind of relationship is a Black man supposed to have with his enemy?

Then this image of being a hard-core brother, a hard-core killer: to me if you're a killer, and you're killing everything that has on red, that wouldn't exclude anybody else that's not Black. That includes everybody that's wearing red; white, Black, blue, green—if you see somebody with red on, you dump on them. The same thing with blue, but the brothers just kept it within the Black community, because that's how it was planned to go.

Think about OSS and CRASH; they have a lot of information. They have pictures of a lot of brothers too. They can just turn their portfolio over to the federal government and wreak havoc in the community. To me, that's what they did when they introduced drugs to us and put it on the street level where we can get it. Now you have young brothers with paper, that don't care about themselves, having as many babies as they can, because they feel they can take care of the babies. It's the image. They didn't come to the set thinking that's what it was about. They watch it on TV, then they want to emulate it. They want to impress that young Black sister. They don't know but one way to get at her, and she's exposed to it, and she accepts it. The same way she does when she sees a brother on "gold ones," as opposed to rolling in a Nova. In my neighborhood people know, we've come through looking wonderful for the people. We had material things, yet the material does not elevate the people. We don't even have any food programs for the homeless.

I look at the brothers in the hood selling dope now, and they see the babies of the parents that are spending their money buying dope from them, and not spending money on the child. Why not take that money and reinvest it back into that child? Buy that child some clothes. Get a program together. You know their parents are not managing their money correctly, so you have to manage the money for them. They think if they worked eight hours a day and got some crack at the end of the day, they'll be fine? What about the rest of the family? We all have to be responsible for one another. We have to cover down for each other. We can't just lean on one person, we have to be able to be strong enough to stand on our own. Get the support from them, and then stand on your own, and then pull somebody else up. The more we do that, and the more people we pull up, the bigger and better we get, then we can just take over the whole community. Reinvest in our community, instead of asking Clinton for some money. Clinton can't do anything for me. Clinton can get caught up in the wrong hood, and him and his people will get hurt. Don't come in the hood, we don't need you. We don't need LAPD, and we don't need the sheriff, they're nothing but security guards. We don't need them, we're all family. I bet if we all get together, somebody will know somebody from somewhere, or we're somehow related.

**Q:** How did the gang peace affect you?

**L:** Brother and sister, that was beautiful. You had to be there. It started April 29. Brothers in the projects, the Nickersons, the Jordan Downs, the Imperial Courts, and the Haciendas, had been talking peace before, but God called it on April 29. The rebellion wasn't a rebellion for Rodney King, the rebellion was an Uprising for unity. I saw people in the streets that had shot at each other just the other day, together doing whatever was necessary. ALLAH blessed a lot of people with a lot of money for those three days. I guess that's what you call the equivalent to Christmas.

It was everywhere, in Watts, on the west side, the Hoovers and the 90's, over where a lot of them brothers don't even know what they're fighting about. The feud between them happened because one of the li'l homeboys named Ony got called, and he got killed over in the other neighborhood, and it came back on this group of brothers, so it separated the two hoods. We used to go to the west side, and I'm from the east side, we used to go over there and party. I used to party so much on the west side that a lot of people think I'm from the west side. I have people from Hoover, founded with Hoover, so a lot of people think I'm from Hoover. I have a little brother that's from Cedar Block Piru in

Compton, a known Blood named Shank. A lot of people from that area would think that I'm a Blood, because that's my little brother, but they've never said anything to me. There's a lot of people that know of me, but don't know my face. Others know my face, but don't know my name. All of us know each other, and we can get along with one another, and God showed us that we can get along with each other on April 29. If you was out there, you saw enemies that were shooting at each other, come together. They gassed up at this little gas station that they had taken control of, and from right there they hit the freeways.

Just think, that was three days of what they call lawlessness. So that means if you was a Crip or a Blood, you could have run through any neighborhood and killed anybody you wanted to. There was very few random shootings like that. On April 29, I lost my homeboy André, and we try to keep everything that he fixed for us, our cars, we try to keep it the way he did in honor of him. I'm going to remember André. I believe that the federal government kicked off the Uprisings expecting one thing, and since they make a plan, and ALLAH makes a plan, and ALLAH is the best of planners, it went a whole different route. It flipped them out, and they couldn't respond fast enough. For those three days, the people got together and was handling their business together, I'm talking about Crips and Bloods together with much love.

Right after those three days is when the peace parties started jumping off. My little nephews and them—one of them is right outside—him and Boo used to go to the truce parties and come back, "Man, we went to the projects, and they was over there partying."

[Leibo goes outside to call in Moon and Boo Capone to join the interview and share their experiences.]

**Q:** What was it like at the peace parties?

**Moon:** One day we was kickin' it, and when we went to the park, some Bloods were up there, so I went to the neighborhood and told my homiez—this was before the peace treaty had jumped—I went to the hood and told my homiez that the Bloods were up there at the park. We went up to the park, and they was deep, so we got at 'em and said, "What are y'all doing at our park?" They was like, "Man, we're trucing, we're ready to peace." We was like cool. Everybody was kickin' it.

**Q:** So your people didn't know anything about a peace treaty?

**M:** We didn't know about any peace. The next morning it was like a peace treaty.

**Q:** Where were the Bloods from that came to your park?

**M:** The Bounty Hunters from Nickerson Gardens. Nobody knew anything about it except the Grape Streets [Crips] and the Bounty Hunters [Bloods]. We didn't know anything about it. It just happened. That was ALLAH right there. I didn't believe it.

The only thing about the peace parties was that everybody was just getting drunk and high every night. Nobody was really coming up with any solutions or anything. Nobody was really talking about making it stronger.

**Q:** What things do you think could have happened during that time that would have made the peace even more strong than it is today?

**M:** It shouldn't be called a "party." If anything, we should get together and talk about something that's going to keep the unity together, because without that we're going to perish.

**Q:** What would you have talked about?

**M:** First of all, we have to start getting at some of the younger brothers. Some of the older brothers have to get at them and let them know that this banging is nothing at all. They are the ones right now that are coming up, and it's going to be their turn. We already had our turn in the streets as far as doing whatever. We have to get at the younger brothers coming up right now.

**Q:** How do they respond to you, because you're not too much older than them?

**M:** I'm twenty-one. I've been in the streets for a while though. I speak to them every day now, and some of them are deaf, dumb, and blind. The rest of them comprehend. I told some of them to come to Savior's Day; Farrakhan had us up onstage, it was way cool. They liked it. That's the only thing we can do for our people, introduce them to Islam. That's the best thing we can do for our people.

**Boo:** We need more of the youngsters to get with it. Some of the youngsters are not with it.

**Q:** How can we reach the youngsters?

**M:** We have to go to them, because they're not going to come to us.

**B:** We have to have something for them, because right now all they have is the brothers in the streets.

**M:** They're not giving up anything, they're not punks, so that's who they're going to go with. Only the strong survive, so that's where they want to be at. In the streets with the strong.

**Q:** How can we get through to the minds of the younger brothers to make them see and understand that their Black brother is not their enemy?

**L:** We have to give them a proper knowledge of self, and we have to let them see that what they're doing is a direct effect, caused by the actual enemy. Then we can go from there. We won't do anything but rise.

We also have to look at that image, look at the so-called leaders of the Black man and woman in America, and then you break it down to whatever city or state that you're from, then these athletes and entertainers, they're promoting a lot of the madness that we have in the community. So in order for our people to realize immediately, we have to use that vehicle that they used to put us in that state, and that's the media, the personalities, Black leadership, and they have to grab the people from the hood. You have to get the people directly from the hood.

**B:** When I was growing up, I looked up to people who was on some rims, they was hopping down the street in their cars. I was young, and this is what was going on in my neighborhood. So basketball players, and athletes, they didn't have me. I was looking at a dope dealer, to be honest. Somebody looking good, with a big chain on. When I saw him, I idolized that, that's what I wanted.

**M:** The young ones today are worse than we were. When we were little, we used to get deep with about one hundred people and just roll to the beach, and we're from Watts, so that was a long way. Now you never see kids on bikes. They're going to grow up worse than us if we don't reach them. That's going to be another generation that we're going to have to watch out for.

**B:** Even us, if we don't do anything for them, they're going to try to hurt us.

**M:** If we're not with what they're talking about, they will try to move on us.

**B:** We have to have something for them.

**Q:** What are some solutions that you speak on to your homiez that can turn around all of the negative that they are surrounded by?

**L:** We would have to do just what the Messenger taught us, and that is to pool our resources, and then the first thing we would have to do is start off with a community market. Providing goods and services for our people, hire our own people. The brothers that have the money can get together, ten of them, and open up a community market. Then turn it into a cooperative, and let that develop. From that market to another market, to restaurants. That way we're creating, generating employment, and creating programs financially for the community.

**B:** We have to have positive alternatives for them.

**L:** We could take that child or individual and let them be around the person that they idolize, but they have to see that person that they idolize involved in a positive interaction, as far as building something in the community, like a business. Knock off the image, and then he will want to emulate what he saw you accomplish as far as starting a business. Take him on a business deal with you, and talk to the brother and listen too. The positive sisters that's with it can deal with the sisters, and the positive brothers can deal with the brothers. Then find out what it is that they would like to do. They have the solutions within themselves, they just don't know how to tap into it yet.

**M:** I see ALLAH working through the gangs, the Crips and the Bloods. ALLAH has changed so much already. He has changed me. Just listening has done a lot for me. It has had an effect on me. Once they tied those blue rags and red rags together, it was on.

**B:** Once they did that, if they go back to doing the same thing, then they was a buster from the jump.

**Q:** What is the significance of the red and the blue coming together?

**M:** There was so much happening over that, I never thought or dreamed that it would happen. I never thought I'd be able to go to Nickerson Gardens. We were straight rivals. I'm talking about brothers running up on me straight knowing me. I cut my hair and everything. Brothers came at me like, "You got at me two months ago." I'm like, "No, man, it wasn't me." Brothers would be like, "Brother, I know you, I know who you are."

**L:** In the hood, nobody really believed it was happening until we did the videotape. I'm telling you there had to be at least five or six thousand Crips and Bloods that night. Every Crip and Blood set in the city was there together. That was just one night when I decided to bring the camera.

**B:** It was so cool, brother wanted to get that on tape, he had to get that on videotape.

**M:** They came for two or three days straight, every night in the projects. It was nothing but ALLAH. Not one man can say that they put the peace treaty together. Nobody can say that. That was ALLAH, and brothers have to know that God has an enemy, and that's the devil, and he's not a spook, he's the white supremist Caucasian.

**L:** We argued last year up and down, "I ain't no Muslim, I'm never going to be that [speaking about Moon]"; now he's talking about getting his X. All praise is due to ALLAH.

**Q:** Let's talk about how we can keep the peace going, and strengthen it, and spread it to other hoods that are not down with it right now.

**M:** When the Minister came, we were going to the hoods and talking to the brothers daily. Trying to get the word across, so we can't stop now, every day we need to get at them. We have to work hard; it's going to take a lot of work.

**L:** We have to keep that open line of communication.

**M:** We go to everybody's hood, Bloods and Crips. We still go right today with no problems.

**L:** We started right where we're from and branched out. We have brothers like Big Phil, Tony Bogard (RIP), and all of them who stand for peace. We just can't get caught up on any one personality. We can't get to the point where if we don't get the credit, then we don't want to do the work. All the brothers from the different organizations, come and let's get together and communicate. Then when we get the money, we have to open up a grocery store, we have to open up banks, so we can get our own loans to get our own houses and get our own apartment buildings, the major necessities, food, clothing, and shelter, and mass transportation for the community. Once we get those four things, everything else will come.

**M:** Right now, the Crips and the Bloods need to come together and think of a plan and try to get some of this money. "Y'all have to give up some money for real, and we ain't playing, we're serious." There are some soldiers right now that, if somebody came up with a plan, I know for sure would straight ride to victory or to death.

**L:** We can't have anybody that would sell us out or set us up with the government. We know who has the dope and everything. Every brother in the hood knows who he has to go to.

**Q:** What should brothers look out for, so they will not be deceived and pushed back into the madness?

**M:** Once we get a group of brothers that are strong enough, then there won't be any more madness, whoever is not with it will get shut down. One set, if y'all think y'all can't get faded or whatever, you will have to go, because y'all are making it messed up for everybody else, and we ain't having it. We are not going to have it.

**B:** Brothers are just looking for guidance, whether it's positive or negative, they will do it, because it's about the love in the hood.

**L:** That brother there [speaking about Moon], when he was in the Crip module at fifteen years old, he was supposed to be in LP [juvenile hall]. He was in the Crip module with the OGs in the county jail. Some of them brothers are stuck right now.

**M:** Everybody on my row was stuck. I was the only person on my row with juvenile warrants. Everybody else had seventeen years and up. Every day, "I just caught the chains, Cuz, twenty to life," and saying it like it was nothing. I'm talking about everybody on the row, and there were twenty-four cells on the row. Everybody in those twenty-three other cells had big time, seventeen years or more. That was in 1989.

**Q:** What was that experience like?

**M:** In the pen I was in, there was not a lot of division, brothers try to stick together. They don't have a choice really. In the pens and in the county the Bloods and the Crips stick together.

They still have the modules, but you have to have a hot one, or constantly be having problems with the Bloods or Crips; if you're constantly messing up on the mainline, then they'll shoot you to the module.

**L:** It used to be as soon as you got to the county, they would look at your shoestrings, or you could tell them you were a Crip, and they would shoot you to the module, but they stopped all of that.

**M:** At first they didn't have the Crips and the Bloods together, but when the peace treaty came about, we got together.

**Q:** What do you see as the potential impact worldwide with the brothers coming together?

**B:** Everybody is looking at Watts. They're looking at the Bloods and Crips from all over.

**M:** I think most of the soldiers are going to come from the Crips and the Bloods. Some of the brothers have seen a lot. I've seen a lot, brother and sister. We're the military, the Crips and the Bloods. When all the Crips and the Bloods unite, that's when they will be the military. It will be the military for real. You won't have to see them unless something happens; then they will come, and they will handle their business.

**L:** I heard there are 66 million Blacks in Brazil. From the teachings, they tell me that first we start in America and wake up the dead here, and then we'll go all around the world. All I can say is that we have to take the attributes of God with us, all around the world, and with the experiences we have had in the world, apply it with the teachings, and take it to the people throughout the world. I haven't gotten over the fact that I met Minister Farrakhan last year.

**Q:** What did he say to you and the other brothers that you can share with us, that helped you, and that might help other brothers?

**L:** He told us that we were greater than him. That we all was greater than him. He said that we all were going to do greater things. What he said was an inspiration.

**Q:** How did that make you feel?

**L:** That made me think there was nothing I couldn't do. I believe him, all I want him to do is come to the people, because they want him bad. They need to see him, they really do. They need to be able to touch, talk, and feel him, just be able to be with him. Everything is going to be all right, I know it's going to happen in time. That's why I'm not tripping. I can just tell by the way my brothers feel now, from what happened October 9 [Savior's Day for the Honorable Elijah Muhammad, brought to Los Angeles by Minister Farrakhan to honor the Bloods and the Crips for coming together], and how they will feel January 9, ninety days after. Things are going to start happening all in time. To me that was the greatest thing that Minister Farrakhan said, that we are the future leaders, and that we will do things greater than him. That should reach every brother out in the streets right now, whether he's selling dope or not, there's something else we have to do. He said, "We all have something to do. Each and every one of us has something to do. . . . You might not know what you have to do now, but just hold on, and don't get caught up in the madness, because it's nothing but madness, and it's designed traps for us; just be steadfast and make your prayers. . . ."

**B and M:** Because it's on, brothers!

**M:** This brother right here [speaking about Leibo], he introduced me to the teachings when I got out of YTS in 1991. I never heard of anything like that. I just got introduced in '91. Some of the brothers right today don't know. Out here Christianity has the brothers and the sisters all tossed up. They're more conscious of the teachings on the East Coast; that's why we have to work hard out here. We have to get at the brothers and the sisters hard. We have to put in work. We have to make them understand.

**L:** That will keep them from running from the police; after a while they will stand up to the police respectfully without getting themselves killed, and then when they unjustifiably kill one of ours, that's when it's going to be on.

**M:** When the brothers see you in a suit and tie, if you're not from the street, they look at you different. But if you are from the street, and you step to them, they respect that, because they see that nothing has changed, I'm still the same homie. I'm just going about things way differently. I'm no punk. I'm following a new God, not that spook God, I'm following a man. I don't have my X yet, but when I do get my X, all the cowards and hypocrites will be weeded out.

The brothers right now on the West Coast, you can't even come at them with religion, you have to come at them with the race thing. It's a race thing right now. In a minute everybody will soon find out. When they find out it's a race thing, then you can come at them with religion. You have to give them a little bit, you have to give them some milk first.

**L:** The one thing we can't do with Islam is take it as, "I'm a mosque man." It's good to go to the meetings and all of that, but you also have to go out amongst the people and spread the teachings. This is just one of the li'l homiez in the hood with some consciousness [speaking about Moon]. Now you can see the change. Back then if somebody tripped, we didn't even think about it, we was moving right then, no questions asked.

**M:** We're some of the first brothers in the hood that have been trying to get the teachings, and some of the other brothers in the hood have been trying to see what we're doing. Now they see that it's the only way to go, now the brothers are coming up to us, asking us what's up. "Yo, get us some books, or let us hear some tapes. Spread the word or something. Don't hide the knowledge."

**L:** It's like banging for Muhammad. That's what I told them. We had a big meeting, and brothers were coming at me like, "Now that you're with the Nation, you ain't with this?" I said, "Hold up, brother, you can't even separate the two."

**M:** The Uprisings showed that there were no plans on rioting for Rodney King. To be honest, Rodney King, you got up there and disrespected us. Saying something like that, "Can't we all just get along?" If anything, you should have kept your mouth closed and waited until everything was over, and then handled your business. Instead, you got up there, and you showed everybody that you was a punk. They whipped on you bad, and you're going to say, "Can't we all just get along?"

I think that speech was given to him. I know what happened, Bush called him and said, "Rodney, all of this is because of you, what are you going to do about this? These are your people. Talk to your people. I'm going to give you this letter, and I want you to say this on national TV." You wimp.

**L:** Think about Natasha Harlins too. [Korean store owner Soon Ja Du shot and killed Natasha Harlins—a young black child, a baby. The murder was on videotape. She served no time in jail and she was not charged with murder.]

**Q:** How do the brothers feel when they hear the teachings of the Nation of Islam?

**M:** When I was onstage at Savior's Day, I saw one of the brothers from the hood in the audience. I was looking at him, and he was jumping up, I didn't know if he was playing or what. The brother was looking excited. I talked to him afterwards, and he said, "Minister Farrakhan was talking on the real." All the brothers in my hood that I spoke with, they all say that the Minister touched something in them.

Minister Farrakhan, if he talks to you, he's going to touch something in you. You can feel it. The Minister can get you in a room and change your whole mind-set. He has that power that can wash you clean and change your life.

**L:** That's what happened to me. When I went, I didn't know anything about meeting Minister Farrakhan, I just knew the streets. When I met him, and then when I saw my picture in the *Final Call* newspaper where it said, "A changed man." I just realized two or three weeks ago what that really meant. It's like he was dictating to me what I'm doing, because I didn't know what a changed man I was, until after the paper. Then I realized that those words in the paper were my thoughts, because now I don't think the way that I used to think. I see the same people every day, but I see them differently now. It's like something new. It can change overnight.

If we can take the sexual energy out of the sisters in the way that they dress, they will have to realize that the way they dress was brought to them from another idea and another standpoint other than God's. That's why God says, "Cover yourself." A lot of homiez got killed behind girls. I've seen a lot of brothers drop, behind a girl. I'm talking about some of my own homeboys, all behind laying up. So it's important to me that the sisters get themselves together and understand what their righteous role is.

**B:** First us brothers have to get ourselves right.

**M:** If you talk to some of the sisters on the West Coast, they're totally dead.

**B:** If you have a close relationship with your woman, that can save your life.

**Q:** What role can sisters play in helping to increase the peace amongst the brothers?

**M:** Sisters have to try to help the brothers the best way they can, and try to help us build this.

**L:** The Black woman, everything comes through the Black woman. God works through the Black woman, so she's the most important conductor; there are two halves that become one whole when you get married. What a sister has to realize is that she has to help her man meet his obligations, and that he's going to maintain her as a husband. Then they have to come together and understand that it's about one family. You have to walk her through the knowledge, you have to deal with her every day, you have to bring the knowledge to her attention every day.

There's a lot that we have to do to bring out a stronger character in every male, because the attributes are all there, we are created from ALLAH, God, so we have all the ninety-nine attributes. All we have to do is tap in to bring that source out. We also have to bring the woman around to realize that she's the co-creator and that she has the same attributes. It's not discriminatory, where the men are elevated and the women are not. No nation can rise higher than its woman.

**M:** We have to get at everybody on an individual level and really put it down. They should start carrying themselves like the mothers of civilization. Then they'll get that respect, we'll make sure that they get that respect.

**Q:** What role can brothers play to help change the sisters for the positive?

**M:** First of all, we have to let them know about all the BS that they're out here wearing. . . . I got at some sisters a couple of nights ago, I was like, "All that is not even necessary." They straight got crazy with me. I told them, "That right there that you are wearing is nothing, you're out here advertising yourself. How are brothers supposed to act, how are brothers supposed to come at you when you're dressed like that? That's an invitation."

**B:** The white man has some of our women so mentally messed up that the things a brother tries to tell them, they don't listen to.

**M:** They'd rather worship a spook God.

**B:** Not only that, but we don't have anything to give our women. We have to make that change ourselves and set the example.

**L:** We have to show them their shortcomings, but don't make it sound like a preacher, "You're going to burn in hell." It's more like, "Sister, you have to understand what you're doing, you have to understand where the root of it comes from," because what does she say when I say you shouldn't dress like that? She says, "I grew up like that, my mama or my sister taught me that." Then you have to go to the root of who taught her mother or her sister that, and every time you'll find that the idea came from another element. The reason why you need to clothe yourself, sister, is so that you won't be talked to as a "b—" or a "whore." You'll be talked to respectfully when you carry yourself respectfully and dress respectfully. You can't be out here following the fashions of the white world, because they don't apply to us anymore. Their rulership and power has been disconnected in the community, so we have to kill the ideologies of the white race's world, so you can go on and become Black Queens, and self-respecting women, and you can raise your children to be self-respecting, and to respect the Black family. It's time to reconnect all of us back to the one family that we were, that one nation of people.

After you get her out of *Days of Our Lives* and *Guiding Light* and all these other white devils' TV shows that they're watching, then they'll start getting into their self-consciousness. They see the madness they are exposed to, they see it daily. You have to let her recognize what's going on when you give her the knowledge, because you don't see it until you get the knowledge.

Once you're civilized, then your duty is to civilize the uncivilized. We have to come up out of these mosques, and we have to hit these communities and let these people know the time. We have to get in the streets with the people, go to where they're at.

**M:** Without that, if you don't get in the streets, you're not doing anything.

**Q:** What are your visions for the future?

**B:** Uprising. A complete change.

**M:** I see revolution. I see complete change.

**B:** L.A., we're going to change this soon. In the blinking of an eye.

**L:** The future is bright. I look into our children's eyes, and into your baby's eyes right now, and I know that they know. You can tell by the eye contact through them, that the future is bright, and they're going to carry the load.

**M:** The young brothers right now are straight-up soldiers. They're out here serious, at twelve years old, and they know this is not a game.

**L:** It brings back to mind the 66 million Blacks in Brazil, and half of them are between the ages of eight to eighteen, street children. The government over there is getting $70 a pop for a head, because the merchants want to rid the community of all the young orphans. That's a major army, and if you expose them to the right ideas and to the right knowledge, they'll bring in a new reality.

**M:** In these movies, everything they put out is for a reason. They believe something, they saw something, they know something.

**L:** Universal change is here.

**Q:** Any further words of wisdom that you would like to speak on?

**B:** To the brothers in the gangs, everybody, all of us, we have to get together and beat this beast, this devil.

**M:** To the brothers in the gangs that still want to gang-bang on the brotherhood, we're coming to get y'all. We're with the peace.

**L:** You're not a gang, you're the family of Muhammad. Just fast and hold prayer, because God is directing us all. If you thought you got yourself out of a serious place where you almost lost your life, it was ALLAH. Keep God foremost in the front and the back of your mind. Minister Farrakhan, I don't care how deep the FOI is, it's not the FOI that's protecting Farrakhan, it's ALLAH that's protecting him, and He can do the same for all of us.

> ***Pay tribute and honor to the Bloods and Crips who are trying desperately to make peace among themselves. . . . It was the unseen hand of the living God that produced the spirit in these men.***
>
> **—Minister Louis Farrakhan**

## SHOUT OUTS

Thanks to ALLAH for coming in the person of Master Fard Muhammad, and raising in our midst the Most Honorable Elijah Muhammad, and those two backing the Honorable Minister Louis Farrakhan. Thanks to Minister Farrakhan for raising me up. Thanks to my parents, and to Linburg for opening up my consciousness. To all the homiez resting in peace:

> ***And speak not of those who are slain in ALLAH's way as dead. Nay, they are alive, but you perceive not.***
>
> **—Holy Qur'an, 2:153**

T. Rodgers—a proud father!

# T. RODGERS

*(T. Rodgers is first and foremost a proud father, along with being the president and CEO of Sidewalk University and a longtime fighter for peace. I'm an ex–gang leader of the Black Peace Stone Nation, currently working on two soon-to-be-released books entitled "Everything You Always Wanted to Know About Gangs: A Parents' Handbook" and "How Not to Become a Professional Victim." I would like for those who read these words in this book to understand that as long as there is life in a body, there is hope. You can change. You can be everything you want to be!)*

**Q:** What role have you played in bringing peace to South Central, and what can be done to strengthen the peace amongst the youth organizations in Los Angeles, and in other parts of the country?

**T:** I have been an advocate of peace since 1969.

**Q:** Nineteen sixty-nine?

**T:** I arrived here in Los Angeles from Chicago in '69, with an open letter from one of the main 21s, to start a chapter in Los Angeles, of what at that time was called the Almighty Black Peace Stone Nation. I did just that, and I did that pretty well. One of the things that my mother always taught me was, "Whatever you do in life, be the best at it." At that time the Vietnam War was going on, it was the time of flower power and free love. It was a time when Black men, not Black males, but *Black men* were not prevalent. They were not truly standing up in our community, and I would guess it was because of the Vietnam War that not many Black men were around at that time. There was a decrease in gangs such as the Slausons, the Businessmen, the Rabble Rousers, the Hat Gang, the Farmers, Blood Alley, and the Gladiators.

While this was going on, I read in several places that the Crips were starting to formulate. That was in late '68, early '69. I can't even begin to tell that story, because I wasn't there.

**Q:** How did you organize yourselves in Los Angeles?

**T:** We were a community-based organization. We started at 2924 Ninth Avenue, off of Mont Clair. We shared our community with the Asians. We would meet at Jefferson and Ninth Avenue, right there on the southeast corner. There's a church there now, but at that time there was a storefront. That storefront was run by what was called the Yellow Brotherhood. They were Asians that wanted to do some positive things, and they were giving us direction in organizing a certain way.

What we found out was that the guys on the other side of the double yellow lines were starting to form also [Crips]. They were into flexing their muscles. The funny thing is, we all went to the same elementary school, and it's ironic that there was competition between the classrooms that were geographically separated. Now that I think about it, the classrooms that we played against in elementary school were the classrooms that developed into Crips. There was always that competition between us. Always that competition between the guys that stayed on one side of Jefferson and the guys that stayed on the other side of Jefferson.

**Q:** How were you received in '69 here in L.A. when you came with the idea of starting a chapter of the Almighty Black Peace Stones?

**T:** L.A. was so laid-back, so into individualism, so into "I do my thing, you do your thing," it was that type of philosophy.

I was something that came into the community, and before the community knew it, I had control of the community, and the situation was out of control. If I had a ten-, eleven-, or twelve-year-old who had paid his dues, and he ran away from his mama, I would put him up at the Hilton. People would trip. We'd ride around in limousines. We did all of the things that kids were doing back East, but weren't doing on the West Coast. So I was a phenomenon. People are afraid of a man who acts wisely, and one of the things that I instilled in the people around me was to just think. Don't just act on emotions, don't just run out there and do something, but think.

We all had a common bond, we didn't like taking out trash; we didn't like combing our hair, we'd have it braided; we liked wearing our pants a certain way, creased, and hung low; we liked our pants starched, we liked our shirts clean, pressed, and starched, we liked our shoes shined. So there was a certain way that we liked to project ourselves. The mothers would say, "Hey, he's a nice-looking kid," but we were controlling their daughters. We were controlling their sons. If they got a $5 allowance, one of those dollars belonged to Black Stone. If he was a representative of Black Stone, then he had to give $5.

I had my first car when I was twelve, almost thirteen. I wore tailor-made suits, and everything I had I would put my initials on. I had custom jewelry. That was the time of leather coats. I had all of my leather coats made, I had leather hats to match the coats. This is the way that we were living. So it was like, what you put into Black Stone was what you got out of Black Stone. It wasn't always about having a gun or beating everybody up.

We controlled the community, and we had a system set up to where if you came across Jefferson, we knew it. If you crossed Washington Avenue, between Arlington and Crenshaw, we knew it. I could leave my mother's house on Ninth Avenue and Mont Clair and get up to Adams without being seen.

We were five hundred strong. We controlled five different parks. At that time, the more parks you controlled, the more powerful you were. If you controlled one park, that was cool. The park was where we went to hang out, and different neighborhoods would come to that park. The five parks we controlled were Jim Gilliam, Vineyard, Jackie Robinson, Queen Anne, and Second Avenue. The communities around those parks we also controlled. We would have the meetings in the parks, so we were very visible to the community.

**Q:** When you first started forming the Black Stones in L.A., what were you teaching them?

**T:** At twelve years old, they had their mothers saying, "Do this," and they had their fathers saying, "I will beat you up," but I was at a meeting twice a week giving them lessons. I was telling them that they are Black Prince Stones, that they are Black People Stones, that they are Black Power Stones, when their mothers were saying, "You're nothing, you look like your father, you make me sick, get out of my sight." The school would say, "You'll never be anything but a janitor," and I was saying, "You're a prince, you'll grow up to be a king, and if you live right, you'll be a god." Now who would you want to be around? They saw that those of us who were leaders and had jobs and responsibilities to the Nation, that had rank, and duties, we were getting compensated for what we did. Brothers were starting to wear different kinds of clothes. Their language started to change. They really started taking time to groom themselves. They had a respectability towards women. Bank accounts were starting to open up. Brothers started to have cars, way before they had licenses. So we started to attract a lot of attention.

One of our lessons was that "Stones don't die, they multiply." If you take a stone, and you pulverize that stone, you have sand. That sand is nothing but little stones. Stones don't die, they multiply. That's where that saying comes from. When we went to jail, you could tell a Black Stone from everyone else, because he stood on a square, he stood on a forty-five-degree angle, with right over left. That was way before X-Clan (respect due). There was something about our mannerisms. Sometimes we would even square corners when we walked, and people would know that there was something different about us.

**Q:** What were some of the early goals you had as an organized Nation?

**T:** One of the first things we wanted to do was to buy property in the community. Mind you, I was sixteen years old. We wanted to get houses, because we found that a lot of us kept running away. We wanted to get legitimate money, especially during the summer, so that we wouldn't have to ask our parents. We wanted to pay our mothers' rents and do the things that men were supposed to do. We knew nothing of the rites of passage, but we were putting ourselves through it without even knowing what we were doing. There were levels that we had to go through; I'll give you a few. You had to maintain a B average, or it was a violation. You had to go to school, or it was a violation. You had to be at the meetings, or it was a violation. Violations ran from menial to very violent. We became the mothers and the fathers of the kids in the community. We became their extended family. We were the ones that made sure that the kids did what they were supposed to do.

**Q:** Was it aimed to be more positive when you first started?

**T:** People say that there is nothing good in gangs; well, that's a lie. I ask you, take a second, name me the attributes of the L.A. Rams. Better yet, name me the attributes of the Los Angeles Raiders, and their whole "commitment to excellence" and Al Davis's "Just win, Baby." "It's not whether you win or lose, it's how you . . ." F— that. "Just win." This is what he instilled in his players. I think Malcolm X said it more profoundly: "By any means necessary." It is the same thing.

We were instilling a sense of self-worth and self-pride, a sense of responsibility and community, a sense of Blackness. "You are not a dog, you're not an animal, you are not a nigger, you're not chattel, colored, or Negro, but you are a prince, in its truest sense."

One of my jobs . . . goals, you ask, one of my jobs was to get legitimate money for the organization, and we did. We got legitimate money. So these are some of the things that were going on. We taught safe sex before it was fashionable. We taught monogamy. If I could put two people together and keep them together, then I did what I was supposed to do.

We became marriage counselors—when I think back, we did a lot of county, city, state, and federal work, right in the midst of Black Stone. We would shoot for scholarships. I didn't care anything about playing ball, and I was good as an athlete. These are some of the things that I was doing and wasn't really conscious of it. We taught economic empowerment, we taught entrepreneurship.

**Q:** Where did some of those early principles come from?

**T:** When I was coming up, we met in a Catholic church, a big, Gothic type of church; it was spooky. A lot of us were devout Christians, but we were taught Islam, and it just progressed over the years.

**Q:** Who was doing the teaching?

**T:** A lot of people. Jeff Ford for one, the Bull, the main 21s.

**Q:** So is Black Stone affiliated with the El Rukins in Chicago?

**T:** That is what we should have evolved into. What happened out here is that brothers wanted to become Bloods, instead of becoming El Rukins. I had grew, and I just wasn't into making people do certain things anymore.

A lot of brothers, if you ask them, they'll say, "BPS," and spell it "B-E-E, P-E-E," or something like that. They're dissing their own set; "P-E-E," what the hell is that? Is that urination? These younger homiez that are coming up now have no direction, and no respect. I was first-generation Black Stone; the second generation got the true teachings, the third-generation Black Stone got the true teachings, and I stayed around all the way until the fifth generation.

The fifth generation—five is the number of man; smell, sight, touch, taste, and sound. It is also Arm-Leg-Leg-Arm-Head [ALLAH]. Love, peace, truth, freedom, and justice. So we studied numerology, we would get off into discussions like that. Then after the fifth generation, I decided to just be a spiritual adviser to Black Stone. Once I did that, and they got away from the teachings, along with a lot of them going to jail and being locked up in the Blood module—peer pressure is something else, and a lot of brothers were not strong enough, their faith, their belief, was not strong enough. That's what you have today, you have the contamination of something which was once very pure. That's the real of it.

**Q:** Coming from that type of background, what happened? How did some of the negative elements get into the organization?

**T:** Getting into the negative aspect of it, or the demise of Black Stone as I knew it, we were infiltrated.

**Q:** How did you feel being a part of this organization?

**T:** It was a sense of power that I can't even describe. It's the closest thing to being God on earth. To stand in front of five hundred people and have them pledge their allegiance to your Nation. That's the upside. The downside is that you set up a platform for death. When you have that many people, and you are teaching self-responsibility and self-respect, you lose people. That responsibility for other lives and deaths became really hard for me to deal with. When things were happening to me, it was different, but when things started happening to people around me, it affected me in a different way.

Here's an example. We were standing on a corner and a car rolls by. The second time it rolled by I said, "Watch the car." The third time the car rolls by, the window rolls down, and shots ring out. Somebody yells "Duck," and everybody was supposed to duck. We used to practice for that. It was called a drop drill. We would yell, "Duck," and those that were not listening would be standing, and we would tell them, "You're dead." This time it was for real, and this kid got shot, and the whole half of his forehead was blown away, his brains, and his body was just pouring onto the dirty concrete. Out of everybody that was standing around, he looked at me, in his dying state, and he said, "T., don't let me die." That's when I realized that I was not God. I don't have the right to play God with anybody's life. That's when the egotism and the arrogance started to leave me. It was a very humbling experience. It was a state of nothingness. Out of all of the powers that I possessed, I could not put him back together.

I had five hundred guys that would move at my command, but I could not put this kid back together. Then there was the turmoil, the trauma, the hardship, the pain, the sorrow, and the families that you had to deal with. It's like, "T., I entrusted him to you, he looked up to you, he followed you, and you let him die. You got him killed. What kind of monster are you? Why would you do this to my baby? I fed you, I loved you like you were one of my sons, and you got my baby killed." I would catch the first anger, the first hostility, the first physical response from the families, and after a while—I mean twenty-five years, man, after a while that eats at your soul. It hurts. You go through this numb feeling about death. It's like, "Well, another one bites the dust. You killed one of ours, we'll kill five of yours."

If we're going through this on our side, then what are they going through on their side? I've been shot four times, stabbed twice, and had more fights than Mike Tyson and haven't been paid for any of them. When I ran Black Stone, we had one other death. Dirty Red got hit by a car. That's the only other death that we had, when I was truly running Black Stone.

I think we had an edge on people because we had a philosophy, an ideology, we had uniforms. Our uniforms were red, black, and green. Depending on your status, you wore red pants, black pants, or green pants, with a red, black, or green stripe, and a matching shirt. We had red berets—we were organized. Then we had the reputation of Black Stone in Chicago. Then there was the third part, of just being intelligent. We would go into another neighborhood, and we would give them certain choices, and a lot of times—human nature just wants to be a part of something, whether it's the Boy Scouts, the Rotary Club, people just want to be a part of something, so they would become a part of our Nation.

**Q:** Expand on how infiltration affected Black Stone?

**T:** At the beginning of Black Stone, they didn't have many, if any, feds that were Black, or any young enough to infiltrate us on that level. What happened is we started separating the males from the females, because we found that the females would instigate a lot of stuff. They would get mad at their boyfriends, and they would talk. There was infiltration among the different sets.

Some kids had fathers who were police, and if he was violated, and he felt that the violation was unfair, he would tell his mother or his father, and we would be infiltrated that way. As time progressed, they would send young officers in on us. It was only in the later eighties that we were infiltrated by the police. It was in the later eighties that we were infiltrated by the feds, and all of the other existing organizations that have networked and hooked up. Now they have very young, baby-face agents, who you wouldn't believe are officers. It's a whole different ball game now.

**Q:** What got the killing started between the organizations?

**T:** Several things; the first fights that ever broke out was over females. The same females that would go and sleep with someone else started a lot of killings.

In the early years a lot of the killings were accidents. Brothers were just loaded and didn't mean to kill, just plain and simple, they didn't mean to kill. A lot of the drive-bys can be attributed to drugs, and liquor. We're not a race of people that are animals, we have a lot of compassion. It is those elements that are put into our neighborhoods that bring out that which would allow us to kill.

I've been in jail when brothers had came out of their high and drunken state, and they're like, "I ain't got a murder, T." "Well, there ain't nobody in here but me and you, and I damn sure don't have a murder." You hear, see, and feel the reality of his soul being lost, and they cry like babies. "I didn't do it, it couldn't have been me." Then the test from the ballistics comes back, because there were three or four guns used. That's the reality of it, and I don't care what anybody who thinks that they're a gangster may say, they didn't mean to do it. Unless it was a specific thing between two specific people. Like a crime of passion for example, or one person who has been picked on for so long that he cannot turn the other cheek, and it gets to a level to where it's either kill or be killed. That is an arguable case for self-defense.

Then they developed CRASH, OSS, and the gang units. Some of their tactics would be to pick us up and say, "I will give you three choices: I will whip you until I get tired, I will take you into the other gang territory, or I'll take you to jail." Me, I was like, "Drop me off. I have good survival skills, but as far as you jumping on me, my mama doesn't jump on me. As far as you taking me to jail and making me a slave, I'm not your chattel. I believe that I am a prince, I am a king, I am of royalty, and you do not treat royalty that way. Take your shackles off of me, and let me run free, and if my God decides that I shall die here, then so be it, but you are not God, you can't be the judge, jury, and executioner over me. You put your pants on just like I do."

They would let me go, they would drop me off in another neighborhood and be mad, because I would make it home. That's when we found out that the police were writing on the walls. Now some of the young police officers can do graffiti, to a level that is passable, to send messages. When I first got here I didn't know about Pinafore, Santo Tomas, Don Felipe, or any of those streets, but my street skills were sharp. I could read the writing on the walls and know what neighborhood I was in. The police, after a while, became aware of that, so they would write on the walls to keep s— going.

Some peace treaties that I negotiated back in '71, '72 were broken, because of the police. They knew that gangs were big business. Without the warring factions of gangs, there would be no CRASH [Community Resources Against Street Hoodlums], there would be no OSS [Operation

Safe Streets], which is the county sheriff's thing, there would be no gang unit, there would be no specialized gang unit, there would be no task force. So crime does pay, and we pay for it with our lives. A brother gets two life sentences, plus forty years, and one day. What is that, a joke? Then the laws change, and they still don't know what to do. They want to charge mothers with being responsible for the kids. If you write on the walls, then your parents are responsible? So they don't know what to do. It's funny, because I've been telling them for years that there is a difference between white culture and Black culture, between white family lives and Black family lives. You can't get a white psychologist to come in and deal with a Black family. It does not work. So this is where the whole level of gang-banging started to change, this is where Hollywood got into the arena, and I'm also guilty, because I'm a part of that. Hollywood's theme is, "Well, it's only a movie, we'll kill twenty of them." That's where the people that have planes, the people that make guns, the true warlords, they sat down at a table and said, "We'll let the niggers have the guns, we'll let the niggers have the dope." Sounds like a movie, huh? But this is true. This is what happened. We don't have any planes. We used to be able to make a zip gun, that's a .22. Then they changed the course, so you can't even make zip guns out of antennas anymore. An AK-47 is not even an American-made gun, so something strange is going on here.

**Q:** What do you feel is the proper approach to bring back the unity and the positive elements within the organizations?

**T:** The same way that I started Black Stone in L.A. You take one person, and you give that person the ideology, the philosophy, the self-esteem, you share the dream, you embrace him, and you listen. Then he will go, and he will bring one, and then they will bring one, and before you know it, you'll have an army. That's how it's done; it's very simple. People are so smart now, they complicate it. It is very, very simple. You take that one person that feels cheated, that feels inadequate, because he's illiterate, or that feels cheated because he gave the state time for a crime he did not commit. You take that one person and give him human proficiency, and training, with a promise of a job after graduating.

Then he has a goal, and he has a choice: "I can go kick it with the homiez, or I can stay with this program, with Sidewalk University, and do something for myself, my family, my mother, my wife, and my baby."

There are those of us who are people, people. They should become the teachers, because they can relate to human nature, and they can take that education and disperse it in a way where it doesn't become like school, because we have been taught to dislike school.

Just by us talking or by us reading this book, that's how we learn, by sitting at a tribal fire and sharing experiences, which is what I call an "expression session." It's giving of yourself to teach someone else. I can relate to things coming from you, as opposed to a professor trying to make me study in order to get an A. I rebel against authority, but if you are my friend, a tribal leader, a scout, a warrior, I have respect and admiration for you, then it becomes a different thing. That goes back to the rites of passage.

Now, mathematically and geographically, it becomes a problem, because how do we deal with individuals on such a mass level? That's what nobody has come up with, that's what we need to do. In my estimation, in my education, in my experience, that is the way to go. If you get personal with a person . . . Check me for a minute: in the fifties and sixties from one corner to another corner, everybody knew your name. If you stole an apple, if you stole a watermelon, in doing those crimes everybody knew who you were. Just like in school, every school has a teacher who has an open door, and all of the kids go in there. The kids will leave their classes that they are having problems with, and instead of going to a counselor or the principal, they go to that particular teacher that has an ear, that understands, that will listen. It's the same thing in the community. I call it the "Kool-Aid" house, that house where everybody comes—the gang members, the unwed mothers, the pregnant mothers, those that have drug problems—everybody will come to that particular house, because that man, that woman, that family unit, understands what that community needs and embraces it. These are the little things that we used to do as a tribe, that we don't do anymore. Yes, I am my brother's keeper, because if I don't keep him, who will? These are the things that we have to get back to. Just in sharing and caring. I want for my brother what I want for myself, as opposed to, "I'm the man, and you ain't, I got mine, and you've got to get yours." The broken promises, the years of tears, the years of fears, of not knowing, of not having a strong Black man who will stand up and say, "This is the way to go. This is what should be done, and you are not a man until you have done this." As opposed to saying, "The more time in jail that I get, the bigger man I am. The more babies that I have, the bigger man I am. The more fights that I've had, the bigger man I am." It doesn't work like that.

A brother will sit up and make $100,000 a year slanging dope and can't spend any of the money. Rides around with the money in his trunk, but doesn't put that money to use. To increase the peace we have to give back, because these are the things that have alienated and increased the envy, the jealousy, the self-hatred, in the community. The "Why are you successful and I'm not?" attitude. So in the sharing of information, in sharing your experience, that is the foundation that we have to build. We have to say, "Whatever you are, you are my brother. Whatever you are, I am as messed up as you are, maybe not in the same fields, but I have my problems too. How can I help you? Forget my problems for a minute; how can I help you?" I've learned that in whatever possessions I've accumulated, if I give them away, I make room for other things to come into my life. That's on a personal level. Now if all

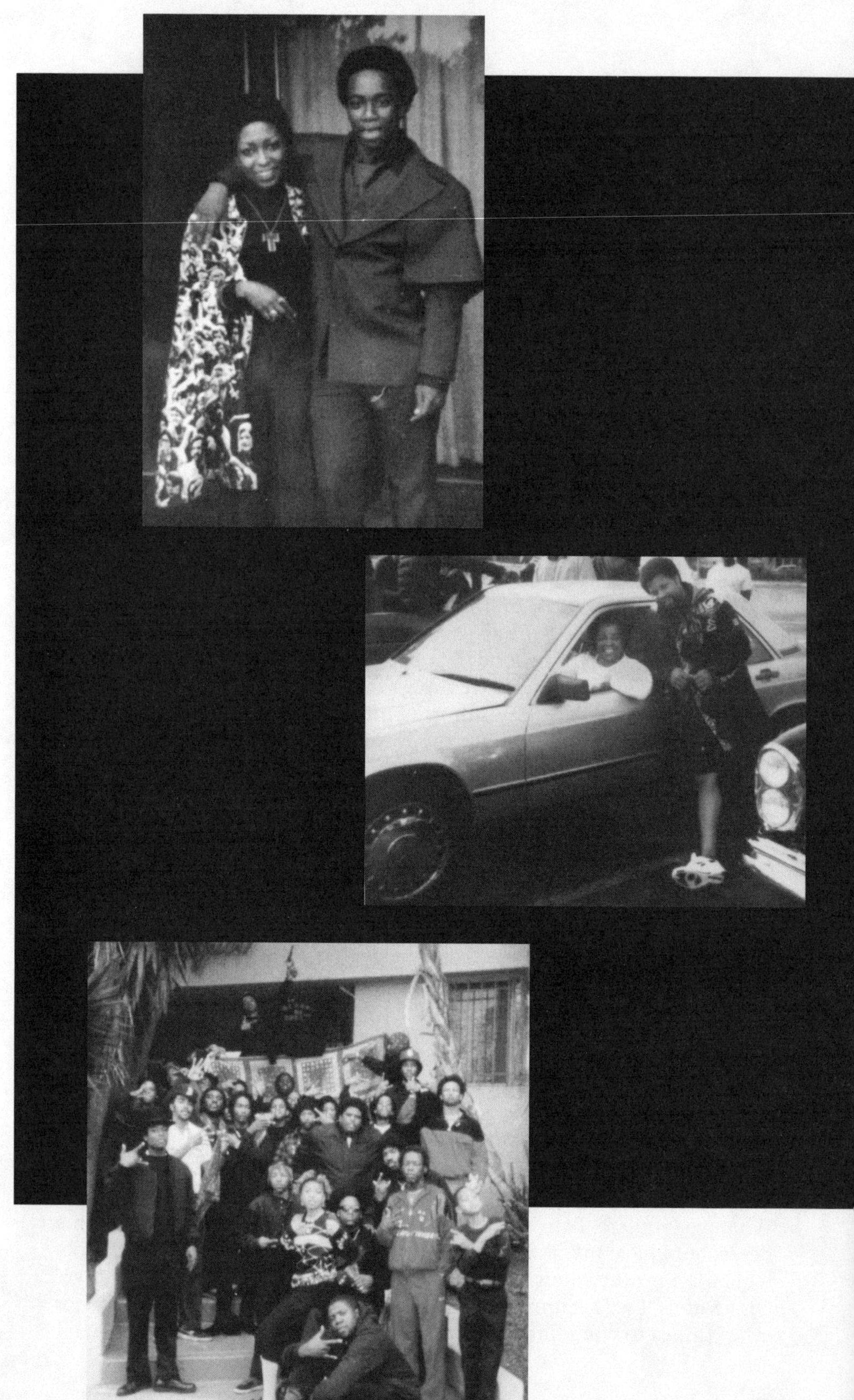

of us did that, look at the exchange and the room that we would leave open for growth. That is what has to happen, and that is what used to happen when we had a common and identified enemy.

Blue is not my enemy, red is not my enemy, brown is not my enemy, yellow is not my enemy; it is those that think they are gods over us. The enemy is called white supremacy, that is the true enemy. Even the skinheads, the neo-Nazis, the Aryan Brotherhood, they are nothing but pawns that are being used. They are nobody. Those are hate mongers that mainly stay in their community, they are nothing but cowards. What is the difference between South Africa and South Central? What is the difference between the ANC and the Zulu, and the Crips and the Bloods? What is the difference between the skinheads, the Aryan Brotherhood, and the Crips and Bloods? The Crips and Bloods stay in their neighborhoods, and the Aryans stay in their neighborhoods, nobody has done any serious killing.

When they busted the skinheads, "the almighty, great, save us, white boys, FBI, who saved us from the Aryan Brotherhood and became heroes," that's BS. They set that up to make themselves look good. That's all they were doing, and that was provoked by the FBI. Let's look at it: who is Chip? He's nobody, and everybody says, "Hey, the FBI has finally done something right." No, man, don't go for the okeydoke, that's the old pimp's con game, that's the jigaboo twist. That ain't happening. They're all in a plot, and the strings are pulled by white supremacists, by people who don't care about any of us.

In the penitentiaries, we come together to fight a common enemy. There's no red and there's no blue in the pen. When the Uprisings jumped off, there was Cuz and Bloods together, in the streets, doing what they had to do. When there is a common, identifiable enemy, then there is no separation. It's funny, because someone had asked me how would the unity come about. I feel there are two ways: in the short term, a war happens, and *we know* who the *true enemy* is. In the long term, those in control will get so arrogant in their genocide that we will just wake up. What is interesting is that they have done both. The Uprisings jumped off in '92, then they started trying to rewrite the laws overnight, and it's just not going to happen like that.

**Q:** How do you define white supremacy, and how is it manifested?

**T:** I will identify how white supremacy is implemented, only to stress how vital it is for us to get out from under it. To truly do for ourselves, as Billie Holiday said: "God bless the child that's got his own!"

I want to start at birth, but let's even take it a step further than that. Under the right circumstances, a man and a woman in perfect harmony can give birth to a god. After the birth of the child—and this is a disaster, but it's a tradition that we do with our children—the first thing that we teach them is how to fight back. If you ask a Jew what is the first thing that they learned, they'll say that the first thing they were taught was to help another Jew. The first thing that we are taught is how to beat up another brother or sister. Think about it. As children: "If he hits you, hit him back. If he's bigger than you, pick up a stick and knock the hell out of him." How far back can we trace that? We are not a violent people. If you trace our history to anywhere that we have been, you will find that we are not a violent people. We're not an aggressive people. We are peaceful by nature.

Where did the violence come from? Look at the cartoons that our children watch. The violence is constantly pumped into the minds of our youth. Look at PBS, with Oscar the Grouch and a freak, mutant Big Bird. I don't even know what the hell it is that's in the trash can, and my child is supposed to love him and embrace him? Then you have Barney, a purple dinosaur—this is some caveman BS that is not relevant to us. That's white supremacy on TV.

The only real Black radio station that we have is Stevie Wonder's radio station, kindness, joy, love, and happiness, KJLH, owned and operated by our own. On all the other stations, if you have a brother or a sister who "makes it" to program director, we're happy? The "slave master" is still in control!

From the very beginning, they've been saying, "I will take you to Jesus." And it was the belly of a slave ship. When we got into the schools, which have messed us up for years, they taught us to do menial jobs, not even knowing that there is a difference between the way a Black little boy learns and a Black little girl learns. Many of the teachers haven't seen a Black little boy until they have reached the inner-city schools, and they think that they are prepared to teach him. They've got to love him before they can teach him, and they have to understand him before they can teach him. They damn sure can't teach that which they do not love. We need higher pay, and more Black teachers. That's white supremacy in the schools.

Why are there more liquor stores and "ungodly" churches in the Black community than anything else? Because if they can't get you drunk off of the alcohol, then they will get you f'd up off of religion having you pray to a twenty-by-sixteen-inch picture of a blue-eyed, blond-haired, pink Jesus. Michelangelo's cousin? I ask them, what color is Jesus? They say, "I don't know what color God is." I didn't ask you about God, I asked you about Jesus. It's in your Bible. (We haven't forgotten about the chapters that have been stolen.) The Bible itself states that Jesus had hair like lamb's wool, his feet were like brass burned in an oven. I didn't write it. But yet you tell me to bow down to a white . . . hell, no. White supremacy at its finest. I know that in the beginning there was darkness, and it was said, "Let there be light." Then my God is Black. My God is Black and Jesus is also Black, and I am a believer in Jesus.

When I read your dictionaries, you force upon me a definition of Black as being evil, black magic, black cat, soot, dirt, bad luck—kiss my Black ass. Then you tell me that white is: pure, that angels are white, with fluffy wings and harps, when I know that from the Bible, it is written that Peter holds the keys to heaven, and Peter was a Black man.

Then you take my money, you rape my mama and my sister within the church. [Begins to talk like a Southern preacher] "It is the church that has been the leader of the Black community," then aligns itself with the NAACP, the National Advancement for "Certain" People. The NAACP was started by a white man. Am I supposed to—because I'm of a warrior state, a warrior mentality, a warrior stature—am I supposed to submit to this BS? Play, pass me. Deal, pass me.

These are things that are there, and once we look at them we say, something is very wrong here.

When you look at the dollar bill—everything on it was stolen from Africa, or from people of African descent. The pyramids, the all-seeing eye, which is the eye of Horus, the number 13, the olive leaf. The eagle in North America was the hawk in Africa, the highest-flying bird. The stars are celestial bodies, then they are five-pointed stars. They have to back up off of me. Then we fight and kill over this dollar, when they say it is just a federal reserve note. So when you get off into it, it's underlying, but it is there.

Let's move back into the schools, because I just touched on it. In the schools the first thing that you give me—"I pledge allegiance to the flag of the United Snakes of America"—that in this U.S., in the Constitution, it still says that we are chattel. The three-fifths compromise. They call Black people three-fifths of a man. Jesse Jackson ran for president, he is not the epitome of Black manhood, but if he would have done what he was supposed to do, then I would have had some type of power. He could have kicked down certain doors that would have said, "Back up, you mf's." Then they bought him. "We're going to give you a radio show, you're a good nigga." White supremacy at its finest.

Hollywood, who will say, "I will take artistic license to change a story, even though it is not the truth," they messed us up through the way that they portray us in the movies and in the media.

Let me try to break this down. The schools teach us how to be slaves, teaching us how to submit. The majority of the teachers are white, and we are supposed to respect and submit to them in a certain way? The books were never written with us in mind. Christopher Columbus fell off the damn boat. There's always a small segment in their books on Africa, and they always have us running around as naked spear chuckers, and jigaboos. They never talk about the Ashantis or the Zulus, or the Mau Mau. None of the great tribes. They never talk about Kemet. They never talk about any of the great contributions that we've made.

We know that Alexander Graham Bell wouldn't have been s— without that brother. Graham Bell hooked it up, and it burned out. The brother came back through there—and I'm saying "the brother" because I want you to find out what brother I'm talking about that invented and perfected the light.

Another point I want to touch on, you'll sit up and tell me that you are a "loc," which is short for *loco,* which means crazy. I guess so, because the way you act, you act like you lost your mind. You will tell me that you're a "dog." "What's up, dog?" B-dog, C-dog, it doesn't make a difference, a dog is an animal. This is what you are doing to yourself. Why would you want to name yourself Capone, C-Capone, B-Capone, why do you want to acknowledge and admire and walk in the footsteps of some Caucasian that died of syphilis? What is wrong with you? This is what pisses me off. This shames me. Then you want to tell me that you're a gangster?

My question to you is where did the first gangs come from? The very first gangs were the gangs that guarded the pyramids—I told you already that they stole everything from Africa. Those were the first gangs. Those were positive work gangs, those were gangs that had meaning. Gangs are now translated over into something vile, vicious, and immoral, and you accept that BS, thinking that you're going to stand up and be something or somebody. Give that a rest. Then they want to know why I'm angry. Because you missed your mark. You want the respect in the community, but you have to become what God put you on earth to be, in order to get the respect that is due to you. You can't kill everybody to get your respect, it doesn't work like that.

**Q:** How do we change this way of thinking?

**T:** One of the first things that I've learned when people would point fingers at me and say, "You need to do this," in the process of pointing a finger at me, they have four fingers pointing back at theirself. You must start with yourself. My class is called *SELF,* Survival Education for Life and Family. If you love yourself, it will be hard for you to hurt somebody else. That's the first thing that happens. If you have knowledge of what you are, and who you are, petty envy and jealousy doesn't even matter. You are aware of it, but it's easier for you to roll it off of your back. You know that God has a plan for you.

The other thing that we have to mention is that there has to be some form of religion, some spirituality in your life. You have to acknowledge that there is something greater than you.

In dealing with white supremacy, I have taken the stand that, yes, there is a racism problem in America. Yes, I am a victim of racism, and from that, eliminate the negative, establish the facts, and start to pick my best options. Regardless of whether you like it or not, you are at war every day that God blesses you to kiss the sun good morning, and you have to make choices during that day. Choices of, am I going towards freedom, or do I remain a slave? It goes back into—I cannot stress it enough, if you start to work on yourself, you get prolific in *human proficiency,* which is life skills. It deals with communication, deals with all types of addictions, deals with self-purpose, decision making and self-answers, self-temperament, emotional control and expression of self, deals with self-relationships, like family, children, wives, mothers, fathers. It deals with self-security, which is financial matters, and dealing with self-occupation, which is whatever your job may be. Getting into that, which sets you up to be proficient in humanity, that's where the progress starts to change. That's when you say, "I'm aware of my worth, and I'm proud of my birth."

There are four things that makes a perfect slave: (1) being loyal to your slave master, (2) having fear of your slave master, (3) when you despise being Black, and (4) feeling inferior to your slave master.

One of the things that I also want to stress, is in identifying white supremacy, I'm saying that it is a key factor but not a scapegoat. I'm not saying that we are only messed up because of this, I'm saying that each of us has a responsibility while we're on the face of this earth to do something about it. Speaking out against white supremacy doesn't make me a racist. If I'm pro-Black, then I'm guilty of racism? Because I love my own Black people, I'm a racist? Something is very wrong.

Some men beat another man, they hit him fifty-nine times. They killed King [Martin], and beat the roots out of Rodney [King]. Then they want to say, "These police are not dangerous to the community"? Well, what community? "We're going to let you out on bail. We'll just give you two and a half years under the circumstances." Then the person who breaks the law writes a letter to the judge and says that the law wasn't really written for the police. Well, who was it written for? This is blatant arrogance. It is a slap in the face of all of us. It is total disrespect. This is the true "coon." This is blatant, open white supremacy. "We write the laws, so we can change the laws to fit ourselves."

While I'm thinking about this, Reginald Denny was beat because he drove through South Central as if he was saying, "F— you, niggers." That's why he was stopped and beaten. Not because he was some white man in a tanker—come on, man, he was in a tractor, he could have run over everybody there, but he was wrong as he drove down Florence, and he forgot to lock his door. That's the truth, and justice got him.

What are the attributes of gangs? If you look at LAPD and what they do, and if you look at the L.A. Raiders, and the skinheads, WAR, and what they do, and if you look at what society terms "street gangs" and what they do, there are no differences. None. The police will jump out and say, "This is LAPD, freeze," and shoot seven warning shots into the back of your head. Something is wrong here.

I knew when I was coming up that if I stood up for what I believed in, my ultimate reward was death. I knew that. I wondered why there were so many Negroes around, and I figured out that it was because they have been browbeaten and whipped into submission of being good "house niggas." "I don't want any problems. I make sixty thousand a year, I'm looking at retiring, I have a car, and a house." F— that. My generation started it, and the generation after me was bred for nothing but change. You've got problems. When the battle cry is, "I don't give a f—, give me death, it's better than living like I'm living, because I'm not promised anything anyway. I'm not promised tomorrow, so I'm going to live today like it's my last day," then my battle cry is, "Bring the noise."

**Q:** What keeps you inspired and motivated?

**T:** I've been touched by the hand of God at least twice, to where I know something has touched me, and each time, it was at a turning point in my life. I've done several things that would make a lot of people happy, content, or satisfied, but there has always been something else, a driving force. I've left the neighborhood several times, only to return, because there's something that brings me back here. It's like my work is undone. I also know that I won't see it through.

Just my name, T. Rodgers. "T" represents absolute, perfect. "Rodgers" is a famous warrior. So when you put it together it's "absolute, perfect, famous warrior." If I spell it T-e-e, it means "to begin to make angry, to disgust." So I know what I'm supposed to do, and they're in trouble.

The police said that they were going to kill me one time, and I laughed. "Kill me, and you'll have ten just like me; kill me." Then one of the Negroes that was with them said, "You're not a martyr." I said, "That's only because you haven't killed me." So on a spiritual level it's real deep.

**Q:** What type of impact do you feel what's going on in L.A. will have in other cities?

**T:** L.A. is the focal point of everything else; everybody is watching us. We're the music capital of the world, when Detroit used to be; Hollywood is the movie capital, so they're watching us here. Over the last ten years we've spread Crips and Bloods across the country. Once there is a redirecting of thinking, then that will spread also. That's where we can get back to what we really are, which is a peaceful people. There are generations that have been bred for nothing but war. I was talking to somebody the other day about the Zulus, who backed up the British, and it's funny, because in the midst of war, you'll never know where an ally is going to come from.

**Q:** How do you feel we can create some economic opportunities in the community?

**T:** That's one of the biggest problems that we face. Again, white supremacy has us so locked into being dependent upon them. My generation is an instant generation. Instant coffee, instant grits, microwave your waffles. We're an instant generation, so we've become dependent upon things that are not natural. Our parents and grandparents own land, workable, farmable land. If we weren't so enslaved mentally, then we could just take a part of that land and plant food. So land is very important, and we have the land. Brothers just don't want to get their hands dirty.

We are a people with so much natural talent that it is unbelievable.

There are brothers that are mathematical geniuses, that know electronics by nature. Architecture, brothers who like to draw. We put together the pyramids because we used *all* of our mind.

If we can be a bookie, without a pencil or paper, or if we can bootleg Gucci, and Fila, or if we can steal a car and strip it, or if we can take stereos out of a car, and if we can burglarize, then all of those things can be turned into a positive, of anti-theft. Just take what God gave you and create a demand for what you do, legally.

In dealing with economics we have to understand capitalism. It doesn't mean that we have to become capitalists, because capitalists are predators, and I say that with much disdain. I am a communalist. If I have a dollar, my community has a dollar. I understand that there has to be those who have an understanding of business, that can be predators against our enemies in business. It takes time. Everybody is not going to be able to knock you out with a right or a left. Everybody is not going to be able to be a marksman. Everybody can't drive, so those who are prolific in those specific skills take that job that suits their purpose. We have to employ them in that way, because they have a value to us. He or she can be a warrior with numbers, they don't always have to pick up an AK or a 9-mm. This is the way that we will soon start to think, because everybody does have a value.

Those of us who have been thrust into a position of power are finding out that it isn't as easy as we thought, and secondly, that we fight against becoming the very same thing. . . . That is the biggest fight that's going on now. The same crimes that they have perpetrated against us, we have to make sure we don't perpetrate against our own people. That is another fight, because we have to remember where we come from.

People look at me on a daily basis and say, "T., you can live anywhere you want to live." My reply is that this is the safest place for me to live. My community loves me. As opposed to going somewhere else, and then having to reestablish myself and become territorial and have them to frown at me, because I am not of their culture. I also understand that when you make a certain amount of money, the first thing they do is sic a white girl on you, and she will demand that you love her more than you love yourself. This is in dealing with economics. If they will "be like Mike," "I want to be like Mike"? Who will sit on a bus after playing the Lakers in Los Angeles and say, "I'm not signing any more autographs, tell them to go buy my shoes." Something is very wrong here. To be like Mike, when Mike says, "Hey, look, I'm one of you guys, get up off of Nike, I've got a contract with Nike." Mike, you haven't contributed s— to the Black community, we don't care about your contract. Then when he does contribute to a community, it is a white community. A youth center in a white area? Mike Jordan, or Mike Jackson—be like Mike? It dawned on me that if Michael Jackson has a skin impediment, why did he go lighter, when he could have gone darker? These are questions that I want to know. All the Mikes [Jordan and Jackson], along with a li'l Magic [Johnson], could come together to buy and rebuild all of the ghettos.

**Q:** You mentioned how we need to rise above our emotions and we need to think—speak on that a little more.

**T:** Most of us come from single-parent homes, headed by our mothers. At times she would say to her kids, "You look like your father, and I can't stand your black ass." A growing boy first sees the world through the eyes of his father, and if his father is not there, then he has to substitute that with his mother, or the men that his mother brings home—I take that back, or the males that his mother brings home. He will imitate or duplicate what is close to him. If he has a certain admiration, or is nurtured by his mother, he will take on the characteristics of his mother. If his mother is not balanced, he will pick up her emotional traits. From the ages of one to three, a child's personality is pretty much locked in. If the child is only around the mother, and the mother is unbalanced, we have an unbalanced child that will stand up, beat his chest, grab himself, and say, "I'm one hundred percent man," and won't know anything about manhood. If true manhood dropped in front of him, he'd fall over it. This is the emotional control that we lack. We have been taught, through example, to be reactionaries. Our fathers may do something, and the mother reacts to what the father does. The son sees the mother react, then he thinks that's the natural order of things. He will be at school, and somebody will piss the teacher off, and then the teacher reacts to what the student does, and he thinks that is the natural order of things. We have been taught, inadvertently, to become reactionary. So instead of doing the things that we need to do to prevent certain things that we don't want to happen, we will allow them to happen, and then react.

I teach kids when I'm in the schools, I say do something that you haven't done in a long time. They'll sit there wide-eyed, and I'll say, "*Think.*"

That was one of the first rules of Black Stone, to be able to think calmly and convincingly in any given situation. You have to do that.

**Q:** What do you say to the younger generations who are still banging?

**T:** This is what I tell them. It reminds me of a poem; the poem goes:

> How tough my life,
> unlucky, lucky life.
> Died twice,
> once in your face,
> and then again alone.
> So lonely sometimes I find myself,
> me, here without you, why?

That summarizes everything. I'm alone a lot of times, and I have to be by myself a lot of times. So I have to tell them to hold on, because I'm working as diligently as I can under the circumstances. Just hold on, don't do anything stupid, don't go and get killed, don't go to jail, just hold on. With sacrifice—you have to give up something to get something. That's it. It's always greater later, it's always darkest just before the dawn. The things that we as a collective community are setting up, just hold on, because there's no quick fixes to this. It took twenty-five years for us to get f'd up like we are, so we have to hold on, we have to pay our dues, we have to sacrifice, we have to give up certain things.

What goes around comes around. You say you're a killer, and you're a G; well, you have to pay for those crimes. If you don't pay for those crimes, then your children will pay for those crimes, your children's children will pay for those crimes. God doesn't make mistakes. If you are an AK-47, or "Streetsweeper" of death, then that death sweeps back around and snatches from you, or yours.

So the whole community is responsible for the development of the children. When you are not responsible, then things like drive-bys happen in your community. Then you say, "Oh, God, God has forsaken me, why has He let this happen?" Because you didn't do what you were supposed to do. I am my brother's keeper. If he's doing something wrong, and he's not one of mine, I'm going to check him. That's what we have to get back to. When we turn our backs on a little boy, and he goes and snatches a purse, then he's crying out. When he snatches the purse of a woman, he's saying he hates his mama. He's getting back at his mother. Then he's saying, "I'm doing this because nobody loves me, nobody pays attention to me. If I have to do wrong to get attention, then I don't want to do right." I know people that have damn near beat the doors down to get back into the penitentiaries and jailhouses, because they're going to get three hot meals, and a cot, and they get clean clothes from the state. This isn't something I'm making up. The readers will know what I'm talking about.

**Q:** What position must the Black family take, Black men and women in relationships, to get us where we need to go?

**T:** The first thing I have to say is that we commit the greatest sin by not saying Black men. When we say "Black male," we never become men. White people will say the white man, or the Caucasian or Anglo, but we'll say "the Black male." A Black male can be a homosexual or a heterosexual. So that pisses me off. I went to a conference in San Diego, and it was called the "Black Male Conference: The Endangered Species." Well, you can kill the males off, but don't mess with the men. There is a difference. The relationships of boys and girls, the relationships of teens; when we get specific, then we know who we're talking about, because we know when we talk about men and women, there are different levels.

When we talk about the family unit, which is something that is very near and dear to me, the family unit is to be valued, and this is coming from an ex-player. At one time in my life all I wanted to do is be a pimp, but when I understood the value of family, when I understood *woman* was a Latin word which means "of man." When I understood that behind every great man there is a woman. When I understood that a man is incomplete without a woman, and vice versa. When I understood that the greatest gifts you can give to the world are children. When I understood that in perfect harmony with your mate you can give birth to a god. When I understood all of these principles, I had to change. It wasn't the cars, the clothes, talking fly, staying up all night, it wasn't the diamonds, it wasn't high-signing, it wasn't the money, but it was principles, it was about developing people. Who says that from my loins cannot come a great doctor or lawyer? Who says that from my loins cannot come someone who will rock the very foundation of the world? So I have to be careful with what I do, and what I say.

The hardest thing that I have found is to be a man. It is twice as hard to be a Black man in America, and it is three times as hard to be a Black father in America. Don't let that father be unemployed. Don't let that father have to apply for any type of assistance, be it Medi-Cal, food stamps, just to get by. "No you're an able-bodied, strong . . . go shovel s—, get out of here." The double standards of America are messed up. To be able to "share" in a family unit, to be able to say, "Okay, I'm not at work now, but my counterpart is at work, so I will cook dinner and keep the house clean, I will braid our children's hair and take care of our children." To say that with pride, and mean it, that's a whole new thing. Not to have my lady stand up over me and tell me that she makes more money than me, or to tell me that she's an independent woman of the nineties or to tell me that she doesn't need me. I don't believe that there's a heaven above, or a hell below, but I believe that my heaven is in my woman, and I don't mean in sexual terms, just the peace that I find in her. That is what the family unit is about. To be able to bring the boys and the girls into the rites of passage, to be there for them. It is unheard of in our community to have a mother and a father in the home. "Damn, you have a daddy?" When my children bring their friends home, they don't know how to act around me, because I am a father. They will disrespect most mothers, or they will run over most mothers, or the mothers are not at home. So that family unit, *family is first.* That is what it's about. That becomes the nucleus of life, and from that, everything else comes out. If it is education or economics, whatever it is, it first comes from that family unit.

**Q:** Speak on the issue of drugs in the Black communities.

**T:** I can trace it back with actual facts, to Prohibition. I'm sure it goes farther back than that. The drugs have always been aimed at the Black community. Prison, homosexuality, not being able to reproduce, self-hatred (Black-on-Black crime), and drugs, these are the five things that keep us from manhood. The drugs were designed to actually keep us from reproducing. With this strain of AIDS, one of the things that they have accomplished is to make people wear condoms, so we won't reproduce. Reproduction is one thing, but to be able to raise a baby, to take care of a baby, is another thing. The drugs were brought in to subdue the more aggressive brothers, to bring down the community. To have one person or a group of people being kingpins over the community. It backfired when they brought in cocaine, because cocaine did not discriminate. Cocaine gave everyone a euphoria, they didn't expect that. When that happened, they realized, "We have a drug problem now," since it crept into the white communities.

In Michigan, if you get caught with a certain amount of drugs, you get a life sentence, without parole. They gave Noriega twenty-five to forty years. He was the biggest drug pusher we know, outside of the president. What about the big drug companies? They manufacture dope. There are double standards in America.

**Q:** What kind of feedback do you get from the youth when you speak to them?

**T:** I've found that from the fifth grade on up, the attention span is there. I've been doing this since 1975. I would climb over the fence to get into the classroom just to speak. The kids wanted to hear me. The things I would talk about were the things that the school board wouldn't allow the teachers to talk about. There's a thing that I call the Trinity: the school, the community, and the prisons. You can't deal with one without dealing with the others. Home, school, and church; if the home fails, then the school and the church have to work twice as hard. If the home and the schools fail, the church doesn't have a chance.

My Trinity is the community, the school, and the prisons. What happens on a Friday or a Saturday night in the hood spills over to Monday or Tuesday on the school campus. What happens Thursday and Friday on the campus spills over to Friday and Saturday night in the hood. Both of them spill over to the penitentiary system, because what happens at Crenshaw High, or Dorsey High, especially if there's a football game, goes back to the 60s hood, the Black Stones hood, and that translates into New Folsom, Old Folsom, San Quentin, Cochran, CMC, East-West, wherever they're at, because the shots can be called from behind the walls. There is more power behind the walls than there is on the streets. My brother is locked up, and I have more respect for him now that he's not with me than I did when he was here with me. I remember when I went to go see my brother in prison, and this big redneck guard with a potbelly and a big old stick, he said, "Rodgers, your visiting hour is over." My brother is a lifer. He has twenty-seven years, flagged with organized crime and special circumstances. "Rodgers, your time is up." My brother kept on talking. The man said it about three times. The third time the guard said it, he said it like he meant it. Now me, I was a visitor, so I was on my way out the door. My brother told me not to go anywhere. He stood up and turned to the guard in the visiting room, and he told the guard, "What the f— are you going to do to me? I've got life. What are you going to do to me? Give me some more time?" There wasn't too much they could do to him. Even the guard backed up. That's power. That showed me that he understands his surroundings, and the guard understood the surroundings and the politics of the prison, and there was really nothing that he could do.

It's funny, because the grapevine in the pens are much better than the phone systems. Something can happen out here on Friday, and I'll get a call from my brother on Monday.

When I speak to the youth, I don't tell them not to get into anything, I tell them what their options are, and what will happen with each option. That's my Trinity, and in that Trinity I would talk about the things the upper-middle-class house Negroes didn't want to talk about, things that were taboo. There's a game that I've devised called Survival. The only way you can win this game is by not even thinking about joining a gang. When we would play the game, the more dominant kids would be the leaders, depending upon their personalities, and something would always happen to them. They could just be driving down the street in their mom's car and get hit by a drunk driver or something, but because they had done some ill to somebody else in the game, that's how life goes. What goes around comes around. The only way you win this game of Survival by T. Rodgers is to not put yourself in a situation where you would be a professional victim, or to not say that gangs were cool. That's the only way you could win. Anything else, you were maimed, in jail, or killed.

By the time we get to ninth graders, that game doesn't work. When you get to the ninth graders, you have to talk about real issues, safe sex, or sex period. I have to talk about safe sex, because they don't care. I would usually take someone else with me when I go into the classrooms, and we would do good cop versus bad cop. If I take somebody that I was training, I would let them be the gang member, and what I would do is be the guy that's trying to get him out, or the guy that wants him to get out, or the guy that cares more about him than he cares about himself. We would actually interact, role-play for the kids, so they would be able to see. Towards the end of the class we allow them to ask us questions. I usually take someone with me who has had some type of experience, who had either been in prison, been shot, or stabbed, and had all of the scars to prove it, so the kids could see the visuals. We talk about parents, child abuse, parent abuse, hangin', bangin', and slangin'. What happens when you're out on the block, and what could happen. I would always make it so that they had the option to be heroes; it was up to them, it's what they want to do.

**Q:** What could you say to a youngster who is on the fence, who has friends pulling him one way to get involved with gangs, and family and other friends who are trying to keep him straight; what do you say to someone like that to keep him out of the gangs?

**T:** The first thing that I do is *listen,* and by listening I figure out what he wants to do. So it's not like me coming in telling him, "You're not going to do this, don't do this, don't do that." I always make them aware of their options. Believe it or not, most human beings truly want the best for themselves.

One of the things that was most effective in my life was not to just sit up there and talk s—, but to get down and dirty, to roll our sleeves up, to come up with something; that's what meant something to me: physical action. So now that I sit in the seat of power, the choices that I present I have to follow through on. Jesse Jackson gives lip service, but to actually roll your sleeves up and get down in there is what you need to do.

I was talking to a Christian, and the Christian said, "I have a lot of respect for the Muslims, because the Muslims will get in there with those guys and roll their sleeves up, and the guys can have an interaction, and they learn." What's wrong with the Christians rolling their sleeves up? That's the key point, that's the thing that I've learned most. Not to be up there and be so articulate and eloquent with my speech; that doesn't mean anything. What means something is to be there, what means something is for them to be able to reach out and touch you, to call you, to knock on your door, to know where you're at if something goes down, or to know that your word is your bond.

Kids now are not from the old school, you can't come to them and say, "Don't do as I do, do as I say." Some of my friends have done up to ten years in the penitentiary, and if it was me in there, the kids would say, "Well, T., you slipped, you got caught, I'm not going to get caught. This is the new style, we've watched y'all put it down, but we have a whole new flavor on this, so we're not going to get caught up." When a kid comes at me like that, it's a direct challenge. I was taught that as a man you have to accept all challenges, even if it means you fight to the death. So I accept that challenge and I go over our options, and I ask that person what he wants to do. The whole key to it is by me not saying to someone that they should be a janitor, when secretly in the basement of their heart they want to be a brain surgeon. That would be ludicrous to them. So I ask the individual—that's the thing, you ask them and you deal with one human being at a time, there's no group therapy to this madness. You can't put all of the Bloods on one side, and all of the Crips on another side, and think that you're going to solve all of their problems at once. Each one of those brothers that got into the Crips and the Bloods had a specific problem that caused them to get into the gang in the first place, and they have to deal with those problems. Sociologists don't seem to understand that. It was an individualistic thing that got them to this point. Individuals that make up a group. You have to deal with them on an individual level.

## T. Rodgers

**Q:** How can the power that brothers have inside the penitentiaries be transferred to the outside in helping with the peace?

**T:** There's this brother named Ton Stone, his name is Salahuddin now; he's a general in Black Stone, he's an Imam up in the prison. What are they doing while they're locked up? You can put fat on your body, or you can put fat in your brain. So the more time that they take to develop their brains, they learn what true power is, what true communication is, what true leadership is, and that same power then transcends to the outside world, through letters, through visits, and sometimes, believe it or not, through the spirit. If I'm truly in tune with my brother, I can feel what's going on with him.

We have to keep in mind that the gangs are big business. Homes are bought, businesses are started, and children go to college from people being incarcerated. It's called recidivism. We have got this thing about being slaves to the point to where some would rather go to jail than stay out here and deal with what they have to deal with as a man. That creates a problem, because that creates a mind-set of, "I'd rather go to jail and get three hots [meals] and a cot, worry about somebody taking my butt, fighting every day, and dealing with a white man who doesn't give two s— from a rat's rectum about me. I'd rather live up under those circumstances than to take on my rites of passage, than to take on being a man, than to take on the responsibility of being a man to a woman, or a father to a child. Lock me up, I don't give a s—. Inside that penitentiary I'm going to watch me some television, I'm going to lift me some weights, I'm going to tell me some jokes, I'm going to have me some sex, I'm going to take Ralph and make him Rosetta, I'm going to get high, all inside this penitentiary." Whatever goes on in the streets goes on inside the pen. We'd rather go to our graves as slaves then to just stand up, because we have learned that when a Black man stands up, his only reward for standing up is death. Rodney King got beat that severely because throughout the whole video all he wanted to do was stand up, and each time he stood up, they whipped him back into submission, back down. Martin Luther King got killed because all he wanted to do was love, and the greatest gratification for love is sex, and if we have sex with white people, there will be no more white people. So they had to kill King.

Back to dealing with incarceration and recidivism—the system gets paid dearly; that's a bounty. If you talk to the brothers in the pen, they'll tell you that they are living in the belly of the beast, they're living in the hells of North America. They refer to the prison system as just that. There is no rehabilitation in incarceration. The only light that they get is when we come to visit them. Mail, money, and visits, those are the only things that they receive in the pens that keeps them going.

The peace comes about the same way everything else comes about, it comes about through the calls home, through the visits, it comes about through the kytes they write to the homiez, and any other publications or communications that are let up in the walls of the penitentiary, or that can leave the penitentiary. That's where it comes from. The system tries to stop that communication from happening.

**Q:** In closing out, speak about the change and the greatness of this generation.

**T:** The Black woman—there's a cliché that "behind every great man there's a woman," and to get back to our greatness as Black people we need to respect our Black women, and our Black women need to be self-respecting.

It all stems from brothers referring to sisters as "my b—" and sisters referring to brothers as "my nigga." We have a problem. She has no true respect for him or his manhood. He damn sure doesn't have any respect for her womanhood, calling her a b—. If that's how he sees his mate, then that makes him a dog. So we're in a very vicious cycle here. As long as we will allow ourselves to wear those jackets and refer to ourselves affectionately by those derogatory terms, then she'll never become a Queen, she'll never become a lady, she'll never become a woman, and she definitely won't become a true mother. That would create another lost generation. Something is very wrong here.

Again, this goes back to knowledge of self, because instead of thinking that she is a dog, the reverse of d-o-g is g-o-d, and if she looks at herself as a Goddess, then she will look for God in a man. That's where we must start.

Up from the ashes of the Uprisings has to come a new phoenix. From the ashes of the Uprisings has to come the first wave, the first generation that will say, "Enough is enough." That will say, "This is my Queen." It has to get back to those simple terms. When Tina Turner said, "What's love got to do with it?" that messed me up; love has everything to do with it. We must go back to one-on-one relationships. The masses of the people don't understand that what we're dealing with is change.

What's so hard about change? I guess it's the four hundred years of slavery, that I can't blame my parentage for. Four hundred years of slavery where we were in the bellies of slave ships. We lost over 100 million during the "Middle Passage." They threw the bodies over the side, and those that they didn't kill or those that didn't die or those that didn't kill themselves were raped. Hell, no. So I'm kind of glad that my mother taught me that if they hit me, to hit them back, because before me, the Black man was castrated. All of these years of oppression, these years of depression, these years of recession, till now we have a generation that doesn't care about anything.

> "Bring the Noise,"
> bring on your elephant guns,
> bring on the helicopters to block out the sun,

and *rat-a-tat-tat* will be the only sound,
and I'll be spreading the blues around.
Bring it on.
I'm not afraid of dying.

I welcome death, because I know as a child that I watched grown men stand up, and when grown men stood up, they were shot down. So I know that tomorrow is not promised to me anymore, and a child that does not have a tomorrow lives for today. Bring the noise. "F— the police" is the national anthem. It's a culture that has gotten to a point to where we're not going to take it anymore. I'm not interested in marching, but if I do march, it's going to be at night from tree to tree, from bush to bush, it's guerrilla warfare. My grandmother can march. I'm not marching. My whole mentality is like the youngsters, the generation that I gave birth to.

***The question of whether violence is going to be used is not a question for the Black community, it's a question for America. 'Cause white America is the one who has used violence for four hundred years, we have been the recipients of violence. We have never lynched, we've never shot, we've never burnt a church, we've never beaten people, we've never taken them to jail, that is the question for white America. The real question is can she civilize herself before we get ready to civilize her.***

**—Kwamé Touré**

## SHOUT OUTS

If you're true to the game the game will be true to you. I have said for years that I'm staying down so that I can come up. This is my time. All of the negative that you waste on being jealous, envious, and petty should be spent on forgiving. I've been a play-her all my life, I love play-hers. They come in all colors, ages, sexual preferences, and I've been played on and I've played. I've gotten millions from the unsuspecting billions. I've never ever, ever, ever been a play-her hater.

I've got much love and respect for those that are true, and I accept and embrace those that want to change, those that allow me to teach them to love themselves and then love their enemies, those that forgive themselves for all of the stupid things they've done to themselves and to those that love them, those that forgive others who have hurt them; then and only then will you find peace, that's self-peace. Then you must accept and embrace somebody else and pass on the formula for peace.

To dislike me is to dislike Black people. To dislike me is to dislike yourself, for I am the epitome of inner city life. I have a Ph.D. from

SWU; I am you. I have gone where no other gang member has gone before. I have kicked down the doors of corporate America so that we could provide for our families as men, yet you see not. But I'm in good company with Malcolm, Marcus, Jesus, and others; yet my heart still holds compassion. There's no way that I could love one brother and then kill another. I forgive you for you know not what you do. I'm a servant of God and my people, and my rewards are spiritual.

I want to thank my wife, who has been with me when I had money and when I didn't have money. My boy babies Bobby and Darryl for completing my manhood. My daughters for completing my appreciation of women. My mother for pushing me out of the house when I turned twelve. My granny and grandmother for my culture and my belief in God. Mrs. Mitchell, my seventh- and eighth-grade English teacher, who made me stay in at lunch and recess and fill my lust for words. Rob Silverstein for my understanding of Jews, Gary Bernstein for *Behind Bars*, Bob Pellegrino for building.

V. G. Guiness for keeping me out of the penitentiary. Allysunn Walker for being my first female friend. My brother Rob for protecting me in my early years. My neighborhoods, the Jungle and the Bity. I've been good to the hood, and the hood's been good to me. Stone Love: Lon Tatum, Long Money Lonnie, Lamont Fletcher, Big Roach, Keith Crawford, R. K. Jones, and all the Joneses. To all the homiez in the pen and all homiez R.I.P. If I didn't mention you I know you're gonna be calling my house collect. This is the first book—the check is in the mail.

Lastly, Jim Brown, for taking my hand and bringing me into manhood and showing me that "I-CAN."

Peace, Jus T.

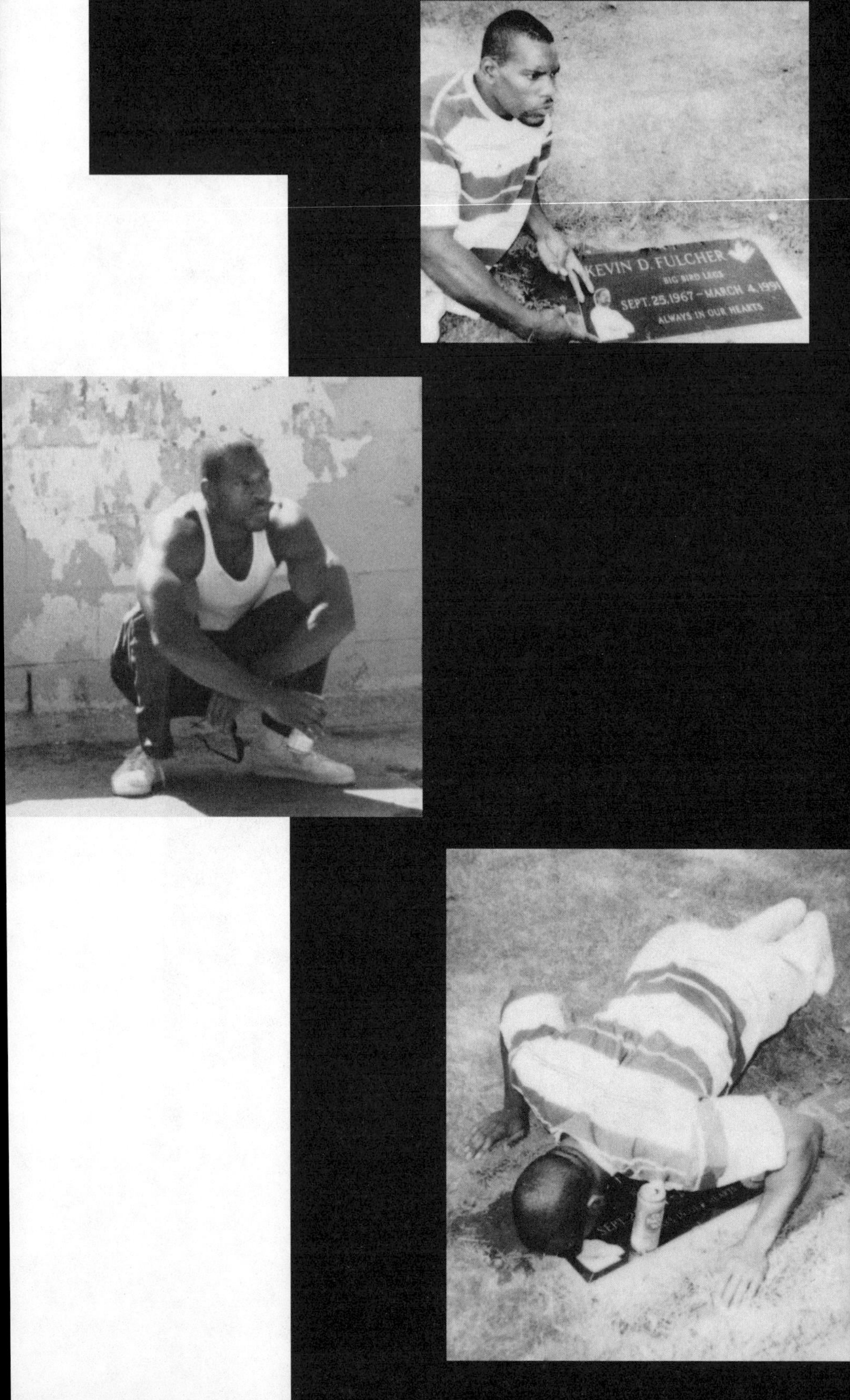
KEVIN D. FULCHER
BIG BIRD LEGS
SEPT. 25, 1967 — MARCH 4, 1991
ALWAYS IN OUR HEARTS

# BIG SHIP

*(When I first started Crippin', there was love in the hood. If you were from Shotgun, there was love from all the homeboys and homegirls. There was so much love that you were glad to be from Shotgun, because if anything happened to you, or if you needed any kind of assistance, the set was there, it didn't matter if you were right or wrong. If you had problems with someone from another set, the hood was ready to roll, it was on.*

*I was a Baby Crip back then. I was young and steadily growing, getting more and more of a reputation for myself. Your name had to be ringin' for Shotgun, that's what I mainly wanted from the set, to have my name known personally. What really got me to start thinking on that level was from constantly hearing names ringin' like R.B., Slate Rock, Rock Bottom, Capone, Hair Bear, Buddha, Poncho, Jobbo; and there were more names like Skeet, Odie, Tookie, Jimel, Raymond Washington. Those names were poppin' and ringin', those brothers had made their reputation, and I wanted to know the feeling of being known all over, in every hood, whether it was my hood or another set in another hood.*

*Most of all I wanted the big homiez to know who I was. So in order for me to get known by the big homiez, and everybody else, I had to start doing things to make my name ring. So I started claiming Shotgun to the fullest, messing up at school, fighting Bloods, fighting other Crip sets, knocking out white boys, whoever wasn't down with Shotgun. I made it my business to stay busy; if I was with my homiez, or alone, I had to get down for Shotgun.*

*A lot of the homiez didn't know who Shiphead was, but they kept hearing my name ringing, and all they kept saying was, "Who is Shiphead?" Different homiez that knew me would tell them who I was. People like Rock, Hawk, Warlock, Sly, Sandman, Fat Dog, Li'l Hawk, Li'l Rocc, Devil, Bootsy, Tyrone, Weather Man, and more. These are the guys I started hangin' out with, they were straight riders. So as time went on, I started getting introduced to all the homiez in the hood, from the nine [139th Street] and the duce [132nd Street]. We were doing so much dirt, I mean much dirt, that my name started ringin' all over, and eventually I started going to jail. In jail I was meeting different people from other sets. As time went on, I became more and more known in the gang-banging industry. Like I said earlier, we were doing a lot of dirt, mostly fighting at schools, like Henry Clay, Gardena High, Washington High, Inglewood High, Morningside High, Centennial High, and other schools that we terrorized. On sight of seeing a "rival," there wasn't any talking, it was about getting down, getting 'em up. There wasn't too much blasting back then, it had to be something really serious in order for some shooting to happen. Back then, if you were talkin' about blasting on someone, you were considered a mark, a punk, because back then it was all about squabblin'.*

*After a while something happened, and there started to be a lot of gunplay, and I mean a lot of gunplay. Out of all that gunplay Shotgun wasn't losing any homiez. Every other set was losin' homiez back-to-back, and our set use to trip off of that. We use to always say, "Damn, Cuz, homiez been gettin' popped on, but none of us have died." It seems like as soon as we started trippin' off of that, homiez started dying. That was around 1978, 1979.*

*I don't remember which homie left us first, but it was out of these top five: Poncho, Lunchmeat, Hawk, L.C., or Patrick. As a matter of fact the Slater brother had left us first, but he had died before I even moved to the set. When we lost the above-mentioned people, a lot more people were coming up missing from our set, and many other sets too. While all the killings were taking place, there was still a lot of fighting too. That was the main object of bangin', gettin' 'em up. You would win some, and you'd lose some.*

*I can go on and on with the way it used to be, but like the title of this book says, this is supposed to be about Uprising.*

*I, Big Shiphead, ex–gang member, am going to close this introduction with a word of advice. I just gave anybody who is reading this book just a speck of what I was into, coming up gang-banging. There has been a lot of lives that have been taken away from loved ones, and you who are reading this book may be a victim of this disease, just like I am. I miss my homiez, very, very, very, very much, but I can't bring them back; neither can you bring back your loved ones. However, what we can do is contribute all of our efforts to the peace, so that no one has to go through what we've gone through: the sadness, the pain, the madness, the suffering, and the vengeance.*

*I know that you can never forget what happened to your loved ones, but we can forgive. Just think about the good Lord forgiving us, and how he died on the cross for our sins. If he could forgive, what makes you think that you're too good, or too hard, to forgive the next man?*

*Enjoy the book, and take everything you read extremely serious, and try to get something positive out of it, because in order for us Blacks to build an empire, we have to change our hearts and get rid of the hate that we have for one another. This is coming from someone who has really lived this life. If you really focus on this book, it will make you think twice about banging. Don't wait until you are on death row to then try and come out of that lifestyle, because then it's way too late. Always remember that everything happens for a reason. May God bless you. Peace.)*

**Q:** How did you first hear about the peace that was happening on the streets?

**S:** I first learned about the peace treaty when I was incarcerated, and at that time I wasn't for it, because so many of my homeboys are either resting in peace or incarcerated as a result of gang-banging activity. However, I began to change my mind while rolling down Crenshaw Boulevard one Sunday with my homeboy Ghost, and after hearing former gang members on the *Peace Treaty* radio talk show on KJLH. My homeboy Keith, who works for NBC, introduced me to a brother named Malik, and they invited me to the radio station. They were talking about real issues and different solutions relating to this violent cycle of gang-banging that is going on in this corrupt world today.

**Q:** How long had you been gang-banging?

**S:** I've been banging since the mid-seventies, since I was twelve years old. I'm thirty years old now, and I'm just now getting my life together. I didn't get anywhere during all of those years of gang-banging. The only thing that I've gained is a reputation, and a CDC number, along with a lot of hurt from my homiez becoming either incarcerated or deceased.

I don't regret anything that I've been through though, nor the lifestyle of banging, because I've learned so much about society, inside the walls and outside of these invisible walls out here on the streets. Now that I've finally waken up and have a broader outlook on life, I realize that I can't keep living the life of a gang banger. I also realize that I can't bring back any of the lives that have been taken as a result of gang-banging, and Black-on-Black crime, that I may have been affiliated with. Nevertheless, I can try to save some of the youngsters that are now coming up in this violent cycle of gang-banging.

**Q:** Is that your mission now?

**S:** Yes. That's my mission now, and I'd like to take this opportunity to tell the world about my involvement towards keeping the peace. First of all, I take time to talk to the youngsters in the neighborhood, and I try to instill in them more positive morals, instead of the negative ones that have kept our people back for so many years.

I'm currently involved in doing radio talk shows on peace, and I've been on television talk shows that have allowed me to speak publicly to youngsters and adults that I'm not able to reach personally. I'm also working with people in the music industry, and I'm managing a group that I helped form by the name of Top Gun. I've been blessed as a singer as well.

These are some of the more positive things in my life that I'm trying to show the youngsters, and whomever else it may concern, to prove that I have made a change in my life, and that there are other things you can get into besides gang-banging and destruction. I'm a living witness.

**Q:** What was it that attracted you to banging in your early years of growing up?

**S:** I was curious about it. When I was young, in elementary school, I used to see other brothers, mostly older, some young, dressed up in hats, overalls, canes, long earrings, biscuits, croakasacks and rolling low-riders with Craigers. I didn't know what biscuits, romeos, ace-deuces, nor what any of those things represented, because I was too young.

One thing that I did know is that it had something to do with being bad, in the coolest way, and that's when I knew I wanted to be just like them. I used to see these guys, I didn't know where they were from, but I used to see them every Sunday at Jim Dandy's Fried Chicken, on Imperial and Vermont. They would be kickin' it, having a lot of fun; there seemed to be so much love between them, and I admired that.

**Q:** How did your involvement start to escalate?

**S:** Well, as time passed, I was steadily growing up, and moving from neighborhood to neighborhood, seeing the same type of brothers that I saw on Imperial and Vermont, at Jim Dandy's. At that time I started really becoming interested in their lifestyle. I began to kick it with young brothers that I felt or heard had older brothers that were gangsters. As time went on, with my parents moving from place to place, I started learning the slang, and learning what the brothers who were hanging out at Jim Dandy's were all about, and I liked it.

I finally reached the neighborhood of Gardena Shotgun Crips. Before making it there, the last place I stayed was on 111th and Western. I went to school at Century Park for the majority of my elementary school years, and my last part of elementary school I went to Purche Elementary. This is when I started to really focus on gang-banging and being from Shotgun. I didn't know too many people in Gardena, except Devil, Tyrone, Squeeky, and Bootsy. I knew them, because we went to school together at Century Park. They had moved to Gardena a little bit before my family did. It was cool to see those faces; Devil has been nutty ever since I've known him. In Gardena I managed to hang out and start learning about different individuals, such as the Baileys, and the Slaters—Jeffrey, James, David, Kevin, and another brother of theirs that I didn't know who's now resting in peace. He passed away before I moved to the hood. Skeet, R.B., Danny Boy—all of whom are Baileys—and the Wilkie Boys. These are the names that were ringing when I first moved to Gardena. I started hanging out with the youngsters my age, youngsters like Warlock, Rock, Sly, Sandman, Li'l Roc, Fat Dog, Hawk, Li'l Hawk, Mad Ronald, Alfred, and John. This was the main crew that I used to hang with. (This was the nine side—139th Street. Then there was 132nd Street, which is the headquarters, The Duce, which is the originator of Shotgun Crips.) One Hundred Thirty-second Street and Van Ness is where Rowley Park is located, which is where we all hung out at. So by hanging out with these guys, I started getting introduced to the Duces, and from then on I always made it to where I could hang out with the homiez.

**Q:** What kept you in that banging mode for all those years?

**S:** It was something I liked to do. I wasn't forced to do it. It was fun, and there was a lot of love that we had for one another back then. If you were from Shotgun, the homiez had your back no matter what. Everywhere we went we were known for tearing things up, whether it was physical or gunplay. I used to like to fight, I wanted that reputation. I wanted my name to ring, so I stayed into trouble until my name was ringing. I felt that wherever we rolled, I had to be one of the ones taking off. Most of all, it was just fun living dangerously, taking chances, and not worrying about the consequences. It was all about Shotgun. That's what kept me going for all those years, bangin' for Shotgun, because I love Shotgun.

It was like a high, banging and believing in what I was banging for—Shotgun Crip. My generation, we felt we had to be harder than our OGs, and I think we were harder than our OGs [says jokingly, and laughs].

Another exciting thing was the fighting, the battles. It wasn't nothing to come home with knots and scars, broken hands. That's really what banging was about, fighting for your set and your territory. There wasn't much shooting then.

**Q:** Did you have both parents in the home when you were banging?

**S:** Yes, I did have both parents and family. I come from a very good and a very spiritual family. They had nothing to do with my decisions on banging. It was just something I wanted to do.

**Q:** When did the shootings start to escalate?

**S:** The gunplay started around '78 or '79.

**Q:** What do you think brought that on?

**S:** Drugs, such as Sherm, Red Devils, Old English 800, Mad Dog 20/20, and Silver Satin. Also the times started changing, and I guess we changed with the times. Then when a lot of the Gs that started this were locked up—there are so many that are gone now with life sentences, the originators, like Jimel and all of them, he's here, but the ones he ran with, when all of them left, a new twist came in. All these guns came in, we had .38s, .22s, .25s, and shotguns. There wasn't that many 9-mm's, and AKs, and all of that back then.

**Q:** How does it make you feel, thinking of some of the things that you used to do, but now knowing you're a changed man?

**S:** I feel great. I don't care where we are, somebody will see me and know me. It's just like that. Which is good and bad, because I know a lot of people who might be considered as my past rivals see me too, and I may not see them. I don't be in fear though, I just ain't like that. It's a trip, man, it makes me feel good. Even the neighbors and different parents tell me to hang in there, because they know how I was growing up. Stevie Wonder's radio station, KJLH, really did a lot. Before that I was singing in clubs, the Grand Slam, Prince's club on Third Street. Doing little things for the community.

I feel like a lot of the things I did was just part of growing up. Everything happens for a reason; the only thing I feel bad about is that I've made a lot of families sad, and that this gang-banging has gotten out of control. I'm a figure that has really contributed to what's going on today. If I would have known that I was going to be on the level that I'm on now, I probably would have been trying to be a positive role model back then like I'm trying to be now. Like I said, I know I can't bring anybody back, but from my experiences in gang-banging I can get at the youngsters that are coming up, better than a lot of these different organizations can, because I've been through it. I feel great that I've changed my lifestyle, and that now I'm helping the youngsters that are coming up in the hood, and other youngsters from wherever else they may be. The same hard-core level I was on when I was banging is exactly how I'm going at the peace.

**Q:** What are some ways we can strengthen the peace and keep it going strong?

**S:** What's going to have to happen is a lot of these OGs that participated and originated this violent cycle known as gang-banging are going to have to come back to the hood and get at the young homiez. The OGs who have positive solutions, who are not just about talk, they must show their homiez what they're about now so they can see that change is possible, and you can be somebody. That's what I'm doing now; I talk to my homiez all the time. I'm always talking to them about something positive. A lot of them shy away, because they remember how I was. What I'm trying to do is change that cycle, because they watched us grow up. We were wild, and they watched that. That's what we used to put in their brain, so they're really with that. People don't understand that's how they were raised. We used to be like, "Crip or die." It was like that. Now, I'm like this, "We didn't tell you young homiez all the other things in life, that you don't have to let banging be your only way out. Change up." My OG homeboys didn't tell me . . . I had a couple, two or three, that would get at me and tell me to have something else going on besides banging, but the majority didn't tell us that. So I'm trying to tell the homiez now since it wasn't really told to me, and after I get through talking to them, I'd say, "I bet you can't count too many homiez that came at you like I just did." It's love, man!

**Q:** When you talk to a young brother, what's the hardest response that you get back that you have to deal with?

**S:** Well, the hardest response I get back is when I'm talking to the young homiez about not going to do some dirt. I get at them and I ask them, "Is it worth it?" They tell me, "Yeah, this is Shotgun." I say to them, "I know this is Shotgun, but you all just had a little gang fight, you're going to have them. That's part of banging. When you're out here banging, you can't just go shooting people up every time you have a quarrel. There ain't no guns in jail, you'll have to get 'em up in there." Their response to that is, "F that s—. Couldn't nobody tell you anything when you were all into this so deep, so how are you going to come at us like that?" That's when I get stuck. That's the hardest response, because it's true. Then I pause for a minute and I tell them, "You're right, couldn't nobody tell me anything, but I was wrong. I wasn't right. My mind was corrupted and that's the bottom line. I wasn't right, homie, and that's coming from the Big Homie, Ship. I wasn't right." Like I said, I don't regret anything I've been through, because I'm blessed to still be here in society to tell the youngsters that you can't let banging be your only way out, you can't win like that.

**Q:** What can the community do to help provide the youngsters with alternatives?

**S:** First of all they have to stop being scared of the brothers, because if you're scared of them, you can't talk to them. The community needs to start pulling over when they see a crowd of youngsters gathered around kickin' it and talk to them about something positive, you know, bring a few job applications, or give them some locations where they are hiring Black men. Just because they're out there hanging out, that doesn't mean that they don't want to work. You'll be surprised at how many intelligent, young Black men are in the streets gang-banging, all they want is a chance. Society and the community fails to realize that if you keep locking these men up, and saying that they're not going to be anybody, the youngsters start really giving up hope on themselves, because their parents gave up on them. So the easiest way to counteract that is to gang-bang, because that's where they're accepted and they feel loved.

**Q:** At the meetings with the brothers are you able to express some of the things that you are saying now?

**S:** Yes, of course. You can express whatever you want to express, positive or negative. That's what the meetings are for. It doesn't matter if the members agree or disagree with what you're saying, you will still be heard.

**Q:** Let's speak on economic empowerment. What can be done to help begin developing economic opportunities for ourselves?

**S:** First of all, we must stop smoking these drugs that the white man has put out here to set us back in life even further than we are now.

Secondly, we need to stop abusing alcohol, because that has us thinking like we're animals with no common sense or self-esteem.

The third thing is, we need to start saving our money and build ourselves an empire and get rid of that self-greed that we have in us and work together. Most of all, and most importantly, is that we must immediately stop this Black-on-Black crime and this gang-banging, because until we start respecting one another as human beings, as well as ourselves, then we won't be able to build up a damn thing.

**Q:** What do you feel it is that makes brothers and sisters begin to use drugs?

**S:** I think what made us start smoking was curiosity and frustration. I know that it wasn't the Black brothers' or sisters' intention to smoke cocaine as a career. It's just so addicting, it's like one hit is one too many, and a million hits is not enough. In my opinion it's the worst drug that ever hit the face of this earth.

**Q:** What happens when we have a born leader like yourself, who during your prime you were banging for ten to fifteen years of your life, and now that you're thirty, what is there for you to now get into?

**S:** If you were on that level of just banging, and that's all you was doing for all these years, and if you didn't get an education or learn a trade, then all you can do is start over. Go back to school, find a part-time job or something. It's going to be a lot harder getting an education now than it was when you were a youngster, because you have to strive harder and be very persistent on your work, you're grown now, you're not a kid anymore. So the teachers of the classes are not going to be checking on you about your homework, nor will they be calling your parents telling them you're not doing well in class, because like I said, you're grown now. You have to stay up with the teachers, because he or she is either going to pass you or fail you. Bottom line. Most of all, you have to *want* to do something for yourself, in order for anyone to help you in whatever it is you plan on doing. Check this out, you have to remember that you were banging to the fullest, and the majority of the lives you've touched, that's all they know about you, so you're going to have to let them know that you want to make it in life and be somebody. Believe me, when people see you trying to change, they will come to your assistance. I'm a living witness.

**Q:** How do you show the homiez another way of life, the positive side?

**S:** Me personally, I tell them what I have experienced through gang-banging activities for the past seventeen years. I tell them to look at me and all the time that I have wasted. Then I try to counteract my presence with the past by not just telling youngsters what I'm doing for myself and others, but showing them the change in my life. I'm not just talking that talk, I'm walking that walk also. That's what you have to do to get your point across, because if they don't see you walking that walk like you're talking that talk, then there's no way that they're going to listen to you or take what you're saying seriously. That's what every role model on the positive tip has to do. You have to show them what you're into just like you showed them how to bang.

**Q:** Talk about your spirituality.

**S:** First of all I'm not a religious person, I'm a spiritual person. I know that there is a God. I know there is because I wouldn't have made it through the things that I've made it through. I come from a very, very spiritual background. My pops has been a minister for thirty years or more, and my moms is the most spiritual woman I have ever met in my life. They both have been a big help to me as far as teaching me, my brothers and sisters, and every man or woman that they come in contact with, about Christianity and the Lord. I was raised in the church. If it wasn't for the Lord, I know that I would be dead or have a life sentence right now. The majority of my homiez that I was raised up with are either dead or in the penitentiary. Some of them aren't ever coming home. In this world you have to have a Supreme Spiritual Being, and the right one, to be able to deal with things out here. You're dealing with physical beings, and you're dealing with evil spirits, and there is no way that a physical being can deal with something that it can't see. So you must have God in your life to deal with these things that you have no control over and things that are too powerful for you.

A lot of corrupt things are going on in this world today because of the lack of prayer, but you have to have faith too. You have to have faith in what you're praying about, and who you're praying to. Faith is the substance of things hoped for, the evidence of things not seen. Always remember that God answers prayers, and don't get frustrated if He doesn't answer when you want Him to, because He knows what you're going to ask Him before you ask Him. He may not come when you want Him to come, but He's always on time because He knows best. You have to have faith.

As far as gang-banging, get out of it. If you're not in it, don't get in it, because I'm telling you there's only two places you're going if you stay in it, either six feet under or in the penitentiary, and you're not promised to come out of the penitentiary either.

**Q:** What would you say to parents whose children are involved, and to the other parents about trying to help keep their children from getting involved?

**S:** Stay close to them, talk to them. Not just on a mother and father level, but as a friend also. Stay close to them and watch for any kind of different changes that they may be showing in their lifestyle. Just because they're making A's or B's in school doesn't mean that they're not affiliated with gang-banging activities. Parents seem to think that just because the grades are good, their sons and daughters are not affiliated, but that's not real. I have homiez who get good grades like that, and I wasn't a dumb gang banger myself. So parents need to stick close to their kids and make sure they know what their children are really into. These kids are coming up gang-banging starting at the age of eight and nine years old, and they're very intelligent, they know what they're talking about. You have to be slicker than your children nowadays, because these young kids that are growing up now are smarter than we were when we were young, so you have to be on top of their program, because it's easy to get involved with gang-banging. The parents be on that level like, "My son was never involved in gang-banging," after they're burying their son or daughter, but they just didn't know, because they weren't watching them close enough. Everybody on the streets knows that their son or daughter was affiliated, but the parents are sitting back thinking that they knew their son or daughter but they really didn't. So the parents have to stick with their kids to the fullest, or they're going to be lost out there. When you get out there, there's so much love, you have some neighborhoods where if you run away from home, and you're a down homie, they take care of you, they have apartments, they put you up in there, you have a sack, and you're kickin' it. You're getting money, so you get deeper and deeper in it, because you've never had it like this. Then you start loving it, and you get attached. Back in the days there really wasn't too much money.

The parents have to stick with their kids and don't be so quick to take them to placement. The thing I hate most is when the parents call the police on their own kids. That's the worst thing. Like they say, "You brought them here, you take them out." Don't let them white people do it. They want to see that. That's all I can say to the parents, *stop giving up on your kids!*

It's rough out here when you have a son and you're a single mother. In the street life you're trying to keep your thing going and watch your kids, but it's hard without a father. Straight up, I know it's hard in this world today without a father. So these brothers really need to wake up and go ahead and put it down. You have brothers out here that are still really wild, banging, and they're thirty-five, thirty-seven, and they've never done anything for their kids. Their kids grow up straight wild. I have older homiez—like I say, I'm not the Double G—I have homeboys thirty-nine, forty years old, some of them take care of their kids, and some of them don't. The kids bang just like their daddies. They dress their kids up in all blue or all red, they dress them like gang bangers. They hang around the whole set and they learn like that. You know kids learn real fast.

Parents also have to watch the movies that their children watch. When I was growing up, my parents didn't let me watch all of that drama. I used to have to sneak and do that. Parents let their kids watch anything now. Their children come in at twelve o'clock, one o'clock in the morning, and they're supposed to be angels? What are they doing out at that time in the morning at twelve, thirteen, fourteen, fifteen, and sixteen years old? They're supposed to be at home kickin' it, doing homework, watching TV, or in the bed asleep; that's how we were. When I came up, the neighbors used to be on us too, like they were our parents. If you were doing something wrong, they would whip you and then tell your people what you were doing, and you'd get another whipping when you got home. Parents must be aware of the kids' wisdom and knowledge nowadays, because these kids are smart, they're dialing 911, saying child abuse when you whip them. So it's rough on the parents. That's why everybody has to show support. You have to treat the next person's child like your own. We need to bring back those good ol' days.

**Q:** Speak to us on relationships. Break down the importance of relationships.

**S:** Well, I feel that a relationship can help or hinder a gang member. It can help the brother if his spouse has a good head on her shoulders, but he has to take time out to listen to her and not be big-headed with a bad attitude. She can be there for him but he has to let her be there for him, and not just when he's incarcerated, you know how the majority of us brothers do it. But most of all a brother has to want to do the right thing, otherwise it doesn't matter if she's giving him some good advice or not. Brothers also just have to beware of the scandalous sisters out there and don't be tricked, because you can do bad by yourself. Always remember that for every strong man there is a strong woman, and vice versa.

Every man needs a strong woman backing him. Just like Magic Johnson; he has a real strong woman backing him. She's still there.

**Q:** [Question directed to Ship's Queen of four plus years, Lynn, who is sitting with us] What would you say on relationships and strengthening each other?

**Lynn:** It's important, you know. I believe that every man needs a good woman and that every woman needs a good man. Everybody needs to have somebody. It helps a lot. You just have to tell them what you feel is right and not what you think they want to hear. I'll say what I really feel. If they don't know what to do about something, I'd tell 'em, "You can do what you want to do, but I feel that you should handle it this way," and it's always positive, never negative.

**S:** She be right there too. She's a big help. Sometimes I might come home frustrated from something happening in the hood, and she'll be like my consultant because she will talk to me and she's not scary. She's not scared to say anything to me even if my feelings may get hurt, you know what I'm saying? She plays a big part, and a real person will take heed anyway. I'm going to do what I want to do, but I'm not afraid to come to her when I'm tripping or mad because I know that she will speak. Instead of me just moving to do something, I want somebody to be talking something for me to think about. When she comes at me positive, it makes me think. I really think about it. I may get mad, but I'll be knowing that she's right. It makes a big difference.

**Q:** You've been there with Ship through his change, right?

**L:** Yes, and it's going good because he's doing what he should be doing now. He's been through too much. Now it's time to kick back and do what's right.

**Q:** What advice would you give other sisters to support the brothers that they are with in coming positive?

**L:** They just have to tell them what's right and don't go along with it anymore. There was a time when I used to kick it and didn't mind if my man was into that. It was cool then and it didn't bother me, but it's not cool anymore. I have children now, and I want things, and you can't get anything living that way. Gang-banging, that's just not it anymore. You just have to let them know and hang in there with them, and eventually it will be all right. That's a little advice that I can give to the sisters.

**S:** I think it would be a lot different if females started asking, "Are you banging?" And if they are banging, then don't mess with them. But you have a lot of people out there that love it when a brother's banging. I'm telling you they love it, and that doesn't help. They need to encourage brothers to stop it.

**Q:** Why do you feel that one brother would not value another brother's life? Where do you think that mentality comes from?

**S:** They are not thinking about the next man's life. It's all about accomplishing your mission when you're banging, at least that's how I took it. I was too young and dumb to think about the life of a brother. I feel that comes from the big homiez keeping that "Crip or die" thought in our heads. Every set that wasn't down with Shotgun had to go, whenever they were caught slippin', and there was no remorse; that's how it was back then. It didn't matter if you were Black, white, or mixed, if you were a problem to Shotgun, you had to watch your back, because we were coming when you least expected it. There was no thought about the next man's life, it was just something in our minds that had to be done Crippin' straight from the heart.

**Q:** Does alcohol and drugs have anything to do with the gang bangers' cycle of violence and retaliation?

**S:** Yeah, that has a lot to do with it too. They are not really focused. Some are and some are not. In the majority of the drive-bys I would say that the person was intoxicated, because they drink before they go anyway. They get that buzz on, and the "Tiger" or the "Bull" comes up out of them. Back then it was that Sherm and that Red Devil that would do it. With the Mad Dog 20/20 or with any alcoholic beverages you get amped. It's something else how they put the liquor stores on every corner in the hood. We need to stop pitching in money for 40s and use the money to start some businesses.

They put the liquor stores and the gun shops out here because they know that we are going to go to them. These white people know that we are militant. Anything that's physical or has some kind of drama in it, you know that Blacks are with it. That's just in us, like the Indians, you know, wild and cool, we like to play. That's something else though, that they put that out here, and with the drinks, they know that we just get sprung, 800 don't even taste the same anymore. They probably put something in there now to make us trip out.

Like with all these guns, man, it's easy to get a gun. They know what they are doing. If they wanted to stop all of this s—, man, they could do it. If they really wanted this gang-banging to stop, they could put it down. They would just put out a law for everybody gang-banging to get life. Just like they come out with all of these other laws. Brothers are not stupid. They probably will come up with another law in a minute after they feel that they have enough of us dead and in the penitentiary. They have all of these liquor stores and all of these guns. That's the Black man's letdown right there. I'm not saying that it's anybody's fault. We do have our own minds, but it's like a disease. It's like a disease. S—, they have every kind of liquor that you can name, and almost every Black person drinks, and we're out here banging and smoking. It's all a part of banging, all the guns and the liquor stores are just a part of banging. A big part of banging.

**Q:** When the Uprisings came up on April 29, all the Bloods and Crips had unity, they didn't see each other as enemies or rivals anymore. What made us come together then?

**S:** It was a Black thing and it needs to stay like that. When they started tripping on us, it was time to get down then.

**Q:** What do we ultimately need to realize in order to come into unity for good?

**S:** We need to identify the ones that are really trying to hold us down. And these OGs need to come out of the closet. The people that have the rank, that everybody looked up to in these neighborhoods. They need to come out and put it down. You may have some that ain't with it, but they can just get rolled up. If you weren't with it back in the days . . . We have to go back to the old law. Bottom line. If you ain't with it, then just stay out of the way. A whole lot of the people that are with this peace are just scared to really get out there. I don't front, my neighborhood knows that I'm with this peace, and if somebody wants to trip, then I'm gonna trip too. I'm not a punk. Bottom line. I'm not going out like that. But I try to stay away from all of that and I'm not quick to just trip. I shun off a lot of things.

**Q:** Speak on the powerful impact that the brothers will have nationwide, and worldwide, by coming together. The red and the blue together.

**S:** Together we will be running things. Just like they were doing. I was locked up when they started the peace, and at first I thought they were tripping. It was cool though. It was just hard for me. The only thing that I had a problem with was . . . you know, I've been Crippin' all of my life, so it was like, damn, they're kicking it with them. That's the attitude I had at first, but I was thinking deeper too. Like, damn, the Blacks are actually together, that's cool. As far as I heard, there weren't drive-bys or anything going on. If we stick together now, man, it will be on.

**Q:** Would you say that there have been lives saved by brothers like you and the brothers in the other neighborhoods who are pushing the peace?

**S:** Yeah. I know I can't save the world, but the ones I can reach, that's good. Even if I just reach a few. I have a couple of homiez that since the *Peace Treaty* radio-station program was on, they went to school and are now working on trades. I have a homie that just went to college and straight got down, man, I'm serious. And that's just from people that I know, ones that I was dealing with.

**Q:** In trying to get your organization started, are you getting any support from the Black community?

**S:** No.

**Q:** How do you feel about that? Here you are, somebody that has been doing this all of these years, and now you're saying that you want to change for the positive and make the community better, something that's going to help everybody in the community, and you get no support from them?

**S:** It makes me frustrated, because I don't have to be doing this, but it's love. Everybody says that I was so wild and crazy all of these years, so I'm fixin' to come at them like this now. I went down to the City Council personally by myself and kicked up knowledge. I've talked to the man next to the mayor months ago, and they didn't come with it. I was like, damn, it's like these people want this s— to keep on going. It keeps the police their jobs. If there's no violence, then the police don't have jobs. When we stop tripping, then the police start something up. They do it now, the police write on the walls and cross out sets and all that. They keep things going, man. You tell me. If that's your job and you've been policing all your life and now you don't get any calls on this hood and that hood, and you're thinking about getting laid off. That's why the police do drive-bys. They know your schedule, they know your whole hood, and they know where you hang out at. They have them hit squads, where they can be off duty, put on some other clothes, get in a bucket [a car], and know where you're hanging out at, roll up on you, and do a drive-by. Bam bam bam, and leave. When the police get the call, they already know that it was their own boys that put it down, so they take their time to get there and give their boys enough time to get out the way, and then they say it's gang-related. With any drive-by they will say it's gang-related. It doesn't matter what it is.

It hasn't been an easy task doing this peace thing, man. I've fought mf's for trying to trip on different people, stopping them from doing what they was trying to do. You've got a lot of people that won't say anything, they'll just let it ride. We have a lot of people that are lost, man. Our people are way out right now. It's going to take a whole lot of people to start participating with this here peace. It's like a Martin Luther King thing, but it's not against the white people to me, it's on the Blacks. We need to start focusing on all the Blacks. I don't know what's happening with us, but we need to wake up. I'm serious, man, I know that if a brother like me can wake up, then I know damn well . . . Somebody's got to do something, man. This is the hardest thing that I ever did in my life. Trying to keep peace and kick it. That wasn't me. You can ask everybody in my family and everybody that knows me. I was wild. I never thought that I would be on this level and be sincere, on the real. I'm telling you this is the hardest thing that I ever did in my life, but that's cool though. I like challenges. There's going to be times when we will have to fight too, you know. It has happened already. There's going to be times like that, but we just have to hang in there. I wanted to put everything down when a lot of my homiez got hurt behind some bull. I was hot, man, it's hard to accept, but I made phone calls and I ran into people that was saying, "You know that you have to hang in there, it's going to be some of that, you know that we're fighting for something that's right, so you know that it's always going to be some s—." So I've been hanging in there, man. I'm not perfect and I do get mad. Like I say, sometimes you have to deal with s—, but as far as being out there trying to trip, I'm not with just killing a Black brother, man, or anybody, period, but especially a Black man. There are too many of us gone already. I have at least thirty of my peoples from my neighborhood gone, dead, from since I've been banging. I know people from everywhere. I know people from sets that have forty, fifty, sixty homeboys gone. There's too many of us gone. We are already short of people, and with this racial s— that has been going wild lately, brothers have got to wake up, man. I'm not prejudiced either, but these white people that are in these high positions with the say or whatever, they are trying to take us out, man.

We're all in the penitentiaries. They've been doing it all their life. I guess a lot of brothers can't see it 'cause they're always drinking and loaded, so they don't have time to kick back and think about it. There's always drama and violence in their head instead. I know brothers that were wild, then they went and did time, and since they didn't get to have all of that ol' alcohol, they came out thinking differently, and I have some homiez that came out and turned back too. It's all this s— out here that keeps you in this violent cycle, and you're always on that level of somebody tying to get you and you always have to be watching your back.

What it is exactly is that all we see is our Black brother, but we don't see the hand behind the hand that's making all of this happen, orchestrating the whole thing, putting all of the guns, the drugs, and the liquor in the hoods to set it off. The system doesn't want it to be too peaceful, but I'm gonna keep on doing what I'm doing. Always. I'm gonna always tell my homiez, whoever, they don't have to be from my neighborhood. I've talked to people who are not from my hood. No matter what we're doing, I would get on a conversation, and peace is going to come up in our conversation before the night is over. That's what time it is with Ship. I'm used to putting it down, instead of talking. I'm going to hang in there, you don't have to worry about me. You're not going to hear about me tripping, just to be tripping.

I'd like to see some kind of recreation facility in the hood. They have some facilities like that, but it's not a Black thing. They need to fund us and help these brothers find jobs. We need vans. Things will happen, all they need to do is get us some material. Get us some material, and we can make it happen. Get us a gym, with some iron. I have homiez that do drafting, that are professionals, that have taught school. I have homiez that have worked in boys homes, that are professionals, that went to college for it. We have professionals if that's what they want. Then we need a spot where homiez can come in at least once a week, and everybody can come in and relate to each other. If you want to talk, or speak, you have a place to come and get things off of your chest. Like the *Peace Treaty* radio program on KJLH. That was working. It was working, that's why they took it off. That radio station was working, that's why they took us off that radio station. I felt it, and I saw it. A lot of people listened to that program. A lot of people that I know that was hard-core bangers were with what we were talking about on KJLH. It was shocking me, just like I was shocking them. Everybody was tuning in to KJLH. It was going on in different neighborhoods like, "Yeah, man, I heard you." Homiez were writing me from YTS. We used to read the letters on the air. They couldn't believe I had changed up.

**Q:** Any further words of importance that you want to express?

**S:** I'm still here. I'd like to give a shout out to the youngsters, and to the old homiez. The best thing for you to do is obey your parents, that's the bottom line. If you don't have any, and you're out there on the streets banging, don't be scared to speak to one of your big homiez that seems like he has some sense. Try to find another way out. Don't be afraid to talk. The only dumb question is the one that you don't ask. Don't let banging be your only way out. I know the majority of Blacks out here doing it, not just in California either, everywhere, need another way out. Some kind of way, find some time in your life to just kick back before it's too late. It doesn't take much. It's easy to get into trouble, but it's hard to get out. Think about your family, your moms, your pops, and if you don't have them, everybody has somebody that loves them. Think about your nieces and nephews, your children, every time you pick up that pistol and go out there putting it down, you're just hurting the next generation. That person that you kill could have been your kin, you never know. Or in the future your daughter could have been hooked up with his son. It doesn't pay; this is Ship: it doesn't pay. I wanted to be at the top, and I got up there, and there's nothing up there. Nothing up there but a f'd-up rep. I was tripping. I don't regret anything I've been through, because it has made me a stronger person. Find another hobby, go bowling or something. Stay Black.

> ***Black people as a nation are in a state of war. . . . It only takes one side to declare war. Black people have an option, you either fight or die.***
>
> **—Sista Souljah**

## SHOUT OUTS

I'd like to send some shout outs to all of my homiez resting in peace, all of my homiez doing time, and all of my homiez that are still out here in society who are trying to make a better life for our kids in the future. I'd like to give a shout out to all the mothers and fathers in the world today who have not turned their backs on their kids. I'd like to give a shout out to the churches that are participating in helping us brothers who are working very hard for the peace out here in these streets. Thanks for your prayers. I'd like to give a special thanks to Hands Across Watts, South Central Love, Hands Across Gardena, and all the rest of the organizations that are participating with the peace. I'd like to thank my girl, Lynn, and everyone else whose name I didn't mention for believing in me and contributing their support, whatever it may have been; may God bless all of you. Last but not least I would like to thank Yusuf and his Queen, Shah'Keyah, and their li'l Queen, Ah'Keyah, for giving me the honors to share my personal opinion, wisdom, and knowledge about gang-banging and what needs to be done about it. Thanks to Uprising Communications. Most of all I'd like to thank the good Lord up above for giving me the opportunity to still be here in society to speak on these issues. Peace.

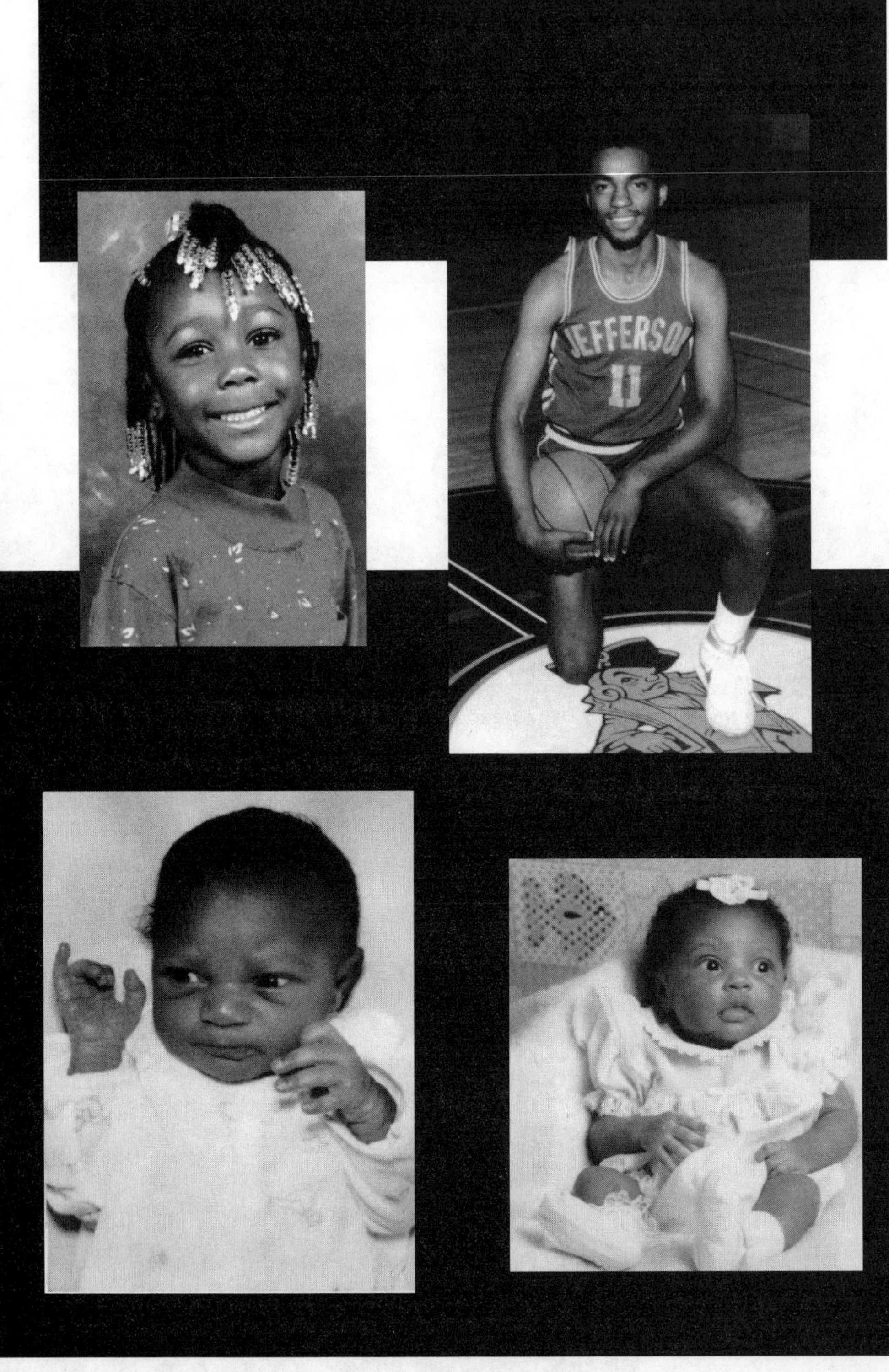
JEFFERSO
11

# LEON

*(My name is Leon, better known as Count. I am a representative of the Pueblos. This is something that all the brothers and sisters out here should listen to and take heed to, because this is something that we all need to be awakened to. This book is very important because it is coming directly from our mouths. There is no cut in this. This is from the actual brothers telling you the real about what's happening. All of these brothers that are in this book have lived through it, and they have changed. I know them all, and they have changed for the positive. They are telling you the real on how not to get caught up and what's really going on out here. When you read these words, I want you to realize that it is time to wake up and help with the problems and get with changing what's happening out here. We must focus in on the young kids that we have out here! Time for positive change! Leon.)*

**Q:** How did you get involved in the gang peace that's going on out here?

**L:** It goes way back. A lot of these brothers out here are partners of mine. We all went to the same high school, Jefferson High School. When we got out of school, we all just went our own ways. By me being a good basketball player, I knew everybody in the school, and so when the peace came about, I felt the opportunity was something I should jump on, because it was a chance to unite some of these people that I already knew with some of my other homeboys. To show them that the person on the other side is not as bad as we portray them to be. That this person over there is pretty much all right. It had gotten to where we were getting caught up in these colors, so when the peace came about, we were realizing that the brother on the other side was a brother just like us.

Back in the day we would get out there and get caught up with our homeboys, and things would happen. You just get mad, and you show out when you're with your homeboys, but once you sit and think about it, you realize that you were just after another brother, and for a silly reason too. Sometimes things occurred because of a female, or a brother would come back and say that a bunch of brothers jumped on him and beat him up, when all along it was a one-on-one fight, and he just got beat down. He involved a whole bunch of other brothers into something that was man-to-man. He couldn't just accept it as it was.

I felt that I needed to get involved with the peace, because we need to go back to the basics of being men. Instead of always getting a team to help you do something, handle your problem on your own. If you have a problem with somebody, that is between you and that person, don't pull everybody else into it. I see the peace as an opportunity for the brothers to step to the problem and settle it.

**Q:** How did you first hear about the beginning of the peace?

**L:** I was standing on the other side of the projects, and everybody was running around saying, "There's a Crip walking through the neighborhood." He was with one of the guys from the Villains [a Blood]. So we were wondering what they were up to. The youngsters were running around preparing to get the dude. The Crip stepped to some of the older dudes that were sitting out there, along with me and a couple of other guys, and he said, "I know I'm in violation, but I think it's time for brothers out here to come to peace. It's time to stop all of this. If you brothers are going to do me, go ahead and do me now. Whatever, man, I just feel like it's time for somebody to step up and say it's time to have some peace over here."

**Q:** Where was he from?

**L:** He was from Five-Tre Avalon. We were like, "We don't want to hear that." He said, "That's the real though." Then at that same time some of the Villains drove through with some Crips in their car. We were shocked, like, "What's going on?" Then we saw some old faces we knew, and they told us that they were all going to South Park. So we sent a few people through there just to look and see what was going on. Then they came back and said, "Yeah, the Villains are in South Park with the Five-Tres, the Broadways, and all of them." So we packed up and went over there, and they was all in the park kicking it, looking at each other, realizing that a lot of us knew each other, we knew this one dude from school, he was a rival, but now we were looking at him like, "What's up, man, we're here." Brothers were hugging and talking to each other. It was a trip. It was a deep feeling. It was the first time in a long time that I saw Black people really caring for each other. The same people who were out here trying to take each other's heads off, now were out there getting along, hugging each other, and enjoying it. It was joyful. Then we figured we just had to do something. So a few of us got together, and we said that something lasting and positive has to come out of this. We started thinking, and we came up with the idea of starting a nonprofit organization, so we could start working with the kids and keep the peace going. Through our nonprofit we were able to get some money to put on a picnic. We threw a big picnic for all of the warring street gangs in this area: the Pueblos, the Villains, the Forty Avalons, the Four-Tres, the Five-Tres, the Five-Duce Broadways. All the main gangs from this area were up there. We had at least six thousand people in the park, packed up in there, Bloods and Crips. Then we had Bloods and Crips coming from the west side; the Eight-Tres, the 60s, the Brims, and all the other gangs were coming in. Then the next day, that

Sunday, we put on another picnic to show whether it was true love or not. For this one we asked the brothers to bring out their families. If it's true, then you can bring your parents out. So the parents did come out, and that's when we started to realize that some of us were kinfolks, and we never even knew it. Like me and Charles [Q-Bone], we are cousins, but we never knew it. It's like, just before that day if something would have happened, me and him could have taken each other out. I would have gone home and saw Moms on the couch crying, and I would have asked, "What are you crying for?" She would have been like, "One of my nephews got taken out." I would have been thinking, "Where at?" Then she would have described the street, and I would have been like, "Damn, I just took him out, my own cousin." It was that deep. You don't really always know who is kin to you out here.

**Q:** How did you find out you and Q-Bone were related to each other?

**L:** Through his brother, my other cousin. Me and his brother had kind of kept in contact a little bit, but I hadn't seen Charles in so long, I wouldn't have known him. We started talking, and his brother came through and was like, "Hey, what's up?" Then Charles looked at his brother like, "You know him?" His brother said, "That's Leon, man, you remember Leon when we were real small." Then our mothers started talking, and it came back to us. A lot of other dudes whose parents were relatives, or best friends in high school, all started kickin' it. It was unbelievable, because you never know who belongs to you on this earth. As Black people, we're all family, because somehow we have a tie to each other in some way. You may never know in which way you have a tie to that person, but you do. That was the great thing about it all.

**Q:** How did you feel when you were going to the park and you saw brothers from the other neighborhoods that you used to war against?

**L:** It was a situation where at first I felt like we can't really trust it. I was figuring, just like the Crips were probably figuring, that somebody was trying to set us up and just wipe someone out. Then I started feeling good when I started to see brothers open up and take other brothers to their parents' houses. That's something way out to do with your rival. To take your rival to your parents' house. Then we started going places together, going over to each other's houses, hanging out all day. The little homiez were going to school tying up red rags and blue rags together, telling the dudes in the schools, "This ain't what it's about." I kept feeling the love to where I just opened up. I had to trust it. It was like if a brother takes me out for trying to do what's right, then that's cool, at least I would go out on a positive note. So I put my heart into the peace and went with it, even if they weren't real with it, I was. Then I came to find out that most everybody was real with it.

There are a lot of people out here that are still real with it, but people have to take care of their families and do what they have to do. Until we come up with another solution, or something else for the brothers to do, then they're going to do what they have to do. If we could come out of this with a situation to where we can employ some people and get some businesses started, then others will want to change. They know they won't make as much money as they were making in the street life, but they also know they won't have to worry about people coming behind them and jacking them up every time they do something, or worry about another brother coming out of the bushes, ambushing them, and taking what they have. They would feel more relaxed and wouldn't have to worry about that kind of stuff anymore. They could do what they have to do in life and raise their kids without having to worry about getting gunned down. When you're in these streets, you can't be at peace with yourself, because you're constantly thinking about something that can happen. You're thinking about something you shouldn't even have to be thinking about. In regular life people don't have to think about that kind of stuff as often as a brother on the street does. He stresses himself out with it. Stresses his parents out, his family out, everybody in the family becomes stressed out.

When I was in that life, my moms couldn't get any sleep, thinking about what I was out there doing. I was coming in the house at four and five in the morning. Now I can see the difference in my mother. Now she's vital, she takes a five- to six-mile walk every morning, she doesn't look all stressed out now. I can see the difference.

One of my sisters who was on crack, this guy slapped her, and she fell back and hit her head, went into a coma, and died. Once I backed up out of that life, of doing wrong things, I saw that my whole family was involved in it, and when I took that lead, then everybody started backing up out of it. Now everybody in the family is straight. Everybody is where they're supposed to be. Everybody is thinking about positive things. My sister has a job, my moms is doing good; she has her grandchildren running around the house now, like it's supposed to be. The family is back tight. It was through my activity that led the whole family into it, so I had to get them out of it.

**Q:** How does that make you feel, to see the steps that you took have that positive impact on your family?

**L:** It makes me feel good, but then again sometimes I think even though it's good that I'm taking this step now, if I had been smart enough to take the step earlier, I probably could have saved my other sister's life. If I had just realized what this life was really doing to us back then.

**Q:** You were able to come to peace, along with thousands of other brothers who overnight were able to come to peace—what do you think it was that made that happen?

**L:** This was meant to be. This is God's work. Nobody else could pull people that had been warring like that together and, at the spur of the moment, bring about peace. It's not possible for any one man to be able to do that. That's God's work. Everybody out here that is a part of the peace should realize that. There's no one man out here powerful enough to say, "Cease," and we all cease. The vibes came through everybody. You have fools that would kick it back up, but even in the fools the vibes came up and said, "Cease." God took the devil up out of us, to let us see how the other side feels. He showed everybody how the other side feels, and a lot of brothers took heed, and they'll say, "It feels good." You may have some that slide back into banging, but the majority are staying out of it. The majority of the people are chilling. In this general area right here, we haven't had any major drive-bys or killings since the peace was called. You'll get an incident here and there, but it's nothing like it used to be. It's to where my mother can take that walk now, a nice long walk. Walking into their neighborhood, come out and walk into somebody else's neighborhood, and back into our neighborhood.

**Q:** Do you think that a lot of the violence that is going on now is gang-related?

**L:** They always say "gang-related," but who is to say who is in a gang? If you let them tell it, all of us are in a gang. If you're from a ghetto area, everybody has a partner that's gang-affiliated. That makes you labeled too. Nine times out of ten, if there are one hundred people in a so-called gang, you may only have five of them that are really gang bangers. I mean really active. The other ninety-five will just be kickin' it with the crew. "The activities in the park are gone, there are no social activities for us, so we go hang with the fellas, because we know that with these fellas we can make some activity." That's what it is.

**Q:** What was it that attracted you to gangs?

**L:** Nothing really attracted me, because I was always a leader on my own. I was labeled by hanging with certain guys, by doing what I wanted to do. I went where I wanted to go, and I hung out with who I wanted to hang out with. There was an incident that happened when I was thirteen years old. I was hangin' with a lot of other homeboys that weren't bangin', we went to this show on Easter, and we all had the same kind of sweatshirts on, but with all different colors. The show was full of Crips. We weren't bangin', but we were from the Pueblo projects. There was a guy that used to stay over here, who moved to another neighborhood, and he turned into a Crip, and he saw us in the show. I could feel bad vibes in the show like something was going to happen. I told my partner, "Let's get up out of here before something happens, and whatever you do, before we leave out of here, don't tell him we're leaving. Let's just leave." Then one fool out of the bunch told the guy we were leaving, and when he said that, so many Crips came, it was a shame. There was twelve of us, and there was a show full of Crips. An uncountable amount. They were beating my young partners up all over the place. It just so happened that I was able to get out of there, while we were all going our own separate ways. That incident led a lot of them into getting involved with gang-banging, because the gang bangers from our area came to the rescue, dealing with them as they caught the bus back through the neighborhood.

A lot of the brothers got with it then. I was still not with it; I was from the Pueblos, but I wasn't with banging. They were still my partners, and we were still kickin' it every day, but they started changing their dress code, and I wasn't changing minc. Slowly, one by one they started changing their dress code. We went everywhere together, these were my partners to the max. So wherever we went, it was on, because they knew that my partners were Bloods; even though I was not one, I was with them, so it was on with me too. People started saying, "You be with them, you're one." I would say, "I'm my own man. I'm going to hang with who I want to hang with. I grew up with these brothers, and I'm going to hang with these brothers." Then it came to a point where they was like, "You're just one then." I was like, "Take it how you want to take it, I am going to hang with the same brothers." Some brothers took it as, "He's cool," while other brothers take it as, "He's with them." That's how it goes. In reality that's how it goes with a lot of brothers out here.

It's like you're forced into something just by being around it, then you get tied into it, then you're with it. In the eyes of the community, there's nobody under the age of thirty that's not involved with it. There are kids that are straight-A students in this community right here, and they're still labeled as gang members. It happens in communities like this one here, the projects; it's different than from being in a residential area. In a residential area you can sometimes escape it, but when you're from the projects, the first thing they will say is, "That brother is from the Pueblos." That's all they want to hear, that you're from the projects. So they can deal with you accordingly. That straight-A student may be defending himself as a man, but it seems like he's defending himself for the neighborhood. That tag is put on you. Then it comes to a point where you really are defending the neighborhood, because you get dealt with so much that you have to deal with it back. Then you're caught up in it, but you really don't want to be caught up because you know better. There's this forcing issue that makes you deal with it like that.

**Q:** How did you come to be in the position of representing your hood now?

**L:** In my neighborhood the brothers have chosen me as a spokesman, not as a leader. They felt that since I was a brother who graduated from high school, spent a little time in college, and played a little college ball, they figured I knew how to speak a little. They figured I could articulate the same things that they try to relate to other people and make them understand. So they felt that I should take the lead as far as speaking up. I'm not speaking up on what I want to speak on. I speak on what I hear from everybody, and I put it together. I speak to all my homiez individually, in groups, however I catch them. I ask them how they feel about things, and I see where their heads are at. I'm just a communication piece for them. It's not like just because I'm doing the talking, I'm the leader. There are no leaders. Another brother may be better at fighting for us. Another brother may be better at getting us something else. You have to utilize people for what they're best suited for, instead of trying to say, "Since he's the baddest one in the gang, he's the spokesperson." He might be the baddest one in the gang, but he might not know how to communicate with other people. It might be the dude in the back that you're calling a little wimp that might be able to get the message across, because he may have a better understanding of what's going on. He probably has a little more education, and he may have dealt with other people before.

I used to take some of the homiez to the college campus with me because they had never been around a bunch of white people or oriental people like that before. I used to take them with me and show them how I deal with other people. I deal with this life, but I deal with other people too, so I know how they think, and how they react to things. I have racial conversations with them too. I voice my opinion, and they voice theirs. They trip off of how the communication is, but when you come back to this community, it's like a wall: "Whites, Mexicans, I don't want to talk to them." But me, when I get out there, I want to talk to them, because I want to figure out what's going on in their head. They just about know everything about us, because they study our people. So I'm going to do a little inventory for myself on them and see where they're at. So that all of us won't be lost when the time comes with whatever they plan to do to us. It's to our advantage to know what is going on when it comes to waking our people up. When something is about to happen to their people, they let their people know. With our people, when we get in a position to warn somebody, we don't. If you have some information that you know, you're supposed to feed it back to me, and I'm supposed to come back at you with a little something. It's not supposed to be where you're always trying to sell game or make me do something for you, to give me a little knowledge or make me pay something just to get knowledge. It should be at a pace where you're trying to share knowledge with as many people a day that you can. Trying to get them to start thinking on that positive wave, where they will start to do something like you're doing something. If you get everybody on that wavelength, then you'll have something positive going on.

The main thing is to get them to think about what they want to do, or where they want to go in life. If you don't get them on that level of thinking, then you're not going to know where they want to go. We have to reach into them, talk to them, and see what's really inside of them. There are some brothers out here that say some pretty deep things to me. Some brothers will say, "I want to be a fireman." This brother is out here gang-bangin', so who is going to believe that he wants to be a fireman? They have dreams. The young girls around here have dreams. They talk about how they want to be computer operators. We all have dreams, but it's hard for some people to get out what they have inside of them. They want to spill it out, but they don't know how. They don't know the words to use to really get out what they're trying to say. You have to have patience when dealing with them and see what it really is that they want. You have to listen to what they're saying. You may have to listen to them a little longer than others, to give them the time to get it out, and they will tell you. A lot of these brothers around here are smart, a lot of them are artists, that's why they write the walls up, there's nothing else for them to write on. Give them something else to write on. Put them in an art contest. Do something with them. Give them a start first, then we can give them that right frame of mind. You have to give them something to want to pull themselves up for.

Like in this neighborhood, I get free tickets to the Lakers games, and I take the youngsters to the games. I had about eighteen youngsters with me, and at least fourteen of them came up to me and said, "Thanks, Count, I appreciate that. I've never been to the Forum in my life." The Forum is right over there [points in the direction of the Forum, which is within a few miles of the area]. Why hasn't this kid ever been to the Forum in his life, and the Forum is right over there? Because we make our own imaginary boundary lines and keep ourselves caught up in the boundary lines. If you look on a map, those lines are not on the map. My set is not on the map. Their set is not on the map. When a brother does get outside of the boundaries, he starts feeling good about himself, because he starts seeing things that he never saw before. Then what happens when you come back to the neighborhood is all the frustration comes back. You've seen what's out there, and you want to stay out there and keep going places, and that's just what you have to do, keep moving.

**Q:** You've been able to go to a lot of places and see a lot of people, but now your focus is on helping your homiez get to other places. What makes that important to you?

**L:** All of us have capabilities to do whatever we want to do, but we're in a condition to where we've been trained for so long that we can't do things, till we start to really think that we can't do them. With my experiences, I can see that no matter what conditions you come out of, good things can happen for you, because good things have been happening for me. I figure if good things can happen for me, what makes me any more special than you that good things can't happen for you? They may not happen for you the way they happened for me, but they may happen for you in a different way.

We have a couple of rap groups over here, so I motivate them. I've motivated them so much that they have cut their tracks, and they're ready to get signed. That's good for the community, because now the little kids from the community can see somebody from their own neighborhood that they can look up to. I tell the brothers all the time that when they make it, they have to come back and give to the kids. Don't act like you don't remember when you came from this same spot. Come back and do some activities with the kids, and let the people know that you're not just out to take the money out of the community, you're out to help the community in return. It's like a cycle, and we're rolling it back in.

We have to start opening up businesses in the community, because if there are three oriental businesses, and two Hispanic businesses, and we have five Black businesses, when the people come down to the community to ask what's needed, since they usually go to the businesses and talk to them, then our voice will start to mean something in this community. We will be able to manipulate the things that happen in this community, to happen the way that we want them to happen. The way we know it's truly supposed to happen.

We can't get our minds caught up in what they set out for us, we have to be concerned with housing, with jobs, and developing entrepreneurs, all of these different areas. Right now, there's nobody concerned about these things, and the people that are trying to be concerned about them are doing too many jobs at one time, they don't have enough hands. So we have to start Uprising people that want to help us to do these things. We have to understand why it's necessary for these things to happen, it's for the betterment of our kids' future.

In my life I've experienced a lot of different things. I think I'm blessed to have lived the life that I've lived, and to have learned the things that I've learned, but I wouldn't want for everybody to have to go through the experiences that I went through to learn what I've learned. Let me tell you about them, so that you won't have to bite into them. A lot of people that experienced these same things with me, they didn't make it up out of 'em. A lot of people got caught up, and now their lives are gone. I am one of the fortunate ones to be able to live this long, to get up out of it and tell about it. A lot of people don't live long enough to speak about it. A whole lot of my friends have died. I'm so cold to death now, it's like if I see a person dead on the ground now, I'm like, "Damn, that brother is dead." I know I'm supposed to feel it more than that. "It's just another brother dead on the ground." I'm not supposed to be feeling that way. We're supposed to feel it. I've seen so many people laying dead it's a shame. For what? For nothing. Brothers wasted, brothers that I was just with fifteen minutes before it happened to them, just before they got smoked. It becomes so regular that I start to not have feelings about this kind of stuff. I get a little feeling, but I'm supposed to get a feeling to where my knees would almost buckle.

**Q:** Break down how important it is for brothers to start realizing that we have to do things for ourselves on the economic level in order to really Uprise.

**L:** Basically we have to take from what we have right now. We have to start evaluating our communities and see who's getting the money out of our community, and where it's going. We need to step into some of these business opportunities that are in our communities. We first have to learn how to sacrifice, because you have to know how to sacrifice to make it work. Like Charles and I, we got into a lot of things, we sacrificed, and when something didn't work, we didn't give up, we just got into something else. We've been sacrificing since we've been out here, but the more you sacrifice, and the harder you try at it, the more the opportunity there is for you to succeed. You start to meet people that see how you're really trying, and they give you pointers on how to do things.

It's to the point now where if we don't step up and start making opportunities for each other, then there won't be anything for us. What I see is them trying to bring slavery back into effect on us, but it's going to be a modern type of slavery. We have to catch ourselves, because there's not a lot of time for brothers to be out here thinking about if they want to change or not. It's to a point in time where you have to motivate them to step up into it *now.* If you've been having a dream all of these years, go on and try it. The only failure you can have is if you don't try. If you don't try, you fail yourself, by not putting yourself 100 percent into the venture to make it successful. It's very important for brothers to get into something right now. Even educational things; we need educators. We need some brothers to start getting educated on the history of our people and then start educating others about what's going on with our people, what our people have been through, and where our people are heading. We have to give the children a sense of pride, and a knowledge of self.

If we only knew ourselves we wouldn't get offended when people say certain things. We have to know how to deal with them and shoot right back at them what they shoot at us, but on a calm level without getting too hype. We have to learn how to catch hold to our emotions and be able to focus in on what we're supposed to do. Things may not be going your way, but you have to hang in there and don't get your emotions too caught up into it. We have to handle our business.

As Black people we're always striving to go straight ahead, but we let distractions on the side make us turn our heads and lose our path of where we're going. If we did like everybody else and went straight ahead, no matter what the people on the outside of us are saying, we let them say it, we'd be all right. We have to make our own plans like they're making their plans. Their plans are only working because they're keeping us distracted, while they're steady working on their plans. So we have to stay focused and work on our own plan, and go in the direction that we want to go in with ours, and do what we have to do for ourselves. Don't let the things that are twice as hard get to you.

We know that it's twice as hard for us already, so why are we still tripping off of that? We know that, so let's go ahead and work twice as hard to make things better for everybody, and make it so that it won't be twice as hard for our children.

We have enough money here to just deal with ourselves, without dealing with anybody else. People just need to come to terms with themselves and realize that we're all Black and we're all here together. Everybody else makes their money off of us, and we don't make any money off of them or each other. So if they're making their money off of us, then we have the money, but we don't even realize it. We steadily give other people our money. We must start realizing that wc can get these brothers that have money to set up businesses and to stop just holding on to their money. What are you going to hold on to your money for? When you die, the money is going to be disputed over and fought over anyway, so go on and set up shop where you can put a lot of people in action.

I feel that after the Uprisings, people like Bill Cosby, Magic Johnson, and other people with enough money should have taken advantage of some of this burned-up property that people were running away from and trying to sell, and they should have built it back up. They could have built Black-owned supermarkets, and for a change we could have had a place where our people can feel like they can go to and feel welcome. We go to these stores now and the Hispanic people have their names on top of the stores, but if you go to a Black store, you probably won't know it's Black until you go in there and they tell you it's a Black store, because they're scared to represent what we stand for. Everybody else represents what they stand for, and everybody else deals with their own. Other people come in and make money off of us, but they're not going to buy anything from the little store we have. They go back to their community to get the things they need for their household. We have to learn to deal amongst ourselves in that same way.

The churches, there's a lot of money in the churches, but they're not doing anything for the community. They're not stepping up for the community. All they're doing is crying about what's happening out here. Nobody is taking the chance to really come out on the streets and talk to the youth to really see what's happening. The churches are not putting money into the community to help it. They just shout about what's going on. What's really going on is you tell these children on the streets that they're tripping, but when the gang peace comes about and everybody starts sitting back and starts thinking about life, all we see is the religions and the churches over there squabbling with each other. The politicians squabbling with each other, everybody is squabbling. Then they want to complain about us squabbling; they are squabbling more than we're squabbling. They have more division than we have. You're crying about me because I've been dealing with you, and then when I also go deal with another brother who has a program over here, you get mad? I'm for all brothers. If I feel like a brother is positive and is going in the right direction and needs help, then I'm going to help him.

We have power, but they have the power all separated. Until we find a way, like Minister Farrakhan is trying to do, find a way to pull all these powers back together and make it one, like a solid ball, only then will we be all right. Until then, we still have one person who wants to take all the glory for making job opportunities, and another person who wants to take all the glory for helping the children—man, f the glory, just make it happen. Let's just help everybody like we're supposed to. You're going to get your glory on Judgment Day, that's when your get your glory, don't be trying to get your glory now, get your glory when your glory is due, when you need your glory. You're reaching for it too soon.

**Q:** What do you see happening with the Bloods and Crips getting together?

**L:** I see powerful Black forces. I see them on the mental and the physical level. Where Black people for a change will be able to move on things and make things the way they're supposed to be, because gang members are the missing element to all of it. Whether people want to face it or not, right now the gang members are the ones that are really waking everybody up to what's really happening. It didn't come from the so-called leaders to wake the people up, it took the people from the streets.

Like when the rebellion happened, it took the people from the streets to make that happen. There were no politicians saying, "Let's go do it." It was the people from the streets who felt that we're not being served justice. The people we call our leaders are not getting us any justice, so we have to do it ourselves. If you look at it, as far as Black people are concerned, what military forces do we have? We don't have any military forces of our own. The only military forces we have is the Crips and Bloods. That is your military force, so you'd better get smart and put those forces together for a positive reason. Let them know what war is about, that when you fight, you fight for a reason. When you go at something, you go at it because you're trying to get something, or you're trying to establish some ground, you don't just do it randomly. The brothers are the ones that are going to make a *universal change* for Black people. The whole world is looking at Los Angeles. We have bad brothers that you've been seeing for years from all over, New York and Chicago, but right now the whole world is looking at us right here in L.A. I have partners in London that live in the same situations that we live in, and they've been through the same things. They've been caught up in the penitentiary system and all of that, and even they're looking at us wondering what we're going to do. Our words, our movements, and our emotions are valuable to them; whatever we do is going to rub off on them. Just like the gang-banging did, it came from here and then it spread. Now we have to be the ones to erase it.

You know what I respect about the Muslims is that when you see Muslim people, you see history. You see real Black people. You don't see them slouching, you see positive in these brothers, these brothers and sisters be glowing. They stand straight and tall. They're disciplined. They know what life is all about. They know that a woman is supposed to teach a woman, and a man is supposed to teach a man. A woman can't teach a man how to be a man. There are things we can teach each other, but as far as the basics, they understand that we have to separate sometimes to get to the point where we want to get to. There are a lot of good principles that they have, the practices, and the studies. The food, how they're conscious about what they eat. A lot of these things we all need to be put up on, our people as a whole, no matter if you want to be Muslim or not. I think that we as Black people need to be following the majority of the Muslim ways. I think we would be a more disciplined people. Every other nationality has something to clinch on to. We don't have anything to say how we do things. How do Black folks do things in the United States? We don't have a culture of doing anything. We do it the way we feel like we should do it. We need to have something to where we can have a sense of pride on how we do things as Black people. There has to be certain principles set, like respecting each other and our women, because we don't have any respect right now. That's why people do what they want to do. That's why all these killings and all these gangs have been starting up like they have.

**Q:** What are some ways that we can help manifest the greatness that brothers have in them?

**L:** It's going to take constant communication. If you see the greatness in a brother, communicate with him for a minute, and then don't give him a chance to slip back into the things that he might have been into at first. If you have constant communications, you have a person constantly thinking. Then you have to come with a solution to help a brother satisfy his needs. You have to find some way for this brother to earn a salary, to where he will be happy, and to where he will want to work with the people of his community, to help them do something. It all revolves around a person being able to take care of their family first, and then we will be able to help other brothers out of their situations. There should be some type of plan implemented for the gang peace leaders to be able to be employed for what they're doing out here. We're doing the job that we are supposed to do, but we are doing the job that others are being paid for, we are doing it for free. I feel like we should be the ones to get paid for doing what we do because you'd see that when a person is able to take care of home, he is able to put more effort into what he's doing. Right now brothers are putting their true effort into it, but I feel that we all have more effort that we can put in, if we were able to feed our mouths and pay our bills. A lot of times we're thinking about our situations, and how we are going to help our surrounding communities, but then we are thinking about the bills that we have to pay, and how we are going to get the money to pay the bills. So we have to put those brothers in situations where they're employed, and then others can see the brothers working to help the community, and they'll be like, "I'm going to help him to help the community."

When I communicate with the youngsters in my community, I communicate with the ones that are being looked up to, and I tell them what's on my mind. Then I let them share with the other ones that look up to them. I know if I can convince that one that what I'm saying is right, then the rest of them will look at him and see him following the right path, then they will follow him because they look up to him. Showing by example. It's like when you have a rotten apple in the bunch, and the rotten apple spoils the bunch, that rotten apple is the one that you make the example out of. You don't have to make the example by punishing the person, you make an example by changing that person. You'll make the ones that are not rotten to become even better people, because they'll see if he can change, then they can make a more valiant effort at what they're doing also. It's about motivation; if you see somebody else do it, and it was somebody that you didn't expect to do it, then it makes you get motivated too. You get an attitude like, "If he can do it, I know I can do it," and that attitude rolls on, and everybody gets to feeling, "I can do it too."

**Q:** What keeps you motivated?

**L:** My little niece Sharon. I have a few nieces now, and I want to see them have it the way they're supposed to have it. I want to see them go to college. I want them to be able to do things that I wasn't able to. I want to see them have a smooth life.

Waking up and seeing my little niece every morning keeps me motivated to do what I have to do. I know I have to do something to help her, and the other little kids in my neighborhood. I see that nobody is really making an effort to help them. Nobody sits with them and talks to them or plays with them. A lot of kids just need some attention, so I feel like I have to be the one to be there for them. I have to have somebody to keep me going to give them attention, so my little niece keeps me going. She constantly makes me give her attention. She keeps me motivated.

**Q:** Speak on the importance of reaching out to the youth, and spending more time talking with our children and *listening* to them.

**L:** They are the future. We have to reach out to them now. We have to catch them right now and start instilling those old principles back in them like when we were young. We can't let people tell us to not punish our kids, by not doing that we let our kids do whatever they want to do. They say, "If you discipline your child too tough, we're going to take your child from you." Who's to say how you should discipline your child? When the discipline was cut out, the children went out of control. When we were in school, the teachers could swat you, and that was one of the best things we had going, because that child realized that if he messed up, the teacher would swat him. Then they would call home and he'd get another whipping when he got home. They took that power from the school, and they're trying to take that power away from the parents too.

When I deal with kids, I make them respect me like I respect them. I tell them, "I will respect you, and I will do whatever I can for you, as long as you respect me as being an adult." A lot of youngsters have lost respect for adults. I tell them why they should respect adults: "Because these are people that have children just like you. How can you feel that you can disrespect somebody that's the age of your parents? Do you want somebody disrespecting your parent? No, you don't want anyone disrespecting your parent, so don't disrespect another person's parent." Sometimes an adult can be wrong, but you have to know how to walk away from them without being disrespectful.

Then we also have to teach the adults how to respect the children. A lot of adults don't know how to respect the children, or even communicate with them. We have to first educate a lot of parents so they can help educate their children, because a lot of the parents aren't educated enough to be able to give their children that extra boost. The child's homework may be over the parent's head, the parent may not even know what to do. So some parents need to get back into schooling so they can learn and be right there to help their children.

**Q:** What are some solutions that you present to some of the younger brothers in the neighborhood?

**L:** One of the main solutions to help us get out of the predicament that we're in is to get some of the grassroots brothers and sisters to start working with the people in the community. Everybody is going to have to just step up and start thinking about the future of our youth and start learning to have heart for them. We need to get people back into church, and into the mosque, so they can gain some pride about themselves. Learn where they want to go with themselves. A lot of people don't know and don't understand the ways of life. A lot of people need to be taught the ways of life. I think that the ways of life are one of the solutions.

Organizations like our nonprofit organization, South Central Los Angeles Youth and Community Services, I think our organization can help the community to get out of the position that we are in, as far as the violence that's happening in our community. I think it can really help us, because we have counselors that have actually been through the same situations as the people that they are counseling. So we can see where they're coming from and see where they're going at the same time. These paid psychiatrists have never lived in the projects or in the ghettos, so how are they going to come to us and tell us how to solve our problems? They don't know.

I feel that through our program we will be able to get a handle on all of these children, because the youth in the community are looking up to us. If our organization was giving a trip, and another youth center was giving a trip, all the kids would rather go on the trip with us, because they know they can communicate with us, and they're going to have some fun and be able to be themselves, instead of always having to be so tight. Brothers have to step up and be that father image for the children that don't have fathers. If not the father image, then the big brother. You have to start taking them up under your wing. You don't have to go in your pocket and cover their expenses, but if you would just take three kids and communicate with them, they'd feel like some older person cared enough to spend some time with them to teach them something, and that made them feel good for the day. A lot of times a child doesn't get a chance to communicate with an adult at all, because their mom may be tired when she comes home from work and doesn't want to hear it. They may have a stubborn teacher that doesn't want to hear it. So who are they going to talk to? There's nobody else there to talk to. There has to be somebody there to communicate with. Somebody they can tell their problems to, somebody who they feel can help them with the problems they might have, instead of somebody who is going to tell them the typical thing. They already know what the typical answer is going to be. They want a new answer, one they've never heard before, something that makes a little more sense. I feel that we're the best people to give them that kind of information. We've lived the life that they are now living, we've experienced it, have been a part of it, and are still a part of it, because we're still here.

**Q:** Speak a little more on the importance of the family structure.

**L:** That's the most important part of all, the family. You have to have a tight family. You have to teach the family to stick together through thick and thin. The family consists of a mother and a father, not just a mom or a pop separately. Even in situations where the father is not there, it's still the father's responsibility to be around and be there for their children to let them know that there is a male figure in their life. That there is somebody there that will stand up for them. The father figure is the one that represents safety. Every family needs that. When you do have that male in the family, you want him to grow up with that same responsibility to be able to take care of his family. It's important for the mother and the father to be there so that a young lady can understand the meaning of a real man, and what her role with a man is, what her responsibilities are when she's with a man. By her growing up under her family and seeing how her mother and father operate, that lets her know how she has to operate also. It's like a trend. When brothers started abandoning their families, that's when the trend broke up, because young ladies and young fellas didn't have that image. You had moms playing the mother and the father image, and the mama shouldn't have to play both roles. The mama playing the mother and the father image is messing the daughter up, because the daughter sees her mother playing both roles and she gets confused.

**Q:** What are some ways we can spread the peace to keep it going and to strengthen it?

**L:** Something has to happen out here. The whole thing is that people feel like nothing is going to happen, so they get laid-back again. When the peace first happened, we all realized that it was going to take for us to put together something. We've been thinking about a major gang summit, not just for gangs, but for Black people period. For a change it's time to let the young people talk to our so-called leaders and politicians. Let the youth voice their opinions to them, so they can get across to them what is on their minds. Sometimes that eases the tension, being able to express what is on their mind.

I feel like we have to get more people from the community to step up. I don't want to just say it's money, but then again it is money. As long as we don't have a basis to work from to generate anything, it's going to be hard to keep peace. There has to be something there to get the young people to come. There has to be something to draw them in, and it has to be more than just words. It's going to take money to make something happen. Let's say for instance that we came up with a way to employ one thousand gang members. We can go and get thirty people from each neighborhood employed. They'll come out, it would start changing the mind-set, they will feel like there's something out there for them.

We just have to find a way to get the cash flow flowing right. That's what a lot of brothers out here are talking about, the cash flow. Brothers say, "If I had a job, I wouldn't gang-bang," or "If I had a business, I wouldn't do this."

**Q:** From your experience of starting businesses, what would you say to brothers on how to become successful in starting their own businesses?

**L:** You have to look out for people who are saying that they want to help you, but when it comes time to help, they want to take over. Look out for people who will actually steal your idea, and people who will front you with the money when all the time they have a plan to take your business.

We were fortunate enough to have people that did protect us from that. People who always told us to watch out for this person and for that person, and to evaluate for ourselves. So we were kind of led in the right direction, but there were times that if we didn't have other people looking out for our safety, we would have been led into something to where we would have been beat out of everything. So you really have to watch who you are dealing with; whoever you do deal with, make sure that they are dealing with you in sincerity. If you feel that they are not sincere, then I feel that you should not do business with them at all.

You have to go ahead and see if your idea will work. They say that sometimes it's good to fail so that you will learn and you will know your mistakes. You just have to go ahead with your idea full steam.

**Q:** What are some steps that brothers may take to get started in forming their own businesses?

**L:** There is a little business that we started over here in our neighborhood with two brothers that are from here. I just really wanted to help them get started, and then I'm going to be out of there and let them have it and I'll go on with what I was doing. It was pure effort that we put into it. It wasn't like you had to be real intelligent or any of that kind of stuff. We just went downtown and inquired and found out about the business licenses and the zones, and what was required for us to run the type of business that we were considering. We found out all of the information, we filled the papers out, we filed everything, and we had a business. It is really easier than people think. People think that business is really hard or complicated, and it's not. Then you also have your people that will say, "What about keeping the books?" And I tell them that there are people out here that will help you keep your books, and at the same time when somebody helps you with your books, you are supposed to be learning about how to keep your books yourself too. There are people that will give you a helping hand to get started and to learn all of these types of things if you are willing to learn. It's just about getting in there and learning about what you want to get into.

The business we started is doing really good now. So it's just about sticking your mind to it, going and doing the research, and finding out what's happening. It doesn't take a lot of money to start a business either. You can take a little bit of money and start a small business to get your cash flow coming in and then work your way up to something big. You can learn with a smaller business how to really run and operate a business so when it's time to take that step up, then with just a little more effort you will already know how to operate and you will be ready for a bigger business.

There are all kinds of hustles out here that other people do that we don't take advantage of. We laugh at them, and sometimes these people are making more money than you would actually believe. I tell the brothers all the time, "You may laugh at the ice cream man, but the ice cream man has three or four houses down in Mexico, the ice cream man went and bought that truck for about twenty-five hundred to three thousand dollars, and he made his money back for that truck in one month's time. The ice cream man is coming through here making about three hundred to four hundred dollars a day, and we laugh at the ice cream man?" I told a brother once to just calculate how much money he would make if he had an ice cream truck and he ran that truck every single day for seven months, making $100 a day. The brother calculated it, he came up with the amount, and he looked at me and said,

"Twenty-one thousand dollars, man." In seven months of just driving an ice cream truck out here, which takes a jive license to operate, you can make good money. Once you add those nickels and dimes up, it comes out to be a lot of money.

Then they wonder why that same truck comes through the neighborhood with a different driver in it. Partner went to acquire some property, and he told his relative that he could rent the truck for a little something and drive the truck until he gets up enough money to buy his own truck. Then when partner returns, he gets his truck back and continues to run the route that they've been running, and his relative goes out and finds himself another new route with his own new truck. He made money off of his truck while he was in Mexico buying some property, and his cousin made his own money to go out and buy his own truck and go on about his business.

We haven't been looking at that, and there's a lot of money in ice cream trucks. That is a business where you keep your own books, and you report what you want to report. You don't have to feed these other folks all of your money, trying to be honest John. They are definitely not being honest John about anything they are doing with their money or with our money. You have to work yours just like they're working theirs.

It's the same as when they laugh at the Mexicans on the corners out here with these oranges and these little fruit stands. We patronize them, and they are making good money on those corners. Those are the type of hustles that we used to do that we now think we are too cool for. We have gotten caught up in this European system and think that we are like them. *We are not them,* and we have to do what is going to benefit our own and stop trying to be like Europeans. Trying to be them will never benefit us in any way. They have conditioned our people to make them think that doing for ourselves is no good, and that working for them is where it's at. When in reality it's the opposite. We're not supposed to be working for any of them people to help build up their businesses. We need to be doing for ourselves and building up our own businesses. We have been taken away from that; a lot of people think that it is hard when it's not, and they just don't know how lovely it is once you do get your own thing going. It's what we've been missing all this time, and it's not hard to get it started and going.

**Q:** Talk about the process you went through that helped you to change your thinking, your ways, and your actions.

**L:** Ooh, that process was rough, man, because some people weren't in agreement with it. The change I was making in the neighborhood was kind of hard on me. I was going to do what I wanted to do with my life, because it is my life. I had to just go forward and not worry about the people who were talking behind my back about what I was doing. Some brothers were saying that they weren't for the peace, and they were calling me a "peacemaker." Some would say that I was just looking out for myself. They just weren't diggin' it. But I knew what I was doing, I was sincere from my heart, and I stayed with it. You get a lot of flak with doing this, but now they see what it was all about. Now a lot of brothers come and apologize to me for what they had said. They would tell me that they were one of the brothers who was talking behind my back, and that they now see it is real.

Me and Charles take a lot of trips; we took 110 kids to Disneyland and then five days later we took 220 kids to Magic Mountain. They were wondering how we did that, with us being two brothers off of the street, but then they saw that we were looking out for their best interest, and the people that we took, we took them all for free. We fed them for free, they didn't have to spend a dime on anything, they just had to get on the bus and roll. Then they started seeing all the other things that we did for the kids, so they knew that we were true.

In doing what we do, we make a lot of contacts, and when we get stuff, we just give it to the community. We get turkeys and other kinds of food and we give it to the people. Congresswoman Maxine Waters gave us some Ben & Jerry's ice cream one time, and we just gave it to the community. We brought a bread truck over here one time and gave away free bread. They see that everything we do is to try to help our people, and we try to do things without charging people, because we know that the people really can't afford a lot of this stuff. We bring it over here and we find families that are in need. We try to help the neediest families. People say that I should look out for my family, but my family is not the neediest family over here. My family is taken care of, so I feel that I need to be looking out for that little kid over there that has a dirty face, whose mama is not combing her hair. I need to be looking out for her, I need to be trying to work with her and get her little stomach fed, and try to get her to focus on what's going on too, because she needs it. There are people over here that are homeless; living in the projects is like being homeless. There are people over here that live just like homeless people live—no lights, no gas, just paying rent and staying in the place. So we have to put an effort into changing that condition too.

So brothers see the effort now, they see that with whatever we are doing we are trying to help in any kind of way that we can. Just like with our friends that rap, we introduce them to people that we know in the music industry, and we don't want any cut out of it. We just want to make sure they get the opportunity.

**Q:** So you have been showing and proving by example?

**L:** Yeah, we have to prove it. It was a long road to prove it, because you get a lot of people who think negative about who we're helping, and they would say that we weren't doing this or doing that, but then it all boils down to them seeing for themselves what we are actually doing. Once they see, then they have to stand up for themselves too, and that's when we'll say, "Man, listen, I'm doing this, but I can be doing a better job with your help." From my neighborhood I was doing this as a one-man effort, taking the kids around in my vehicles. So they also started seeing us dealing with the kids and taking them places, like to the museums and to basketball games.

Instead of these white organizations or oriental organizations coming in and dealing with our kids, coming through and trying to pick up our kids, *no,* let us deal with our own kids. Let me deal with our kids. I'll have fun with them without any money, so just think if I did have some money, I could probably have them all straight with the help of the other people in the community. There is nobody better to work with ours but us. There's nobody better to help the problems in the community but the people in the community, because we live the problems 24-7. Other people come and try to solve these problems in fifteen minutes, and that's not taking enough time. If you haven't been here all of your life, then you can't solve these problems. You have to know this lifestyle. This is not something that you can just come and pick up on in one day or two. It may take somebody else twenty years or better to sit here and figure out what the problem is and how we can even think about trying to solve the problem. So since I have been here for twenty years, then go on and let me and the other people that are from here try to solve the problems, since we already know them. We are right here, and the time is now, and we already know what needs to be done, and how to go about doing it.

**Q:** What really moved you to make that change and to start doing what you are now doing for your hood and for the community?

**L:** Well, even before the peace I was already a Pop Warner football coach. I'm coaching a little basketball team around here now. In high school I was an all-city basketball player, and I saw how the actions that I took in high school kind of stopped me from going to places that I wanted to go. I had recruitment letters from Washington State and UCLA, you know, big-time colleges, but my attitude and the things that I was doing on the side made people fade away from me. Even though I was real good, they just didn't want to deal with what I was into, and they backed up off of me. So now I let the kids know that if they get the opportunity that I had, then they have to do what's right, and I know that I have to stop them from doing what I did so they can go on and make it. It's to a point where I'm trying to help guide them because I see where I made my mistakes, and where I can stop them from making their mistakes.

**Q:** What's the main thing that keeps you out here striving to make a positive change?

**L:** It's the kids. They show me respect, they shoot a few jokes with me and play around, and I shoot a few jokes back at them. I let them know when enough is enough though, and they know when to raise up. They know that they can come around me and have a little fun. They know that I am serious about the things that I say, so I don't have to say things too forcefully.

We went to the Laker game and we were in the nosebleed section, and the little dudes wanted to try to go all the way down by the courts. I told them that if they can get all the way down by the courts and sit down, without the people trying to throw them out of there or mess with them, then they could go on ahead and sit down there. Other people would have tried to stop them from even trying, but you know how kids are, they can get past anybody. They won't get stopped like an adult would, so they were down there three rows from the floor watching the game, and after the game they were like, "Man, did you see A. C. Green? I tried to give him a high five when he came through the runway!" I let them go on down there and try to get their cards signed. You have to give them some freedom sometimes and release that rope from around their neck and let them do some things. With me, I tell them like this, "You know that you don't get a chance to go anywhere, the only time that you go out of the neighborhood is with me, so you know if you mess up, then you're not going anywhere with me anymore." They say to me, "Come on, man, I'm not going to mess up." And to this day I have only received one report about one of them messing up, and I let him sit out for about two trips, and then after that he didn't want to mess up anymore, because while he was just standing on the side of the street watching everybody pulling out to go and have some fun, he knew that he had to straighten up to be a part of the fun activities. So we let him come back out with us after that and he was cool.

It's real cool to be around kids, they keep me going, and they keep me young and alive, they keep you ready, and they keep you wanting to teach because you know that they need it.

**Q:** What are some ways that brothers can start to make positive impacts on the community like you're doing?

**L:** A lot of times they just need to step up and be real men. Some of them don't understand what the definition of being a real man is. The real man is a man that is going to lead his own path and go in the right direction to do what he has to do. A lot of brothers claim to be men, but you're not a man until you control you own destiny. You have to control where you are going. You have to control what's going on in your life. You can't say, "I think about wanting to get up out of this, but then the homiez want to do it like this." I tell them, "You better think about yourself first, your surrounding conditions, and your family who is with you. You have to deal with them first. You have to make things right for them first and then think about the homiez."

That's what my father always taught me, because my father was

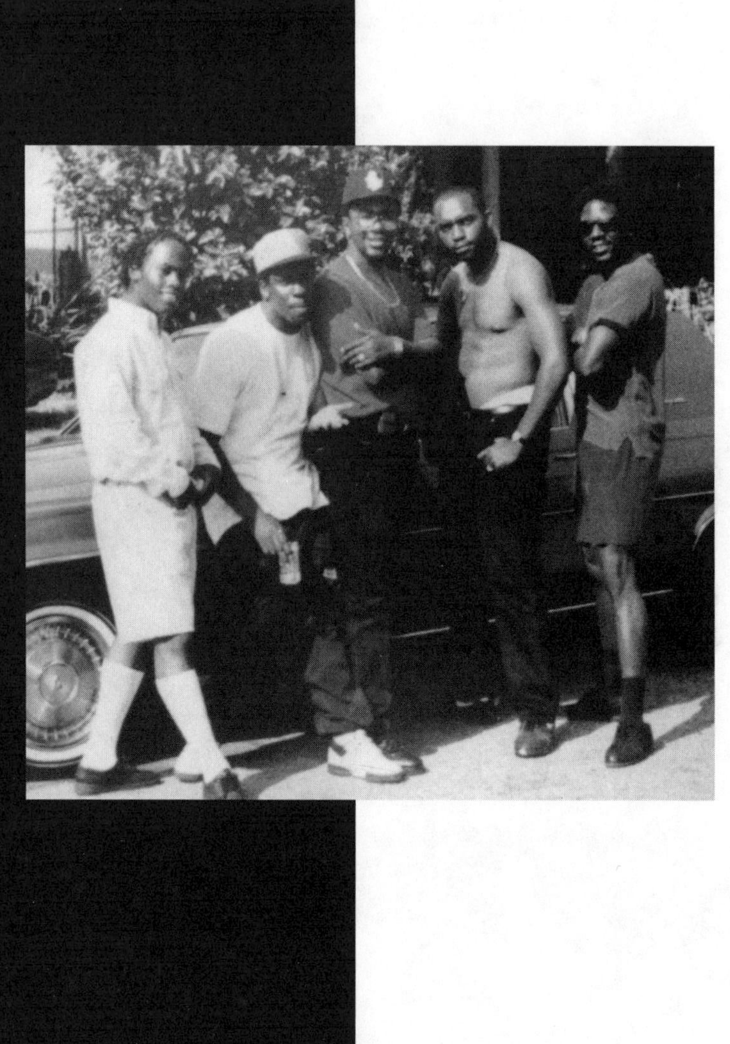

around until I was about fifteen, but me and my father always did and still do keep good communication. My father always taught me about things, and I know that you have to have somebody there to be able to communicate with you and guide you in the direction that you need to go in, because if you don't, then it's going to be kind of rough for you. The parents play a very important role, because parents bring you up all the way from the bottom to the top, and they are supposed to mold you into the person that they think you should be. For the children that don't have parents, that's when we need to step up and be big brothers to them. I try to play that big-brother role, I go get them and say, "Come on and roll with your big brother today."

When we have trips, I take the so-called "bad ones" with me. Everywhere we go I keep them with me and I handle them. People ask me how can I do that, and I don't even trip with them because I know how kids are. I'm not all on their back for every little thing that they do. Kids will be kids, and I know they will thump each other on the back of the ear, but that is natural. I just make sure that they don't go overboard to where they get hot or want to start to fight or something. I just keep it under control and let them have their fun. That's what is going to make them respect you more. They know that they can have fun and they know not to go overboard with it and it's cool. It's a communication thing.

**Q:** Any further words that you would like to say in closing?

**L:** I just think that the brothers and the sisters in the community, we need to just stand up and take charge of our community, and take charge of our youth, to redirect them and send them in the right path. It's time to stand up! Everybody that is sitting down, it's time to stop sitting, you've got to rise to the occasion. We have to do this as a unit. We've got to move as a whole. We can't just do this separately. You know that with our own great collective efforts we can progress much faster, and in a more positive fashion, with everybody else joining in with this. I'm saying that we need more input too, because I am not the only man in the world with input. Other people have input too, and they need to step up and put theirs in.

> ***You cannot have fear and win. You cannot have fear and be number one, you must understand that nobody is more powerful, more special, or smarter than you are, and when you understand that, you will have no fear.***
>
> **—Congresswoman Maxine Waters**

## SHOUT OUT

To all my family and all the homeboys and homegirls.

Mia, Charles, Ebony in Washington, D.C., 1993: my little friends who belong to the Youth Task Force

Congressional Black Caucus 1993: Charles with participants in Kid Witness News

# Q-BONE

*(Brothers out there know me as Charles Rachal, but brothers also know me as Q-Bone, from Five-Duce Broadway. I would say to the children and to the families that read this book, to the nation that reads this book, take it as a tool that can better our community, better our lives, and better the Black race. This is something that you can read coming directly from us, and not from anyone else. This is not to excite or to entertain, but this should be taken as a lesson, and a teaching on what not to get involved with. To the children out there, live for your future, you have to make your own, nobody else can make it for you. Peace.)*

**Q:** What motivated you to get started with the peace?

**QB:** In '89 I was incarcerated for a parole violation. I kept going back and forth to jail. During that time I did nine months, and I did a lot of thinking. I started finding myself getting closer to a lot of brothers that I didn't get along with in the past, just on the strength of being in that place. First I did three years and nine months; I got out, and went right back. Every year from '87 to '89 I kept going back for little petty violations. While I was in there, I kept thinking that I was in there for a reason. I kept thinking that, in order to keep myself going for my release date, instead of me going off and tripping. I was attached to a lot of the brothers in there from different gangs, and the majority of them were Bloods. I looked at the Crips, and we fight each other, and we wear the same color. So I looked at it like, if I can get close with the Bloods, I know I can get close with the Crips from different sets, because they're somewhat close to me already in a sense. So I got to thinking one day, "Why am I still doing this? I just wish that all of us brothers would drop our rags and come together." I knew brothers who were trucing from years ago, still trucing today. Some brothers don't do things to other brothers anyway; I consider that peace.

One day I was locked up in my cell, and I got to reading *Chains and Images of Psychological Slavery,* then I read the *Autobiography of Malcolm X* three times, then I started reading the Bible, and I started getting inspirational thoughts about what I was reading. I even started reading the Nation of Islam's books. I was trying to get an insight, and an understanding, so I could teach myself, not have someone else teach me from a classroom. Then one day I was reading, and it just hit me, all of a sudden, I felt like something had to happen: "I have to get out of here and not come back." So in '89 when I was getting out, I said, "If I have to come back in here, I don't need to go home. But if I go out now, I want to stay out there and do something in my neighborhood that's different from anything else." That was my goal. I didn't want to go out there selling drugs, because I had too many people that were smoked out on drugs, and that hurt me, to see them like that.

Right before the Uprisings happened in '92, it was one week before Easter, I was at a hamburger stand at Fifty-fifth and Figueroa. This is what really made me have a feeling that something different would take place, because a little girl walked up to me, she was about five years old, and she handed me a flyer. On the flyer it said, "Let's have a no-killing weekend for Easter. From twelve o'clock midnight Friday to twelve o'clock midnight Sunday, let's have a no-killing weekend." Then she walked away. I looked at her as she was walking away, and I was saying to myself, this little girl is asking us not to kill, and I prayed to God right then and there that He would grant her that wish. Then I looked across the street, and there were some more kids and parents walking, just passing out flyers that day, but it wasn't an adult that passed it to me, it was a little girl that passed it to me, and it meant something to me. That we have youth crying for us to stop. Not the adults begging us to stop, so they can have a clear path to do what they have to do, but we have kids, crying out for their future. I prayed that she would get her wish.

The weekend went past, and there wasn't any killing. So I felt good about that, and then the next week the Uprisings took off, which took me by surprise. Then, in the midst of the Uprisings, what really made me feel that something was about to change with the Bloods and the Crips was when the brothers came out, running to get with each other. All through the city, Bloods and Crips were running to each other. I saw Bloods come down my street that never came down my street, unless they were ducking.

So a couple of days after the Uprisings, I was at the movies with my cousin and one of my other homiez, we left and was on our way back home when we stopped by this little bar to kick it, and a brother walked in and said, "Wasn't you just at the park, man, you got here fast." I have a brother that looks identical to me, a lot of people think that we're twins. He said, "Wasn't you at the park just now, those Bloods were up there deep, huh?" I was like, "What are you talking about? What park?" "South Park, man, you was up there." I said, "Man, that wasn't me." My cousin and our friend on the side was looking at him like, "What is he talking about?" He said, "Man, I'm telling you, there are Bloods and Crips in the neighborhood together. They're all up at South Park kickin' it. Your homiez, and my homiez." He was from another neighborhood that was close to us. I'm from Five-Duce Broadway, he was from Fifty-third. We have the Pueblos, the Villains, the Four-Tres, the Five-Tres, and Forty Avalons, and the Four-Duces. All of us live in this little area, so for all of us to come together with everybody else and kick it, we had to solve our differences, because we're all from different sets, we are to the east side. So during the peace we solved 'em, and we went to South Park, which is the Crips' park, and then we went to Slauson Park, which is the Bloods' park. We kept going back and forth to the parks, and then during the daytime we started hanging out in the Pueblo projects, so the police wouldn't crash us while we were in the residential areas. We stayed up till five o'clock in the morning out there, every day for the first two to three weeks of the gang peace.

**Q:** Where was this taking place?

**QB:** This was in South Central. The peace in Watts was going on at the same time, but people were branching off. Then later on at night we'd all meet in Watts. We would go down to Watts, all the sets together, in the cars together. It wasn't, "There goes one hood, and there goes another hood." When we came, it was like, "What hoods are that?" We had El Caminos with Bloods and Crips in the back together. Some of the homiez would leave, go get something to eat, and come back, these were Bloods, and they'd come back. "Where are the Five-Duce Broadways [Crips] at?" There were other Crips and Bloods in there too saying, "Hey, man, give us some of them burgers." "Man, this is for the Five-Duce Broadways. We have to look out for our prople." They were giving us burgers right in front of other Bloods. The other Bloods were saying, "Hey, man, we're Bloods." They was like, "I'm from down the way. We're taking care of our people. You go to your enemies and buy them a burger." It was very inspirational to me, and it took me by surprise.

**Q:** How did that make you feel?

**QB:** I felt like, "I can take this jacket off. I feel good now." That was the best thing that ever happened to me in my life of living on this earth. To see what took place. I know what took place deep down inside. Not from the outside looking in, or from the outside guessing what really went on. I know what really went on right here.

When I first went to the peace-treaty party, it had been going on already. They were in the park hugging, and I was at the movies not even knowing about it. Nobody paged me and said, "Q-Bone, come on in, we're with the Bloods." Normally, if anything happened in my hood, I would get to the call to come, because I'm one of the oldest ones here, and I'm highly influential verbally. I can speak to the youngsters, and they'll either take off, or they'll sit down. I don't try to make them or force them, I tell them it's their own will.

It really took me, because when I first got to the park, everybody was gone. It was kind of funny, so I was like, "Man, there ain't no peace-treaty party going on, there's nobody at this park, that dude lied to us." So I go to my neighborhood, and I couldn't find anybody. Nobody was answering my pages. So I thought they were out in the street somewhere. There were a few people riding around, and they said, "Hey, Bone, they're over there in the Pueblos." I said, "Well, why aren't you over there then? Don't be trying to set me up." I was thinking they were playing with me the whole time.

Me and my little sister were in my grandmother's car riding around in different neighborhoods, so we cruised over there since we were in a low-key car. I wasn't in my car, because they know my car. So we were rolling through there, and we got all the way to the projects. I had never gone that far before without a gun out. I was still looking, but I didn't have a gun out, because something was telling me that I didn't need it, there's peace going on. We didn't call it a truce, we called it peace.

So when we went over there, I saw five girls walking across the street. I said, "Hey, where's the party?" They said, "There ain't no party." I really thought there was no peace going on then. "There's no party?" If there was peace, and there was a party, these five girls would have known.

I went on home and tried to sleep on it, but couldn't. I could not sleep. I was paging my brother and everybody, and they didn't call me back, because they were over there partying. Nobody was answering their pagers now, because they were embracing themselves with the Bloods, and the other Crip sets. So the next day about eleven o'clock, I got up and rolled over there to the projects. I was still curious. I even called other neighborhoods, and I couldn't find anybody. At about eleven-thirty, three of my homiez were on their way over there. They said, "Come on and roll with us, we're going to take you over there. We know where they're at, we just left from over there. Everybody is over there. It's about eight hundred Bloods and Crips over there." They named all of our rival sets. They said, "Bone, you're the only one from the hood that hasn't seen this yet. You have to do this, man. You're our man over here, you represent us. You speak for us." They were playing with me on the way there, talking about, "We're going to get off when we get over there. We just had to get you in the car." So when we get there, we go all the way to the back of the projects. I'm thinking they're trying to set us up, to kill us up in there. My legs got to trembling. I was in fear, but I wasn't going to show it. I felt like I had to do something, I wasn't going to die crying.

Then when we hit that back street, man, my dreams came true. I saw Bloods and Crips together shooting basketball, lined up on the sidewalks, hugged up, kickin' it, blue rags and red rags on. I was looking at rivals who had been shooting at each other, hugged up. My legs were still trembling, because I hadn't warmed up to the feeling yet, but I wanted to. I loved it. I wanted to cry right then, but something held it back, something said, "You don't need to cry, man, just keep rollin'." From that day on I took the mission for my neighborhood to keep the peace going on.

What really made me get involved with it was because everybody got down with it, and it was something that I always wished would happen. It was something in my heart that I wanted to stop, but I just didn't have the power or authority to stop it, but then I had the power and authority to keep it from starting back up again. I took that lead, we were one of the first groups to form a nonprofit organization. Our group, and Hands Across Watts. Amer-I-CAN was already out, but we didn't use their credibility, because they had already been established. We were South Central Blackness then, and there was Hands Across Watts. We met up, and we started building programs daily. One night I was talking to some brothers in the projects, I pulled about eight of us to the side, from all the different neighborhoods, and I said, "What can we do to keep this going in the days ahead, because this ain't going to get it, we're partying, and we're drinking too much. This is summertime, I can understand it, but what about when the summer is over with. We need to get back to responsibility, we have too much to focus on right here. We need to go out there and get what we deserve for doing this. Not that people are obligated to give us something, but somebody out there deserves to give us something for stopping this, because we're saving lives. We're doing something the police can't do, we're doing something the churches are not doing, we're doing something the people as a whole in the community are not doing, we're doing something that's unbelievable, because it's coming from the man up above."

I believe that God placed peace within my heart in order for me to forgive the next man that had done something to me. He placed peace in all of us, because all of us forgave that day. I saw ten thousand brothers and sisters in Watts forgive, not by getting on the stage speaking. I saw brothers that didn't walk the yard, walk the yard. I would walk and hear brothers say, "Brother, I'm glad we're together; remember you shot my leg off, I'm still in this chair for that, man, but I forgive you for that, because I want my kids to have a future." I kept hearing kids, kids, kids, so I felt that we needed to start a nonprofit of our very own, to take care of the kids that look at us as role models. If we let another organization do it, that wasn't doing it before, then all they would be doing is misleading another generation that would end up like we did when they grow up, not caring. You know they really wouldn't care. So the brothers and sisters that were there thought it was cool, and they said, "Let's do it."

**Q:** How did the brothers and sisters respond to you when you told them that y'all would have to carry the peace on and keep it going?

**QB:** They loved it. They challenged me. They said, "What can we do?" There were four brothers and three sisters that were involved. The three sisters were from one of the neighborhoods, and one of the sisters ran the neighborhood. Right now to this day she runs the neighborhood. Straight with it, right now to this day, and she's smart, she teaches computer classes at our center, and all of that.

So I went over to the gang services the next morning, since they were a gang service, and I wanted to see if they could help us with what we needed to do, plus I knew them. I went over there and told Ed Turner from the gang services that I had about five hundred brothers and sisters that want to form a nonprofit and do something for our community, like remove the graffiti off the walls and do a lot of other things that need to be done. We're old enough to realize what needs to be done. He said, "Bring me forty brothers back, and we'll see what we can do." So I went back and told the brothers, and at five P.M. that evening, one hundred of us went up in there, straight up into the gang services.

We just wanted advice about how we can go on with our nonprofit, and how we could keep the peace together amongst us. They gave us some office space there, and we worked it. The brothers liked that, and they saw that it was real. So we started painting the neighborhoods, painting walls up and down Central, Alameda, and Compton Avenues. We started going to schools, tying blue and red rags together, telling the kids not to get involved with gangs. We went on Crenshaw with red ties on, to show love for the Bloods. We took the lead in South Central, which made a lot of brothers from the west side come through.

Watts had already committed to the peace, but South Central was still tripping a little. They didn't really know what was up. They were in a whole different atmosphere. We were on the east side, and we had the same feelings as the brothers in Watts, because there's a straight line from there, all the way to downtown. We accepted the peace, and the brothers cherished it. We had a van, and brothers would get together every morning, and we would go out to schools and churches and get involved more. Then we gave a Unity Day where we played football against each other. Not the Crips playing the Bloods, but Crips and Bloods playing Crips and Bloods. It was the Pueblos, the Five-Tres, and the Four-Tres, playing the Five-Duces, the Villains, and the Avalons. So it was a three-on-three game. Then the second day, we wanted everybody to bring their families; your children, your mama, your niece—bring your whole family. It was a family reunion, so we could know who is who out here. I felt that would make brothers think twice, and it did. I saw brothers that were kin to me, that I didn't even know, brothers that I would have probably shot the day before. Two thousand to six thousand people came out. We had food, a big barbecue pit set up, rap groups came out, Compton's Most Wanted, Mad Circle, brothers spoke, and church choirs sang. We had things to enlighten everybody that was out in that crowd. Something spiritually was going to enlighten you. At the same time, brothers started to build themselves up.

Then a brother pulled up in the park and said, "Hey, Charles, Coretta Scott King wants you to come to Atlanta. She heard about you." I was like, "Aw, man"; that was like a dream to me. Now I knew that God had answered my prayers. I thought all the way back to that prison cell and brought it all the way up to that day, and I said, "I'm on a mission." The brothers accepted it and cherished it. So we went out of town, and we started traveling to different places. We started seeing things out of town that weren't in our town. Coming back to LAX [airport] is like coming back into a naked city, with people in it that you can just talk to, go to the movies with, chill out with. So we saw things we had never seen before. I started seeing business developments. I saw 75 percent Black-owned businesses in Atlanta. I saw 85 percent Blacks in Washington, D.C. They may not own the government part, but everything around the government part is Black. They have caterers, street entrepreneurs, hot dog carts, every corner is Black. They have it going on. Why not L.A.? L.A. is the robbery capital, and all of that.

In memory of my brother Lamont: OGs only

Chillin' in the hood

So I started searching, and businesspeople were talking about starting businesses. So we decided to create a newspaper to fund our nonprofit, the *South Central Los Angeles Post.* Eight of us, we contributed to it, we got a lot of writers to contribute stories. Then the printing didn't go through, so we had to leave it alone. After that we started another business; we had eight businesses lined up to start at a lower capital level.

We started a hand car wash, and then once we got the capital, we wanted to make it into a big car wash with the machines. We'd start from the ground first. So we went on to Compton, us and the Bloods, and while we were painting, we talked to Luke Skywalker's brother, Stan Campbell. He came out here and helped us. We got to walking into buildings, talking that business talk, and then we'd be out there across the street in the parking lot just kickin' it. "What's up, Blood?" "What's up, Cuz?" We were having fun, trying to get that out of us, to where if I say that around the brothers, it would be just another word. I don't want it to be like, if I hear you say "Blood," I have to say "Cuz" back. If you say, "What's up, Blood?" I might say, "What's up, Blood?" back. I want to be able to say that. If I say "Cuz," you're my cousin too. It's all in that cycle.

At the same time we had the car wash, we thought about a maintenance service, because a lot of brothers come out of the penitentiary with janitorial skills. I was in YA [Youth Authority], so I know this. We could be the best maintenance service in the city. They don't know how we had to do the maintenance in the administration building in the prisons. I mean, they have to look spic-and-span for when the secretary, the governor, and the warden come in there. So we had certificates in maintenance. Then we thought about a security business, because we have big brothers that are not scared to fight. So we started thinking of businesses that we would put brothers from the streets in, to get them off of the streets. We had several different projects.

**Q:** What help could y'all have used at that time in building those businesses? Did you get any other help?

**QB:** There wasn't anyone from the business world that came forward to say, "I'll match y'all with this." Nobody offered us an accountant. They offered us a building. What were we going to do with a building that might not be with the codes? I know that much. Give me an accountant so that when my money comes in, it will be right. Give me the ropes. I talk to the rappers all the time out here, and they talk business, and they say what they want to do to help. I don't ask them. They don't have to give me money, don't give me money, give me some advice on how I can take the money I can get and make it like you made it. That's all I want, advice. I don't want a handout, just give me advice. Then let me flow, because I know I can get with different brothers and get three of them together that have some money, and we can do it ourselves. A lot of brothers in the past that have made money legitimately are not coming to brothers out here in the streets. They may portray in their videos that they're with brothers out here, when you see a thousand people in their video. Well, there's a million people out here. So a thousand is nothing compared to the million. TV can make them look like the baddest person in the world, but I've seen them off of the screen straight drop their act. Their word of bond is not there anymore.

There are some brothers that have come back. The brothers in the Playground store, on Florence, Keitarock, and them brothers. Someone invested in them, had faith in them, and it helped them out.

So I had to use what I was learning, because I had a lot of people with me, I was in a leadership role. I was a gang leader for positive change. I wasn't a gang leader for violence, I won't ever let them label me as that. I had Bloods that were behind me now, that were looking for me to do this. When the Bloods were asking me to speak for them, I was like, "You speak for the Bloods, I'll speak for the Crips." "No, you speak for all of us, because you speak positive." It was the role that I had to play to build a business that brothers wanted. I was just a spokesman, going to the delegation to speak for what the brothers wanted. We tried to start our own clothing line. We were thinking of high stakes, a future for the kids, and ourselves too.

The only thing that's going to eliminate the violence in the streets is jobs, businesses, and help. We started doing that, and a lot of help started coming in once we started showing them that reality. We started focusing and coming to them deep, knocking at their doors. They started waking up, and after listening to us, they realized that they had passed judgment. "These brothers are smart. These brothers need degrees." I don't need a degree, just give me the degree to where I have to go. You can keep that paper stuff. I did my twelve years; that's all Mama asked for, after that I could go to college if I wanted to. So *if* is a big word. I didn't go to college then, so I'm not going now, it's too late. I'm twenty-nine years old. What do I look like going to college, and I don't have anything out here? Let me set up a business, and then I'll go to college, because I know I'll come from college directly into what I built up. I'm not going out like that.

You see a lot of brothers that make it, have backgrounds of making it, they have backgrounds of people that made it. What about the brothers that don't have those backgrounds? So we had to try our best to build a couple of businesses. We're in the process right now of striving to build another one. Right now we're working with street entrepreneurs to put hot dog carts in Los Angeles. If that's the last thing I do, I'm going to see Blacks out here with hot dog carts. I'm going to try to get Blacks out here involved in the businesses that I see when I go to Atlanta, Washington, New York, Louisiana, St. Louis, Detroit, Philadelphia, even Seattle. So it's not just the East Coast without businesses, other West Coast cities are doing it. Seattle, Portland, and all those Black towns are doing somewhat better than Los Angeles. We're lost. We've "Lost" part of "Angeles." It's time for us to wake up. The Hispanic brothers are coming to their senses, so we'd better come to ours. We're on the same level. It's time for us to have that economic empowerment. I meet a lot of topnotchers. I've met with everybody around here. Everybody I've ever wanted to meet in my life, all the way up to Michael Jackson. I met Nelson Mandela twice. I met Jesse Jackson three times. All that is good, but it's like walking up the yellow brick road with nothing, coming back, and getting my people ready to lay something down. I'm ready to make the grass green on this side.

**Q:** The leaders that you met, what type of support have they offered to help in the community?

**QB:** On the business part I can name it on one hand—Danny Bakewell, Maxine Waters, Ice-T, Ice Cube, and the Nation of Islam, who have all helped by trying to tell us what we need to be doing. Those five that I've named have helped us in business. Support and spiritual endurance have come from Reverend Eavy Hill, Minister Louis Farrakhan, Coretta Scott King, Betty Shabazz, Maxine Waters, and Diane Watson. There are a lot of people that have helped in different areas where we needed it, but there are a lot over here that are just talking. Talking the talk, not walking the walk, not living the life. They're just full of talk. There's a lot of brothers out here that have potential of doing right, and a lot of brothers don't want to fight, but if they don't have any alternatives, they're going to fight, kill, stab, no matter what color you are. They're mad and angry. We have a past that makes us mad, we have a present that makes us mad, and if we don't have a future, we're going to be mad. So we have three mad categories of life that we go through, that haunt us every day of our lives as we walk out the door. I learned to adjust to it, now I speak to those who haven't yet.

**Q:** What would you say to brothers in different neighborhoods who are not at peace right now?

**QB:** To each his own in thinking, and to each his own in what he wants to do. No matter what neighborhood you're from, you have your own thoughts, and you know what you want to do, deep down inside your heart. Let's take the masks off, we're not Batman and Robin. We're going to always be ourselves, so let's take these masks off, and these costumes that we've been wearing, and take these rags out of our pockets and start living. Every brother in the neighborhood, I don't care what neighborhood he's from, there's another neighborhood that he doesn't get along with, which has a brother in it that he personally does get along with, and that he personally would embrace if he saw him outside of his neighborhood, by himself. Brothers need to stop letting that pride, stop letting that mask, stop letting the stupidity and ignorance, keep them down. All those brothers who went to Watts that day that are now back fighting, are fighting over something from the past. When they know in their heart that they embraced somebody from the other set. I saw it for a fact. Check me if I'm wrong. I know there were brothers there that wasn't with the peace, but I know brothers that were there who was with the peace. In every neighborhood there was somebody there who was really for the peace, and those brothers should take that lead. Why? Because brothers idolize them for doing that, and there are brothers who need their help in order to stay with it. When they give up, the brother who really didn't want to do it anyway is going to really give up. Just look at the hurt that we're doing to each other.

Let's face reality: we're hurting ourselves, and we know it. We can play Billy Bads out here all we want to, but none of us are badder than the next person, because all of us can get caught slipping. We all have lost at lcast ten homiez each, from our neighborhoods, and some have lost more. The Hispanics are starting a gang peace off of what we started, because they saw the opportunities that came from it, and they kept rolling with it. Don't slip and fall and mess our opportunity up, because we're not going to get this again. I would love to see these brothers come back to peace. In their hearts they know it's time. Brothers, just wake up. Let's do this.

**Q:** What do you feel moved people to get with the peace in the first place?

**QB:** It's simple, that was God. People call Him a lot of names, ALLAH, the Lord, all of that, because you didn't find ten brothers in the streets that would have said that they were made to come together. Rodney King didn't do this. Rodney King just happened to come at the time when Armageddon was almost here. It had to do with the time, I believe, because the whole city was in violent rage. When it came to that day, it was spiritual all around the board.

In the prison system you see red and blue together, living right next to each other. Some may fight, but the majority don't. What it was that day was spiritual. If we take everybody back to their elementary school days, every brother that gang-bangs, I bet you he will find a brother that he doesn't get along with, that he has killed or shot at, in that school yearbook, that he went to school with when he was a little kid. He could say, "I've been knowing him before I met my own homiez."

I think the peace in South Central happened after the unrest, and not before the unrest, because if you look at a city that's in violent rage, the whole city, the whole community, what's the best thing to do to solve a whole city at rage? What could be done to make a whole city that's at rage calm down? The police can't do it. The National Guard can't do it. They can keep people in or out of buildings, but inside their hearts, they can't stop that rage. Two days after the Uprisings, peace was called with the Bloods and the Crips. I believe God used that tool of violence, that tool of rage, that tool that people knocked for a decade: "They're not going to be anything in life, they're nothing but thugs and hoodlums." So God takes the most violent people and places peace in them, which made everybody else wake up. People in the neighborhood would only act up if we act up. That's the reason they gave us the publicity. They blamed it on the gangs, they blamed it on the wrong people. Blame it on your system, don't blame us.

**Q:** Do you feel that the rage has been removed from the brothers?

**QB:** I feel the rage is gone as far as the colors are concerned, and that's a big step. There are Crips that wear red now. I wear red now. Before, you couldn't get me to wear anything red. I have homiez that wouldn't drink punch because it's red. That's a part of the process that shows that the brothers are taking a step ahead. Then again there are brothers who were in that park for peace that are back killing right now, but killing doesn't always come from gang violence. Personal stuff plays a big role. The brothers that I've seen slip back into it was because they had no alternative. There's a lot of brothers that want to go farther, but they don't have any help to go farther. They know my position, so it's like, "Man, you can go tell them people to come help us, but you can't give us the help that we need as a whole. You can help us by speaking for us when we need it, but we have to help ourselves too. But how can we help ourselves, if we don't have somebody to help us?" Somewhere down the line everybody that has done something got a helping hand from someone, some advice, or has been given something.

**Q:** What steps can brothers take to do for themselves, and to make things better for themselves?

**QB:** Let's say we take a six-month grace period for planning, and in that six-month period, each one of us in a gang puts up a dollar a day. That way no one is putting more than the next person. After six months you calculate that money. I know there's at least one hundred people that can contribute a dollar. That's $100 a day for six months. Thirty days that's $3,000. If we can do that, then during the same six months, we can train for whatever we're going to do with that money. When the sixth month comes, then we're ready. That's the only way I believe it will work, capitalizing the money, investing into a business, and making everybody feel on the same level. If one brother gives $2, and another brother gives $5, then the brother that gave the $5 is going to feel that he has to be the president and think that the other brother should be the deliveryman. When in fact, the brother with the $2 may have the potential to be the manager, and the one with the money may have to be the deliveryman, or do marketing or something. Let the broke one be the manager, because the broke one usually has the most sense, because he has a lot more time to think.

That dollar a day will create some businesses. We need to get involved with basic things like ice cream trucks, and things that our people use. We shouldn't care what society says. The Hispanics do it. If they have to sell oranges on the corner, and if the Nation of Islam has to sell bean pies and newspapers on the corner to support their cause, then brothers can start doing something to build that money up. We also need some successful people that the brothers look up to, to come down and help us, even if it's verbally. There's stuff that we can do on our own, so we need our own people to come and sit with us. So we can help each other. If we go to the white man to help us, we're going to feel bad walking away, because we had to go to somebody outside of our culture. Accept the help, don't get me wrong, but don't accept it to the point where you believe you've made it. You're still to the curb, until you sit behind that desk, twelve stories up, and you look down on your own building. Some brothers in the projects have over one thousand brothers down with them, and everybody is hustling. So a dollar a day could go a long way. The only way we can help ourselves is to give to ourselves. If we keep waiting for people to fund us, corporations, and loans, we're still going to owe them back. I believe right now if brothers wake up and go for what they know, they'll get what they want to get.

**Q:** What role can sisters play in bringing about the economic development and increasing the peace in the hoods?

**QB:** Most sisters out here that I see are involved in management fields more than brothers are. A sister can handle that type of business. A brother can be out here in these streets making sure the sales are being made, but a sister is going to keep the management together. Brothers can stack a bunch of money on the table, but a sister will know how to count it, handle it, and manage it. The management part should be done by the sisters. Why? Because brothers love the streets, they stay out in the streets, and they can change the streets. Then the sisters that are willing can come out too. If a sister has the potential to be a founder of a business and can bring these brothers up, then the sisters should take that lead. There's a lot of brothers that look to sisters, but pride keeps brothers in front of the sisters with the big chest. There are brothers that will stand behind a sister, and sisters that stand behind brothers, but we really need to start standing at each other's side. Not one behind the other, but at each other's side. She reaches out, and I reach out. We need each other, we have to work in collaboration. We have to learn to respect our sisters to where they can understand why we're out here. Sisters don't understand why brothers stay out in the streets, so they seem to have a tendency to quote negative accusations to the brother when he comes through the door. Sisters need to respect brothers more too and help brothers more in getting businesses created. Then the brothers will feel more confident if the sisters are handling their part also.

**Q:** In your opinion what has made it so easy for a brother to take another Black person's life?

**QB:** That comes from the past, from being angry. All the way from the slavery days to the teachings that have been taught to us in school when we were young. We may not have known what was going on then, but we have been lied to. So, once you get older and realize what you have learned, it makes you angry. Secondly, it makes you angry when you see the neighborhood that you lived in as a kid, and the same kids that were with you then are with you today, but now we're older, walking that same street, and people seem to jump back from us. Society seems to not want to mess with us now. So brothers get angry. That's like when a lady rolls up in a car and locks her door, brothers get mad. Then you have law enforcement that's on us real hard, and we're looking for help from our community, to come slide right through the middle and help us, and they don't. So you have brothers with all that rage, and who do we have to take it out on? Each other, because we're around each other. We're not around other races. Most of that rage comes from a lot of that tension from the past, and from learning the truth and being frustrated.

Our image is put out there as some monster-type figures. We put the frowns on, to let a person know we're with a gang; we put the stroll on. At the same time, all that is nothing but a costume, and brothers will use that costume to do violence, because that's the image, the stereotype that's been placed on us. Not by just us, but by generations ahead of us. The Black man is always portrayed as angry, we're portrayed as drug dealers, as shooters. Before I got involved with gangs, back when I was a kid, looking at movies like *Cleopatra Jones, Hit Man, Trouble Man,* I wanted to be cool too, growing up. Nobody told me, you don't want to be like that because tomorrow you're going to be like this here. Nobody gave me the real.

**Q:** What did you want to do when you was coming up?

**QB:** I wanted to be an entertainer, a singer. I dreamed of singing. When I was young, I used to sing a lot in talent shows, I danced, and I played drums for a band that I was in. Then when I was ten years old, I was looking at *The Ten Commandments,* and I went to the kitchen, opened the curtain enough for the moonlight to come in, and I got on my knees and prayed. I said, "Lord, one day can I be your next messenger? When I get older, I want to do what you sent Moses to do."

I believe that I now have that job. Why? Because we have people that have been kept in bondage, in a city with opportunities, and now I have a leading role to get them out of that, and I'm going to do that. I've taken my homiez to places that none of them have ever been. I've gotten fifty of them jobs. I've taken them to the *Robert Townsend Show,* I took two hundred kids to Magic Mountain and Disneyland. I take kids to camp every summer. Some are kids from out of state that they bring in for me to counsel, and they go back with a smile. So I'm on that mission that I prayed for. That's what I really wanted to be when I grew up, what I'm doing now, because if I didn't, I wouldn't be doing it. I would have accepted other jobs, and believe me, people have come at me with jobs. People that wanted me to stop doing what I'm doing. They didn't say they wanted me to stop, but I already know. The new style is to not even tell a person what you're doing, just give him the job and give him the benefits. Most people would think you looked out for them, but you didn't look out for me by sending me out to Marino Valley somewhere because the houses look good, and you think you could have my dreams and hopes on looking for a so-called better future for tomorrow. Man, I'm talking about today, where I live at. This is the foundation. I'm cool right here, you're not pushing me out. The Blacks are moving out, but we have to start coming back in. There's a lot that has to be done to clean up, and there are a lot of us that can do it. If each one of us grabs a broom, the streets would be clean. Nobody wants to grab the broom, everybody wants to grab the bag.

Then the brothers that are willing to put in the work and handle the responsibility are not being called upon, and they are the vanguards. That's the brothers who are going to be tomorrow's future. We have brothers and sisters in college, we have brothers and sisters in jobs, but we also have the majority of our brothers and sisters in these streets. In a quick snap, they can loose that job and be right back in the streets. There's a lot of work that has to be done. The only way we're going to do this is by coming from the heart and working together as young Black people in our community. Let the older people give us advice, but let the older people understand that *we have to do this.* We have to take the lead. We can't be taught leadership if we don't have leadership. Don't teach me about something that isn't going to be real when I graduate.

**Q:** What made you first get involved with gangs?

**QB:** What got me was when I was in junior high school. I was going to a school where the Bloods lived, but I lived in a Crip neighborhood. They never messed with me, I was cool with them. I say Bloods now, but they weren't Bloods then, they were just like me, just going to junior high school. So one day some Crips from my neighborhood that lived on my street, that went to elementary school with me, they came to the high school. They started hanging with me. There was three of them; they weren't tripping up there, but they were showing their colors. I used to tell them, "Look, there's Bloods up here who ain't with that, I know these Bloods, but I know what they'll try to do." They was like, "I don't care, we're right here too." So one day they got into a fight, and the Bloods rushed them. The Bloods beat them up, and they took off running. I knew the Bloods that beat them up, because they had just joined the Bloods. It was five brothers that was in the same class with me; we used to talk, draw together, I used to go over to their house. When they started banging, I backed away from them, because I lived in another neighborhood, and I didn't want to bang. If I wanted to bang, I could have done that right where I lived at. My father gang-banged, he was the man in his neighborhood, he was from the Businessmen. He practically ran the Businessmen, he was the biggest one in that neighborhood. My father is in prison right now. He had a lot to do with my strength, because I saw the leadership role he took when I was growing up. He was the man. I remember when they had thirty people come over to my house in low-riders, and they took me to Brookside Park, and a lot of other places. That right there helped me with the fear, I didn't have fear of gang-banging. I just looked at it from a distance.

So when those brothers jumped on my people, they tried to jump on me. I told them, "Why y'all jump on them, why didn't y'all fight them head-up?" They was like, "What you talking about, you with them or something? You banging now?" I said, "Look, you know I don't bang, but I ain't no coward either though. But it's wrong what y'all are doing, why don't you fight them head-up? You just started because somebody influenced you." So we got to fighting, and they tried to jump me, so I hit the gate and was gone. On the way running home I thought about it. I said, "These brothers were my friends, and they turned on me for this; it's on."

I really didn't want to join the gang stuff, because I knew there was a better life. I had been through it with my father, so I was a step ahead of the average gang banger out there my age. I kept thinking, these are my friends I helped out, I know I'm labeled now, I know I can't go back to that school. Then again I thought they might not trip. So I went back to school. A few of them said, "Bone, I heard you banging now." I was like, "I'm not banging, but I'm not going to let anybody jump on me though." One thing led to another, and one day I just said forget this, and I started hanging with the fellas.

There were about fifteen brothers that I went to elementary school with that lived in the same neighborhood, and they would say, "Why don't you be with us, man? You know you want to be with us, man. You can't help it." So I got with it. I wasn't initiated in or anything like that, I just ran with the same crowd that I ran with when I was growing up. I had no alternative though. If I didn't hang with them, who was I going to hang with in my neighborhood? A bunch of cowards? I don't hang with people that try to run out on me. There are people that try to take your money when you're walking home from school, and I wasn't the one. I wasn't going to be with anybody that was going to let that happen. So it was the crowd that I had no choice to be with, because I'm like that. That was my crowd.

My parents were there for me, telling me not to get involved. If anything, when I would see Pops, he would hit the corner and say, "Hey, what you doing out here? Oh, it's like that." Mom and Pop were my strength while I was out there. They knew they couldn't take me from it, so they taught me to be strong in it. So I was strong in it.

I always wanted to be an entertainer though. I worked at Hollywood Race Track when I was twelve years old. I lied to them and told them that I was seventeen. I got my grandmother in the racetrack while I was working there. I was selling the *Herald-Examiner* when it was fifteen cents. While I was working with that, I kept seeing the gangs grow. I've seen this generation of OGs grow. I looked at it from a distance. Then when it grew to where I felt it had leveled off, that's when I jumped in. It was just that mutual way of life that got me in it, that gets anybody in it. It's from that, "Mom, can I go out and play?" Then the kids you play with are the kids that form that neighborhood. Kids that are born under mothers that were involved in gangs are 90 percent more likely to get involved with gangs themselves. A rich kid that's born into a rich family, what is he likely to become? Rich. He will automatically have his money. A poor Black man that's born to a family in poverty is going to be what? Addicted to drugs, crime, gangs, because that's what society offers you. If you take the gang away, what else am I going to do? Nothing. A gang to me is society's label to identify a group of young men. That's all it is. If you ask the people in that gang, they're not going to say "gang," they might say, "Five-Duce." If you change Five-Duce into a different form, then it's no different from the Dodgers or the Lakers. It's just what we do is so wrong. Now if we could turn that into a national football team, we'd have another team in the league.

I know brothers that own their own business right now, making plenty of money, they're still in their neighborhood. I also know people who own big businesses that grew up in our neighborhood, that have never came back since, to help out.

**Q:** Did you find more positive then negative in your experience with the gangs?

**QB:** There's a lot more positive. Negative only comes when you're angry. Brothers be out there thinking positive. They only start thinking negative as soon as something happens, a shooting, or they lose a friend, or the police come by tripping, then the anger comes in. Who are you going to take the anger out on? You can't take it out on the police, because you know they're going to trip, so you take the anger out on the closest thing to you, and that's "the enemy" across the field, and that's the same thing they're doing. So it goes back and forth. A lot of things happen over girls. You'll be surprised. A lot of it happens over girls who go with one brother from one neighborhood, then wants to go to another brother in another neighborhood. Then when the other brother from the other neighborhood that she's been messing with for six or seven months accidentally or purposefully hits her, and she has to report back to the one brother, because she's with him too, and he sees that, she's going to tell him a different thing. Dudes are the same way. They get beat up in a neighborhood by one person, and the first thing they do is go back to their neighborhood and say they got jumped on by five or six people, because they don't want their homiez to believe that one person can beat him up like that. So everybody goes back, or even if one guy goes back, he'll go back, "Five-Duce," and shoot somebody. Then they come back on Five-Duce, and the person that did it is probably at home somewhere, and an innocent brother walking down the street will get shot and killed. Not even knowing why they were shot, but they're dead.

Then you want revenge. You figure a drive-by was done by your rivals, so you go do a drive-by on a gang that you don't get along with. You think it was them. Yet all the time it could have been the police. Brothers are starting to get intellectual. Like when the peace treaty started, and a couple of brothers got hit, brothers weren't tripping, we thought it was the police who did it, because brothers were together. What did we have to shoot each other for, when we were together? All of a sudden one of my homiez gets shot in the face, and I'm supposed to think the Bloods did it, and I was over there with them that day? If it is them, then somebody is doing it behind their backs, trying to mess it up for all of us. We have learned our lessons, and we'll receive our blessings.

**Q:** What are some of the ways that we can strengthen the peace and keep it tight?

**QB:** Spiritually is the first way. You've got to make a brother that is pushing the peace believe that what he's doing is right. You can't make him believe by giving him money right off. He won't believe in that, because you can go back to your neighborhood and be shot with a million dollars in your pocket. It has to be spiritual, but it has to be brought to the light by brothers that are out here in their neighborhoods. You can't always take a brother from another neighborhood and have him speak for the other neighborhood, because he doesn't even know that neighborhood. You have brothers in each neighborhood that can come out and speak, and other brothers will follow. Like yesterday, we had a little meeting, and we were talking to these people in our community, and nobody said anything but me. One lady said, "You're speaking for yourself." Then about four or five of the brothers said, "He's speaking for us. Like the president speaks for the United States, just like you are speaking for something right now. He's speaking for something." It has to come with the understanding that we have to do this in order to hold that peace together. It won't happen with just coming together and hugging each other, and somebody telling us to "stop banging." You have to come righteous with it. I believe the Nation of Islam is fixin' to do that, because they've committed to help the brothers create some things. I respect that. They're the first group that came as a mass and said that. Churches may come one at a time, one person at a time, but the whole church doesn't come out and say, "We're willing to help you brothers." Some people feel like they're not obligated. They say, "Those brothers should change. They need to change. They don't need to be rewarded for changing." That's something Daryl Gates would say: "They don't need to be rewarded, they were supposed to be doing that anyway. They're not citizens." At the same time a brother needs to come and say, "Look, brother, I know it's wrong what y'all have been doing, but, brother, we have to make this better, so this is what I'm going to do." All it takes is brothers to come and say they're creating a business, and brothers will be down with it, because we all want to create something. Help us to create that. Don't just tell us, help us. It takes a lot of spiritual inspiration and endorsement from the brothers in the community. Not just gang bangers, you could bring a whole Black college down here, and I bet you brothers will stop fighting. Why? Because they would see the concern. Not a person here coming, and a person there coming, but if the Blacks in the whole city got together and pleaded for these brothers to stop and offered them some food when they come to the table, then brothers would stop. I don't think giving up a turkey to save twenty lives is asking too much. It has to be spiritual, and there has to be economic growth.

Economic growth and spirituality are the two keys, along with respect, in order to keep the peace together.

**Q:** How much did your set mean to you once you got into it?

**QB:** As I started getting deeper into it, it meant family. It was people who I could share my problems with outside of home. As the record by Cherelle says, "Giving you something that you're missing at home." I have six brothers and sisters, and I'm the oldest. I like a mass of people. My mother raised me that a group of people gets the job done. I grew up family oriented. I could cry on my homiez shoulder. They would come to my aid if I was stuck somewhere. If I didn't have them, who would I call when there was twenty other people after me? We fed each other. Nobody starved with us. If I didn't have a dollar, I could get a dollar from them, and vice versa. I didn't want to take it from my mother's mouth all the time. So I have brothers out on the streets that are just sharing their lives with me, and I'm sharing mine with them. It was the family value that made me adapt and feel more and more with it. I started feeling like it was my last name. Instead of using the slavery name, I felt like this was my name. I choose my own name in America. I had a family at home, but my home is different from the streets. I have to take it that way. I have to have a family out there as well as at home, because what if I lose this? I'm back out there. I need to have someone to turn to. We don't have society set up where all our cousins and uncles are on the same block. Then it would be cool, but then it still would be gangs, because then there would be family feuds going on. It was the family that impacted me. It was something where Mama said, "Go out and play," and I went out to play with it, and I grew up with it. It's my family. I look at everybody as brothers and sisters, so I hung with the big family. I'm a part of that big family, and I still am.

**Q:** Is that why it's so important to you, now that you're coming positive, to bring all of your family with you?

**QB:** Right. I don't want to leave anybody behind. I'm like the usher at the door, sending people out, and not letting anybody else come in. We don't accept anybody in our neighborhood anymore. Anybody that tries to join Five-Duce in our neighborhood, we won't accept them. There may be some youngsters that grew up with us that's already in it, but don't realize it, but we're not letting anybody else in. Any young ones we let in, we're letting them in to teach them. I'm from a neighborhood that's really hot on the map, because of the ambush with the police. That was my homie that died out there that night.

CRASH took a brother from another neighborhood over there; they've been doing that. Then you have brothers that just don't like the police. Things took place between the brother and the officer, but the brother got the jump on the officer, before the officer could get the jump on him, and the brother let him have it, and his partner let the brother have it. At the same time there was a street full of people out there, and now everybody is suffering. They're just booking people now. Arresting people for anything. They've set traps up around the neighborhood, just looking for brothers. They're looking for the young ones. They're just snatching young brothers. They snatched one young brother and just gave him the case, and he's booked right now for murder, and two counts of attempted murder. They don't have a gun, evidence, or anything. That goes to show you how their justice works. Somebody is going to suffer. Now if it had been one of us who was shot, would they be out there looking for people like that? They would have put the yellow tape over there and labeled it "gang-related." Case closed.

We talk to the officers that work in our community and let them know that we're not animals. Sometimes I like to see them come through the neighborhood, because they don't know how many lives they've saved from a brother not turning up and doing a drive-by, because they came up the street. They need to realize that. There are some Black officers in there that I talk with personally. I have family that works in law enforcement. So I don't have a personal grudge against the police, but I personally have a grudge against an individual that disrespects me, I don't care where he's from or what he does. That has a lot to do with it too: the people coming to patrol in our community come from way out and don't know anything about where we live. They don't even respect us, because they don't know anything about us. Their chief officers that are teaching them are teaching them that we're their enemies. We're not their enemy. Every officer probably has a family member that's in a gang. It's a matter of respect all around the board. Brothers out here are not ambushing the police, that's personal, isolated stuff between one brother and another individual. It's a matter of disrespect. Sometimes they grab people the wrong way. You can't just grab anybody like that. I'm not going for them grabbing me any kind of way. My mama told me not to ever let anyone hit me. You don't have any authority to be hitting me. If I did something wrong, then you handcuff me. I'm not fixin' to let them pop on me like that, because they will try to do that. They actually abuse their authority. They think brothers are not smart. I fool their little assumptions now. They thought I was crazy and ignorant in my past days. Now if I have a problem with an officer, I go straight down to the police station by myself. If I can't deal with you personally, one-on-one, man-to-man, to resolve this confrontation, when you roll away in your squad car, and I walk up the street, I don't have to see you tomorrow with a frown, I'll go to the police station, and I bet I'll talk to you in front of your captain. I don't want to write a grievance, I just want you to hear what I have to say right there, now let's see what you have to say. So we have to play it like that in order to get our justification. You may not ever see justice as a whole, as far as a people, but you can get your justice as an individual if you demand it, and I'm going to get mine.

The only difference is they have a uniform. I want to be the police of my own nation. I'm glad I did take this way of life, because I don't have to go to the service. If I fight, I'm fighting for my Black race, I'll fight for my people in Africa. I ain't fighting for no other folks that's not giving me a dollar. Give me a dollar to go and kill a good man? For what? There's a lot out here that brothers are waking up to. It's not the gang. The gang is not the problem. The problem is that the society needs to start accepting the gang members back into the community as human beings and take that label off of us.

I'm glad I did tattoo myself. It's not like a T-shirt, I can pull this T-shirt off and never put it back on. I can take the tattoos off right now and never put them back on, but I don't want to. Like the record says, "The corner may not promise you a future, but it gives me my props." I'm out there, but I'm out there positive. I'm not packing, I'm not shooting, I'm not serving, I don't have any warrants. I'm just out there kicking it now, just like I wanted to. That's what I got into a gang for. I got what I wanted to get out of being in a gang. To me, I'm never going backwards again. Before I would go backwards and fall on my knees, I would die.

**Q:** Speak on the potential impact of brothers from all over getting with the brotherhood.

**QB:** That right there is a must. The East must meet the West, and the West must meet the East. Why? That's another thing that can help brothers out in their peace efforts. There are brothers out on the East Coast that are Vice Lords, Disciples, that have development. They may not have the best type of houses down there, but one thing that they have, that we don't have here, is development amongst our Black people. So we need them to come out here to show us development amongst our people, and maybe we can show them what they need, to go out there and build on the way the neighborhood looks. Their cities are real tight and close together. Maybe we can show them how to stretch the houses out. Not by the framework of the house, but the value, because we should value being around each other. We look at all of this as nothing to us, but it would be nice, if we made it nice. We need to start bringing brothers from the East Coast and the West Coast together. I believe it's time brothers started to intermingle, teaching each other, and establishing our own. If it takes the nation to open up a school for just us, then do it. "Boystown" or "Gangtown," I bet you any kind of money brothers will stay up in there for about a week or two, just training. We need that, to teach us all the things that we don't know. People would say, "You're putting the gangs too much into high positions in life, you're rewarding them with too much. A school—come on, they don't deserve that." Well, we don't deserve a $2-million freeway that's out here right now either, that we don't have any parts of economic growth in. Don't tell us what we don't need. They put large sums of money out here for small things and don't even get the job done. Now put that large sum to a large thing, and I bet we'll get that job done.

**Q:** Are there any points we didn't ask you that you want to express?

**QB:** We need our future, and it's today. We have to look out for the children, because they don't have a future without us. When I say "us," I mean the Crips and the Bloods, without us they won't have a future. Why do I say that? Because if we don't come to them and help them, then they're going to come to us, and we sure won't be able to help them then, by us being out here acting as Crips and Bloods. We're building an army, but we're tearing our own selves down. We know history, we let one brother guide the Europeans out of the caves to show them Africa, which is the reason why all Blacks are in the conditions we are in today. So one brother rocked the boat. We have to stop that. He's dead now, four hundred years ago. Now we have another brother that can counteract that, by the masses though. Brothers, we can't keep looking at the white folks and clown at our brother because of what they have done; they've done it, let's counteract that with intelligence. Like Too Short says—a lot of rap words mean a lot, I quote rap words, because it's the rap words that inspire me—like Too Short says, "Be intelligent when you put people in check; if we're ignorant, they treat us that way. If they throw us in jail, we have nothing to say." That goes to say, be intelligent when we're placing each other in check, because if we pull these guns out, we really won't have anything to say. We have to be intellectual, loving, and caring towards one another. As men and women, not as gang members. Gang-banging is over with. Believe me, it's over with. There's a new generation coming, involved with some other stuff. So we have to really look out for each other in a positive way.

***We must also realize that the problems of racial injustice and economic injustice cannot be solved without a radical redistribution of political and economic power.***

**—Martin Luther King**

## SHOUT OUTS

I would like to give special thanks to God Almighty for spiritually placing PEACE within our hearts to forgive each other, and to all who was a part of the peace treaty.

I also want to give shout outs to the Five-Duce Broadways, my home team. We did it! My allies in street life!

5 Tray Avalon
40th Avalon
43rd Street
42nd Street
52 Villains—Bloods
52 Pueblo Bishops—Bloods

I know we still have some differences, but keep the faith within your heart, and we can do it again. If we want, you all know how we kicked it, and we knew some obstacles would come our way!

Special thanks to Theresa, Pam, Tawanna, Devera, and Gwen for the homegirl input!

To Lonely Man, Kenney Fly, Lemon Head, Theodore, Leon, Batt, Kay Dee, Raven, you're my home team from the perspective of unity. And that's a lot. We started something good. Let's continue.

All thanks, courage, effort, and prayers goes out specially to —OG Bull Capone 53—for going to the Pueblos and the Villains. You did it with the first step to change the nonsense! Much love always to the man!

To the rest of the loved ones incarcerated, on the streets, or resting in peace, you all are the true children of God. Peace-out.

# TWILIGHT

*(My first name is Anthony. My last name is not important. I go by the name of Twilight Bey. A lot of people ask where I get that name from. TWI is an abbreviation of the word "twice," and the word "LIGHT" is a word that symbolizes knowledge, which you find in the Bible, the Holy Qur'an, or any spiritual doctrine that you read. So it means that I have twice the knowledge of those my age. My last name Bey is an African tribal name, and it basically means that I take action minus emotion when at war, that I am a doer and not a talker.*

*I was born in Dallas, Texas, and I was raised in California from seven, eight years old. I lived in the Nickerson Gardens Housing Projects on 115th Street and later moved to Hacienda Village, where I lived as a member of the Cirkle City Piru gang, and I am now an inactive member up to this day. I sold drugs for five years and had committed numerous crimes. I've almost lost my life on many different occasions, so I've always thought that God had something planned for me because I'm not dead yet. So in my search to give myself a better life, I found that a lot of times your homeboys won't like it when you choose right. But then comes the decision, are you living for yourself or are you living for them?*

*I decided that I was living for myself, and the only thing that mattered was what I thought of me and not what they thought of me. Then came the rude awakening that to care for myself was to care for my brothers, because what I want for myself, I want for my brothers.*

*So in working with the Amer-I-CAN Program, I've learned life-management skills and how to manage my life successfully. By knowing my history, I've learned what it will take for me and my people to succeed. And with all of my experiences, traveling, and dealing with business, there's one thing that I've learned and that is: Nobody can save the Black man but HIMSELF, with the help from God!*

*Everything that I've learned, I offer to my brothers and sisters with open arms, so that we all may succeed. May you gain the most of insight and understanding from reading this book so that you may know to take heed!*

*P.S. Ya'll can teach me too! Still got love for all ya'll!*
*Time for work!*
*Twilight)*

**Q:** When you got started bangin', how old were you?

**T:** Nine or ten years old, running around in Nickerson Gardens. I moved here from Dallas/Fort Worth in '78. I didn't know anything about Los Angeles, but living in the projects with my family, everybody said Blood, so I said Blood. Everybody had all of this red stuff that looked good, so I wanted to wear red too, because I wanted to fit in. One of my people, he shot at the police one day, and he laughed about it, so I felt maybe that's the thing to do. I didn't know, I was a kid. I was growing up in this. Nobody was telling me that there was a flip side to this. Nobody said, "Hey, there's this gang neighborhood that calls themselves the Crips, and they don't like us." So I'm growing up, and I'm conditioned to be a Blood. I'm watching the way my OGs treat women, I watched the way they made money, I watched everything that they did, I studied them. I checked out the ways that they got over on the police. So my mind was conditioned to live a certain kind of way. I've learned that children are conditioned by their basic environment, perhaps as young as two years old. That includes home, school, community, church, everything that they deal with.

**Q:** How did the gang peace treaty first come about in your area of Watts?

**T:** A peace document was actually drawn up by Daude Sherrils, and Brother Tony X, but what happened was that the treaty was discussed only amongst the older generation, and even though they may have agreed to certain terms, it never got down to the younger generation. In Watts, I can go anywhere, but my younger homeboys can't, because you have bad apples in every bunch. You have a few bad apples out here who have a few followers who are creating problems. One of my homeboys got shot recently, and the guy that was behind it is older than me, but he just doesn't want peace. He's manipulating the minds of the younger kids from his neighborhood and sending them on these missions. It's hard, because my younger homeboys look at me and say, "What are we going to do about this?" And me being an advocate for peace, I don't want to go to war. That's not the answer, it has never been the answer. I've been doing this since 1979. I've come up in this, this is all I know. They have their good points, but gangs are not like they were back then.

**Q:** What are some of the differences between now and then?

**T:** Back then brothers bonded together strictly out of love and respect for each other. Then came the drugs, so now it's all about money. Their loyalty is to the money, and not the love or the brotherhood anymore. So what happens now is that the ones with the money become the ones with the power. Brothers respect them because they have money, and they get money from them. They become dependent upon them. Whereas before, we helped each other because of who we were, and where we came from, because we all came out of the same boat.

I remember when all of us had raggedy clothes, and our mamas shopped at Zody's. We had a bunch of cheap clothes, but we had each other. That's what mattered. But now it's like if you don't have any money, the homiez don't want to talk to you. If you're not helping them to make money in whatever game they try to make their living, then they don't have anything to say to you. This is my generation. I'll say between the ages of twenty-one to twenty-seven. It's real shaky now. Nobody really backs anybody up on anything anymore. I look at my homeboys that are my age, and they're concerned with selling their drugs, they don't care about the younger homiez anymore. They just want to come up. What I see now is what happened in '74; a lot of people don't know that they had a peace treaty in '74. Back when they had one leader of each L.A. gang, all of those leaders came together. Then they were shafted by the people they were dealing with, by the government officials that were involved, different city officials that were involved, and different community organizations, such as reverends and people who represented the church community. Some of them were there, and they basically messed over these guys. They had agreed to keep the peace, but when the things that were promised didn't happen, those who we now call the OGs got to selling PCP, cocaine, and made a lot of money. Some of them moved out in the Valley, Rancho Cucamonga, they moved out of the neighborhood.

**Q:** What happened then in the hoods?

**T:** They left the younger ones here to fend for themselves. So what do they do? They go back to the only thing they've ever known, gang-banging, warfare. Then from watching the older brothers get on their feet, from rolling with the dope the way they did, that made everybody want to get a piece of the action. And as everybody started getting their little piece of the action, more deceit came in. There is a saying that "the love of money is the root to all evil." Not having money, but loving money more than anything else, brings about evil, because then that dollar becomes your master, your God. Life is not important anymore, and that's what happened.

I see the same thing happening now. My generation has gotten together and said, "We can squash this, we can have peace." And that again leaves the younger generation out there to fend for themselves. That's one way that I look at myself as being different from a lot of the other brothers that are my age: I'm not going to leave my young homiez to fend for themselves. I'm going to teach them the right way, make sure they understand what has to be done. That death and murder is never the key to anything.

**Q:** Before you came to L.A. and got involved with gangs, what were your goals and dreams?

**T:** When I was in Dallas, first of all my father was in the house. He was a disciplinarian, an ex-Marine marksman; he didn't take any mess. Then my family was very religious Pentecostal Christians. It seemed like there wasn't a day out of the week that I wasn't at church. In school

I remember being bullied. I remember when some guy took my lunch one day, and somehow my father found out about it, and I got the beating of my life when I got home. In Texas I was a humble, quiet kid. I liked to sing, I used to sing in a lot of the school plays. I wasn't concerned with anything but growing up. Back then the only thing I knew and understood as something I could do was become a preacher. I was in church all the time. My father had gotten his minister's license, that's all that I knew. I didn't know much about police. Police didn't even come down my street where I lived in Texas. I had never seen a cop in Texas. I liked music, I was into Michael Jackson. But being bombarded with church, and understanding righteousness from my parents, that's where I was moved to go, that's what I wanted to do.

Then when I came out to California, first of all I was like, "Man, where am I?" I left a big house. We had four different sections to the backyard, raising chickens and ducks. I had dogs and all that. I was a little country kid. Now I'm in the city with nothing but concrete. In Texas I could go out in the backyard and walk down the street to the river. I could fish. When I came out here, I didn't see any of that.

So how I got here to L.A. was when my father started indulging in negative dealings. The electricity was turned off, the water was turned off; I remember helping my mother haul water from the neighbors' yard down the alley, chopping firewood, and cooking in the fireplace in the house. My mother got fed up with it and decided to come out here to where we have relatives. I was a little more mature than the kids my age, because I had been forced to take responsibilities before I got here. I mean hauling water, chopping firewood, looking after my brothers and sisters. I have two brothers, and two sisters. When we got out here, my mother was running around trying to find out what she could do to get on her feet, so I was left a lot with my brothers and sisters to look after them.

Hanging around with the guys in the neighborhood, I found that if you want to make it in the projects, you have to be a fighter. You can't sit back and just exist. It wasn't like Texas. I couldn't just go to school and have a problem out of one person; everybody in the projects was going to try you in one way or another. Everybody gets along, but if you're new, everybody is going to try you, so I got to fighting. My mother would make me do pull-ups, she was the one coaching me, telling me, "You need to make your muscles bigger. You need to get bigger." So for a long time I was really into working out, and I became a very violent young man, because things had changed. One of the people that my mother met was a known drug dealer in the neighborhood, and he did his thing, and I watched him. All of my cousins—I have a very large family in L.A.—and my cousins would fight and sell dope, so I got caught up in that. It was Blood this and Blood that.

Then we moved from Nickerson Gardens to Hacienda Village when I was in the fifth grade. When I moved to Hacienda Village, it was strange again. The Nickerson Gardens were so big, you have over two thousand people living in those projects. Everything that you need is right around the projects. The stores and the school was on the inside of the projects. I never had to leave outside of the projects, so when I moved to the Haciendas I was getting to know the homiez down there and checking out where they was coming from. I saw that I was still in a Blood environment, because everybody was saying Blood. I go to the elementary school, sixth grade rolls around, my last year in elementary school, and then I start hearing from my cousins from the Bounty Hunters, and a lot of other guys that I grew up with, "Hey, when you get to Markam, there's going to be some dudes up there that are Crips. The Crips are going to try to kill you." I remember getting out of school in the sixth grade on Fridays, and every Friday there would be a shoot-out at the junior high school across the street. We'd be ducking and wondering what was going on. As time went on in the summer of the year that I went from the sixth grade to the seventh, that's when I got into my first gang fight. Which took place right here at Will Rogers Park.

I realized that a lot of the guys that I was cool with when we used to play basketball for the sheriff's league in elementary school had now become Crips. They went to 102nd Street Elementary School down there by the Jordan Downs, Grape Street Crips, and 92nd Street School, East Coast Crips. Back then I went to 112th Street School in the Nickerson Gardens, and then I went to Compton Avenue school, which happened to be in the Haciendas, which deals with the Cirkle City Pirus, the Bounty Hunters, and the Hacienda Village Boys [Bloods]. My first day of school at Markam I get into a fight with three Crips. I beat two guys up and ran the other one off, but then when I got back to school the next day, it was a trip, because I didn't know that the Bloods did not come to school for the first month. [Laughs] I was the only Blood there.

My mama didn't know what was going on. So when I told my mama that I didn't want to go to school, she said, "Boy, you better get your behind out of here and go to school." So I was paranoid and scared, not knowing what I was going to do. So I started carrying butcher knives and little miniature Dodger bats and all kinds of stuff to school. I couldn't think about educating myself because I was thinking about protecting myself. But I never was a dumb kid, I kept my grades up and everything. I would do my work in class, but, man, when the bell rang, it was a different thing.

So it just got to the point where I was ditching school a lot; my mother found out and beat my behind real bad. So what happened was, when I would get in trouble with my mother . . . you know I didn't know how to explain to her what was going on, so I would get so mad that I would take it out on the Crips. That's when I bought my first gun. It was constant war, and that's all I wanted to do was go to war.

I went through seventh grade, and that summer I caught a case, went to jail, got out of jail, and from then on my life was just caught up in that warfare, that's all I knew. Then I started drinking and smoking weed, and in the neighborhood the homiez would dip the marijuana in PCP and start trippin'. We would smoke those things, man, and I can remember the days when we would go to Watts on 108th and Central and take over the welfare office, and when the Crips would come up there, we would fight them with trash cans.

**Q:** Back then it wasn't about shooting, was it?

**T:** No, back then there wasn't a lot of shooting. Only now and then you may have heard a few gunshots, but it was mostly fighting.

What happened with me is that over the years I caught another case, I got kicked out of Los Angeles Unified School District, and I had to go to school in Compton. Now in Compton the school was different, you had Bloods and Crips, but it was different. I was in Davis Junior High and it was an all-Black-run school. I had a teacher named Mr. Littles, my science teacher. I will never forget him; he was a Black man that didn't take any mess. If you were late to his class, then you were punished. If you didn't have your notes, you were punished, and if you didn't have over a certain average on your tests, you were punished. We didn't have that over at Markam. The teachers were scared of us at Markam, because they were white folks, and they didn't understand us, but the Black teachers knew what was going on and they didn't take any mess.

So the first day of school I got kicked out for ditching. My mother found out, and she was back home in Texas because my grandmother died, she was my favorite grandmother, which was another thing that just made the negativity in me grow. My counselor got me back in the school, and I then made a reputation for myself at that school. I had maintained a 3.5 to 3.6 grade point average. But the whole point about it was that I still found time to fight with the Crips in Compton. I'm not bragging either, but I never got beat in Compton. We had a large percentage of Bloods from Watts going to Davis Junior High School, because we would get kicked out of Markam and that was the next school that we all went to. The principal would look at us because we didn't have permits to go to the school. We were using friends' addresses that stayed in the neighborhood by the school. One day she got us all in the office, and we all had on All-Stars with the tongue flipped down, and our neighborhoods written all over our shoes. We had our khakis sagging, with Pendleton shirts, and we had on these red belts that we called khaki belts with the buckle of the belt in the back, because the Bloods wore their belts to the back. So the principal, Ms. Grant, she looked at us and she said, "I don't know what it is about ya'll, but ya'll are not from Compton." She knew that we didn't stay in Compton, but she couldn't prove it. Man, this lady would just constantly watch us.

I was in the choir, and with my reputation at school, even the teachers called me Twilight. Everybody remembers me as Twilight. It was at that time when I was at Davis Junior High School that I started to notice the change. It was in '84, '85 in my ninth-grade year that I started seeing a lot of my comrades rollin' in Mercedes and Cadillacs, making barrels of money. I was wondering where they were getting the money from, because I was in the school, but I was also in the gang warfare, and I never really thought about the money aspect.

At that time to be a gang member was the thing to be, because the gang members were considered the men on campus. We had all the respect and all the women, and if you got out of line with us, we would break your neck. Then came all of the drugs, which just made things better, we thought. That's how our attitudes were back then. So I started selling weed and guns at school and started making my little money. Then I started dressing better and looking better.

When I graduated from Davis Junior High they wanted to send me to Compton High School, which was an all-Crip high school. My first day there I walked in wearing all white, but the Crips knew who I was. So I was telling my pops, I said, "Look, man . . . ," because he came out here when I was fourteen, when I caught a case and they were trying to give me nine years. My mother didn't want me to get locked up, so she said she would rather send me back home to Texas. So my father came to California to see about me.

I left Compton High and found myself at Morningside High; it had predominantly all-Black teachers. The teachers were very interested in who you were, and what your goals in life were. When my counselor there saw that I had the ability to sing, she put me in the upper echelon of the choir, called the Chamber Singers, instructed by a teacher named Jeffrey Pearson, who grew up in Compton, went to school in Compton, and knew all about gang-banging. He was in his twenties so we couldn't run game on him. The Chamber Singers did a lot of traveling, and if we wanted to go with them, we had to keep our grades up. So every day after school Jeffrey would have a meeting with us, make sure our grades were up, make sure we were doing our classwork. The first year I was there, he wouldn't let me get away with anything. What would happen is we would do performances for the school, and my homeboys would tease me. I would see them, they would be in the audience: "Hey, Twilight, what's up, Blood? The singing gang banger, right, Blood?" So the following year, my eleventh-grade year, I dropped out of the choir, and I went back into gang-banging and tripping real tough.

The summer came, and a lot of my friends had died. That was the summer of '87. This is when I started thinking about a lot of things. My brother and the homiez talk about me all the time, because they look at me now that I don't bang, and they remember when I said, "Gang-banging will never stop." That was my attitude. That summer of '87 I lost so many friends, so many homeboys, and I didn't know if I was going to live or die, and in a lot of cases I didn't care.

**Q:** So you didn't see selling drugs and living that life as your career? Was it just a phase you were going through when you were young?

**T:** Yeah. It was something I was doing when I was young. But like I told the homeboys, "When I turn eighteen, I'm not going to jail anymore." I knew once you turned eighteen, everything that you did was going to follow you for life. To this present day I don't have any felonies as an adult. I was thinking about these things, and then my daughter's mother became pregnant with my daughter. So that was on my mind. I was listening to Public Enemy, and I was checking out what Minister Farrakhan had to say.

Everybody listened to L.L. Cool J and Slick Rick when they first came out, but I said, wait a minute, PE is trying to tell us something. "Black Steel in the Hour of Chaos," "Rebel Without a Pause," I was listening to this stuff. I was telling the homiez to check 'em out. I quit wearing a curl, I've been wearing braids ever since '88. I realized that we're always conforming to what they're about. What about me? Who am I? Where do I come from? Eighty-eight was the first time I heard about Malcolm X. I was eighteen years old, and I started reading about Malcolm, checking out what he had to say. I told the homiez, "Maybe we've been doing this all wrong." They were drunk: "Man, what are you talking about?" I was the only one sitting there sober, really brainstorming on this. Wondering, why are we killing each other? I couldn't understand it. Then as time went on, I did a lot more reading, and I started meeting new people.

**Q:** What books were you reading?

**T:** I read *From Babylon to Timbuktu, They Came Before Columbus, African Presence in Early America.* Then I was like, they've been lying to me all this time.

**Q:** What inspired you to seek that knowledge of self?

**T:** I would hear about different stuff from Public Enemy. I checked out Minister Farrakhan because of Public Enemy. They played certain excerpts of his speeches in their rap songs. Then I met a brother named James, and he was telling me that I should start reading. I was tired of reading, because in school I did a lot of reading. Then in the twelfth grade another thing I came to realize was that everything the schools were teaching me was BS. It has been a repetition of the same BS for twelve years. When are y'all going to really give me something that I can benefit from? I remember the only good thing I heard about my people in history books was Martin Luther King. Everything else had to do with slavery. I didn't know anything about Queen Nefertiti, King Amen Rah, and all of our other great African kings and queens. I was really trying to figure out what was going on. Who am I? Where do I come from? What's happening?

Then in the summer of '88 I was approached by some people that wanted to give the Bloods and the Crips a forum, to come to the table and talk about their problems. To see if there was an opportunity that we could have peace. I took that opportunity, and I represented my neighborhood at that meeting. It was a gang summit, 1988, in the city of

Carson at the Ramada Hotel. We met with some Crips, and we talked about what was going on, and we found that there was no real major problem between us. We all felt like we could get along.

So when we did a television interview, and the white media wanted to ask all of these quesetions, I said, "You know what, it has been a long time that we've been killing each other. But we're basically the same people. I always thought that they were different from me in some kind of way, but there's no difference. So right now today I can shake this man's hand, because a man can stand with another man with no problems at all."

I shook the brother's hand, and they snapped the picture, and in the paper the next day it read, "Twilight, the leader of the Bloods . . ." I never said I was the leader of the Bloods. Why did they say I was the leader? It was enough that I shook a Crip's hand, the homiez were able to deal with that, but that little sentence, "Twilight, the leader of the Bloods," just blew everything out of proportion. That got a lot of my own comrades upset who thought I told those people I was the leader. I didn't tell them that. I told them that "I am a representative of my neighborhood. I'm here to listen to what you all want to do, and what we can do to help my homeboys. My concern is my neighborhood. If we can be at peace with everybody that we're warring with, then we have the time to listen." If we're at war, we're not listening to anything, we're worrying about living.

That lie that the media told had created a whole mess within itself. Homeboys would come down to my house pulling guns out, talking crazy. I stood there with my gun, and I said, "Who sent you?" They would tell me who sent them, and I'd say, "Is he your daddy?" I'd say, "No man is my daddy except my father, and my father is not here. I make decisions for myself. No man can tell me to go kill another person."

Our OGs kick back and stack paper, and they make deals with the Crips. At one point in time the Crips had the biggest dope sack. So Bloods were dealing with the Crips, because Bloods had all of the guns. So they were making exchanges on the top, but on the bottom we were killing each other like it was the thing to do. I told them, "I've seen our Gs in the pen kicking it with the Crips. They're not at war. We're out here fighting each other, and you're going to let another man tell you that you should kill me? All of y'all know me. I grew up with all y'all. None of y'all have I done anything wrong to. So why do you want to hurt me?" They couldn't answer the question so they left it alone. But constantly I was approached by different things.

I was approached by a G from another Blood set who wanted to sweat me about it. We got into a fight, and God must have been with me. A lot of the fights I had, God must have been with me, because I don't know how I won. This cat, I kept telling him, "Look, man, I love you, I don't want to fight you." He kept running up in my face, so I hit him, and he hit the ground before I even knew I hit him. So the word

4 5 6
CIRCLE
CITY
Circulo

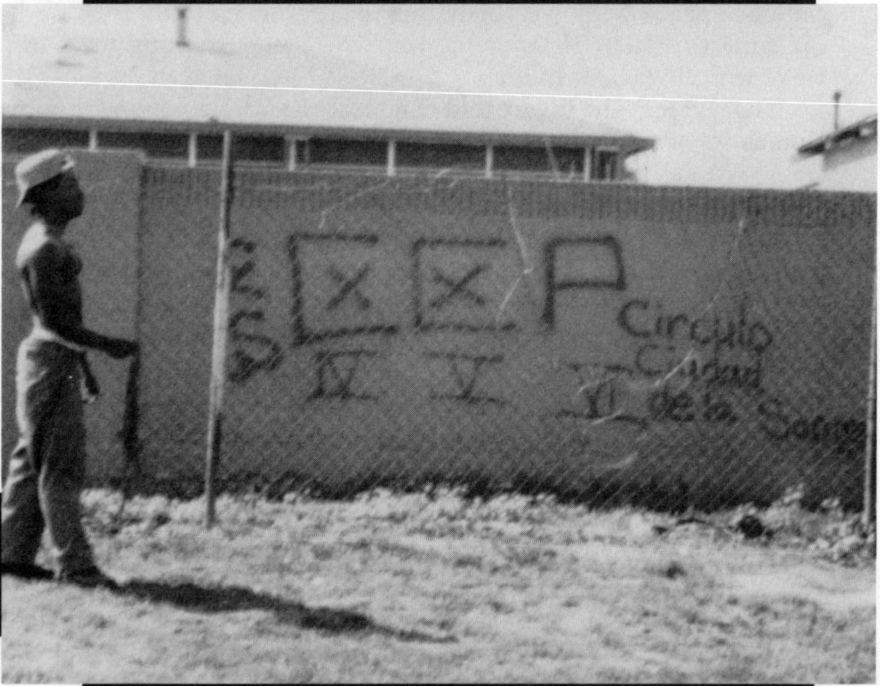

traveled—I said, "You know how I feel about the neighborhood, you know how I feel about this red flag. I will die or I will kill for this. That's the same way I feel about peace. You will have to kill me, or I will kill you so that peace can rule. I'm not fixing to let y'all push me over." When some of the guys heard what was going on, they backed off. Ever since then I started making strides.

I hooked up with the Moorish Science Temple. When I made that move, I was enlightened to so many things, I was energetic with all this new information. It was a whole new world that I didn't know anything about. So I started getting off into all these different things, I started doing speaking engagements at different colleges. They showed me how to use what I knew, and my experience, to my benefit, so that I didn't have to sell drugs.

Coming out of gang life, a lot of gang members retire to become drug dealers. If you don't want to be a drug dealer, what can you do? Every job that's offered can't give you what you really need to sustain yourself. So here I was, I had become a father, my daughter was one year old, and I worked with this church organization . . . by the way, I want to make sure you get this too. Some of the people who were involved with the gang summit in 1988, they worked with another organization that received half a million dollars from the city. This half a million dollars was supposed to go to an anti-gang program dealing with education, and money for the brothers while they were going to school. A lot of us had kids, and we didn't want to sell drugs. So if we were going to be in here catching up on the work that we didn't finish in school, we had to have some kind of paper in our pockets.

To make sure that the money went where it was supposed to go, they said that they would have a watchdog who was going to be paid $60,000 in the course of a year to watch over that money. I was supposed to be the watchdog, I never saw $60,000. Yet, all the homeboys thought that I was making big money. I wasn't making big money, this was something that the media confused. The church people supposedly gave us a building to have meetings. They said that we could have the building. I had the keys for a little while, we had meetings there, but when they saw that we were going to say something serious, that we were going to demand that they follow our lead, they wanted to sit us down. They wanted to tell us how we should feel, tell us what we should do, without listening to what we have been through. How are you going to tell us what to do if you don't examine the problem first? They had all this money, and only a few brothers went through the program, a few brothers made a little money, but the rest of the money all of a sudden disappeared. Five hundred thousand dollars gone in less than a year. Come on, man, what did y'all do with the money? The program never got implemented, and now the money is gone?

They had homeboys thinking that I had stacks of money somewhere. People were threatening my life. I was out there and real confused, because I was like, "Wait a minute, churches are not supposed to do this type of thing." I started thinking back to my upbringing when I went to church. The churches in Texas were so much different than in California. I notice that a lot of the ministers out here drive these big cars, and they have gold rings on their fingers. The pastor of the church that I went to back home didn't wear a lot of flashy stuff. His job was purely to teach the word, or the gospel, and to assist the people in his church.

A lot of these ministers out here are having fund-raisers to build up their church to make them bigger. You have all these big churches . . . that's another thing I started looking at, how I can go down Central Avenue and see more churches than anything, and they're not doing anything in the community. A lot of people don't know this, but gang members probably know the Bible better than a lot of those ministers in the churches. When we began to pull them on God's word, what they were teaching, I said, "Wait a minute, God said that the church was a place of worship. That your work was out amongst the people. Jesus was in the streets with the criminals, the murderers, the gamblers, the whores, he wasn't behind the church wall. Y'all are scared of the community that you have the church in. So how are you going to say you're representing Jesus Christ?" They couldn't answer the questions, then they'd tell us that we don't know what we're talking about. I was like, "Wait a minute, look, I know better than this. You took the money, you lied to us, and now you want me to stand here and believe that you have our best interest at heart. I'm not going to do that." So a lot of the guys wanted to kill the people that we were involved with. But I stopped them from doing that. Killing them wasn't going to change what they did.

As time went on, that's when I got more involved with the Moors; I learned a lot there. That experience with the churches made me very leery of any type of minister. I just lost trust in preachers. It wasn't just one church, it was ministers from several different churches, and that one minister who's on cable, a real big shot. As time went on, I started seeing what was going on, and I tried to enlighten as many people as possible. I tried to educate my own homeboys.

**Q:** How did your homiez respond to you when you asked them, "Why are we killing each other?"

**T:** Back then, everybody was delirious, laughing. They weren't really tripping on what I was saying. They weren't concerned with that. What happened was, as the years went by, certain brothers started coming back, "Twilight, I see what you were talking about." I guess it took them having to get a girlfriend, get married, have kids, and still have to worry about somebody trying to kill them. They started to see what I was talking about, but they didn't know what to do about it. I would tell them, "We have the respect, we have influence. Y'all sit back and talk about the youngsters, and how they're robbing and killing everybody, we're the ones who taught them how to do that. It should be us that stops them. Now you sit back and act like you're scared of the very baby that you created."

That's the difference between me and them, I'm not afraid of these little knuckleheads. I will slap them upside the head and tell them that they're wrong, and then sit them down with love and try to show them the right way. Everybody doesn't do that. Everybody has their problems that they go through. There are a lot of brothers in the twenty-two-to-twenty-five age group, if they are not addicted to drugs, they're alcoholics, slowly getting to the point where life is of no concern to them. A lot of the brothers have been victims of violent crimes, and they go and get that money that victims of violent crimes can get. Some of them get social security because they have bullets in their necks, bullets in their backs, and they can't do hard work, because it may paralyze them. So they have no concern, no focus, or no guidelines on what to do, and when you try to tell them something, a lot of them, they can't hear you because their minds have been altered by alcohol, and they just can't hear you.

**Q:** What role do the drugs and the alcohol play in the violence that goes on?

**T:** I can tell you from my very own experience, my mother can tell you, every homeboy that ever kicked it with Twilight, we all know the things about each other's lives. I remember when I would drink alcohol, very, very potent alcohol, and get stoned out of my mind. Instead of the alcohol taking the pain away, the alcohol magnified the pain and made me feel it even worse. I'd get intoxicated and start thinking of all the homeboys that are dead, how they died, actually seeing the murder scene in my mind, and who was behind it. This is what went through my mind when I was drunk, so the first thing I wanted to do was kill. I'd get drunk, I'd think of all these terrible things happening in our community, to my homeboys, to their mothers, to their girlfriends, to their children, because of their deaths, and all I wanted to do was go out there and kill the punk mf that did it. That's all that was going through my mind.

The reason for that way of thinking is because, come on now, sit back and look at this world that we live in, look at society. I grew up watching *The Rifleman.* If the rifleman had a problem, he grabbed his rifle, right? If I had a problem, I grabbed my gun. This is what I grew up watching. Not only that, look at all of those movies, if you go into any house where you have a large group of young men, guaranteed you will find these movies: *Terminator, King of New York, Scarface,* most definitely *The Godfather,* and *Mobsters.* I sit back and watch Scarface kill everybody and still live. The media plays a major role in all of the killings. Look at Charles Bronson, he played the good guy, and if he had a problem, he was a renegade cop that would just kill up everybody, solve the case, and he's the hero. Okay, fine, if America has a problem, what do they do? They blow up the country that they have a problem with, and everything is cool.

Going through the Amer-I-CAN Program, you're trained to examine the whys and the wherefores of past behavior patterns that have negatively affected your life and see why you acted the way you did. Now I see very clearly what gave me the f'd-up mind-set I had, but then I can also see back even further at what gave me the foundation to go back to righteousness.

**Q:** What was that foundation?

**T:** My foundation was my upbringing in Texas. I was basically a good kid. I never wanted to hurt anybody. My mother told me to always put God first. Even in all the years of me gang-banging, and I'm going to tell it, because I don't know if anybody else told it, yes, a lot of Bloods and Crips pray. We have a strong belief in God, even though we're out here doing all of these terrible things, and going stark out of our minds, a lot of us believe in God. That foundation of knowing right from wrong, what's good and what's bad. Everybody by nature knows better, we just choose to deal a certain way, because if you look at the society that we live in, it tells us that this is the way to do things.

**Q:** What is the root cause of brothers getting into the negative activities?

**T:** The root cause is a condition of the mind. A lot of people don't want to look at it and really deal with it. But we've been messed up from day one in America. From the day they put our ancestors on the boats and brought us over here, we have been messed up ever since. That's the truth. When I look at the history, and I read back and find out things, the woman did what she was supposed to do, the children were looked after by the whole entire village, and to be taken from a situation where we were controlling our own destiny, our own leadership, we were taken and reduced to lower than animals. I read certain books, *The Secret Relationship Between Blacks and Jews;* a cow was priced higher than a Black person. What kind of condition does that put on the mind? I think back, and I look at this, and I look at the plantation. They have the brothers out there picking the cotton, some of the sisters picking cotton too, and some of them raising the children, not only their children, but the slave master's children too. The slave master fed everybody, and when the Black man got out of control, he beat him, and in some cases he cut off his foot or cut off his head, it depended on what it was that he did. Then for the man to sit there and have to deal with the embarrassment and the indignity of seeing his woman raped. Dealing with the embarrassment and the indignity of seeing the Black woman go to the white man. They f'd us up. When I look at today, and I put it together with today's times, we have the same thing. The plantation is just called the "projects" now. Instead of brothers picking cotton, brothers are peddling white rocks and killing each other, picking each other off, and the sisters are still in control of the household. Then we have the county building, which we might as well call it what it is, the slave master's house, who still takes care of everybody.

Now they wonder why men and women can't get along, why they argue, fuss, fight, and bicker. What is it? Why does the Black man have such a strong hatred for his own self and his own woman? Let's check out the history, and maybe we'll find out where it went wrong. Look at how slavery played a role in tearing us down as a people; all of that has an effect on what's going on right now. To lose our language, to lose our culture, and to be reindoctrinated into something that's totally alien to us, it's only natural that we reject it. It's not natural to us, so we reject it, and we rebel against the society.

You take the Black man and supposedly take him out of slavery. The Black woman gets what she wants, because the white man loves her. She can get a job quicker, so the Black man is not the breadwinner in the family anymore, and he's depressed. Then they have alcohol everywhere, so he drinks. The same conditions exist today, it's just that it's not in a brown jug, it's in a clear bottle called 8 Ball. The same problems exist today. If I can't be the breadwinner for my daughter, if I can't find certain jobs because of whatever stipulations they have set against me, or if I'm a felon, then I can't get hired. The majority of Black men in the Black community are being charged with felonies because there is no economic development out here. There is no growth, so therefore they go out and rob, steal, or kill and do whatever they have to do to survive. Then they go to jail, and they're locked down totally.

I remember myself, I took care of my child for the first six months of her life. Her mother didn't have to get on welfare. I had a job. Then I got laid off of my job and couldn't find another job, so ultimately she had to get on welfare. With her being on welfare I couldn't stay in the house, because I'm a man. The man can't stay in the house if you get on welfare. However, I went there anyway. I was trying to get in school, trying to find ways of getting myself some type of employment, and also talking to the brothers in my community, dealing with the problems of my community, because I knew if we could stop the violence and bring some type of unity to the community, then some people would invest. So this is an around-the-clock job, something that I have to invest my time in.

My woman sits at home looking at the soap operas, where this guy claims he's going to work, and he's out doing something with some woman, so she thinks I'm doing the same thing. I come back and there's an argument. "You dog, get out my house. This is my house. My name is on the lease." What did you tell me that for? I don't even want to trip on you, because you don't even know what's going on. But now I see it, they put you in a position over me. Well, I'm not going to have that. If I'm going to leave, then I'm going to leave permanently, and I will create my foundation, build my own castle, and uplift myself. Then I will have my own power, they won't control me, I'll control myself. I will develop the things that are needed for my daughter to live, grow, learn, and become who she is to be in the future.

What I just talked about, as far as the problems between the Black man and the Black woman, is something that goes on in these projects every day. You'll be surprised how many brothers try to restrain themselves from hitting their women. I sit and watch it. Somebody I know, his girlfriend was cursing him out and yelling at him because he didn't bring a certain amount of money that she needed at the time. She comes out of the house, hits him upside the head, and calls him out of his name. He says, all right, that's enough, just leave me alone. She keeps pushing the issue. So when he gets up and goes in the house and physically beats her up, she calls the police on him. The police come and take him to jail, and now the European has made it a felony for spousal abuse. So if you didn't already have a felony, you have one now. If they don't get you from a normal crime, they get you when you're having problems with your wife. Now he goes to jail, and she calls him, crying and wanting to apologize. The cycle just starts over. Then the children grow up looking at this.

I've learned that if a child lives with hostility, the child learns to fight. That was the main reason why I didn't want to deal with the arguing and fighting anymore. When I became aware that children become conditioned by what they see us say and do, I realized that I don't want my daughter to be messed up. I don't want her to think that fighting is the thing to do. I don't want her to think that fighting against a man is the thing to do. I don't want her to think that men are worthless. So I'd rather not even live in the household. I'd rather go out there and work, do what I have to do for myself, and when my daughter comes to see me, I can sit her down, teach her how to read, and show her positive things to do. Document all the things that I do, so that if I die before she becomes a young lady, she'll be able to read about what her daddy did. She'll have videos, she'll have picture albums, she'll know that her father was worth something, her father did try to do something, in spite of all the things her mother might say about me.

So with all of the problems that go on in the community, I can almost understand why some brothers are unable to get to the level that I'm at right now. My reason for being able to get where I'm at is from my foundation as a kid, and knowing right from wrong. Knowing that there are two worlds: a spiritual and a physical. Knowing the history and the knowledge that was brought to me through the Moorish Science Temple. Understanding all of this, now I can see that if everybody is not equipped with these particular things, it's hard to be strong, and it's hard to stand up. If a Black man does not know the extent of damage that was done to him during slavery, and how it plays a role in today's society, then how can he stand up against it?

**Q:** How do we turn that around? How do we counterattack what we are up against?

**T:** I believe that people need history and things of that nature. A lot of our people reject their history, because of self-hatred. So let's take it back to something that's more common and doesn't have anything to do with history, that doesn't have anything to do with anything but life. That's what I found in Jim Brown's program, Amer-I-CAN.

Amer-I-CAN deals with specifics, life-management skills. Africans that I know, and me myself, were unable to manage life successfully. I didn't know what it was to set realistic, worthwhile, and attainable goals. As a matter of fact I couldn't have even told you that goals needed those three characteristics. I didn't know this. Even though I maintained a 3.5 grade point average through school and got to the first semester in the twelfth grade with a 3.5 grade point average. The second semester I dropped out, two classes short of graduating, because I was fed up with school. But if I understood how to manage my life correctly, with proper communication skills, problem solving, decision making, goal setting, emotional control, job search and retention skills . . . These are things that people need in order to live a successful, productive life.

For example, as a gang member coming up in my youth, if I had a problem, the quickest way to solve it to me was to kill it, beat it up, destroy it. That's all I knew. That was the first thing that came to mind. If you're not going to give me what I want, or you're not going to do what I ask you to do, if you want to rob me, I'll kill you. In the program it tells me to eliminate the negative, establish the facts, and choose your best option. Now that makes you think.

One of my homeboys was killed, and everybody was upset about it. When I heard about it, I got upset too, but then I had to think, and I had to eliminate the negative. There's nothing I can do about his death, I can't bring him back. So what are the facts of the situation, what happened? They say, "Well, he got killed on 108th and Clover, so the Front Streets must have killed him." How did he get on 108th and Clover? "He was at 108th Street police station." Why was he at the 108th Street police station? "His people called the police on him." Why? "Because he stole some money." He had a dope problem, he was hooked on crack. So what you're telling me is that he stole money from his family, and so they put him in jail. How did he get released? "He asked his family to drop the charges, so they came to the police station and dropped the charges, but they didn't wait to bring him home." But he knew he couldn't walk home, he knew he had to walk through three different rival neighborhoods to get back to his house. He knew this, but he still wanted to walk. So in the process of walking back home he got killed.

Now, let's check it out. What options do we have? We have all the facts, now what are our options? If he would have never stole the money in the first place, he would have never went to jail. But he did, and he got killed, but the real reason for him being killed is because he stole money from his family. So is his family reponsible? Are we going to kill his family? Can't kill them, they did what they were supposed to do. They didn't want to kill him so they sent him to jail for stealing from them, because that was wrong. Are we going to go over there and try to kill the

Front Streets for killing him? That wouldn't make sense either. Because first of all he knew he couldn't come home through there. He was responsible for putting himself there. If we go over there and kill a Front Street, we're going to create a war, and a whole lot of other people are going to die. So the best option is, he was wrong, let him rest in peace, and all of these other youngsters out here thinking about doing drugs, let this be a lesson to them. That's what we did, we left it alone.

Now, if I would have never had those particular problem-solving skills, the first thing that would have come to mind, "Let's go kill those SOBs," that would have been the first thing that came to mind. The program teaches that when I set a goal, I must first have a burning desire, enthusiasm, and perseverance. Then I must set my goal. If I don't have a burning desire, then I don't have the motivation to push it through. If I don't have enthusiasm, if I don't feel good about what I'm doing, then I don't have the focus to push it through. Then if I don't have the perseverance, I don't have the commitment to push it through. So therefore if I don't have those three things first, then don't even think about it. It's going to be a waste of time. But if I do, then the goal has to be realistic. Is it realistic for me to think that I can go to school and get a worthwhile education? Yes, it is realistic. How do I know this? Because people have been to school before me, people have gone in their golden years, handicapped people, and people who were formerly illiterate have gone back to school and got degrees. So I know if I can read, see, hear, walk, I can do the same thing, and I'm young. Is it worthwhile? Yes, it's worthwhile for any Black man to have a degree in this country, especially looking at the fact that we have to uplift our own community. We can't keep looking to other people to give us something, so in order to give it to ourselves, we have to have the knowledge. Is it attainable? Of course it's attainable. With the proper time commitment, and sitting down and strategizing what it is we have to do, it can be attained.

I hear from the guys a lot of times, "I can't go to school and learn this, it's going to take too long." All of these excuses. Well, I heard Farrakhan say at Cal State Northridge that God made us in His image, not to make this religious, but this is a great example. God made us in His likeness, in other words we're like God. God is not stupid, so he didn't create you for you to be stupid. If we're made like God, God has mastered all of the things that we're trying to learn, so that tells me that I am capable of mastering those things. When I look at myself, I am everything that we study. I am mathematics, I am science, biology, chemistry, physics—now what is it about myself that I can't master? If I am mathematics, why can't I master mathematics? Anything is attainable once you put your mind to it.

In the Amer-I-CAN Program it tells us that success may not come to us the first time we seek it. You have to keep applying yourself. For every obstacle there is a creative solution, and if you think this way, then you will react this way. If you know that for every obstacle there's a creative solution, then when you run into a brick wall, you're either going to go through it, around it, or get you a hook and a rope and go over it. If you haven't been taught how to think, or how to manage your life, then it's hard for you to go out there and make any kind of change, realistic, worthwhile, long-lasting change.

That's the problem in our community, we don't think. Most women on the county fill out the CA-7 form, wait for their check, go to the food-stamp place, they go get their groceries, go shopping, pay their rent, and pay their bills. A good percentage of them go to school or attempt to go to school, but then when they run into obstacles with baby-sitting, with time management, that's usually what forces them to give up.

For every obstacle there's a creative solution. If you sit back and think about it long enough and come up with a way to get around these little problems, you can still attain your goal.

**Q:** What kind of impact has Jim Brown had on you?

**T:** First of all when I first met Jim, I looked at him as being another hustler coming down here talking about some BS, because I had just got out of the problem that we had with the ministers. My involvement with them had everybody looking to kill me, and things like that. So when Jim came down and talked about what he had going on, I got with T. [Rodgers] and talked to T., and T. said, "You know, Twilight, I'm going to check it out, why don't you come up with me." So I caught the bus over there, to hook up with T., and we went up to Jim's house. I checked out the program that he had, and while checking out the program, I had the opportunity to talk to Jim. What I noticed about Jim that I haven't noticed from any of the other Black elder men in the community is that Jim sat and listened. He didn't tell me how I should feel, what to say, or what I should think, he didn't say anything like that. He took in what I had to say, and he basically asked questions about different things. In my answering his questions I learned something. Instead of him telling me, he asked me a question and showed me how to find the answer myself. It was already in me. Which is what I do now when I work with the program, facilitate.

I'm not a teacher, I'm not a mentor, all I do is guide people through the material and let them find the answers for themselves. That's all it is, bringing out what you already have inside of you.

The day that I met Jim I really didn't know who he was. Once I started finding out who he was, checked out his background, I said to myself, "Damn, this is a bad mf right here." This man played for the Cleveland Browns, ran all these yards, and that didn't mean a thing to him. He left the game in his prime. Evidently, football didn't make him, he made football. In dealing with Jim, and going with him to a lot of different places on business, and in talking to him personally, I found that he gave me a lot of things that I should have gotten from my father, but I didn't. He gave me a lot of insight on the problems that I had.

Now I'm starting to grow and understand why things are the way they are. Jim has his attitude that if there's something he wants to do, he's unstoppable, and uncompromising. That's something that I've realized, in order for a Black man to achieve anything, he has to have that attitude of being unstoppable and uncompromising. The program that he has offered, he uses in his own life. When he was faced with problems, when things would come up, he would use the material from the program.

Before you can make a decision you must have full knowledge and understanding of the problem that you face. When we would run into problems, Jim would get full knowledge, find out what was going on, and then he would go in there and basically diffuse the whole problem. Then he would show the arguing parties how they all can work together.

That's another problem amongst Black folks, we all have our little organizations, but all the organizations are jealous of each other, and they don't work together, so we don't get s— done. Everybody is doing their small little 10 percent, so we're still falling short all the time.

For me to have Jim sit on the couch and say to me, "You know, Twilight, what I have is yours. You can come up here anytime you get ready. If you want something to eat, my refrigerator is always open." A man of his stature, and his level of life, I'm like, "Why would he want to let some gang bangers come up here in this big, pretty house, lounge around, and eat food? Come on, man, what is it about you? What are you after?" I wanted to know what he was after. But Jim was never after anything, all he wanted was for us to be successful.

Then when you look into his history, back in the 1960s he had what they called the Black Economic Unit, BEU. What that organization was all about was taking young Black MBAs, and people from the community, putting them together, and building Black businesses to uplift the Black community. He had received over a million dollars from the Ford Foundation to fund that operation, using who he was, and his knowledge of the business. He worked with Richard Pryor and helped develop his business. What I see is that all Jim wants is for us to stand up and take control of our communities. He wants for us what we want and what we need for ourselves. He's developing an opportunity for us to do that right now.

Jim Brown has gone broke many times while investing and helping in the community. He would give and give and give, until it hurt. Some brothers will talk bad about him, some brothers will say things that are not true about him, but yet he still continues to do this. When I see what he is doing, coming up the way I did, I think of my foundation.

Let's deal with the philosophy from the story of Jesus Christ. He was persecuted by his own people, abused by his own people, but yet he was the one to bring the way for his people. So I look at what Jim is going through, and what it shows me is a strong desire to achieve. His perseverance is unbelievable. I've traveled with this man; this man hops on planes, goes into seven or eight different cities in less than four days, and will still be up and going strong, thinking all the time. So I'm like, is this what I have to develop within myself in order to win? The desire, the perseverance, the energy to go forth and achieve?

**Q:** How do you answer that question? Do you feel that's what you need to develop within yourself in order to win?

**T:** When I look at it, I say, "Exactly." Jim is my professor; he teaches me, he educates me, and he shows me what he sees, the big picture as he calls it. I'm going to take everything that Jim has to offer, and I'm going to uplift myself, and I will stand on his shoulders to see even a bigger and greater picture. That's my focus. That's my drive. To maximize everything that Twilight has the capability to do, and what I don't have the capability to do, I will go and get the full knowledge and understanding of it, to come back and make more change.

**Q:** What things are you doing now to make a change in the neighborhood?

**T:** I've been working with the Amer-I-CAN Program for six years. My first step with any group of young people that I deal with is that they get the life-management skills. Because if they get the life-management skills, then I know they understand that it's about the responsibility of self-determination. What is self-determination? You're free. It's about you being responsible for your freedom, and using it for whatever you want to do. Remember, you're responsible for what you do, and how it affects the community that you live in. No longer is it just about you. When they go through this program, they understand that they don't just have a responsibility to themselves, but they have a responsibility to their families, and to their overall community, to develop themselves in a certain kind of way to bring about change.

I get with these young men and take them through the program. Several of them I've taken out to the Indian reservation. The reason for that is because as a people of African descent we have very little, if any, of our own original culture. My way of looking at it is that the closest thing in America to getting to our culture is the way that the Indians live. So I take them to show them the humanity, the oneness with the earth, the respect of nature. I go to other places, and I can hear the birds when I wake up in the morning. I tell people when they come to Watts, "You won't hear any birds around here." The kids around here kill the birds. I've seen kids that would get a BB gun and go out to kill the little birds in the neighborhood. Birds are scared to say something around here [laughs].

While they're up there at the Indian reservation, they learn the Indians' culture, they learn how to get along with those of so-called Hispanic backgrounds, the Mexicans. Because when we're there, that's all who is there, the Mexicans, the Blacks, and the Indians. We're all people of color, we've all been stepped on, misused, and abused in some kind of way by the European. So up there on the top of that mountain, in the valley, on the Indian reservation, we find a type of peace. I know for myself, from waking up in the night and looking up into the sky, you can't see the stars from down here. You may see one here and there, but up there, man, you can see so many stars it's unbelievable. You can see the star dusts. The thoughts that generated in my mind was deep. Just think, some people believe that there is no God. In the morning you can see the quails running, the rabbits running, the bears, and things like that. Look at creation, look at all of this, nature. We get out of the concrete jungle and go up into nature, and we see what's going on. Me myself, I honestly believe that civilization destroys. . . . [points towards the projects in the background] I would go back to nature any day.

To me, over the years that man has developed, man has gotten weaker, man has gotten lazier, because of so-called progress. The progress is destroying the earth. I just show them these things, and when they come back, they're totally different. Let me not forget about the sweat lodge. We take them in the sweat lodge. It's like, "Wait a minute, it's hot in here." "I know it's hot in here." When you go into a sweat lodge and sit in there, there are four different stages, each stage is about five minutes long. Of course it's hot, but if you come in and you pray, and you meditate and deal with your mind, you'll find that you can endure that heat. You can endure it, sit there, go through it, and probably go through it a few more times.

**Q:** What does that teach you?

**T:** For me it teaches that if I can take my mind and control my body and deal with all of this heat, and not come out of there and pass out, or fall out, then there's nothing I can't do once I put my mind to it. So they learn a lot of things at the Indian reservations.

Sometimes we have book readings, I try to get them to read as much as possible. Some of the kids can't read, but Amer-I-CAN works with the Hooked on Phonics Corporation. So we have a lot of their materials. I take them through the Hooked on Phonics course and teach them how to read. Get them back involved with school. "Go back to school; I know how school pisses you off, but they won't take you in college unless you've been through high school first. So go to high school, finish high school, and along the way let's check out what your dreams are. Tell me what your dreams are. Tell me what it is you want to do." When they start to tell me these things—the money that I earn from Amer-I-CAN, I do the same thing that Jim did with us. I invest it in these kids that I deal with. One kid wants to get into the music industry, he wants to develop his skills as a musician and a producer. So I buy equipment, I give him the equipment, and I put him in a position where now he can deejay and learn that business. Then he can generate his own money by deejaying for other people, to buy the equipment that he needs while he's going to school. One other kid is an artist who wants to silk-screen T-shirts. He had buyers for T-shirts, all he needed was the materials, so I got him the materials. Now he's developing that. He now has stores ordering T-shirts from him. He now has his own business to put a little money in his pocket, and into the pockets of a couple of the guys that work with him. Not only that, the art that he does—I got him with another guy, and this guy has canvas, he wants him to put the art on canvas. Graffiti art sells. I don't know why white folks talk about it when they see it on stuff, but when it's on canvas they want to buy it. Now we're in the process of trying to develop a street-art gallery.

If a kid doesn't have food or clothes, how can he think about education? The program has helped create a situation where I can feed these kids, where I can clothe these kids. Some of them go to schools that are pretty far away, and they need bus fare. Their parents don't have the money. I give them the bus fare. Then if there's a problem at school, I sit down with the counselors and find out what's going on. Then if the school is not doing something they're supposed to do, and we have talked to everybody up there the way we're supposed to, then I go up there and sit down with the principal, lay out all the facts, and lay out the options that we are left with. "You can either get on the ball and make certain things happen, or I can take you to the school board, and if the school board doesn't want to do anything, we can take it to another level, where we can fight it in legislation, whatever has to be done." The Amer-I-CAN Program has given me a power base. Speaker of the House Willie Brown, he backs us up 100 percent. We have one of the best lawyers in Beverly Hills. It gives me something to use, to fight for these kids.

**Q:** What motivated you to first get involved with some of the positive things that you're now into?

**T:** I had an idea years ago for a publication that deals with youth organizations. In Chicago they call them nations, in L.A. they call them gangs, in Florida they call them posses. My reason for that is because now that we have a certain level of peace in Watts, what is going to keep that peace going? Communication. Young brothers need to be able to hear some of the brothers they respect, talking about the peace. That's the problem. A lot of them don't talk about it. A lot of them don't keep the thought fresh on the minds of the people in the community. They get bogged down with whatever little problems they're having at home, and they basically forget about it. We don't want to forget. That's another problem: we forget, and we leave things alone, and the next thing we know, it comes up again.

It happened in '74, and we had another peace treaty in '88 that didn't last, because of lack of communication. Now we're in the nineties, let's try to make this stick. We have to be able to communicate. My thing was to have a publication that has a section dealing with brothers in the penitentiary called "Behind the Wall." What's going through their mind? What do they think about what's going on out here? A lot of these youngsters in jail respect these men, and these men need an outlet to the streets themselves, because they don't know what's going on. Nobody cares. This may be the only thing they have, that keeps them with some sort of sane mind, because in some of these penitentiaries where they are living, it's hard to stay sane. Then we have another section in the paper, we call it the "YG's Corner," the young gangster's corner, because this is where they get an opportunity to talk. When they talk about what's going on with them, that brings the older generation in touch with the younger. They hear what's going on, so now they have something to deal with when they go in and get with the younger generation. They'll have some type of idea of what's going through the youngsters' minds.

We have another section that I call "The Zone." It's basically my section, but I call it "The Zone" because as it has been proven through the history of our people of African descent in America, that every time you have a brother doing positive things, you have those who are either jealous, envious, or have some type of problem with that brother. I find a lot of brothers don't like me, because I was approached about the peace before they were. I don't know what it is. The main thing is, I have their best interest at heart. So don't rag on me, because they approached me first, respect me, because you know that I'm not going to lie. I will tell the truth, and I will represent what the problems are, and what needs to be done. I also feel that much too often the negativity is given an ear. Much too often they're putting the camera in the face of some brother that says something crazy. "The Zone" is Twilight's zone. That's my zone. This is my time to say what's on my mind, because a lot of y'all out there don't know me, and if you did know me, you will find that I'm not the person you knew six, seven years ago.

When you remember that I smoked weed, drank, got high, and all of that, I don't do that anymore. I don't drink, I don't get high, I'm not with that anymore. You remember me as being willing to fight at the drop of a dime. Being willing to shoot a brother as soon as he said something I didn't like. But no, no, no, that's not Twilight anymore. Twilight is a different man now. Twilight understands that he has to go forth and bring about change. He has a responsibility to his daughter, his family, and his community to bring about change. I am a man.

Far too long have the women ran the communities. I go in Nickerson Gardens, and this is nothing against women, but when you go into Nickerson Gardens, you have old women running everything. You have brothers my age, grown men out here hustling on the corners, selling drugs, being a bad influence on the younger generations, whereas a lot of us are not stupid, we have influence, we can bring about change, we can turn the whole community around. But now we have to fight with the women in our community, because we haven't been men for so long, till now they don't even respect us when we do choose to be men. So "The Zone" is an opportunity for me to talk about some of the things that are on my mind. This is a chance for me to ask the questions.

# Twilight

**Q:** When you go to schools and speak, how do the youngsters respond?

**T:** When I would go to the junior high schools to speak, the young Crips and Bloods would talk all this crazy stuff about them gang-banging, and I would let them know that the Pirus have a constitution, and the Crips have a constitution. These organizations at one point and time were grassroots revolutionary organizations. They were too young to become Panthers, so they created their own thing. But the youngsters now don't know that, and they don't know the history, how they were pitted against each other by outside forces.

Certain OGs whose paths I've come across, they tell me the information, and they give me the insight on the things that go down. Piru and Crip are acronyms. At one point in time in Compton, Pirus and Crips were one gang. There wasn't really a Blood and Cuz [Crip] thing until later. The gangs that are now known as Bloods were just independent gangs when they first came about.

CRIP stands for Community Revolutionary Inter-Party Service. This is a revolutionary organization for the grassroots people. The Crips' and the Pirus' jobs were to protect their neighborhoods, feed the kids, take care of the elders in their community. PIRUS stands for Powerful Intellectual Radical Unit of Soldiers. This is where the mind-set of the homiez was at, back when the gangs first started.

The Brims go even further back. One of the first gangs was the Brims, they came into the new generation. First we had Gladiators, Rabble Rousers, Roman Twenty's, Businessmen, and all those brothers. Then came the Brims, then the Crips. The Crips didn't want to be Brims, because it seemed like everybody was Brims. Then in the beginning it wasn't even Crip, it was Crib.

During the time period in the city, everybody was in a revolutionary mind-set. You had the Black Panther Party, the US organization, all these organizations doing things. So the youngsters that wanted to be Black Panthers but couldn't, they created their own organizations, which became known as so-called gangs. The Crips created their thing, they brought their constitution, and the Pirus created their own constitution.

As years went on, that's when the conflict was brought about. What happened was, I remember there was a neighborhood called the Bishops. A Bishop was killed, and the reason he was killed is because a Crip's car was stolen, shot up, and set on fire. The police were the ones who stole this Crip's car, and they spray-painted *Bishop* all over the car. So when the Bishops came to a party in a Crip neighborhood, a Bishop was killed. Then the Bishops made a vow that never again will any of their homeboys be killed and nothing be done about it. That's what kicked off the war on the east side.

The Bishops linked up with the Bounty Hunters, the Denver Lanes, the BeBops, the Swans, and the Pueblo Bishops, and that's when you got the Blood thing. Everybody said Blood, and when they went through the correctional institutions as juveniles, everybody that was identified as a

Denver Lane, a Bounty Hunter, or a Brim was sent to a certain camp and was given a bandanna that was the color red. At that camp that's what they could wear, and when they would come down and go to the juvenile center to get ready for court, they would have to wear this bandanna, and that was how the Crips could tell that they were Bloods. Then the Bloods could tell who the Crips were, because the camp where they sent most of the Crips, the Crips got a blue bandanna. This is how they were able to identify each other. They were given these bandannas. It wasn't an idea that they wanted to do, because in the beginning you identified the Bloods and the Crips, and the different sets, by the hats that they wore: acey-deucey, derbies, brim hats, and by the way that they dressed. Now it's gone to colors.

In Compton, the first war that broke out between the Pirus and the Crips was initiated because of a girl who was dating a Piru and a Crip at the same time. Both of them were brothers of influence and leadership within their different sections, although they were together. When they found out, they fell out and got to fighting, and people got hurt severely. That's when the Pirus and the Crips from Compton split up. Then the Pirus started rolling with the Bloods, because the Bloods went against the Crips. So now this young lady that they fought over is still alive, but the sad part about it is that she's a drug addict now, she's a "strawberry," she's strung out, but look at all the young lives, and innocent people, that have died, because of who she was, and because of who she was dating.

We find ourselves at this point to where the Crips' thing is to say "Cuz" to each other. The Crips use the word *Cuz* because when they would get into a fight, the rules on the street back then was that you couldn't help your homeboy or help a person unless they were related to you. So to be able to get involved in a fight, they would always say, "That's my cousin." That's where the Crips get the word *Cuz* from.

As the years went by, the numbers changed, and the Crips became the more dominant factor. The Bloods had to stay together and have more of a brotherhood with each other in order to fight the Crips. In the beginning the word *Blood* was even used by the Crips. Then over the years it became a word that only the Bloods could use.

A lot of times the youngsters don't understand the history, they don't know what's going on, and I always ask them, "If *Blood* means brother, and *Cuz* means cousin, and both words come from the word *family,* which means unity, then why are brothers and cousins killing each other, since they're all related from one family?" They can never answer the question. I say, "You're out here fighting and don't even understand what you're fighting for." When I found out why the Pirus and the Crips were fighting, and I'm a Piru, I was like, "Oh, no, man, not over a woman. All these years we've been fighting over a woman? It has to be more to it. You're not telling me anything." The homiez would tell me this, and I would get part of my information from an OG that was an original east side Bishop, who started the east side Bishops, and one of the OGs from Leuters Park Pirus from when they first started, he had given me part of the information that I have on the Pirus. Then I get some of my information from an OG Eastside Crip, and an OG Compton Crip.

A lot of times people say, "That didn't happen, this is what happened." Well, I talked to people that was there when it happened. People that have the pictures and all of the information to back it up. A lot of times people just don't understand what's going on, or what went on.

**Q:** How can we get it back to how it used to be, with the love and the family unity?

**T:** I really believe that the OGs and the Triple OGs that are still alive need to come back. A lot of them still haven't come back. Some are dead, and some are in the pen, but the ones still here need to come out.

**Q:** Do the OGs still get respect from the youngsters?

**T:** Let me speak on my neighborhood. I'm in the Cirkle. The Cirkle is strange, because right now I'm considered an OG, and I'm only twenty-four. A few of my other homeboys from the hood are considered OGs too, and they're not over thirty. Our OGs are only in their early thirties, they're not that old. If the OGs were concerned with the lives of the youngsters who are now representing something that they created, then they would come back twice a week to tell them, "Y'all really need to be working on trying to get this peace thing together." At least if they said it to the brothers my age, because the brothers my age, we respect our OGs. We listen to them, and they listen to us. We're more like men to men now. That's even better, so when the youngsters see that everybody else is with it, then they will have no choice but to get with it. We have to embrace the youngsters with the love and respect that they need. We've taught over the years that you don't let anybody call you boy. You don't let anybody step on your shoes. You don't let anybody call your mama out of her name. Certain things. You don't let any man talk to you like you're a punk. Now what their interpretation of what a punk is may be different from what our interpretation is; you may say something that he doesn't like, and he may shoot you. In order for this thing to be turned around, it's going to take a collective effort on every front. The Jim Browns, the Minister Farrakhans, the Twilights, the OGs, all of us.

I call my generation the Gs. I don't look at myself as an OG. I'm just a gangster, I haven't gotten to be original yet. The Gs, and OGs, the Double OGs, and the real fighters, like Jim Brown. See, Jim and them didn't fight each other, they fought them crackers. The Nat Turners, those brothers were for real. We're out here BS'ing. I tell my homiez all the time, when I see them get into an argument with each other, over name-calling. I'd say, "Wait a minute, if the police call you a name that you don't like, you wouldn't say anything, you'd sit on the curb and shut up. Yet, if your brother calls you the same name, you want to tear his head off." Why can't you tear the cop's head off? Not saying that you should kill a cop, but why should the cop be allowed to disrespect you, and he's not even one of you? He's one of the ones who have been disrespecting you for four hundred years. His granddaddy disrespected your granddaddy, and his great-granddaddy disrespected your great-granddaddy. So this is a thing that he has been doing for a living, and you give him the opportunity to do it, you allow him to do these things. Yet, we say that if we were living in the 1960s, they wouldn't have been siccing dogs on us and watering us down with water hoses. You're lying; they would have done the same thing, because you're scared of them now. I'm not saying that we have to go out there and peel caps, but what I'm saying is we have to go out there and stand up. Quit depending on these fools.

I tell homiez not to go down there and get on GR [general relief] and work in the park for $285 a month, when there's enough houses around here to where you can do yards. You don't have to work for that little bit of nothing that they're giving you. There's always something for us to do for ourselves.

**Q:** What would you say to brothers still dealing drugs?

**T:** For the brothers who are ballin' out of control and brothers on the street who generate sixty, seventy, eighty, ninety thousand dollars in just a short period of time, it only takes about $15,000 to open a little minimarket. When the Koreans and all those folks got burned out during the Uprisings, they came right back, but they didn't have to come back. Some of these street hustlers could have come up off of $15,000, bought the store, remodeled it, and set up their own shop and let their li'l homiez work for them, to get the li'l homiez off of the corners. What is the fascination with selling drugs anyway? I don't understand it. I guess it's because you think that you can sit at home and not really have to do anything. That's a lie. It's the same format. If a baller had his own store, he would be doing the same thing he's doing now. He'd get up in the morning and call his workers and make sure they're working. He goes by the spot to check everything and makes sure the product is where it's supposed to be, he collects whatever money he has to collect, and he pays his people at the end of the week. It's the same thing, the only difference is you have to pay taxes. Just keep track of all your receipts, which shouldn't be hard, because you keep track of all the numbers you get at the nightclub. It's nothing but numbers, keeping track of the numbers on pieces of paper. It's the same thing. I always try to make sure that they can put both of them together and see how one relates to the other.

**Q:** What role did you play in helping to bring about the peace, and have you had any help from the community?

**T:** When it first jumped off, we had a meeting at the Masjid on 112th and Central. Jim Brown asked for us to work on peace, because of the constant deaths that were taking place on the streets. Looking at myself, I had been through that boat before, so I was like, "We could probably pull it off this time, but it's going to take a lot of work and a lot of talking." Daudé decided that he was going to go and talk to his homeboys, he said if we could get the projects together, then we can get everybody else together. I told him that we have to include my neighborhood, because even though we have houses and we are not a project development, we have earned the same respect that all the projects have earned. If you're dealing with this square block, you go north of Cirkle City and you hit the Nickerson Gardens, if you go west of Nickerson Gardens you hit the Imperial Courts, when you go around that square area, this is where you have to hit. The Bounty Hunters, Cirkle City, Grape Street, and Imperial Courts [PJs] have much respect. So if you're going to deal with the power brokers, deal with the power brokers, and let's all come together.

So what happened is a meeting was called at the Masjid, and I brought my homeboys from three different generations, because that's the way it is out here now. In each generation you have a man that's respected and has influence. So in order to make sure that it gets to every level, you need to bring representatives from every level. So we came in and dealt with it from that standpoint. What happened was, as time went on, we talked about the peace documents that were drawn up, and everybody agreed to those particular things, but then when they got to taking homeboys from one neighborhood to the other, they got caught up in partying. When Negroes get caught up in partying, they don't have any time to think about the work that needs to be done. They just want to party: "Pass the 40s. Look at all the women we haven't been seeing all these years," which I can understand, but still business has to be first.

That's why I'm thankful to Amer-I-CAN, and the Moorish Science Temple, and my foundation, because it all taught me to have discipline, and to take action on the work at hand, first. We can always party and play around later. You're not promised the next day, so whatever business is at hand, you need to take care of that business first. Right now that's what we find ourselves going back to, taking care of the business. That's why the publication that I put together is important, because it opens up a line of communication between the gangs in L.A. that are not yet a part of the peace, and the gangs who are at peace and trying to maintain the peace.

I feel that eventually it will get back to the point where everyone will have to come to the table once again. If I had it to do all over again, I would bring in the representatives from all these different neighborhoods to lay down real simple guidelines, and if everyone can agree to those guidelines, then each one of the representatives can go back to their neighborhood and have their homeboys agree to those same guidelines. So when the homeboys in each neighborhood, every member of each set has the guidelines, and agrees with them, then they will know that this is the law to maintain a lawful society. The OGs will deal with disciplining those who are out of control in their own neighborhoods.

So what happens is if one of my homeboys goes and does something in a neighborhood that he doesn't have any business in, and the neighborhood notifies me, I'm going to go take care of it. I'm not going to beat him up or shoot him or anything, but I'm going to sit him down and let him understand the seriousness of what he could have created from his actions of stupidity.

**Q:** How is it different in Watts now with the peace than from how it used to be?

**T:** Since the peace, people are happier now, children can walk down the streets and play, people can go anywhere they want to go. And we are not going to let anyone single-handedly bring Satan back into the neighborhood, hitting up the babies and killing folks again. No, we won't have any of that. If I had it to do all over again, that's how I would want to set it up. Everybody would have some type of responsibility and control. I would make sure that the Amer-I-CAN Program is in every neighborhood, that Hooked on Phonics is in every neighborhood, that everybody understands the importance of family and community, and that everybody understands the importance of responsibility, of self-determination. Then in understanding that, and bringing about those certain thoughts in the mind, a person will automatically want to gravitate towards change, for themselves, for the better. Attitude changes motivation, because it's the only motivation that lasts.

Right now in America, things are not getting any better. They just passed the Brady Bill, they're taking nineteen different assault rifles off the shelves, they want to do background checks on people buying guns now, so the people are being disarmed, and now all the entry-level jobs will be moving out of the country since NAFTA has passed. So in other words, life is not going to get any easier for brothers. So whether we like it or not, we're going to have to start dealing and working with each other. Either the conditions of the country will force us to get together and continue to maintain our peace, or we will decide for ourselves that it's the best thing to do. That's something to come about within the next few years. As we all can see now that it's not getting any better, it's getting worse.

On March 17, 1994, at about 7:30 P.M., I was in the Jordan Downs housing projects and I was attacked by two brothers. Their names are not important, they know who they are. One thing that I realized at that point in time is how twisted and demented the minds of some of our own people are. These brothers knew who I was, they knew the work that I have been doing for the past six years, and yet and still they did attempt to rob me and came at me with a firearm. However, I did not seek revenge, I did not retaliate, I kicked back and I waited. In the time that I waited I started to think, and I realized something, I realized that if there is going to be peace, love, and strength amongst our people—every nation has its security force, every nation has a team or an army of individuals that stand to fight for what they believe in, and if our brothers do not feel that they can come from under the ignorance of self-destruction, which has been perpetuated on them systematically by the society in which we live in, then the only thing left for those of us who love peace, who love our people and each other is to stand firm and strong and defend ourselves. If love and acceptance is not a strong enough force, then by any means necessary we must do what it takes to maintain the peace, the love, and the security of our community, and ultimately our nation. I don't have much to say about the things that go on in our community, because we all know what they are, but one thing I can say is that there are groups and groups of brothers everywhere who stand for peace, who want to see peace, and who believe that peace can bring about great things for our community and our nation.

We must band together and reach across this vast country, reach across these streets, work together and support each other truthfully. Stop hiding information and start truthfully coming to each other, telling what's really going on, dealing with each other in a truthful and brotherly manner. Therefore when the brothers that attacked me did what they did, they wouldn't have been able to run back into their neighborhoods and find a safe haven, or find brothers that would secure them, hide them, and keep them out of sight from being able to be dealt with for the crime they committed against me. Their own people in the community should bring them to the front lines and make them answer to the crimes that they committed. I'm not seeking bloody revenge or anything of that nature, all I would like to see is for those brothers to deal with me face-to-face and give me an explanation for what they did, and to see what I've been through and what I've suffered because of their acts. However, this is not something that I'm used to doing, looking at my background and where I come from, I was always taught that if they hit you once, you hit them back four times harder. But I'm willing to let that go, to strengthen the peace, and to find a way of dealing with these things without always resorting to violence and gunplay.

**Q:** Any further words that you want to say to your homeboys and to the world?

**T:** My homiez are homeboys from everywhere. Twilight doesn't put down anybody for being whatever they want to be. All I have to say to any man that's out there walking is, "Are you truly a man?" If you're truly a man, then you're going to take control of your household, your community, and your nation, and you are going to make sure that they grow and develop themselves, in a successful and self-reliant way. Now is the time for brothers to wake up and quit playing around, stop jaw jackin' and skirt chasing, and really get down to business. I have a daughter and I'm not about to sit back and give her something worse than what my father gave me, because what he gave me wasn't all that great.

# UPRISING

We have to look at the original gangs in Africa; some gangs were called the Craftsman gangs, because of the craft work that they could do. One thing that I noticed about the history of these particular gangs is that they were brought together and united by a great African king, and out of that came the Egyptian empire. These gang members were the builders of the pyramids, the architects, the security force for many nations. Not only that, they were the teachers of the children, and they are the ones who developed the science of astrology, mathematics, and all of the different sciences which makes the world what it is today.

This is the power and the potential that gangs have, but until we bring about some force that can unite these gangs on a positive level, and take them back into the direction that our ancestors went in, then we'll be lost and we will end up behind. I always felt that the Egyptians were far more avanced than present-day society, they only came together in unity because they knew that certain things would bring about destruction. If we can take one lesson from our people and the history of our people, let's take the lesson of the unity and the strength which brings about a great nation.

In closing, the final words that I would like to bring to the people reading this book, or who are having this book read to them, is that even though we have a history here in the United States that is not a good one, because our spirits were broken, our families were destroyed, and we were taught self-hatred, *we can come up out of that.* In coming up out of this condition we will have to restore everything that was taken from us. A lot of times brothers want to put culture first, but it's hard to take five hundred years of culture and put it on the shoulders of the young men of today, who are dealing with the stress that this society has put upon them. What I would like to say is, if we can start out first with self-determination, if you can be determined enough to free yourself and take responsibility for yourself, and learn to manage your own life, then maybe you can make your life better, and your children's lives better, and all of those around you. I think it's very important for everybody to remember that when we make our decisions, we must keep in mind how those decisions will affect us and our overall community. And remember that the only way we can find true freedom is not from being able to buy all the things that we want to buy, or not being able to go into a company to possibly own it one day, but just through having self-determination, freeing our minds and freeing ourselves mentally of those things which distress us of our past. If we can do that, then we can have the world.

***Good vs. Evil, Right vs. Wrong, God vs. Devil—WHAT SIDE YOU ON?***

**—Public Enemy**

## Twilight

# SHOUT OUTS

I'd like to give a shout out to my homeboys in the Cirkle, Cirkle City Pirus, much love to all the homeboys over there. We've had many years of fighting and hardships, trying to put the Cirkle City Pirus on the map for the city of Watts, but now I think it's time that we put love and unity on the map for the city of Watts, and try to take it a little farther. I'd like to give shout outs to my homeboys from 1-5-1 OBP, y'all know who y'all are, much love for all of y'all. The homiez from Westside Campanella, all my relatives in the Nickersons, y'all know what's up, got a lot of love for y'all too. I'd like to give a shout out to the homeboys on the west side, the Black P. Stones. T., you know who you are, you know where we're at. I'd like to give a shout out to my homeboys from Park Hill Bloods in Denver. The homiez up north, the east side Pirus in Seattle, Washington. To the Lincoln Pirus in Denver and in San Diego. All the homiez, I have love for all of y'all. My people in Florida, y'all know who y'all are, working with Amer-I-CAN, much love. Last but never least, I'd like to give a shout out to Big Jim, the only one who took the time to believe in the brothers, and putting his money and his heart on the line to give us a chance to be real men. Much love to all the strong Black men in our community. Peace!

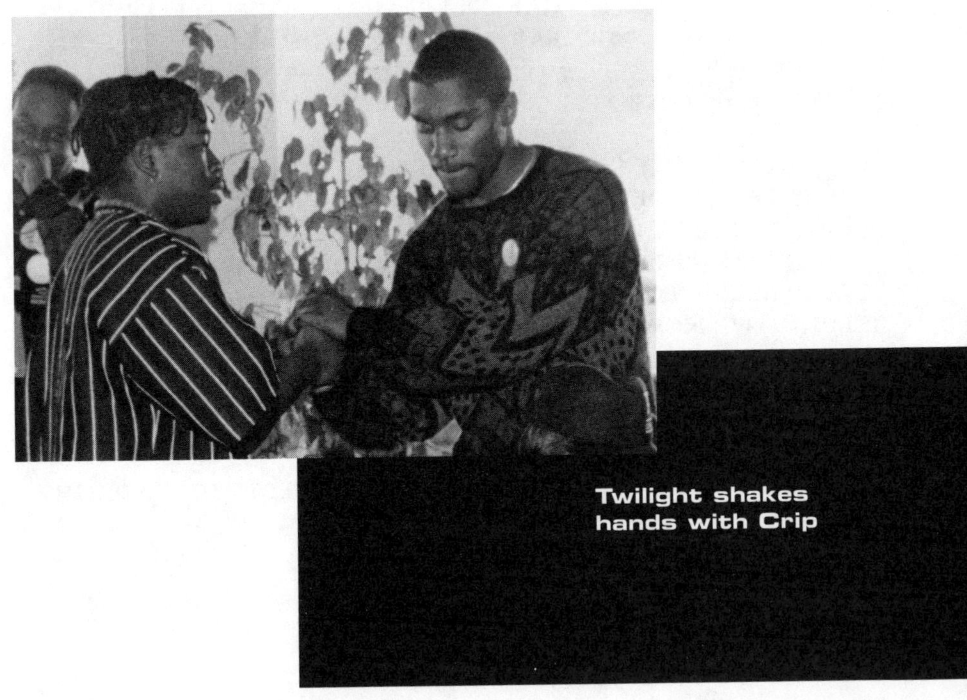

Twilight shakes hands with Crip

# THE TWILIGHT

## (LIGHT TO DARK, DARK TO LIGHT)

MY LIFE IS OVER I SUPPOSE
NOW THAT MY LOVE HAS GONE AND THE TWILIGHT HAS AROSE
WE HAD SO MUCH FUN TWO KIDS ALWAYS TOGETHER
DIDN'T MATTER THE TIME, THE DAY, THE WEEK,
IT DIDN'T MATTER THE WEATHER
I ENJOYED HER LAUGHTER AND COMPANY
I ADORE HER SENSUALITY AND BEAUTY
I DREAMED THAT WE WERE KING AND QUEEN OF A BEAUTIFUL CLOUD KINGDOM
WE DANCED, HUGGED, AND KISSED IN A MOONLIGHT BALLROOM
IT SEEMED LIKE THIS COULD NEVER END
LIKE WE WERE IMMATERIAL ETERNAL FRIENDS

THEN CAME THE YEAR OF THE TWILIGHT
EVIL CAME AND DARKENED MY WORLD OF LIGHT
THE LOVE WAS GONE ALL OF A SUDDEN
NO MORE HUGS AND KISSING
AND WORSE THAN THAT, NO MORE LOVIN'
I GAVE UP SINCE MY HEART WAS SHATTERED
BROKEN INTO A THOUSAND PIECES THEN SCATTERED
BECAUSE OF THE DARK TWILIGHT I HAVE NOTHING
NO LOVE, NO HEART, I CAN'T EXPLAIN HOW I'M FEELING
WHERE ARE YOU, MY DEAR, I'M LOOKING FOR YOU
I WANT TO TAKE YOU WITH ME TO ECSTASY
AND FALL IN LOVE TOO

I FOUND HER, MY SEARCH IS OVER
SHE IS THE TIP OF BEAUTY, SEX, AND CHARM
I CAN'T HELP BUT LOVE HER
THE TWILIGHT IS GOING FROM DARK TO LIGHT
GOD WALKS WITH ME AND HE SAYS IT'S ALRIGHT
I'M IN LOVE NOW
SINCE THE LORD TOOK MY HAND
I'VE FOUND A WONDERFUL FRIEND
AND MY SHATTERED HEART IS BACK TOGETHER AGAIN
DARKNESS CAN BECOME LIGHT
SO DON'T GO BLIND, KEEP SIGHT AND ACCEPT THE TWILIGHT

LI'L BRO. J.B. WATTS RECKIN BOY'Z

# AFTERWORD

*(The following pages are the exact words from letters that we received from men in the penitentiary who have read excerpts from "Uprising" and have been changed and/or affected in some positive way from reading these words.*

*All praise is due!)*

Coming from the streets of South Central L.A. and in-and-out of jail, I've met and kicked it with a lot of my brothers who are and was affiliated with different hoods, and knowing them and the streets, I feel that the soon-to-be-released book *Uprising* will be an insight to all younger brothers, as well as the little sistas in the hood, that gangs are not cool and that they can find people who love them in other outlets of life.

—Richard F. Butler

I didn't know or couldn't even begin to understand. Although I don't totally agree with everything that I have read in these excerpts, I do find myself with a much better insight to a world of thoughts that has pretty much been alien to me. Being a white male, most people would think my knowledge on this subject would be nil, but having been brought up in the pen and on the streets, my knowledge is probably 100 times that of the "average white male." But these excerpts made me realize how little I do know. These are Black men's words from the heart, the mind, and the soul. I thought I knew, I wasn't even close! I truly want to read this entire book!

—Anthony Pendleton

West up, my name is Li'l Red from Hoover Criminal Gang. After reading *Uprising* written by a number of ex–gang members, all OGs from their hoods and actually talking to one, gave me a new outlook on gang-banging and how deep some of our OGs be thinking. A real man stands alone and now it's time for me to stand on my own two feet and look out for me and my family, because taking a life over a word, a street, a name, or a color is not worth me spending the rest of my life in the pen. I'm not belling out on my homiez because they will always have much love from me, but it's time for me to help them come up a different way, and stand on my own two feet and be a man and a leader, not a follower. It took words from some real OGs that been to the pen on the foe yard for murder and then had to kick it with the same set that he killed a person from—so it's time to stand up and be a man because we need a few good ones.

Thanks to Big Hoover Red and Big Bruno from Brim to help me see that life has more to offer me.

—Lonnie French

# UPRISING

My name is Abdul-Akbar, also known as Young Cuzz, from Compton Twilight Zone Crip Gang. I am now currently a member of the Nation of Islam.

My main objective and goal is to help teach and communicate with young Crips and Bloods my age, eighteen and under. The youngsters of today are of the downest and most serious generation. Most of them need and want a change, they just have to be guided, so that is what the brothers in this book are contributing to. I'd like to say one more thing to my fellow youngsters: I don't condone gang-banging, but the unity and strength that we have in our neighborhoods—we need to *keep* it, *develop* it, and channel it toward the right path.We will find that by doing this—nothing or no one will be able to stop us economically, physically, and mentally. Please take heed to *all* the words in this book, so we can *Uprise* and revolutionize the world.

The gang truce among the Crips and the Bloods is a very needed experience. It gives the Brothers and Sisters in the Black community a chance to come together and realize that we are not enemies. In fact, it gives us a chance to see who the real enemy is.

The gang truce is also important in terms of the *future*. By us coming together we also have a chance to get rid of the negative guidance, and begin to teach ourselves, our children, and our grandchildren how to grow up in an atmosphere where there is self-knowledge and independence.

It is critical that we re-educate ourselves and come into the knowledge of self and the enemy. The need for re-education is important, because of what the youngsters are being taught today. It is relevant toward our *rise* above our current condition. If we re-educate ourselves about our past accomplishments and history then we'll be able to see the position that our ancestors held before slavery.

Positions as kings and queens, the first mathematicians, scientists, and doctors, etc. Knowing these facts, we'll have something to work toward. This is the reason that re-education is important to the building of our independent nation!

Having the knowledge of the enemy is important because it enables you to dodge and shut down all the obstacles that your enemy may put in your path. For example, during the peace treaty, the government sent a lot of young and old government agents among the Brothers and Sisters to start division and confusion. By having knowledge of the real enemy, knowing that his purpose is to keep us divided, we can then be aware and not fall victim to his weak traps. The police and the U.S. government know that our "Rise" leads to their "Fall." They can only keep us oppressed as long as we let them! This they know and know it well!

The teachings of the Most Honorable Elijah Muhammad is what's going to raise the Black man and woman out of our wretched condition. The teachings of the Most Honorable Elijah Muhammad, which are now being taught to us by the Honorable Louis Farrakhan, teaches the Black man and woman that, no matter if you are Christian, Muslim,

Jewish, Blood, or Crip, to "Do for self" and help build our own independent nation. The Most Honorable Elijah Muhammad also stresses for you to develop yourself spiritually, mentally, physically, and economically.

Reasons for spiritual development is to get you in tune with yourself and God. It gives you the patience to persevere through the hard times in order to get to the times of ease. Religion and spirituality also forbids you to get drunk, to smoke, or to have dealings in the things that will keep us in our condition.

Mental strength is important because without a strong mind and knowledge of things going on around the world, we cannot have positive dealings with nations across the globe, to get the things we need to help further the development of our nation. We must have a broad mind and understanding in order to build a nation.

Physical enhancement is important because by being physically fit it contributes to and balances out your mental and spiritual growth.

Every nation and government has an economy. The reason for this is that a nation has to provide jobs and comfort for the people, supplies for the military of that nation, and build hospitals, schools, and farms, etc. We can have these things if we would just pool our resources together under the right leadership and build!

The solutions to the problems of the Black man and woman in America is to pool together our resources, develop ourselves mentally, spiritually, and economically, put our differences aside and do for self together!

—Your Brother in the struggle,<br>
As Salaam A'laikum<br>
Abdul-Akbar Islam

## SHOUT OUTS

Shout outs to the Islam family, the Brotherhood and Sisterhood of Compton Mosque #54, my homeboys the Twilight Zone Crips, the whole Nation of Islam, and the entire Compton Carr. I most of all thank Almighty God ALLAH and Brother Yusuf and Sister Shah'Keyah who made this possible

# INDEX

# INDEX

# INDEX

# INDEX

# INDEX

# INDEX

# INDEX

# INDEX